PAINT, PIGMENT, SOLVENT, COATING, EMULSION, PAINT ADDITIVES AND FORMULATIONS

PAINT, PIGMENT, SOLVENT, COATING, EMULSION, PAINT ADDITIVES AND FORMULATIONS

Written By

EIRI BOARD OF CONSULTANTS & ENGINEERS

ENGINEERS INDIA RESEARCH INSTITUTE

4449, Nai Sarak, Main Road, Delhi - 110006 (India)
Ph: +91-11-23918117, 23916431, 45120361, 23947058
*E-Mail: eiritechnology@gmail.com & eiriprojects@gmail.com
*Website: www.eiriindia.org & www.industrialprojects.in

PRINTED & PUBLISHED BY

ENGINEERS INDIA RESEARCH INSTITUTE

4449, Nai Sarak, Main Road, Delhi - 110006 (India)
Ph: +91-11-23918117, 23916431, 45120361, 23947058
* E-Mail: eiritechnology@gmail.com & eiriprojects@gmail.com
*Website: www.eiriindia.org & www.industrialprojects.in

Distributors:

EIRI PROJECT CONSULTANTS AND PUBLISHERS
4/54 Roop Nagar, Delhi-110007
and
Industrial Technologies, India
Nai Sarak, Delhi-110006

Revised & Enlarged Edition

ISBN: 9788189765156

Printed in New Delhi (INDIA)

₹ 950/- or US$ 100

Printed & Published by Sudhir Gupta for
"Engineers India Research Institute", 4449 Nai Sarak, Main Road,
New Delhi -110006

Preface

Paint, Pigment, Solvent, Coating Paint, Additives and Formulations Hand Book is published by EIRI Consultants & Engineers. As these all paint and allied products have got good demand in India and also having export, potential. The invaluable book is covering depth manufacturing technology with various formulae on different paint items.

The book covers various methods including Flavours and Its Study, Changes of Food Flavours Due to processing, Flavouring Materials Made by Processing, Natural Flavouring Materials, Flavouring Materials of Natural Origin, Manufacturing Technology of Flavours. Food Colourants.

The book has been written for the benefit and to prove an asset and a handy reference guide in the hands of new entrepreneurs and well established industrialists.

The book **'Paint, Pigment, Solvent, Coating, Emulsion, Paint Additives and Formulations'** covers various methods including Paint Additives, Solvents, Pigments, How to Formulate a Paint, Inhibitive Primers for Metal, Paints for Ships, Drying and Curing Additives, Light Stabilizers, Foam Control Additives, Additives for Powder Coatings, Calcium Aluminium Silicate and Magnesium Aluminium Silicate, Paint Stainers, Painting of Aircraft, Anionic Bitumen Emulsions, Rheology Modifiers in Waterborne Paints, High Performance Coatings, Bio-Diesel-Opportunities for the Coating Industry, Road Marking Paints, Emulsions, Silica Gels, Emulsion Paints, Paints and Varnish Removers, Spray Painting, Paint Bases, Paint, Varnish and Enamel Removers, Paint Mixing and Grinding, Pigments Formulae, Paint Making Machinery Suppliers, Paint Mixer Suppliers, Chemical Storage Tank Suppliers, Ball Mill Suppliers and Triple Roll Suppliers..

The book has been written for the benefit and to prove an asset and a handy reference guide in the hands of new entrepreneurs and well established industrialists.

Director

EIRI Board of Consultants & Engineers

4449, Nai Sarak. Main Road, Delhi - 110006 (India)

E-Mail: eiritechnology@gmail.com & eiriprojects@gmail.com

Website: www.eiriindia.org & www.industrialprojects.in

CONTENTS AND SUBJECT INDEX

OTHER RELATED BOOKS

- Fruits & Vegetables Processing Hand Book
- Fruit Beverages & Processing With Mango Products
- Food Processing & Agro Based Industries
- Manufacturing Technology of Snacks Food, Namkeen, Pappad & Potato Products
- Preservation & Canning of Fruits and Vegetables
- Hand Book of Food Dehydration & Drying
- Meat Processing & Meat Products Hand Book
- Technology of Food Preservation & Processing
- Hand Book of Food Packaging
- Agro Based & Processed Food Products
- Potato & Potato Processing
- Technology of Maize & Allied Corn.
- Technology of Food Processing
- Technology of Sweets (Mithai)
- Hand Book of Organic Farming And Organic Foods With Vermi-Compost-ing and Neem Products
- Hand Book of Fish Farming And Fishery Products
- Hand Book of Mushroom Culti-vation, Processing And Packaging
- Hand Book of Spices & Packaging
- Start Your Own Cold Storage Unit
- Hand Book of Bakery Industries
- Hand Book of Confectionery
- Breakfast, Dietary Food, Pasta & Cereal Products Technology
- Hand Book of Modern Bakery Products
- Modern Bakery Technology & Fermented Cereal Products With Formulae
- Technology of Confectionery, Chocolates, Toffee, Candy, Chew-ing & Bubble Gums, Lollipop and Jelly Products with Formulations
- Hand Book of Poultry Farming & Feed Formulations
- Hand Book of Pig Farming
- Agro Based Hand Book of Planta-tion, Cultivation & Farming
- Agro Based Plantation Cultivation & Farming
- Agro Chemical Industries (Insecti-cide & Pesticides)
- Modern Bee Keeping & Honey Processing
- Technology of Modern Rice Milling and Basmati Rice
- Hand Book of Goat Farming
- Floriculture Hand Book
- Aloe Vera Cultivation, Processings, Formulations And Manufacturing Technology
- Hand Book of Dairy Formulations, Processes & Milk Processing
- Milk Processing And Dairy Products Industries
- Hand Book of Dairy Farming to Produce Milk with Packaging
- Hand Book of Ice Cream Technology And Formulae
- Hand Book of Milk Processing Dairy Products and Packaging
- Dairy Farming for Milk Production
- Ayurvedic & Herbal Medicines
- Hand Book of Ayurvedic Medicines With Formulations
- Technology of food chemicals, pigments and food aroma compounds
- Modern Technology of Agro Processing and Food Packaging Products with Project Profiles
- Technology of Soya Milk, Tofu, Hydro-lyzate, allied Soyabean Products with Project Profiles
- Technology of SOYBEAN Products with Formulae
- Technology of Wine Production and Packaging
- Modern technology of Food Additives, Sweeteners and Food Emulsifiers
- Poultry Farming, Hatchery and Broiler Production
- Modern Technology of Tomato Processing and Dehydration
- Technology of Chicken Meat and Poultry
- Modern Technology of BIO GAS Production

1

Paint Additives

In its simplest form mixing pigments with binders can make a paint. One of the easiest compositions would be as follows:

Pigment (organic or inorganic)	50
Drying Oil	50
	100

A brush could apply this composition, it would also dry and form a film, but the performance would be unsatisfactory on several counts.

For example during storage, the pigment may completely settle out, even hard settling may result. During application, the brushing may not be easy. If a thick film is applied it may show pigment separation. It may take several days to dry; the film may not produce gloss. If some dust particles gather on the surface during drying, they would become permanent part of the film showing it as a defect. The hardness and adhesion of the film may be inferior.

To improve the process of paint preparation, its storage, applications, performance and economics of a paint system, additives are necessary almost from the very beginning. An additive is a substance, organic or inorganic, that alters the characteristics of paint or coating disproportionate to its concentration. We may also say that Paint additives are materials that when added at about 1% concentration affect 100% performance.

For example, a drying oil such as linseed oil may dry in about 250 hours after application. Converted to a long oil alkyd, the alkyd may dry in about 12 hrs. without driers. An additive in the form of a cobalt soap crman accelerate the same process and reduce surface dry time to just about ~ an hour, and this too at a concentration as low as 0.05% as metal on solids of the alkyd.

The improvement is about 50;000%. In this case, the cobalt acts as a catalyst to accelerate the drying process. In most other cases the mechanism of the action of an additive is selected by deep understanding of the root cause of the deficiency.

The capability to alter a given property at a very low concentration makes these materials very powerful. These belong to the class of products known as "performance chemicals". As we know, power corrupts and absolute power corrupts absolutely; an additive used in a quantity larger than the minimum required has negative effects on the other properties of paint. Use of an additive, therefore, must be made judiciously. One rule must be remembered. "There is no additive without side effects."

Any scientist takes considerable time to develop a right product for a right application. At times, several man-years have been spent in developing and perfecting performance chemicals. Such research is expensive. Further, the efforts required to generate data as part of the technical bulletins and product support information, user education and trouble shooting are time consuming and eat up the resources still further. The manufacturer likes to recover these costs and make profit as early as possible. For this reason, most of these products are sold in their trade names with very little information on their chemical nature.

The best policy to use additives is:

- Use minimum number of additives.
- Use smallest possible concentration (not essentially recommended by the manufacturer)
- Never add another additive to cure the side effects caused by an additive; i.e., the additive should be able to perform what is expected of it without affecting any other property.

For example, zinc oxide is used as an additive to white enamel to prevent yellowing. Zinc oxide has two major side effects:

- It causes rapid livering (gelling) of media with high acid value.
- It causes reduction of gloss and causes bloom on the applied paint film either immediately or over a period of time.

Both are caused by reaction of zinc oxide with the free acidity of medium. An alkyd is a polycarboxylic acid and zinc oxide is a difunctional base. Bonding of molecules at multiple sites causes gelation. Migration of low molecular weight acid salt to the surface causes bloom.

One option is to modify the medium such that it would not react with ZnO any more. The other approach is to find an additive that would react with the acidity of the resin and prevent gelation. Some of such additives could be amines, butyl titanate etc. These very effectively prevent gelling, but cause severe yellowing of the paint. Thus, one can travel a full circle without ultimately achieving the objective, but after having spent the money for the additives.

All additives are to be used with care. These are like very potent medicines that must be used with caution. Selection is an important process where supplier's information plays a vital role. Depending on the need, a right product should be selected. The job is as delicate as that of a surgeon. He must choose his surgical instruments carefully. A sword need not be used where a needle would do. Same is the case with a doctor. Either he can use his skills of clinical diagnosis and treat a fever for its exact cause or use a broad-spectrum medicine to cure all infections together. The first approach is the most desirable in the case of a paint chemist. This helps to sharpen his skills of formulation to cut costs and make his products performance oriented."

Skills of addition

Most additives are used in small volumes. Care must be taken in:

- calculation,
- weighing/measuring, and
- actual addition.

This part of work can not be delegated to unskilled personnel. Additive once added can not be taken out. I have seen several cases where caution was blown to winds and unskilled person added an additive in double or larger quantity. The only available option after such an event is to enlarge the size of the batch. This would result in considerable over-production and losses.

Matrix dilution

A simpler way is to store additives in diluted form. This is but done in a harmless solvent. For most of the post additives, the solvent quantity can be adjusted in the formulation for the portion, that would come from the additive. A three to five times dilution reduces the risk of erroneous addition considerably. For very sensitive products that are required to be added in ppm (parts per million concentration), further dilution up to 1-5 mg/ml (or g/l) is recommended. Thus, if for a batch of 1000-lit. 10 or 20 g. of an additive are required, one might add 1 to 2 lit. of this additive solution containing 10-20 g/l additive in a solvent.

The journey of the paint additives starts from the very beginning of preparation. Several raw materials already include additives. For example the new class of pigments comes with surface treatment to reduce the requirement of wetting and dispersing agents. The exact requirement of a dispersing agent must be ascertained before deciding the composition.

The additives in a paint system can be broadly listed as follows:

a) Additives for paint processing
   - Wetting and dispersing agents (surface active agents, defoamers)
   - Viscosity control.

b) Additives for improving paint application properties
   - Anti skinning agent
   - Driers
   - Mattening agents
   - Gloss improvement (leveling and flow control) agent
   - Wet edge additives
   - Thixotropic agent
   - Mar resistance
   - Anti-foam

c) Additives to improve storage properties
   - Anti-settling agent
   - Desiccants
   - Anti-rust agents
   - Protective colloids
   - Biocides

d) Additives for improvement of performance of the film
   - Mar resistance
   - Biocides

- Weathering resisting agents
- Adhesion promoters
- Surface renewal agents

e) Additives for special effects

- Wrinkle finishes
- Hammer tone finishes

One of the best source materials for additives is the Handbook of Coating additives by Calbo(1). Next source is the product literatures of manufacturers. Some of the most important additives have been discussed here.

WETTING AND DISPERSING AGENTS

The pigments can generally be classified as:

- Processed organic or inorganic substances
- Processed minerals

In the first case, the products have seen various stages such as precipitation, washing drying, grinding followed by packing. During precipitation, the particles come out from a saturated solution as individual fine particles. If these are immediately surface treated, these will resist flocculation. Since fine particles pose difficulty in filtration and the pigment manufacturer would like to maximize his production and yield, exactly opposite action is required. A flocculating agent is added to increase the particle size and hence the filtration efficiency. After filtration and washing, the cake is allowed to dry in either tray dryers or flash dryers. As the moisture between two particles leaves, it causes primary particles to come closer to each other due to capillary forces.

In the process of drying the pigments, water from the interstices of the bulk of the pigment is removed by application of heat. As we are aware, the surface of the particles has excess energy that needs to be neutralized. As the water leaves the space between two particles, it brings them closer due to, the surface tension exerting a pressure as high as 1 T/cm^2 of the surface. This phenomenon is fairly similar to film formation of polymer emulsions. Since the pigment particles are hard and can not deform under this pressure, they only stick to each other by a high degree of packing. Even though, it is expected that all particles are uniform in size, in reality there is a considerably wide distribution of particle sizes and this helps these to pack closer. This is evident during the drying of solid cake where several cracks develop and the lumps get separated from one another. This gap is the cumulative movement of particles present in that lump. The particles are held together as agglomerates. Grinding df the pigment in a hammer mill before packing is not able to break down the agglomerates. Further work is required to separate them to primary particles. At times, pigment manufacturers also agglomerate the flocculated particles for ease of packing, transportation and handling and reduce tendency of dusting at the users end. Primary particles, though highly desirable for user would actually make the material very light, difficult to handle, bulky to pack and transport, will take larger space for storage, would heavily dust during loading in paint preparation. It would also lead to problems of contamination of colours. For example, black pigment particles are most undesired in any clean-shade. Opening a bag of black pigment in production area increases risk of cross contamination. For these reasons, the pigments are supplied in granulated form.

For avoiding the problems stated above, the best feature of precipitated pigments, the fine particle size, is lost. A paint manufacturer has to, break down the agglomerates and flocculates to primary particles all the way. One good way of avoiding these problems was a range of products called "flushed pigments". These were obtained by displacement of water from the voids and the pigment surface by a liquid, that could wet the pigment surface more easily. Typically, linseed oil was used in the past. If a wet cake of pigment was kneaded with linseed oil, all the water got separated and a ready dispersion of pigment in linseed oil was obtained. The advantages of this technique were many. The slurry required no dispersion or grinding, the colour value of the pigment was highest with very little risk of flocculation. Even though "flushed" pigments offered highest surface area and colour strength, it was not feasible to supply them in all possible resins. (Imagine the number of products to be carried as inventory if there were 50 pigments and 25 commercial resins, atleast 1250 products would be needed).

Over the years, as several new resins became commercially available, cross contamination of linseed oil or other materials used for flushing were not acceptable. Supplying every pigment in different media such as epoxy, urethanes, polyesters, alkyds, was not feasible. The technology had to clear way for drying and grinding in place of flushing.

Of all the additives, the most important class is wetting and dispersing agents. They primarily control the ease of dispersion, thus saving energy. They extmctthe best performance from a pigment or colourant. During application and storage they provide trouble-free performance from products. A right wetting and dispersing agent enables a pigment to provide highest hiding, colour value, prevents settling during storage and controls defects such as flooding, floating, flocculation, reversal of finish, bittiness etc.

The terms wetting and dispersion are used concurrently. Effectively it means covering the entire surface of the particle with the vehicle or binder by complete adsorption of the binder on the surface. Since most binders may not be able to wet the pigment surface, they require a more acceptable inter-phase. In their dry form, most pigments are flocculated. Also for the ease of packaging, handling and avoiding dusting, the manufacturers agglomerate the pigments. The paint manufacturer is required to reverse this process. For increasing the ease of dispersion, the pigments are surface treated to be able to wet and disperse easily. In their primary form most pigments have very high surface area (50-100 m^2/g for most of the inorganic pigments with density 2.5-3 g/cc and up to 200-500 m^2/g for organic pigments, carbon black with density 1.5-2 g/cc). Even if a mono molecular layer of the oil is adsorbed on this surface, the requirement would be about 4 mg/m^2, that translates into *0.2-0.5* g linseed oil /g pigment for inorganic pigments and upto 2 g/g of organic pigments or carbon black. This would pose serious problem of contamination to a wide range of modern products.

There is a virtual explosion amongst the type of wetting and dispersing agents available in the market. Various manufacturers such as Byk Chemie, Efka, Tego Chimie and others have concentrated on finer aspects of the physical chemistry of these products and contributed significantly to the development of new products. New classes of surfactants with properties unique to the new products have helped solve problem not surmountable with conventional materials.

Two categories need special mention - polymeric dispersants and hybrid surfactants.

In the first case, block copolymers of acrylic monomers with varying functionality such as ester, carboxyl or hydroxyls are prepared with low molecular weight of about 2000-3000. These are flexible molecules that can adsorb on the pigment surface from hydrophilic part while extending the hydrophobic part away frcm the surface:

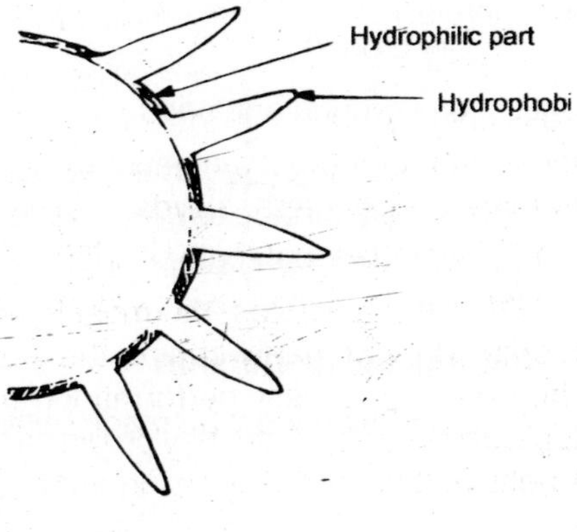

The number of variants possible in the composition are so large that one can generate a very large number of unique products.

The other class of surfactants is hybrid surfactants. The hydrophobic part of these products is derived from synthetic substances such as silicone or poly fluorinated hydrocarbons.

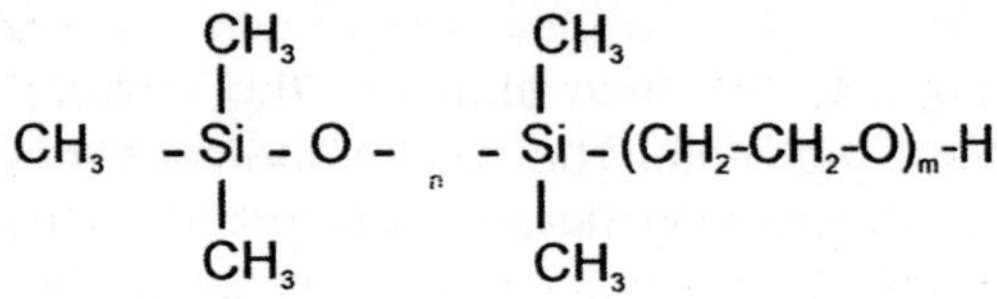

& $CH_3 - (CH_2)_n - (O - CH_2 - CH_2)_m - OH$

The commercial products are available from Byk Chemie and DuPont respectively.

The dispersion process thus requires following actions,

- Displacement of the gas (air) filled in the voids with binder.
- Displacement of adsorbed layer of water, other gases from the surface of the pigment.
- The displaced water may not be soluble in the binder and needs to be compatabilized.
- Completely covering the individual particles with binder, dispersing agent and separating the particles from flocculated form to primary particle.

In the case of processed minerals, these may be supplied in two basic forms,

- Dry ground
- Wet ground and dried.

In both the cases, the fine particles contribute large surface area with unbalanced surface forces. These are neutralized by adsorption of water or any polar gas molecule such as CO_2, or sulfur compounds. All of them may even be simultaneously persent.

Wetting and dispersion

Distinction must be made between wetting and dispersion.

Wetting

If we place a drop of mercury on a filter paper, the individual particles stay away from the surface and retract. If these were forced to contact the surface, they would break rather than penetrate. If a drop of water is placed on the same filter paper, it is spontaneously soaked in the filter paper. If the mercury is brought in contact with a clean galvanized iron surface (coated with zinc metal) the surface becomes shiny.

Let us examine what has happened in the three cases. The nature of mercury is completely different from that of the filter paper and we say it does not "wet" the paper surface. In the second case the surface of filter paper is completely covered with water since the paper can adsorb as much as 10% by weight of water. It has great affinity for water. As soon as water is brought in contact with paper, it wets the surface easily and is absorbed quickly. Mercury can dissolve zinc metal. As soon as clean zinc surface from the galvanized steel is brought in contact with mercury, it dissolves in it and spreads thin like a mirror surface.

The importance of "clean" zinc surface must be emphasized. If the metal is not pre-cleaned with an acid before contacting with mercury, wetting does not take place: This is because the metal surface is completely covered with inert layer of metal oxide, that is not soluble in mercury. Only after this layer of metal oxides is dissolved by acids to expose fresh metal surface, can mercury wet the surface of zinc. Once the surface is cleaned, the attraction forces between zinc and mercury are so strong that they can overcome the resistance offered by liquid water, that may be present on the surface. Due to the great density difference between mercury and water, water is conveniently displaced and floats over the surface of the amalgam (solution of metals). For the wetting process of the pigments this is what is needed to visualize.

The surface of all pigments is covered with a thin layer of water. So much so that the chemical composition of a few angstrom thick layer of a pigment particle may be a saturated solution of the pigmentary substance in water. Since the solubility of all the pigments in water is very low, it may be nearly pure water, containing dissolved gases like CO_2, 02' and N_2 that will saturate the water to their solubility. In the wetting process, this surface layer of water needs to be displaced with the wetting agent; that makes the job of the resin to wet the surface easier. Thus wetting agents are necessary only for oil- based system where the layer of water strongly adhering to the pigment surface needs to be displaced and an inter-phase is required to facilitate wetting ofthe pigment particle with the resin. The wetting agent might also facilitate dissolution of the disrobed water in the organic medium. For water-based systems, wetting, agent may be necessary only if the pigment surface is hydrophobic. This may be so in case of some organic pigments that do not adsorb water. It would be apparent that such pigments would need no wetting agent for oil-based systems.

Dispersion

Having provided a wetting agent in a medium, one is equipped to wet the surface of the pigment with the vehicle. The primary particles that have agglomerated together need to be broken down to primary particles. The imbalanced surface forces that hold these particles together need to be balanced. For this, polar organic or inorganic molecules that can neutralize these surface forces are added to the medium. It is expected that these molecules would penetrate deep into the agglomerated structure and separate the particle to be covered with the wetting agent. The medium can then be coadsorbed on the pigment surface. Once this process is completed, the particles that should ideally have achieved primary form, should stay independently, apart, adequately separated by layers of dispersing agents, wetting agents and the medium.

Adsorption is a surface phenomenon that is equilibrium-limited, strongly dependent on the concentration of the adsorbed moiety in the solution in its physical contact. It is absolutely essential that the concentration of dispersing and wetting agents should be highest when the process of dispersion is carried out. As discussed earlier, no additive should be added more than the minimum, essential concentration. To be able to apply them at highest concentration in the minimum amount, the composition of the mill base should be suitably optimized.

The surface energy of the pigmentary particles is not same on its entire surface. The excess energy at the edges and corners forces pigmentary particles to stick to each other. As a result, the primary particles do not stay as primary particles, but tend to gather together. These are termed as 'flocks'. Flocks tend to intermingle with each other and form aggregates. Clusters formed by the collection of aggregates are called 'agglomerates'.

The situation is more easily explained with the help of a marigold flower. The individual petals in a flower are the primary particles. When these are held together in the form of a flower, it is a flocculate. If we take a bunch of flowers and convert them into a garland by stringing them, the resulting garland is an aggregate. If this garland is placed in a basket with 10 other garlands and allowed to intermingle, the product would be an agglomerate. The job of a paint chemist is to start with an agglomerate and go back all the way to the petals, i.e. primary particles, to get the best of the properties of the pigment. Chemicals that can get adsorbed on the locations of high surface energy and reduce or eliminate the tendency of flock formation are required. This is achieved by tailoring the molecular structure of chemical compounds by incorporating two parts of the molecule that have different chemical nature. Organic chemicals can be broadly classified in two types of products - water-liking and water-hating. The former are termed as hydrophjlic or lipophobic, and the later are termed as hydrophobic or lipophillic (derived form Greek, *philos* meaning dear or loving and *phobos* meaning fear). Functional groups such as sulfonic acid, carboxylic acids & their sodium salts, hydroxyl groups, primary amines are water liking and if they are part of a molecule, they significantly affect the property of the molecule in that direction. Aliphatic long chains do not like water and would stay away from water. Thus, if a molecule had two parts, one a sulfonic acid sodium salt and another a hydrocarbon chain, it would orient itself in water such that all ends liking water face water and all the ends not liking water will stay away from it. Such materials do not make true solutions in water and dissolve only to a limited extent. This can be found out by relationships of solution properties as a function of their concentration in water or a solvent The solution viscosity, refractive index, surface tension, osmotic pressure depend on.solute concentration for ordinary solutes. In the case of surface active agents these properties change linearly only up to a certain concentration. Beyond this concentration, the properties do not change linearly. This is because the molecules do not mix uniformly in the solution beyond this point, but would form aggregates by orienting themselves in water liking and water hating ends. These groups of molecules' can take different shapes at different concentration and are referred as 'micelles'.

The shape of a micelle depends on the concentration of the surface-active agent in water. The concentration at which the micelles first appear is known as critical micelle concentration (CMC). At CMC the shape of the micelle would be spherical (most typically 1-10 g/l). When the concentration exceeds this concentration, the shape changes from spherical to cylindrical and on further increase of surface-active agent changes to plate like and then to bundles of rod-like structures. These concentrations may be real high, up to 100 g/l. At this concentration, the solution resembles a dispersion that is very often seen in the household detergents sold under the umbrella of liquid toilet preparation such as shampoos, liquid cleaners etc.

On the basis of the chemical structures, the surface-active agents can be classified into four categories - anionic, cationic, non ionic, and amphoteric.

The surfactant (short for surface-active agent) gets classified as anionic when the organic molecule has a negative charge, cationic when it has a positive charge, and non-ionic when it has no charge at all. Amphoteric surfactants have both charges. on the same molecule. One of them is more easily ionized than the other.

Anionic Surfactants

$Org X = Org^- + X^+$

where X may be Na, K, NH_4 or any other cation, that easily dissociates in water and Org is organic residue. Examples are:

- Soaps of fatty acids, such as sodium or potassium stearate, potassium oleate, sodium laureate, ammonium soaps of fatty acids,
- Sodium soaps of alkyl aryl sulfonates (active matter of the household detergents), such as alkyl benzene sulfonate,
- Alkyl sulfates such as sodium lauryl sulfate, castor oil sulfate also known as TRO (Turkey red oil)
- Alkyl ether sulfates such as sodium lauryl ether sulfate that is prepared from ethoxylation of lauryl alcohol followed by sulfonation. Sulfosucceenates di 2-ethyl hexyl or di butyl, that are remarkable wetting agents.
- Sodium or potassium salts of polycarboxylic acids such as sodium polyacrylate, sodium polymethacrylate, copolymers of styrene and maleic anhydride and a host of other water-soluble monomers converted into low molecular weight polymers. These are water-soluble and are used in only water-based systems.
- Inorganic salts of phosphoric acid and polyphosphoric acid such as sodium hexameta phosphate and sodium tripolyphosphate, sodium and potassium silicate. These are also used only in water based paints.

Cationic Surfactants

$OrgY = Org^+ + Y^-$

where Y is a typical anion obtained from a mineral acid such as HCl or H_2SO_4' HNO3 or even organic acids such as acetic acid or formic acid.

- Derivatives of ammonia, such as tetra alkylammonium bromide, where the alkyl group can be selected from a large number of alkyl chains, such as methyl, ethyl, benzyl, lauryl, cetyl, steryl and their combinations. Since, a quaternary nitrogen compound can have four different groups, the number of possible compounds is very large.

- Derivatives of diamines such as sterylpropylenediamine diacetate. These are derived from cyanoethylation of primary or secondary amines, followed by hydrogenation and neutralization with acetic acid.
- Derivatives of vegetable oils converted into a mixture of diamines without isolation of individual components. These are referred to as cocodimethylbenzyl ammonium chloride or tallowdimethylbenzyl ammonium chloride depending on the starting material that may be coconut oil or mutton tallow.

Non Ionic Surfactants

These are products prepared from organic substances that have great love for water by combining them with water hating substances. None of the components are capable of ionizing. The structure remains stable in solution and also high temperature since the bond between the two components is covalent. These may or may not be soluble in water depending on the proportion of the two components.

This, by far is the most important class of products required by the paint chemist. These are prepared by condensation of ethylene oxide or propylene oxide with molecules such as alkylated phenols, fatty acids, cardanol, silicone oils with hydroxyl end group, alcohols, fluorinated alcohols, castor oil etc. The ratio of the weight of the ethylene oxide to the organic molecule determines the properties of the finished product. Water solubility of the product depends on the ethylene oxide weight content. The products also act differently depending on the relative weights of the two parts of the molecule. Other products in this class are derivatives of fatty acids with polyols such as glycerol, pentaerythritol, sorbitol, manitol, etc. These may be oil-soluble or watersoluble type depending upon the weight of the fatty acid in the composition. Many paint manufacturers, who also produce resins, utilize the monoglyceride interm~diate in alkyd production as a good wetting and dispersing agent. Coconut mouoglyceride is one good example.

Amphoteric Surfactants

These are molecules in which both types of ionizable groups are available. The functional groups, however, are not very highly ionizable and are selected from tertiary amines, carboxylic acids etc.

These are surfactants that have both charges on the same molecule. Examples are alkyl imidazolene monoacetate, lauryl diethanolamine sulfate, soya lecithin etc.

From the foregoing, it would be noticed that the possible number of compounds that can be used as surface-active agents is infinite and the selection of the products can become extremely difficult without the structural knowledge. Most often, the suppliers are reluctant to disclose the chemical nature of the products. They would, however, provide gross information about the chemical nature of the product, except for the commodity chemicals. The question then arises, as to how does a paint chemist distinguish one product from another? There is a simple parameter that the supplier is obliged to inform the user and this is termed as hydrophil-liphophil balance (HLB) value.

There are several ways in which the HLB value of a given chemical can be determined. In one method, various structural groups are allotted a number that indicates the intensity by which the group affects the water sensitivity or water repellency of a compound. The contribution of both the types of the groups is combined together to arrive at the net HLB value of the product.

Table 1-1 lists the contribution of various structural groups. The HLB value is calculated by a formula:

$$HLB = 7 + \Sigma H - \Sigma L$$

Table 1-1 **H And L Numbers For Representative Hydrophilic And Lipophilic Chemical Groups**

Hydrophilic groups	H Numbers	Lipophilic groups	L Numbers
$Na\ SO_4$ -	39	-CH-	0.47
KOOC-	21	$-CH_2-$	0.47
NaOOC-	19	$-CH_3$	0.47
HOOC-	2.1	=CH-	0.47
HO-	1.9	$-CH_2-CH(OH)(CH_3)-$	0.11
-0-	1.3	$-(CH_2-CH_2-O-)$	0.36

Sample calculation

Take the example of sodium lauryl sulfate (SLS). The chemical formula of SLS has one sodium sulfato group, eleven methylene groups and one methyl group. Thus we have $\Sigma H = 39$ and $\Sigma L = (11 * 0.47) + 1 * 0.47 = 5.64$. Inserting these values in the formula, we get the HLB of SLS as 40.36.

Similarly, we can calculate the HLB value of various other surface-active materials. For example:

- Oleic acid ($C_{17}H_{33}COOH$): HLB = 7 + 2.1 - (17*0.47) = 1.11
- Sodium oleate ($C_{17}H_{33}COONa$) : HLB = 7 + 19 - (17*0.47) = 18.01
- Sorbitol monooleate (5 hydroxyl groups of sorbitol are available) : HLB = 7 + (5*1.9) - (17*0.47) = 8.51
- Propylene glycol monolaurate [CH_3-CH(OH)-CH2]-OCO-(CH_2)1O-CH_3: HLB = 7 + 1.9 - (13*0.47) = 2.79

Other methods

(i) For derivatives of fatty acids, that have saponifiable groups, HLB is given by an expression:

$$HLB=20(1-S/A)$$

where, S is the saponification value and A is the acid value of the recovered acid.

Thus, for propylene glycol monolaurate, the sap value is 217 and the acid value of lauric acid is 280.5. Putting these values in the formula, we get the HLB of P^G monolaurate as 4.52. If we take an ethoxylated sorbitol monooleate, with saponification value of 50 and the acid value of lauric acid is 280, the HLB is 20 (1-50/280) = 16.42.

(ii) When the hydrophilic portion is only ethylene oxide, the HLB value is calculated by the equation,

$$HLB=20 * W$$

where W is the weight fraction of ethylene oxide in the surface-active agent.

Thus, for 10.5 moles of ethylene oxide condensed on nonylphenol, HLB = 20 *[44x10.5] / [218+(44x10.5)] = 13.58.

Significance of HLB value

HLB value tells us the chemical character of the surfactant. Lower values indicate low water solubility and higher oil solubility. Higher values indicate higher water solubility and lower oil solubility. It is not possible to exactly demarcate where a deemulsifier ends and a wetting and dispersing agent starts on the HLB scale or where a dispersing agent ends and an emulsifier starts. The general guideline is:

- Deemulsifier's HLB is in the range of 2 to 4
- Wetting and dispersing agent's HLB is from 4 to 8
- Emulsifier's HLB is between 7 to 40

The surface active agent that is to be added would also be decided by what needs to be the continuous phase and what needs to be the dispersed phase. Selection of the wetting and dispersing agent would also depend upon the nature of the pigment surface. Organic pigments would require totally different products compared to inórganic pigments, which, in turn, would be completely different from carbon black.

How much wetting and dispersing agent would be required for the pigment would depend on the surface area of the pigment primary particles. It is recommended that the surface-active agent should form a monomolecular layer on the surface of the pigment. Depending on the area of cross section of the molecule of the surface active agent, how it gets adsorbed on the pigment surface, and what is the molecular weight of the surface active agent, the requirement of the surface active agent would vary from 2 to 3 mg/m^2 area of the pigment. Thus for a pigment with 50 m^2 surface area, the requirement of surface active agent would be about 100 mg/g pigment, but for a fine particle carbon black with surface area of 500 m^2/g, the requirement of surface active agent may be up to 1 g/g of pigment.

Many a times, the medium in which we are dispersing the pigment itself acts as a good wetting material for the pigment. The requirement of the actual wetting and dispersing agent in such cases reduces considerably.

Method of addition

Surface active agents need to be adsorbed on the pigment surface for achieving maximum benefits. These must be added in concentrated form with minimum solvents directly to the pigments. The optimum requirement is best worked out by Daniel Flow point method, described later.

Side effects

Surface active agents are water sensitive. Too much additive that is not fully adsorbed on the pigment surface causes the film to be water sensitive. The film may develop blisters or white spots on immersion in water. These substances also reduce surface tension of the liquid medium. Formation of stable foam, reduction in paint density due to air entrapment, bloom on the dried paint surface, impaired flow of the paint are some of the defects caused by excessive addition of surface active agents.

Caution

Cationic and anionic surface active agents have opposite electrical charges. They should never be added together since they would neutralize each other, become completely insoluble and become totally useless.

ADDITIVES FOR VISCOSITY CONTROL

Viscosity of the paint depends on the molecular weight of the resin and the total solids present in the composition - higher the molecular weight of the resin, higher the viscosity.

The viscosity of the resin also depends on the type of the solvent. Good solvent to a resin is able to open out the chains completely and the viscosity of the resin is high. A poor solvent does not allow polymer chains to open out and the viscosity of the resin reduces. Invariably, this phenomenon is not correctly understood and the poor solvent is erroneously called "cutting solvent" because its addition considerably reduces the viscosity, at times disproportionately. Typical example is n-butyl alcohol in a long oil alkyd where its addition at even 1% level causes a steep drop in the viscosity of the alkyd solution. This property can be used for controlling the viscosity of the paint. Similarly, higher viscosity of the resin can be obtained by using a true solvent that would extend all the polymer chains and increase the viscosity of the medium. In pigmented systems, deficiency or wrong selection of surface active agent leads to flocculation of pigment that leads to increase of viscosity by a process called "bridging". This can also be used to control the viscosity of the coating material. By addition of adequate surface-active agent the lowest viscosity of the system can be obtained. Another technique is addition of very high viscosity polymers or associative polymers. These affect viscosity of the medium at very low concentration. These are separately discussed in additives for control of flow and leveling.

Side effects

If a solvent has been used for lowering of the viscosity, its boiling point must be lower than the true solvent so that it evaporates before the true solvent goes out. The flow and level of the paint thus will remain unaffected. If the viscosity reducer stays in the film longer than the true solvent, the flow and leve1ing of the film are seriously affected.

Scratch, mar, slip and abrasion resistance

Mar resistance is the ability of a coating to interact with the environment without incurring relatively fine surface scratches that spoil appearance(2) of coatings.

The scratches referred to here are much shallow compared to the deep scratches that may extend to full depth of the coating. To give an idea of the order of magnitude, if a coating is about 40 microns thick, the scratches being referred here are 2-3 microns deep. To mar means to spoil the appearance(3). A scratch would be anywhere from 50% of the depth of the film to complete exposure of the bare metal.

These are surface properties of a film highly desirable in coatings that come in regular contact with human body parts or other moving objects. Automobiles, especially in India, are prone to scratch formation by deliberate efforts of street urchins as 'time pass' activity while crossing a road. This is without a realization that it causes annoyance to the vehicle owner who cannot get the fault rectified, even if he wanted to.

When an external sharp edge comes in contact with a painted surface, it can cause damage in two ways - by penetrating just the surface or by cutting through along the plain surface. The second case appears when the body with the sharp edge is also moving. There are two ways to prevent the scratch formation:

- Increase the hardness and toughness of the coating.
- Increase the lubricity of the surface so that the penetrant slips and damage is avoided.

Since the formulator is constrained by other parameters such as flexibility and impact strength of the film, the hardness can not be indefinitely increased. One way to tackle it is by addition of perfectly spherical fine particles to the topcoat that are order of magnitudes smaller than the film thickness. If the film thickness is 10 micron, very fine *(0.05μ)* and transparent particles of a hard substance can prevent formation of scratch, by prevention of indentation(5).

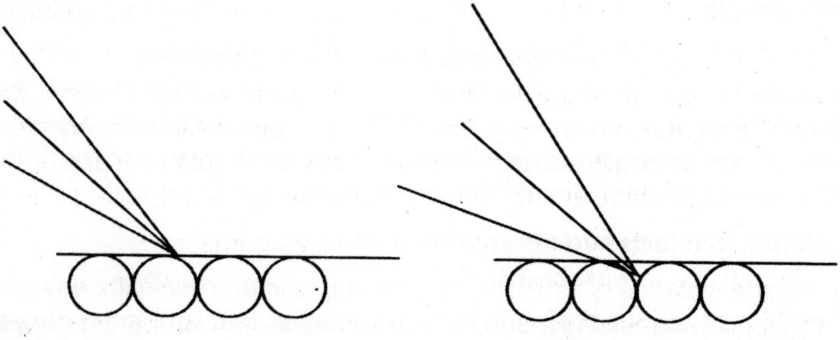

Further damage is prevented

For better bonding *of* the fine silica nano particles these are chemically converted to reactive particles that become a part *of* film by chemical reactions.

Siloxane methacrylate - nano composites are prepared by condensing (trimethoxysilyl) ethyl methacrylate with silica nano particles.

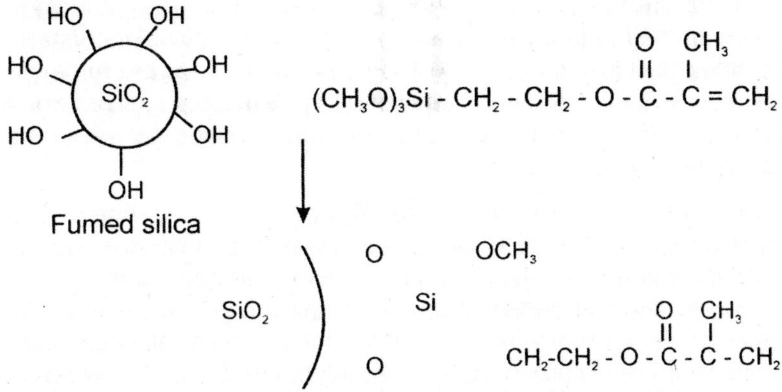

These silicon dioxide particles are quite hard being high (7-8) on the Mohs scale of hardness (talc-l, gypsum-2, calcite-3, fluorite-4, apatite-5, feldspar-6, quartz-7, topaz-8, corrundum-9, diamond-10) and too small for an indenting tool, abrasive particle *or* steel wool to be able to dislodge them from the surface. Moreover, the spherical shape of the hard surface makes the gripping of the surface for propagation *of* the scratch very difficult. For this reason, surfaces modified by the above particles in a cured film offer extraordinarily high abrasion resistance and retain gloss even after several thousand revolution *of* Tabar Abbraser ($H\text{-}_{10}$ rollers *of* 250 g. weight, gloss retention of 98% after 8300 revolutions for 20μ thickness against about 53% for a coating without these spheres at only 2700 revolutions).

Additives other than the silica nano spheres are mainly waxes. These work by making the surface slippery. These are low melting polycrystalline products that melt locally due to heat created by friction, lubricate and prevent scratch formation. There are two types of waxes available to the paint chemist:

- Natural products: Vegetable waxes such as camauba wax, rice bran wax, soyabean wax, bees wax
- Synthetic waxes: Polyethylene / polypropylene wax, microcrystalline wax, fluorocarbon waxes.

Natural Waxes

Wax is present on the surface *of* .leaves of all plants as a thin film to prevent evaporation of water from the large surface area *of* leaves. These waxes are fatty alcohol esters of long chain saturated or partially unsaturated fatty acids. The chain length of alcohol is up to C_{36} and that of the fatty acid C_{16} or C_{18}. Thus most of the natural waxes are triocantanol palmitate or triocantanol stearate. Similar variety of waxes is also present in vegetable oils. Due to their high melting point, they become insoluble/ crystallized in vegetable oils at low temperature and cause haze. They are removed from vegetable oils by a process called "wintering" that comprises storage at low temperature (about 5°C) for long duration followed by separation by centrifugation.

Melting point of most of the natural waxes is in the range of 58-65°C, highest being about 82-85°C for carnauba wax that contains a hydroxylated fatty acid. A variant of these waxes is hydrogenated castor oil that can mimic some of the properties of carnauba wax due to intact hydroxyl groups. A peculiarity of natural waxes is that the fatty acids or alcohols both have only even number of carbon atoms. Probably nature can add only two carbons at a time!

Synthetic waxes Petroleum wax

The mineral hydrocarbons that are the chief feedstock of the chemical industry contain a wide variety of structures. The crudes found around coasts of India are rich in linear hydrocarbons, particularly in the range C_{40}-C_{60}. This is a good source of wax (about 50%) that is mostly being burnt as a low sulfur heavy stock (LSHS) fuel. Certain refineries (e.g, MRL) are equipped to distill this fuel and separate the paraffin wax in the melting range of 50-60°C.

These waxes dissolve in chlorinated solvents at high temperature and also nonpolar solvents. Solubility in polar solvents is restricted. Also, solubility at lower temperature is rather low.

Microcrystalline wax

When paraffin wax or higher residues of the distillates of crude are further distilled under high vacuum. or are separated by techniques called "dewaxing", higher melting waxes (mp 60-90°C) result. The carbon number may range from 40 to 50, in a straight linear chain. Due to presence of long straight chains, they easily crystallize into very closely packed bundles of molecules and are harder than paraffin or carnauba wax. As they rapidly tend to crystallize from a solution, they offer better mar resistance, and give a harder feel to touch.

Polyethylene and polypropylene waxes

The manufacturing process of polyolefins, whether high pressure or low pressure, produces low molecular weight by-product. These are detrimental to the properties of the plastic and are therefore removed by hot hexane extraction. This extract contains oligomers with carbon numbers ranging from 70 to 200. These waxes are high melting, less soluble, harder and therefore provide less resistance to slip. These are therefore, blended with other lower melting waxes to get the desired properties. Being byproducts of polymer industry with a large base, they are relatively cheaper.

PTFE waxes

Polytetrafluoroethylene (PTFE) is one of the most inert polymers. Its low molecular weight product displays similar properties such as chemical inertness, high melting point and high density (2-2.2 g/cc). Because of its high density and poor wetting, it tends to settle down in low viscosity media and cannot be found in the final application where it is most required. Its use is, therefore, restricted to very high viscosity coatings or powder coatings. Since the melting point of the waxes is also high, they do not melt in the curing system. All the properties imparted to the surface are dependent on the particle size of the wax. Particles in the range of *2-31-1* provide good performance. Coarse particles are a waste and nuisance, as they cause large particles to appear on the surface or even choke the spray equipment.

Like all fluorocarbon resins, these are very expensive (- Rs. 1,000/kg), not still produced locally and are used in special applications demanding high gloss. To improve upon some of the drawbacks, they are melt blended with polyethylene wax. One major advantage to these waxes is their water resistance, chemical resistance and out door durability. Where all other waxes disappear from the surface fairly rapidly, PTFE waxes stay long enough to provide continued slip and mar resistance.

All the waxes find application in glossy and semi-glossy paints, automotive paints, furniture and wood coatings, white goods coatings including coil coatings etc. where they impart longer blemish resistant life to the coatings.

Addition method

The wax is heated in a solvent (except wax that melts above 300°C) and allowed to cool under good agitation. This precipitates the wax as a micro crystal below *3-5μ*. The dispersion is added to a well-agitated system and would be one of the last additives added to the paint system. Adequate stirring is required to disperse the wax thoroughly so that agglomerates of crystals are not formed. PTFE waxes are used as received under good high-speed dispersion.

Side effects

Too coarse particles and too much of the wax can cause bloom and problem of overcoat adhesion. Problems of film slippage on vertical surfaces, particularly for thick coatings can be observed if too much of wax is a part of the formula.

THIXOTROPIC AND ANTI-SETTLING AGENTS

Thixotropy is useful in a coating formulation for attaining three sets of properties:

a) Ease of transfer

b) Ease of brushing or application

c) Flow, leveling and sag control.

Imagine a paint that is highly viscous and flows like honey. If the painter dipped his brush, the paint would continue to drip in form of a thin string that never-wanted to stop. In this way, the painter will have to wait for a long time before he could transfer the brush to the object. Even while doing this, he would spill plenty of paint on the floor. In his next operation of brushing, the drag would be so high that his arm would easily get tired and the painter would not be able to spread much of the paint. Soon after the painter has removed his hand from the object, the paint would continue to flow down causing sag marks. The thixotropic agent alone provides remedy to all these problems.

By definition, the thixotropic agent causes lowering of viscosity as the shear rate is increased. The viscosity builds up as a function of time after the shear is removed. Let us examine how the shear rate changes in the above three operations.

As the brush is dipped in the stationery paint, the shear rate at the surface of the brush is high. This causes thinning of the paint in direct contact of the brush. The paint can easily penetrate the brush. As the penetration of the brush is stopped and the brush is pulled out, the paint inside the brush has thickened and the shear rate between the layers of paint surrounding the brush becomes high. As a result, a thick coat of paint gets attached to the brush. As soon as the brush leaves the liquid paint surface, the paint already contained in the brush thickness and the string is broken. The painter can easily transfer the paint up to the wall or the surface he intends to paint.

As the brushing operation is started, the paint thins down and the effort required for spreading the paint reduces. The painter can comfortably spread the paint on a large surface without getting tired.

As soon as the brush is removed from the surface, the rate of shear becomes zero and the viscosity of the product starts to build up. The rate of rise of viscosity can be so adjusted that the paint finds enough time to flow and level but does not drip or sag on the surface. All these three properties are very conveniently obtained with organoclays.

Settling

As we know, paint is a dispersion of particles in a viscous medium. The particles size is finite and there is a definite pull dull due to gravity (F=mg). This causes the particles to settle down. For a well formulated paint this settling may be negligible, whereas for a poorly formulated paint, the settling may be too hard and severe. The thixotropic behaviour of the paint helps to reduce settling. As soon as the paint is filled up in a can and reaches its storage space, the shear rate is zero. This allows the viscosity to build up. The settling velocity, also called terminal velocity of a particle, is a function of its density, particle size and viscocity of the medium. Whereas the first two will directly affect it, the viscocity has inverse relation. As soon as the viscocity increases, particles settling velocity reduces. For very high viscocity medium this velocity may approach zero. Since the particle size of most of the paint is very small (~1μ) the viscocity of the medium required to completely prevent settling is not very high.

There are three types of products for solvent based coatings. Organoclays, organic products, and metal salts. For water based systems polymers of natural origin are modified to meet the need. These include HEC, CMC etc.

Organoclays

These are the most important thixotropic agents added to paint system. These are derivatives of naturally occurring clays that have a highly crystalline structure and have an exchangeable cation on the edges of the cyrstals. The cation is replaceable by typical ion exchange techniques. Of the several minerals only a select few are suitable for this application. Two main members are :

Montmorilonites : Chemical structure —$Si_8(OH)_4Al_{3.34}.Mg_{0.66})O_{20}$; some portions of the crystal lattice have a charge imbalance, this has been offset by a metal cation, usually, Na, K or Ca that are exchangeable.

- Hectorite: Chemical Structure — $Si_8(OH)_4Mg_{5.34}.Li_{0.66})O_{20}$; with a difference from bentonite that it has Mg & Li in place of Al & Mg and has no calcium. It is relatively less frequently found in nature, is a valuable source of lithium and is rarely used for preparation of organoclays.

The clays are hydrophilic due to the presence of the four hydroxyl groups on the edges of every crystal. These can associate with a large quantity with a large quantity of water and swell in water to a great degree. None of these clays show any affinity for solvents or oils and do not swell at all the organic medium.

Exchange technique is used for obtaining the hydrophobic behaviour in the clays. The exchangeable sites of Na+ or Li+ are exchanged with organic cationic molecule. Nitrogen containing compounds that have a positive charge are the modifying agents. There are several quaternary ammonium compounds that can be used for exchanging with cation of the clays as already discussed in surface active agents.

$$\text{Clay } O^{-}Na+ + R_2 - \underset{\displaystyle R_3}{\overset{\displaystyle R_1}{\underset{|}{\overset{|}{N}}}} - R_4\ CBr^{-} \longrightarrow \text{Clay } O^{-} - +\underset{\displaystyle R_3}{\overset{\displaystyle R_1}{\underset{|}{\overset{|}{N}}}} - R_4 + NaBr$$

where R_1, R_2, R_3 & R_4 are methyl, benzyl steryl or other radicals derived from tallow, fatty acids or vegetable oils. A blend of different quaternary ammonium compounds is practiced to tailor the properties of the product. Suspending the clay in a dilute solution of the quaternary compound or directly mixing the wet clay with concentrated surfaceactive agent can carry out the exchange reaction.

An organoclay swollen in a solvent is thixotropic.

How to use

The organoclays swell considerably in a solvent and are first swollen in a solvent before addition of other paint ingredients.

The product is obtained as a fine powder and is first suspended in the solvent to break the agglomerates with high-speed stirring. Solvents may be high aromatic/mineral spirits. Small quantities of long oil alkyd may be added to improve the wetting. If the paint is based on epoxy or polyester resin, the alkyd would act a contaminant and is best avoided. In such a situation, it is recommended that the organoclay be wetted with neat solvent before adding any resin, since these resins are not very good wetting agents. The time required to wet the clay varies from a few minutes to about 30 minutes depending upon the resin. For better deagglomeration a combination of wetting and shear is essential.

For actually swelling the clay, polar activators are required. These are polar solvents such as methanol, ethyl alcohol, propyl alcohol and propylene carbonate. These solvents may be used neat or with traces of water (up to 5%). The activator requirement is about 3 to 5% of the weight of the clay. Larger quantity if added, can interfere with the process of hydrogen bonding by blocking those sites. This, in turn, affects the thickening capability of clays. The viscosity of the clay dispersion increases with increasing concentration of the activator up to a level and then falls off.

The concentration at which maximum viscosity is obtained is the optimum level.

After activation, the clay is delaminated by application of shear. A high shear high-speed disperser does this best. If the system is pigmented, the shear required to disperse the pigment is generally enough to disperse the clay as well.

For poorly wetted system, the organoclay can also be swollen in only the solvent with activator at 6-8% concentration. This forms a gel that can then be added to the other constituents of the paint. A typical composition would be: Organo clay 9, Activator 3, Solvent 88.

As the mixture is stirred, it thickens up. It would however not be able to completely delaminate and would do so when the other ingredient of the paint are subjected to high shear. It is a better procedure to be able to optimize the concentration of the organoclay since the addition must be very accurate.

Side effects

Gloss is reduced by excessive addition. The loss of gloss is minimized. by careful adjustment of the composition by pre-gel technique. Excessive addition can seriously affect both, flow and DOI.

Corrosion resistance may be affected by presence of residual chloride or bromide ions left behind by the ion exchange reaction. Both these ions are corrosive to mild steel. The levels of organoclays are fairly low in the paint composition; of that chloride or bromide ions are a small component. These can affect the corrosion resistance of the coatings.

Organic thixotropic agents

Organo metallics - aluminum stearate, octoates, calcium linoleate - function by swelling in solvent as gel.

There are different grades of metal soaps. The aluminum is a trivalent metal and it can react with one, two or three moles of stearic acid. As monostearate, it produces highest viscosity in hydrocarbons. This may be attributed to the possibility of intermolecular hydrogen bonding that results in much higher molecular weight

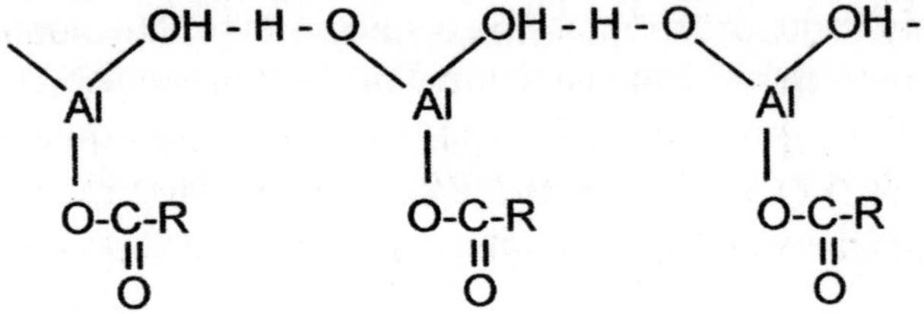

In the case of distearate, the possibility of forming long chains of such molecules does not exist.

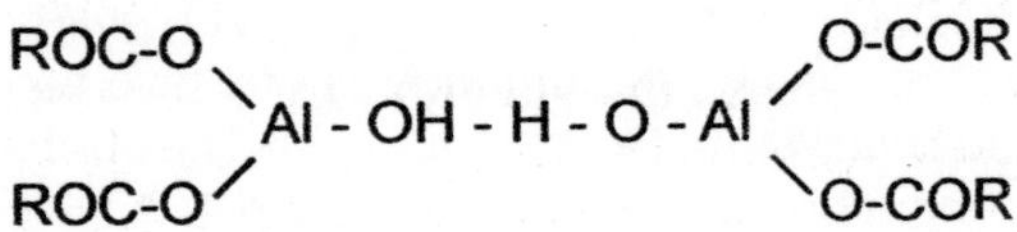

In the tristearate the possibility does not exist at all. Even for economic reasons, monostearates are preferred more than di- and tri-stearates. The hydrogen bonding can also take place with pigment or resin component. Since these are shear sensitive, weak and non-specific bonds break down easily under high shear of high-speed agitation or under a brush (shear rate up to 20,000/sec). As soon as the shear stress is removed, the bonds can form afresh. This process takes some time. This is the time available to the film to level. By the time the level is attained, the flow should reduce and prevent flow and sag. It is quite obvious that aluminum monostearate would best do this job and aluminum tristearate may not be able to perform at all.

Needless to say that these products can not perform universally. They would strongly depend on the type and concentration of pigments and binders.

Method of addition

The organo clay based. products are first swollen in a suitable hydrocarbon solvent with the help of an activator. It may also be mildly heated if necessary. The gel so produced is mixed with the paint composition. In the case of aluminum stearate, it is added to a hydrocarbon solvent, heated to about 60-90°C and the resultant gel, that can also be stored conveniently, is added to the composition with adequate stirring.

Thixotropic agents for water borne coatings

There are several derivatives of cellulose, starch, and animal products such as gelatin, chitin and natural gums that can be used for this purpose. There are several issues dictating the choice of thixotropic agents such as viscosity, bacterial degradation and the effect on the final film properties.

Of the products listed above, derivatives of cellulose are the most stable to degradation. Cellulose is a polysaccharide with anhydroglucose repeating units. Each unit has three hydroxyl groups available - of these one is primary and two are secondary hydroxyls. Chemical reactions are carried out to convert these functional groups to solubilize cellulose in water. The reactions of methyl chloride, ethylene oxide, propylene oxide and chloroacetic acid sodium salt produce products with varying degree of substitution. Ethyl chloride, on partial substitution produces alcohol soluble products suitable for printing ink application. The extent of substitution is described by "Degree of substitution" or DS. The highest number for DS is 3. Most of the water-soluble materials have DS = 2.1-2.4.

Except CMC (carboxymethyl cellulose) all derivatives are non-ionic in nature. These are supplied in powder form.

Dissolution

It is preferable to add the thickener in the form of solution rather than a solid power. The manufacturer's literature must be used to choose optimum temperature and pH for dissolving a product. A variable speed drive with turbine blades is the most recommended equipment. The agitator must be fully dipped in solution and air should not be allowed to entrain. Products are generally hygroscopic and must be stored dry. Powder is added quickly without allowing it to form lumps. The pH is raised to the recommended level that causes a marked change in viscosity. The mixing intensity should be adequately increased to cope with the change. Mixing is continued till a clear solution free of air bubbles is formed and undissolved suspended particles are absent. A preservative is added to avoid microbial contamination.

The other varieties of thickners for water based paints are polyacrylate and associative thickners. Of these acrylics could be had as aqueous solution or emulsion. The emulsions are preferred as they have high solid contents and low viscosity as raw materials. Whenever these are neutralized by ammonia, dimethylethanolarnine or any other acceptable base, the polymeric particles dissolve and a solution results. These are quite popular products in the Indian paint industry. Low odor, almost no colour, and very high viscosity at low concentration characterize these. These products are highly pH sensitive.

Associative thickeners

The structure of these polymers is similar to surface active agents in that they have hydrophilic and hydrophobic parts in it. The solubility of hydrophilic part is high that pulls the hydrophobic part in solution. The type and frequency of the hydrophobic groups and the molecular weight decide the viscosity of the solution. Polymers from acrylic, vinyl acrylic, ethylene vinyl acetate or terpolymers'with acrylic acid belong to this group.

Problem faced with associative thickeners is colour distribution, especially in gloss and semi gloss paints where the colour distribution may not be uniform. Poaming is another problem that can be caused by increased level of surfactant present in associative thickener during its production. Seeding, just like in cellulosic thickeners is also caused by improper mixing of associative thickener with the base paint. Repainting of objects previously painted may show lifting of the film and the associative thickeners are known to do that.

In spite of the problems, associative thickeners have shown promise.

Side effects

Excessive use can result in flocculation of pigments that has its own contributions to defects such as loss of colour value, seeding and in extreme case reversal of finish.

ANTI-SKINNING AGENTS

The air-drying paints are supplied in containers of various sizes ranging from as low as 50 ml to as high as 20 l. Most users do not use up all the paint in one go. They either transfer a part of the contents in another vessel to use or directly use from the container; after that they place the lid back and store it for future use. As the paint is packed in a factory the container does contain a small volume (about 5- 1 0%) of air at the top of the paint. This is a problem for the paint formulator. The surface of the paint has everything that is required to start the process of drying. There is a surface, there is air and the paint contains driers. If an additive that can prevent drying of the paint is not present, a thick film is formed on the surface that represents loss of the paint. Whenever the user reopens this can, the skin is required to be removed and discarded. If the use of paint is spread over a long period with small usage every time, the waste of paint may be up to 50% for small packaging. This loss needs to be prevented. Thus the formulator is faced with a contradictory situation. The additive must fulfil two demands.

- It must retard drying of the paint in the container
- It must not retard drying of the paint when applied on a surface

Invariably, the twin objective can be achieved by suitable combination of antiskining agents and driers. Most additives for anti skinning are temporary antioxidants. They either get consumed or destroyed when exposed to air or evaporate. Though they may prolong the drying time a bit, that can be compensated by adjusting the quantity of drier.

Most commonly used anti skinning agents belong to two classes.

- Phenolic - phenol, cresols, xylenols
- Oximes - MEK oxime, cyclohexanone oxime

When the paint is contained in the container, a small amount of air is present on the surface. The antioxidant, that has certain vapour pressure, distributes itself in liquid and vapour and causes inhibition of oxidation in full measure. When the paint is applied as a thin film and exposed to plenty of air, the phenolic antioxidant evaporates and is lost from the film over a period of time and the paint dries normally. For this reason, higher substituted phenols can not be used for this application. Also, phenols produce dark coloured products on oxidation.

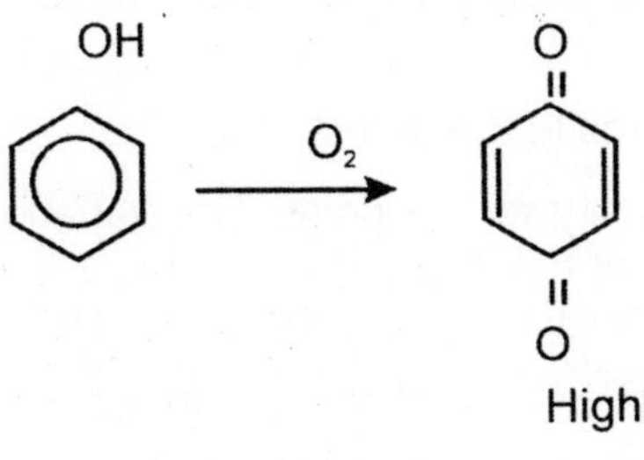

Highly Coloured molecule

These can seriously discolour light coloured paints and should be avoided.

The oximes may decompose with atmospheric water into a ketone and hydroxylamine.

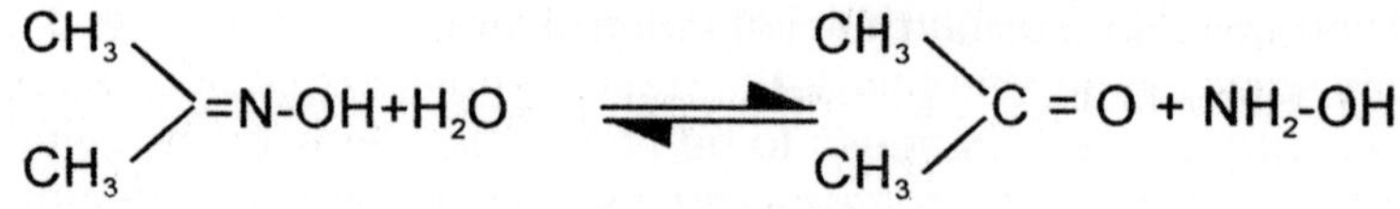

Or

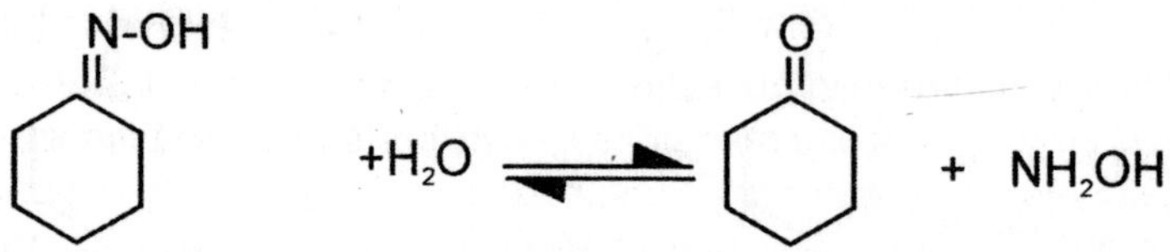

The solvent methyl ethyl ketone evaporates from the surface when the film is exposed and the inhibition, that is similar to the hindered amine type, is eliminated. The drying can then proceed smoothly.

Side Effects

The most significant side effect of anti-skinning agent is retardation of drying. This is acceptable and must be overcome by additional cobalt and lead driers.

ANTI-FOAMING AGENTS AND DEFOAMERS

Foam is a dispersion of large volume of gas in a relatively small volume of liquid. The phase ratio may be as much as 99% air + 1 % liquid or small part of air entrapped in large volume of liquid. For a coating technologist both situations are troublesome. During manufacture, if the agitator does not dip completely and creates a vortex, it can pull in large volume of air. With the energy of the agitator, the air gets broken down into finer bubbles that do not easily break.

This foam creates two problems to the user:

a) It reduces the apparent density of the paint. The variation may be significant since the density of the dispersed air phase is very small (0.00116 *g/cc* compared to about 1.2 *g/cc* of the paint). Therefore even a small amount of air dispersed in the paint can cause it to become off specification.

b) If the foam is stable and persistent, it causes film defects on application. Small bubbles lead to problems such as fish eye, pinholes, and larger bubbles cause formation of craters as they break. At times, the air bubble may remain entrapped through the process of drying or break too late during drying and cause orange peel effect.

There are two ways to get over this problem:

a) Not allowing the foam to form during manufacture by addition of anti-foams.

b) By additives that break the foam even after it has formed.

In all coating systems, surface-active agents are present that cause lowering of surface tension. Lowering of surface tension stabilizes foam. The ability of different surfactants in different media is not same. The effect of same surfactant may be completely different in water and organic media.

Anti-foaming agents

Anti-foaming agents are generally sparingly soluble in the medium they are put. They are also added in very low concentration. To improve the accuracy of addition, they are diluted with solvents. Surface active agents may be added to improve the wetting and spreading.

Following are the classes of compounds suitable for antifoam applications.

- Block copolymers of ethylene oxide/propylene oxide (more PO than EO)
- Amides of fatty acids, hydroxy fatty acids, esters of fatty acids, metal salts of fatty acids
- Silicone oils of intermediate molecular weight, also used as emulsions for water-based systems
- Organophosphates
- Fatty alcohols (C_2 to C_{18}) and esters of hydroxy acids such as castor oil.

Solvents can be chosen from the wide range of available solvents known to the organic coatings industry. Any solvent that can suitably dissolve the anti-foam is acceptable. Surfactant may be ethylene oxide- nonyl phenol condensate, sulfonated fatty acids.

Defoamers

The chemical defoamers are compounds that are able to destroy the foam even after it is formed. One good material is *Surfynol 104,* an acetylenic diol, that is very effective for water-based systems.

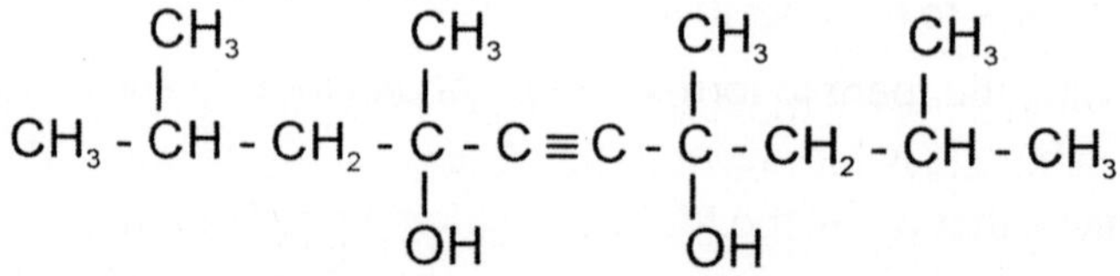

(2,4,7,9-Tetramethyl - 5- decyane-4,7-diol)

For water based formulations suitable materials are dipentene, pine oil and combinations of hydrocarbon oils at low concentration.

Application Method

Antifoam compounds should not be included in the formulation. If, on manufacture, the paint appears to have foaming, suitable defoamers may be added in a quantity that is exactly required. This being a critical component must be added with matrix dilution.

Side effects

The anti-foams may produce side effects such as loss of gloss, and adhesion and may also adversely affect the flow of the film. Excessive addition may cause pin holing, cratering and dewetting

COUPLING COMPOUNDS (Adhesion Promoters)

Coupling compounds were initially discovered for use in fibre reinforced plastics to improve adhesion between glass fibre and the unsaturated polyester resin. These, products have become very useful for the paint technologist. These impart following properties to the coating:

- Improve adhesion to the substrate, particularly inorganic/metals
- Increase the film integrity by chemically bonding on the pigment surface.
- Improve flow and reduce flow defects
- Reduce flocculation.
- Increase wettability of pigments and the pigment loading

Coupling compounds are so called because these can chemically react with the surface hydroxyls of the pigment. Once incorporated, they change the bond between pigment and binder from physical adsorption to a covalent bond that is much more difficult to break. Even though the bonding between fibre glass and polyester resin appeared satisfactory initially, it was realized soon that the bonding was lost due to exposure to atmosphere and water. When the industry started using trace amounts of these products, improvement in the performance was drastic. From then on these have been increasingly used in coatings, inks, sealants and several other automotive products, that broadly.suffered from poor adhesion and poor flow.

There are primarily two types of coupling compounds - (1) silanes and (2) titanates and zirconates.

Typical silanes have the general structure

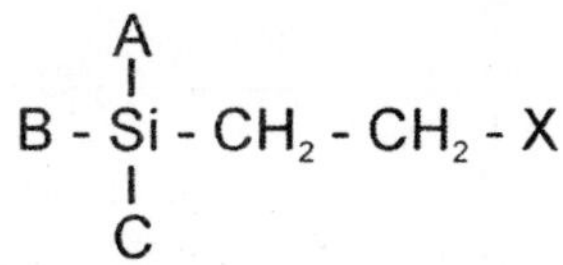

where A, B C are short chain alkoxy, aryloxy groups or hydrolysable groups such as Cl, or OH. X is a functional group such as amino, azido, methacryloyl, epoxide or carboxylic acid or its anhydride. Some times the entire alkyl group (CH_2-CH_2-X) can be replaced by a vinyl (CH_2=CH-) group. Several functioned groups can be used as a blend.

Titanates and zirconates are organo metallic compounds of Ti and Zr with combinations of groups from alkoxy, sulfonyl, carboxyl, acetylacetonate, phosphate, and a functional group such as amino, epoxy, azido, or methacryloxy. The substitution may be restricted to one or two groups, the balance being methoxy or butoxy groups.

Aluminum compounds of similar nature are also recommended.

Mode of use

The coupling compounds are partially hydrolyzed prior to use. This is accomplished by addition of calculated and measured quantity of water.

Suppliers

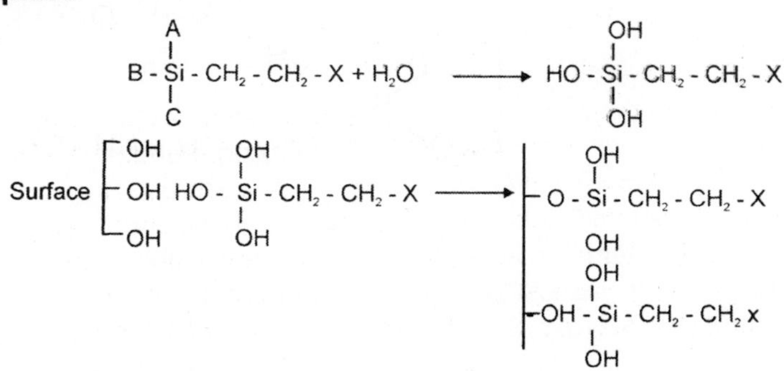

Cont.

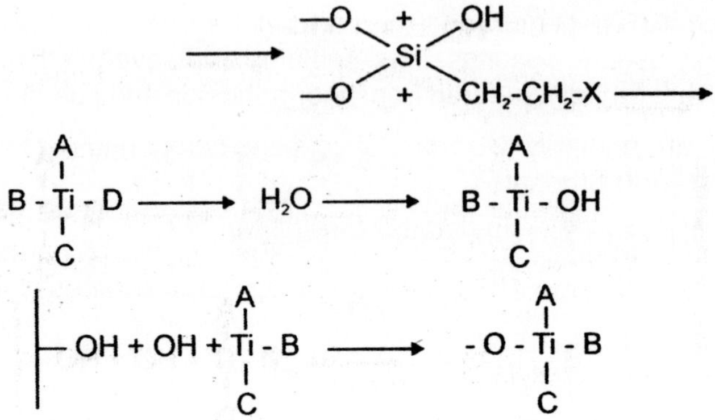

ABC may react with -OH, -COOH or other functional groups of the binder and act as a bridge to chemically link the surface with the medium.

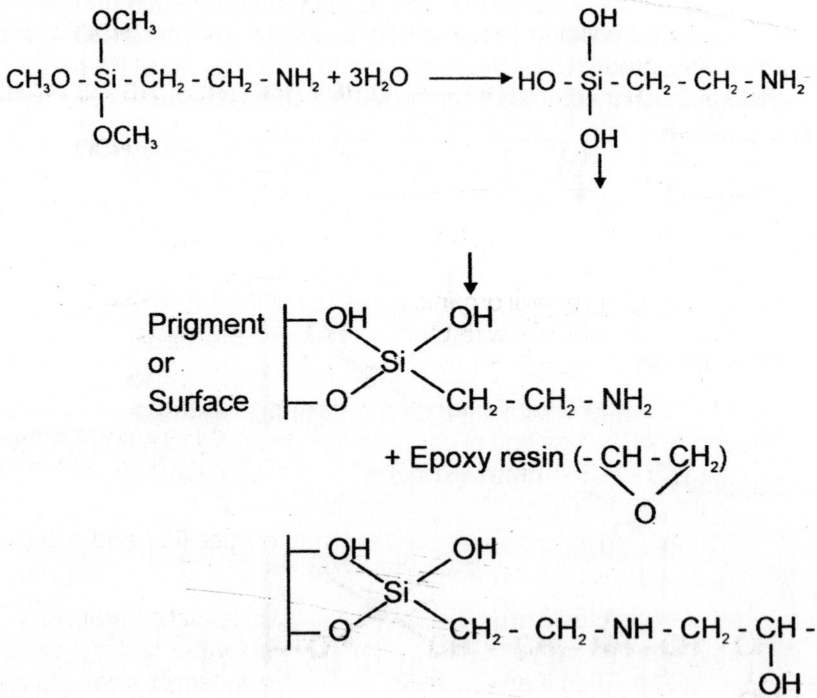

- Silanes - General Electric, Union Carbide
- Titanates & Zirconates - Kenrich Bayonne NJ Petrochemicals, Coatwell Paints (India)

DESICCANTS

Water is an important impurity in the coatings. Except water based coatings, it is expected that all the ingredients of the paint should be as dryas possible. Inspite of this, there are three major sources of water in the formulations.

- Moisture adsorbed on the pigments
- Moisture contained in the solvents
- Moisture contained in the medium

As we have discussed under wetting and dispersing agents, the surface of all pigments is covered by moisture. When wetting and dispersing agent gets adsorbed on the surface, it displaces water in the continuous medium. Depending on the surface area and density of the material, this moisture may be a few percent of the weight of the pigment (1.5 mg/m^2 for a monolayer). If the surface area is about 50 m^2/g, which is most often the case, the equilibrium moisture content of the pigment would be 75 mg/ g or about 7.5% on dry basis. Most pigments are dried before packing and may have moisture ranging from 1 to 5%.

Even though several organic solvents have no apparent water solubility and water does not mix with them, they all have finite water solubility that increases with increasing temperature. If the solvents are processed by distillation these contain saturated concentration of water. This will depend on the chemical nature of solvent. Hydrocarbon solvents may contain less water, while alcohols and esters may contain some more. Water soluble-solvents may contain large concentration.

Solvents, therefore, need to be carefully specified and tested before purchase.

Most of the media are produced by polycondensation reactions such as polyesterification, polyetherification etc. where water is the molecule split and removed. Even if an entrainer is used for water removal, the returning entrainer is at a boiling temperature where water solubility is high. This concentration restricts the completion of reaction if the reaction is reversible and as the equilibrium is reached, the reaction is stopped with the traces of water still present in the final product. Thus, alkyds, polyester polyols, epoxy, phenolic, melamine (MF), urea (UF) any resin that has not been used as a solid dissolved 'in a solvent, contains water in trace level. Thus, if all ,the',' constituents contain water to the extent of 1-5%, the resulting paint may contain w,ater up to 1% depending on the composition.

This water may have several detrimental effects on the storage and performance of the coatings. Following are the possible consequences:

a) Corrosion of metallic container

b) Dewetting/flocculation of pigments

c) Water separation

d) Hydrolysis of the medium leading to higher acid value

e) Livering due to reaction with basic pigments

f) Loss of isocyanate groups in the case of polyurethane coatings.

Whereas others may not be very serious, (a) and (f) are the most detrimental. Corrosion of steel container produces iron hydroxide that can become part of binder by reacting with carboxylic acid. Iron compounds are highly coloured. If the coating in consideration is a light-coloured product, serious discoloration may result. If a polyurethane coating is formulated with about 12% isocyanate content, only 1% total moisture can destroy nearly 90% of the reactive functional groups leaving behind carbon dioxide and cured polymer. For these reasons, it is absolutely essential to remove mois ture from coating composition.

There are two ways to remove water from a paint. The first is by a chemical reaction, that leads to product that is harmless in the system and the second is by adsorption

Materials such as high purity calcium oxide react even with traces of water irreversibly and produce lime as a product. If the other constituents are tolerant to the presence of lime, calcium oxide serves the purpose very well. The most prevalent difficulty is in getting a right grade at right price. CaO derived from seashell is one good possibility, others being derived from calcite.

One precaution is essential here. On hydration CaO produces $Ca(OH)_2$ by following reaction:

$$CaO + H_2O \rightarrow Ca(OH)_2$$

Whenever this coating is applied, the $Ca(OH)_2$ that is a part of film may react with atmospheric carbon dioxide.

$$Ca(OH)_2 + CO_2 \rightarrow CaC0_3 + H_2O$$

The water may diffuse out of the film. The net change in weight of $Ca(OH)_2$ with a density of 2.2 glee is about 35% when it becomes $CaCO_3$ of 2.93 or 2.71 glee density in its two crystal forms. Thus even if the weight of $Ca(OH)_2$ increases by 35%, the volume of the composite film remains the same (74/ 2.2 ~ 10012.93) and there is no damage done to the film. If in place of CaO, MgO is used, the product of hydration. Mg(OH)2 (density 2.4 glee) on carbonation becomes $MgC0_3.Mg(OH)_2.3H_2O$ (density 2.16 glee) by following reaction:

$$2Mg\ (OH)_2 + CO_2 + 2H_20 \rightarrow MgC0_3.Mg\ (OH)_2.3H_2O$$

The volume of Mg(OH)2 increases in this process by about 68%. The expansion of particles can cause damage to the film and ruin some of its properties. On the part of suppliers, calcite ($CaC0_3$) and dolomite ($CaC0_3.MgCO_3$) make little difference as raw materials. Care must be exercised to ensure that the lime is free of MgO (the reason why CaO derived from seashell, oyster shell is recommended). The difficulty arises while locating suppliers of these materials and these may have to be specially developed. If composition permits, 3-5% of gray or white cement could also be used to do the same job.

Molecular Sieves

Molecular Sieves, also called synthetic zeolites, are highly crystalline, fine white powders with particle size ranging from 1 to 10 microns They are aluminosilicates with.general formula: $xNa_2O.xAl_2O_3.ySiO_2.nH_2O$

x/y = 2 to 6 and x ranges from 0-8.

The sodium in the crystal is exchangeable by other cations such as K^+, Ca^{2+} to yield different products. When fully activated, these powders can hold 25-28% moisture of their weight.

The term molecular sieve is not to be mistaken for any sieving equipment. This is a figurative term meaning material with openings of molecular dimensions. These dimensions are of the order of magnitude of 3, 4 or 5A ^{o} units and are able to distinguish molecules based on their shape, size and polarity. All molecular sieves have very high affinity for polar substances, that may be liquids or gases. They can adsorb moisture from air and, therefore, must be stored in closed condition. The process of removal of adsorbed water is called activation and is carried out at temperature ranging from 300-

500°C. These products should be purchased in activated form, adequately packed to exclude all moisture from air in contact with the materials. If the formulation permits, the product can also be obtained as a slurry in a low molecular weight hydroxyl terminated polyester resin or even castor oil. The principal use of these products is removal of moisture in urethane coatings to prevent unwanted loss of functional groups.

Same products are useful for removal of moisture from solvents in the form of extrudates or spheres of 3-5 mm size formed with the help of a binder. These maybe repeatedly activated inside the equipment or can be taken out for activation. Moisture levels can be brought down to 300 ppm or less by suitably designed equipment. For drying air for spray application, equipment made from molecular sieve operates in pressure swing mode. If molecular sieve is brought in contact with high-pressure air, the moisture gets removed tothe required low levels. When the container is depressurized, it removes the moisture from molecular sieves. For improving the efficiency, the regeneration can be carried out under vacuum and is called vacuum swing adsorption cycle.

Molecular sieve powders are free flowing white solids and can be easily incorporated in resin systems. These are alkaline in nature and may leach some sodium in contact with high acidity media. These are stable in neutral and alkaline condition, but do not resist highly acidic conditions.

Another application of desiccants is in solvent-based coatings containing metal powders that react with water - typically non-leafing aluminum and zinc powder. If packed as a single pack, the metals react with water and produce hydrogen gas. This can at times explode containers and cause livering of the medium.

Mode of use

Molecular sieves are fine powders and can be incorporated as such during grinding. The level of use will vary depending on the moisture content of the composition, but should not exceed 1 to 3%. Addition is preferably done at the earliest opportunity so that system remains dry through out the manufacture and storage.

Side effects

Addition of molecular sieves and lime increases the alkalinity of the medium. Their presence can affect alkali sensitive solvents such as esters and ketones. Of the two, ketones can discolor due to formation of aldol condensation products. Esters can get hydrolyzed if all moisture had not been removed.

Manufacturers

IPCL Catad, Zeolites and Allied Products manufacture activated grades. M/s. TNPL have a large facility to produce detergent grade zeolites that are available as non-activated materials. Their material can be used after heating in a furnace at about 350-400°C and cooling it in closed condition.

WET EDGE ADDITIVES

The wet edge problem

As a painter paints a surface, he can not finish the entire job in one stretch. He can then divide his area of work depending on his approach (with the ladder, painting equipment etc.) He has to leave the job at a certain point and restart at the same point after a gap of 30-40 minutes. If the edge of the previous patch has dried up, as he applies another layer, the coat thickness at this point will increase and the appearance of the entire job would be patchy. It is therefore expected that the edge of a coat should retain its wetness till the job can be restarted and a good level is obtained.

Solutions

Advantage is taken of the property of the thixotropy of the coating. Due to very low shear at the end of the coating device such as a brush, the spreading of the paint on the edge is minimal. The edge remains thick unless specially spread. The thickness of the edge may be 3 to 5 times more than the normal spread. The thick thread contains more solvent and stays wet for longer time, particularly in water based systems. The problem is solved by addition ofa true solvent to the system that retards drying and can hold solvents for little longer time than normal requirement.

Following additives are recommended for coatings:

- For water-based, emulsion paints: Ethylene glycol, diethylene glycol, triethylene glycol, cellosolve, carbitol, sorbitol
- For solvent-based paints: High boiling true solvent for the resin selected from esters, ketones, (2-ethylhexyl acetate, isophorone, celloso.lve acetate, diethylene glycol diacetate, etc.)

Manufacturers

These are common solvents and could be obtained from any solvent dealer.

Side effects

Serious retardation in development of all film properties may occur as the slow evaporation rate of these solvents may allow a certain concentration of the solvent to linger longer than that is necessary. In the case of water-based system, enough time may have to elapse before adequate water resistance can be developed. The films may remain soft for little longer. Since these additives are required to be added to architectural coatings, that are not put to use immediately after application, most ofthese side effects are acceptable.

DRIERS

Driers are catalysts for acceleration of polymerization reaction of various air drying products when they are exposed to air. The discovery was based on an observation that paints not containing lead pigments tended to dry slower than the ones, which bore lead based pigments. It was then realized that a part of the lead from the pigment had reacted with the free acidity of the medium and thus had become soluble in the organic medium. The soluble metal was catalyzing the drying process.

If ordinary drying oil is applied as a thin film on a surface, it may take 3-7 days to become surface dry. Hard drying may take place over a very long time strongly depending on film thickness. Thicker films may contain liquid or highly viscous liquid closer to the surface for several days or months. There are two reasons for this:

1. The reaction of drying requires oxygen. If no catalyst is present to accelerate the process, the drying takes place where highest oxygen concentration is present, i.e. on the surface.

2. As the drying progresses, the diffusivity of oxygen through the dried film reduces, This reduces the oxygen concentration in the bulk of the film and the process of drying is retarded.

The need for acceleration of drying arises due to several reasons.

- The job may be required urgently, or in a manufacturing process one can not afford to wait indefinitely for the paint to dry.
- Even if the painted object is stored in a closed environment, certain

amount of dust collection on the painted surface can not be avoided. As the dust falls on a polymerizing surface, it sticks to the surface and becomes a permanent part of the film. If the surface remains wet for too long, the dust collection may be bad enough to completely spoil the aesthetics of the film.

Based on the observation that lead pigments accelerate the drying process, other metal salts of fatty acids were also investigated for their drying activity. The fatty acid salts of Co, Mn, Pb, Fe, Cu, Ni, Zr showed considerable increase in the rate of drying of air drying or stoving systems.

There are some basic rules governing the selection of metals, that can form suitable driers:

- The metals must show polyvalence
- The difference in the free energy of the different oxidation states should be small (of the order of 3-5 Kcal/g mole).
- If the difference between the two oxidation states is high, the metal does not function as an effective catalyst at low temperatures. It will, however, function as a drier at elevated temperature.

In an air-drying paint system, there are three types of drying requirements surface drying, through drying (hard drying) and tack-free drying

These duties are not carried out adequately by anyone metal alone. It is, therefore, customary to use a combination of metal soaps to achieve an all round desired performance.

Following are the activities of different metals:

- Cobalt - Surface drying
- Lead - Through drying
- Mn - Auxiliary for cobalt where colour is not objectionable
- Zr - Auxiliary for cobal! and lead where light colour is desired
- Iron - High temperature, dark colour, low cost.

The other constituent of the metal soap is the fatty acid. In the earlier years, fatty acids derived from vegetable oils were used. These had relatively low acid value and therefore, the metal content of the driers was low. In addition, they displayed higher viscosity. As smaller fatty acids became available, the industry shifted to C_7 to C_{11} linear, branched and highly branched (neo) acids that are products of the petrochemical industry. These acids are produced by Koch synthesis that uses olefins, carbon monoxide and water to produce highly branched acids. (Table 1-5).

The chain branching helps to reduce viscosity, crystallization and increases solubility in hydrocarbon solvents. Acids with 6 carbon atoms and lower form crystalline soaps that have low solubility in hydrocarbon solvents and resin media and can not be used. These acids are available as individual components and also as mixtures under various trade names such as iso acids, neo acids, versatic acids, and cekanoic acids that are trademarks of different manufacturers such as Exxon, Shell, and Kuhlman.

Most commonly used acid in India is 2-ethylhexanoic acid derived from butyraldehyde by aldol condensation followed by oxidation and hydrogenation.

Table 1-5 Synthetic fatty acids produced by Koch synthesis

Trade Name	Chemical Name	Manufacturer
Varlaric acid	Neopentanoic acid	Exxon
Valaric acid mixture	Versatic Acid 5	Shell
Octanoic, Nonanoic and	Neo decanoic Acid 10	Exxon
decanoic acid mixtures	Versatic acid 10	Shell
Cekanoic acid 8,9 and 10		Kuhlman
9 & 11 mixture	Versatic 911	Shell

Iso nonenoic acid is 90% 3,5,5-trimethyl hexanoic acid produced from hydroformylation of Di isobutylene + CO in 83-86% H_2SO_4 at 20° C and 70 kg CO pressure 2,2,4,4-tetra methyl pentanoic acid is also produced similarly.

Also popularly used acid, derived from ozonolysis of oleic acid is pelargoric acid (C_9 acid)

Over basic driers

The economics of driers are dictated by the prices of materials. The manufacturer would like to include maximum concentration of the cheapest ingredient. The more expensive the metal, lower would be its concentration. The cheapest metal oxide is calcium (Rs. 3/kg), followed by lead (~ Rs. 20/kg), zinc oxide (- Rs. 70/kg), and zirconium (- Rs. 300/kg). The most expensive metal used in paint driers is cobalt (~Rs.1 ,200 to 2,500/kg). Most of the C_9-C_{11} carboxylic acids cost about Rs. 100/kg in India. Thus, there is a strong incentive to manufacture driers with Ca, Pb and Zn that are richer in metals.

The theoretical metal content is equal to the stoichiometric equivalent of two carboxylic acid molecules since all these are divalent metals.

$(R\,COO)_2\,Ca,$ $(R\,COO)_2Pb,$ $(R\,COO)_2Zn$

It is recommended by manufacturers of branched acids that if carbon dioxide is present when metal oxide is being dissolved in carboxylic acid, the metal precipitates in the form of micro crystals in its carbonate form and the metal content can go much above the stoichiometric equivalent. Thus a cheaper metal can be solubilized by less quantity of acid, bringing the cost down.

The technique does work as described by product literature of fatty acid manufacturers, but the logic is not acceptable. For any size and shape of the carbonate of the metals (Ca, Pb or Zn) its carbonate is not soluble in hydrocarbon solvents.

As per the procedure, a metal oxide is reacted with the fatty acid. As the dissolution is taking place, carbon dioxide is added as a gas. If we consider carbon dioxide as the smallest dicarboxylic acid, carbonic acid, it can be expected to take part in the reaction as follows:

$$H-O-\overset{\overset{O}{\|}}{C}-OH \quad \text{or} \quad HO-\overset{\overset{O}{\|}}{C}-OH$$

$$CaO + R\,COOH \longrightarrow \underset{\text{(Intermediate)}}{R-COO-Ca-OH}$$

$$2\,R\,COO-Ca-OH + CO_2 \longrightarrow R-\overset{\overset{O}{\|}}{C}-O-Ca-O-\overset{\overset{O}{\|}}{C}-O-Ca-O-\overset{\overset{O}{\|}}{C}-R + H_2O$$

$$2\,R\,(COO-Pb-OH) + CO_2 \longrightarrow R-\overset{\overset{O}{\|}}{C}-O-Pb-O-\overset{\overset{O}{\|}}{C}-O-Pb-O-\overset{\overset{O}{\|}}{C}-R + H_2O$$

Thus, the calcium or lead content of the drier can be much higher for the same weight of fatty acid. This is my own hypothesis. I have no experimental evidence to prove what is written here, but I believe it stands to logic better than a crystalline substance getting co- solubilised. The over basic driers do not precipitate out the carbonate for up to 1.5 times metal content based on fatty acid.

Addition norms

For most oil based products such as boiled oils, polymerized oils (stand oils) cooked with rosin derivatives, and medium & long oil alkyds air drying type products following combination are suitable:

- Cobalt - 0.05% on resin solids
- Lead - 0.5% on resin solids

For light coloured stoving systems with no urea or melamine resin curing agents, the following combination is suitable:

- Co - 0.02-0.04% on resin solids
- Pb - 0.3-0.5% on resin solids

For stoving systems with dark colours the following combination is suitable:

- Co + Mn combination (1 :2) 0.05% metal on resin solids
- Pb 0.2-0.4% on resin solids

For air-drying or stoving systems with light colours Zr octoate is recommended for better gloss and lowering the cost.

Alkyd emulsion based architectural coatings do require driers. In such cases the driers may be added to the resin prior to emulsification, or to the aqueous phase in the form of water-soluble salts such as cobalt acetate or lead acetate.

Primers and undercoats that are formulated at high pigment volume concentration (PVC) (40%+) do not require surface driers; this also helps to reduce cost.

Side effects

Following coating systems do not require driers:

- Saturated alkyds (alkyds made from coconut or castor oil without dehydration) cured by urea or melamine resins
- Chlorinated rubber and nitrocellulose based lacquers or other lacquers where air oxidation is not required
- Epoxy, urethane silicones that cure by alternate chemistries
- All plastic emulsion paints

Side effects

Cobalt drier accelerates the surface drying. If the cobalt drier content is more than required, the surface dries faster than the bulk. This results in formation of wrinkles on the surface. Lead is a through drier. Excess of lead drier causes haze in the coating. It can also cause livering, formation of gritty film and flocculation.

ACTIVATORS

Cobalt is the most effective, but most expensive, metal used in paint compositions. Efforts have been made in the past to add activators to improve the efficiency of cobalt. In certain complex forms with organic heterocyclic compounds, the effectiveness is doubled and it is possible to reduce cobalt concentration by half.

1,10 phenanthrolein is one such compound that complexes with cobalt

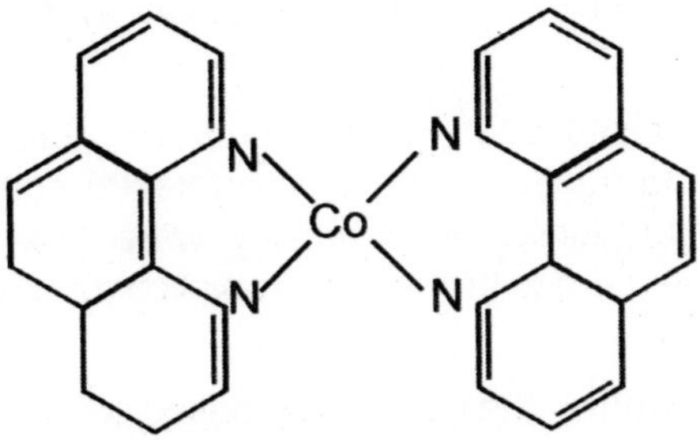

1-10 phenanthrolein cobalt complex

Difficulty is experienced in keeping the complex in solution in hydrocarbon media. Alkyl substituted derivatives might possibly work better.

BIOCIDES

Life is not possible without microorganisms. Human body contains millions of bacteria/cm^3 of the fluids in stomach and intestine. There are several harmless and friendly bacteria and there are several others that are very harmful and cause various diseases. Human body has resistance to attack by several of them, but can also be gotten by several bacteria and fungi.

All organic products around us are susceptible to attack by bacteria and fungi and need preservation. Earlier practices included drying, preservation in salt solution, impregnating with spices and vegetable oils.

Elemental chlorine, iodine solution in alcohol, compounds of mercury (mercurochrome), copper were used for prevention of foul odors from wounds. Phenol, cresol and xylenols, derived from coal tar have been used as disinfectants. The bacteria are present in all the media surrounding us - air, water, etc. - produce enzymes that are catalysts for degradation of organic matter. For prevention of degradation, bacteria need to be controlled. This is possible by heating the contents to a high temperature, removal by filtration or by chemical killing.

The early efforts were targeted for preservation of wood, particularly wood that was constantly in contact with water. Cresol, mercuric chloride, copper sulfate and zinc chloride were used for this purpose for centuries.

Bacteria, fungi spores are extremely fine and can not be seen by the naked eye. The filtration required is of such high order that only very special filters capable of filtering out particles up to 0.2 micron may be necessary. Equal care is necessary for avoiding recontamination. The pH, temperature, oxygen concentration, presence of nutrients and moisture are some of the most important factors governing contamination and proliferation of microorganisms.

Apart from lime based coatings, paints were primarily oil based till emulsions came on the scene. with environmental concerns, need for reduction in cost, and reduced inflammability, water based systems have entered. without proper care to prevent microbial contamination, paints can have two major problems:

1. **"In can" preservation:** The early water-based paints contained natural proteins such as gelatin, gums, and casein as binders. On storage, these degraded to cause foul odors. The degradation resulted in loss of viscosity, staining and discoloration, development of pressure to the extent of disfiguring the containers or even bursting and spillage. These are primarily caused by enzymes secreted by bacteria for predigesting of food for them to breed on. Enzymes are polypeptides that are biocatalysts and are capable of degrading a large variety of molecules. Most interestingly, they do not consume themselves and continue to degrade the host several thousands of times. Thus, even a very small concentration of enzyme can, over a period of time, degrade a large volume of organic substrate. The reactions are rather slow at room temperature and any effective change in viscosity, presence of malodorous gases or generation of pressure would become apparent only after a couple of weeks. The contamination of enzyme may occur from atmosphere, water, or any raw materials used in the paint preparation.

2. **Film Protection:** Once the film has been applied, it would continue to remain a source of food to the micro flora. Algae can easily hook on to the micro irregularities on the surface, particularly when the surface is wet. They may continue to grow and proliferate to other areas. In the presence of sunlight, it would behave like vegetative matter. Similarly, fungus can grow on wet surfaces. If the surface gets periodically wet and dry, the developed algae or fungi dry out and cause black stains. Even an otherwise well painted surface looks ugly. Since most of the exteriors of buildings are painted with low cost cement based paints where the manufacturer can not afford to put any biocides, we are

destined to see large structures, that get disfigured within one year of complete painting. The stains can be removed with a wire brush and plenty of water. This causes loss of film and creates new sites for anchorage. Cleaning of large exterior surfaces can prove expensive. These problems are best attended by inclusion of chemicals in the formulation called biocides.

In the past, when environmental awareness was low, two products most popularly and very effectively used were sodium pentachlorophenate (SPCP) and phenyl mercury oleate. Both of these have now been banned - SPCP due to its tendency to accumulate in live bodies through the food chain (vegetables to insects to birds to fish to human) and mercury because of its high toxicity. Several new organic biocides have become available over last 10-15 years that very effectively prevent bacteria growth during storage and algae and fungi on application.

Testing and selection of a biocide

There are six major issues related to selection of biocides:

1. A microbiologist is a desirable member of the team to identify the type of organism present in water, air and raw materials. He should be able to carry out the efficacy studies of the various biocides available in the market.
2. The best way to control microbiological problems in storage is to avoid contamination. For this good housekeeping is essential. No raw material should be subjected to undue exposure of water. Overall cleanliness in the work atmosphere and complete segregation of food products from the work area are some essential precautions.
3. Insist that all raw material suppliers, particularly those of water-based and watersoluble substances, supply bacteria-free materials. If the raw material already contains enzymes, any amount of biocide would not be able to prevent degradation of cellulose derivatives. One way to deactivate enzymes is heating to 80°C and rapid cooling. It may not be possible to expose all raw materials to this treatment.
4. Raw material supplier's literature guides selection, dosage level and economics of use. Invariably, suppliers would recommend certain dosage that needs to be verified for the effectiveness in a given formulation. The supplier is in no position to evaluate his product in all possible combinations of raw materials. Using his information as guideline, the selection and dose both have to be optimized by actual experimentation.

It is to be noted that these studies are laborious and time consuming. No results can be expected in a short span of a few months. If effectiveness is to be tested for outdoor coatings, the time taken may range from 3-5 years. A careful study including controls must be planned and reviewed several times before deciding the course of action. Omission of any parameter, that may turn out to be very important one, can prove very expensive.

5. The facilities for testing a biocide are special. Some of the requirements are separate work station, artificial source of day light, bacteria-free working conditions, high degree of cleanliness, restricted entry. It requires trained manpower and commitment of the management to invest in the training and time.

6. The interaction of two biocides may result in interference (where they kill each other) or synergistic. Combinations of several biocides have been studied by suppliers and are available as blended products. It is best to follow suppliers advice since developing your own blends may be a time taking exercise that may or may not be fruitful.

Some biocide suppliers are Rohm & Haas, Thor, Bode, Zeneca, Nipa, Albright and Wilson, BASF and Indofil.

UV, LIGHT AND HEAT STABILIZERS

The rising cost of capital goods makes their replacement a more difficult job. Protection from sun, rain and weather is very essential. In the past, corrosion due to rain alone was important. Over years, environmental pollution has pushed manufacturers of white goods and automobiles to specify paints that must resist a pH of 2 for extended hours. This became necessary since acidic gases in the air dissolve in the dew and cover the complete surface of the automobile. pH of this liquid may be 2 or lower. This dew may remain present for 4-6 hours every day for at least 6 months of the year. If the paint is not able to resist this condition, immediate corrosion may result. In India, where people do not like to change a car for at least 10 years, a good corrosion protection is expected.

The automobile manufacturers like to reduce the thickness of the metal to reduce material cost and also the dead weight for better fuel efficiency. The inherent corrosion allowance gets sacrificed and the need for a better corrosion resistant and stable coating gets emphasized. The depleting ozone layer also allows more UV to reach earth surface and that is an issue of serious concern.

There are eight factors in nature that cause rapid degradation of coatings:

1. Ultraviolet light and sun light
2. Ozone
3. Acid rain
4. Repeated wetting and drying Pollutants
5. Oxygen
6. Microorganisms
7. Heat

Any or all of them can affect adhesion, gloss, DOI and colour. It is difficult to find coating systems that would be able to resist all the factors on their own structural strength. They need reinforcement by way of additives. It is not conceivable that only one additive would be able to take care of all the ill effects. One would need UV absorbers, and antioxidants to take care of some of the problems stated above. Anticorrosive agents and other additives may be necessary to overcome all the problems.

Oxidation catalyzed by UV

It is said that strength of a chain equals that of the weakest link in it. In the process of polymerization, we use different monomers that have a definite structure. Some portion of the monomer or the polymer during polymerization process happens to be weaker than the rest of the polymer. When any external attack takes place, the weakest part is affected first of all. Invariably such reactions lead to scission or breaking of the chain. The net result is the molecular weight of the polymer becomes lower. If the cleavage takes place at the center, the molecular weight is reduced to half.

The properties of a coating material are strongly dependent upon the molecular weight of the resin. On the one hand, the coating chemist has been forced to look at low molecular weight high functionality polymers to overcome the problems of low volatile organic compounds and high solids, on the other hand demand for long life have increased. The only way out is to arrest degradation of the polymer.

Sunlight contains ultraviolet light from 190-400 nanometers (nm). Of this the most energetic part, 190-290 nm, is absorbed by the top-most layer of the earth's atmosphere converting O_2 into O_3. This O_3 further absorbs ultraviolet light and the radiation reaching earth is above 290 nm.

UV light is classified in three parts:

1. UVA (315-400 nm)
2. UVB (280-315)
3. UVC (<280)

UVC is not commonly encountered on the earth's surface, except in the polar regions where there is no ozone layer.

UVB is the most commonly found radiation and is the most damaging to paints and coatings.

1. The reactions catalysed by UV light which result in degradation are as follows :

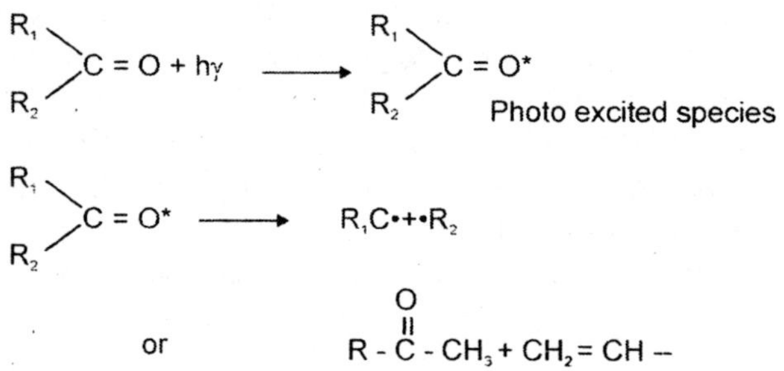

In the above case R_1 and R_2 are polymeric chains and the terminal double bond is created by cleavage of the chain.

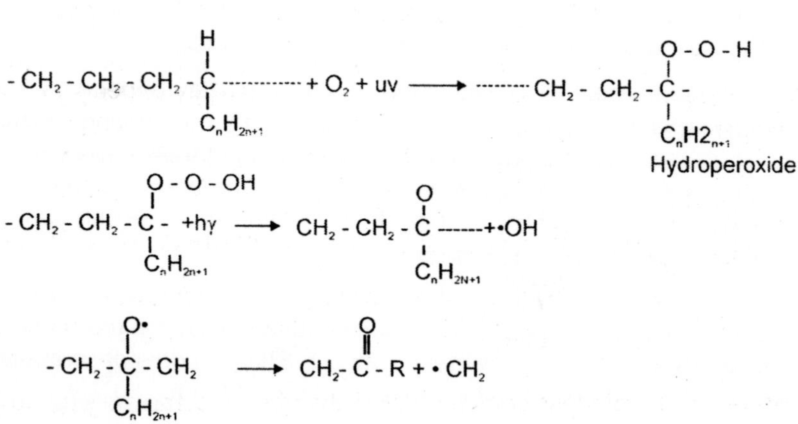

The above reactions are valid for polymers of different chemical structures from vegetable oils, to acrylics to aromatic polyesters or polyurethanes. For superior performance all of them require stabilization.

There are two types of additives to prevent UV degradation - UV filters & UV absorbers.

Pigments that are opaque to UV are the simplest additives. All of them colour the film, which may not be the desired colour. One of the best substances is carbon black. The cheap plastic polyethylene or the rubber tyres are so well stabilized against UV attack that the water tanks made from polyethylene are in service for over 20 years installed on the roof tops without degradation. Bý definition, incorporating pigments also makes polymers opaque. In applications such as clear topcoats, metallic finishes, transparent colour coats, use of pigments to stabilize against UV defeats the purpose. In high gloss coatings, pigments are considerably below the top surface since the gloss is provided by clear polymer. The protection is available just below this surface. Loss of gloss is inevitable in such systems.

UV absorbers are certain organic compounds, which can completely absorb UV, particularly in the range 290-330 nm. These compounds are generally aromatic ketones such as acetophenone, benzophenone, salicylic esters, cinnamic acid ester, and substituted benzotriazoles.

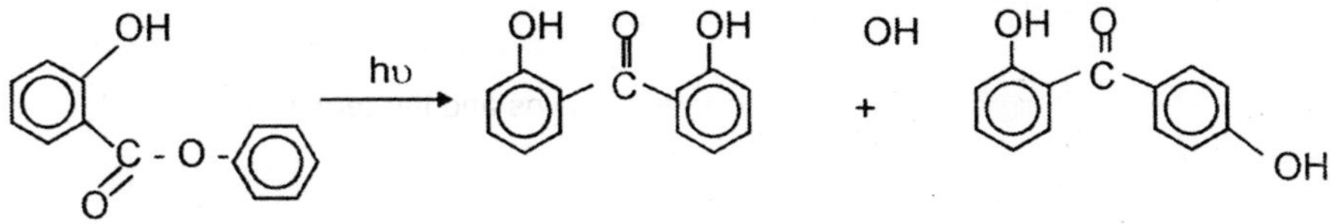

The dehydroxy accept ophenone hydroxyacetophenone is a better UV absorber than phenyl salicylate formed by photo catalyzed Fries rearrangement.

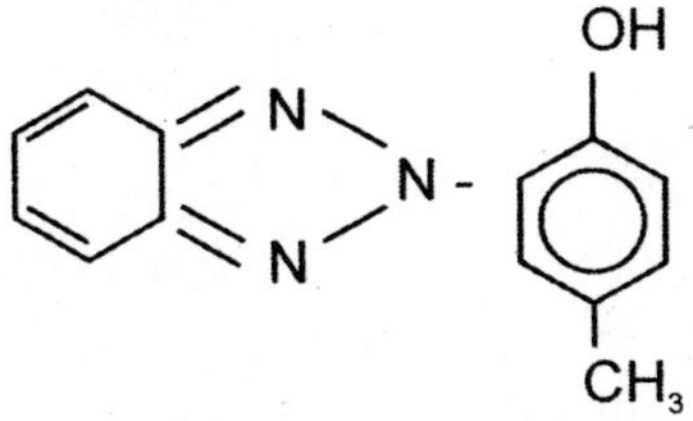

2-(2'-hydroxy-5'-methyl1) benzotriazole

It is a nearly colorless compound and absorbs UV completely (up to 400 nm) even at a low concentration of 0.05% for 1 cm path length.

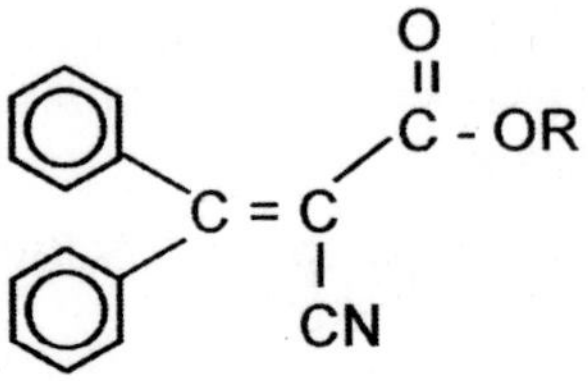

2-cyano-3, 3-diphenyl alkyl acrylate

The R group may be a long chain alcohol or a branched alcohol to reduce volatility and increase entanglement of chains.

ANTI-OXIDANTS

The free radicals caused by UV degradation of the polymer or the residues of initiator molecules used for polymerization can start the degradation process.

If these free radicals are not terminated, they initiate further excitation of oxygen molecules and cause degradation. There are two types of compounds, which are useful as radical scavangers - hindered phenols and Hindered amines' based light stabilizers (HALS).

In the first case, a tri-substituted phenol that has oxidation stable substituents is used. Of these two are tertiary butyl groups. The third position is occupied by a long alkyl chain, which increases the entanglement with polymer and reduces its volatility.

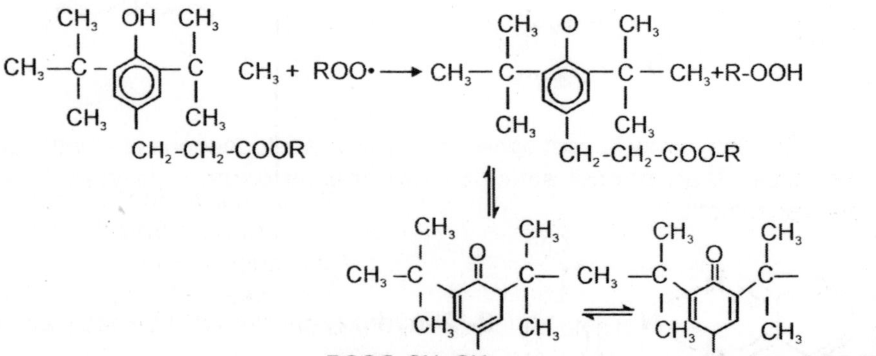

The phenoxy radical so formed is stable. The alkyl groups attached to the 0- and p- position decrease its ability to abstract a hydrogen from any neighboring molecule due to steric hindrance and limit the oxidative chain reaction.

Hindered Amines light stabilizers (HALS)

Most of the commercial products are substituted or polymeric derivatives of 2,2,6,6- tetramethy lpiperidine

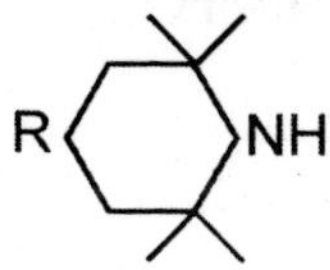

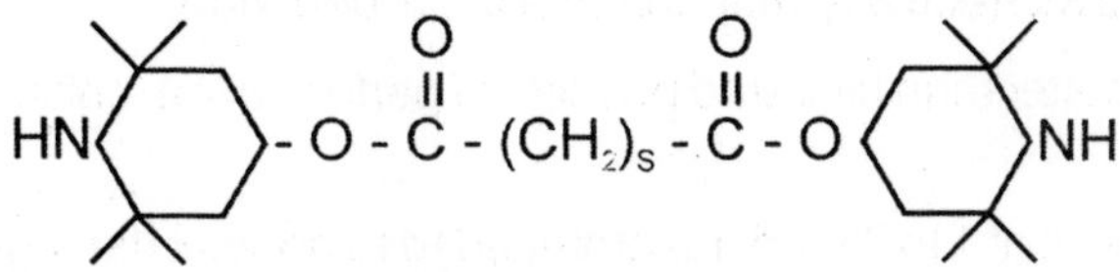

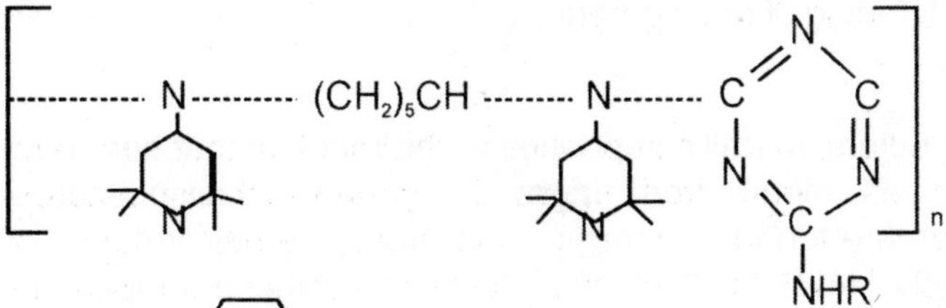

Chimassorb
CIBA 994

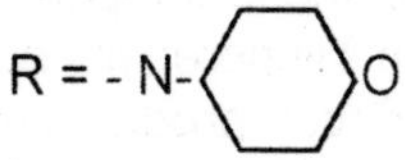

American Cyanamide
Cyasorbuv 3346

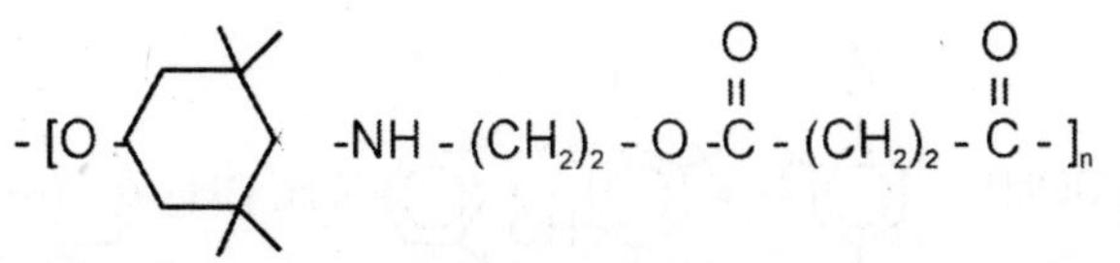

Tinuvin 622
CIBA

The purpose of attaching a long alkyl chain or converting the structure in polymer form is to reduce its vapor pressure and its loss from the polymeric films by volatilization! extraction. The product literatures of several manufacturers claim 90-95% retention after 5 years of outdoor exposure with no change in colour of the treated product.

Hindered phenols and amines both are capable of retarding UV degradation and thermal oxidation. It has been observed that polymer compositions, from which entire HALS has been consumed still remain stabilized. This has been attributed to the antioxidant action of the first stage reaction products of HALS.

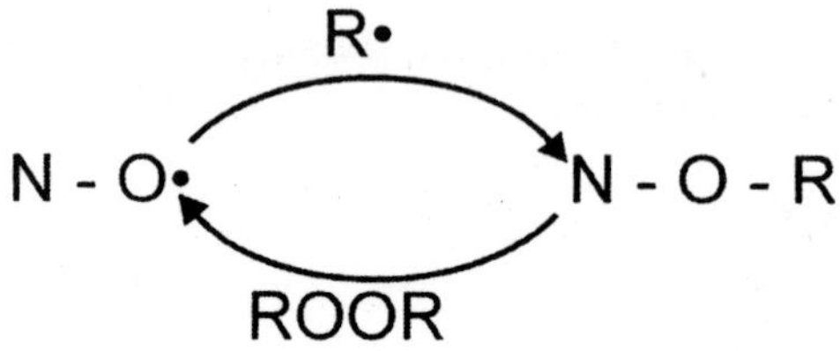

as if they are effectively able to stabilize a peroxide.

HALS are better than hindered phenols in performance, colour and colour retention.

Addition levels of 1 to 2% are recommended to prevent damage to various properties of the coatings such as gloss, DOI, flexibility, elongation at break, yellowing, adhesion, fading of the pigment.

Side effects

Acidity of the medium, metallic impurities in the medium that can react with secondary amines, metals from driers, isocyanates, thioisocynates, phenolic substances are found to interfere and affect the performance of HALS. Simultaneously, HALS do affect the performance of these components if these were added as desired ingredients of the paint film. Hindered phenols, which act by trapping free radicals produce stable oxidation products that are highly coloured.

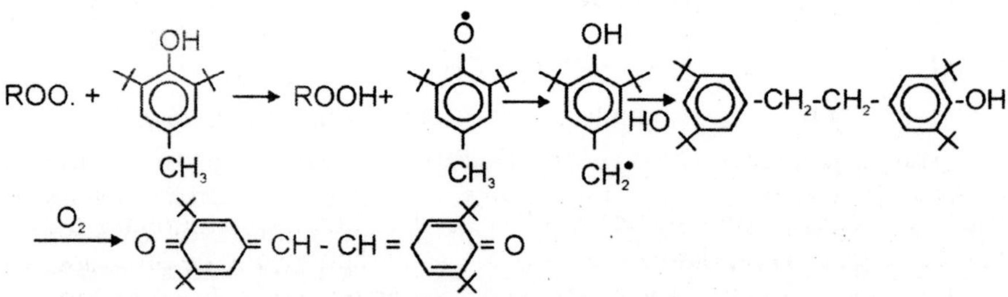

This is a very highly coloured product and even a concentration of 5-ppm (parts/ million) can impart yellow colour to an otherwise white coatings. This may not be always acceptable.

Other derivatives of phenol are

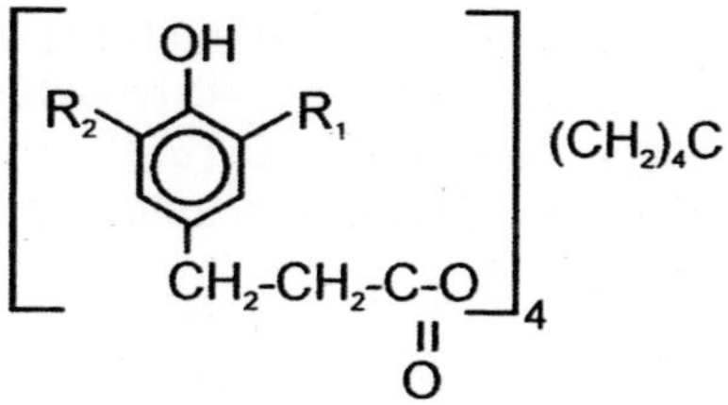

Irganaox 1010

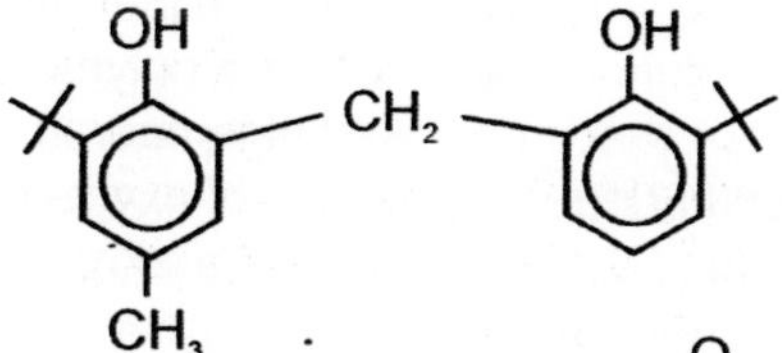

Cyanox 2246

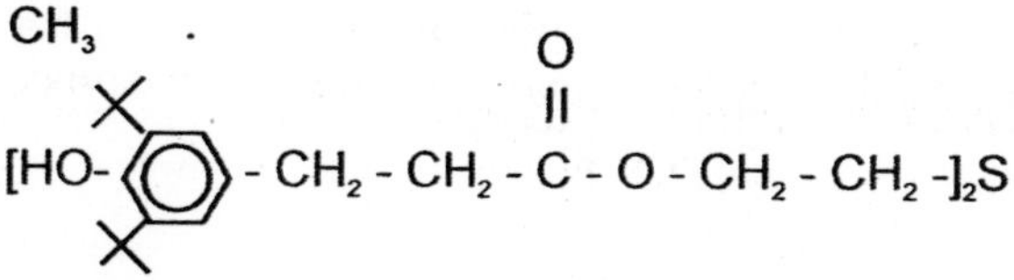

Irganaox 1035

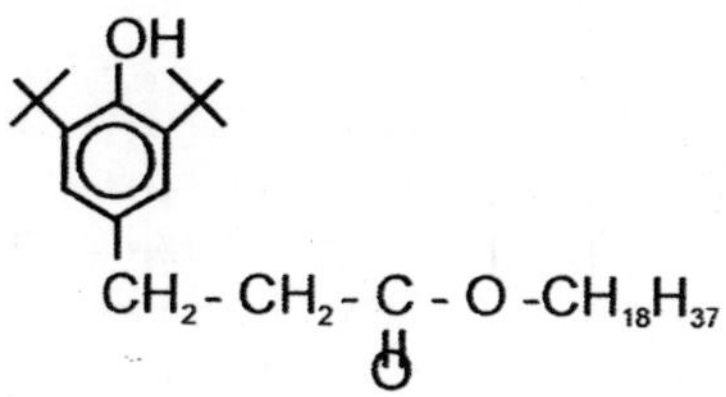

Irganaox 1076

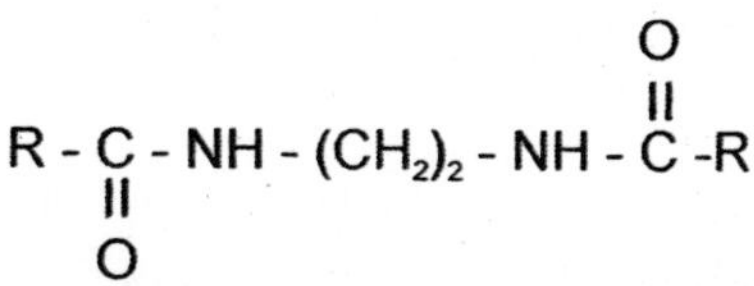

Irganaox 1098

Other less popular antioxidants in paint industry are listed below.

Aromatic Amines

Aromatic amine condensates such as aniline ketone condensate or substituted p-phenylene diamine or derivatives of diphenylamine are dark coloured products. These are very effective and can be used only where the colour is not objectionable. The mechanism of the action is not fully understood primarily because these are not simple single compounds, but a mixture of their oxidation products.

Organic Sulfur compounds

Metal salts of dialkyl dithiocarbamic acids like zinc salts and esters of long chain fatty alcohols such as lauryl, myristyl, stearyl of thio dipropionic acid are important commercial antioxidants. They show synergy with hindered phenol antioxidants or aromatic amines and are useful up to 160-165°C. The recommended level is 0.4-0.5% with a ratio of phenolic to this antioxidant 1 :3.

Phosphorous compounds

Phosphites are effective at temperatures above 160°C and are therefore useful for prevention of colour development during manufacture of polymers. Typically, alkyds, rosin esters and polyesters, that are cooked at temperature in excess of 200°C tend to develop dark colour due to presence of oxygen in the atmosphere. Tris nonylphenyl phosphite (TNPP) is a low cost antioxidant of choice. They are used with hindered phenols to minimize change of molecular weight and colour development during high temperature processing.

2

Solvents

Solvents carry out following primary functions in a paint system:

- Reduce viscosity of the resin to ease processing and wet the pigments better
- Enable ease of application
- Improve flow level, gloss and wetting of the substrate

Solvent is not a part of final film and is only a member during the journey of the paint from production to its final destination. But it leaves its indelible marks on the final product, that stay up to the end of the life of the paint. Selection of the solvent, therefore, is one of the most important jobs of a paint chemist.

If the solvent or solvent combination is not right, it could cause serious problems in the final product and cause defects that reduce the utility of the paint film. This may require reworking or even complete scrap out.

The most important factor to be considered while selecting a solvent for a polymer system is the solubility parameter (§). It is a mathematical expression to quantify the secondary forces and dipole forces, which hold molecules together. All molecules, either polymers or solvents; are held together by two types of forces - Primary bonds & Secondary bonds. Of the two, in organic chemistry, the first is invariably a covalent bond and rarely a coordinate bond. Secondary bonds such as hydrogen bonds, dispersion forces and ionic attraction contribute to most of the properties - desirable and undesirable - to polymers and solvents.

When a polymer is heated, the secondary bonds slowly break and the polymer melts. If it is heated beyond melting, covalent bonds break and the polymer either depolymerizes back to monomers or degrades to fragments of uncertain structure. It is the magnitude of the secondary forces that determines the melting point of the polymer, its solubility, adhesion to surfaces, etc. If these forces are too strong and do not allow the molecules to become free from each other, polymer solubility gets restricted. Such a polymer has high melting point and in extreme cases where these forces become very large, the polymer may not melt at all and chars if heated. Polyvinyl alcohol, cellulose, polyacrylic acid are some such examples. These polymers have very high frequency of polar groups on their backbone, which does not allow them to melt. If heated beyond certain temperature, they decompose without melting.

Solvents being smaller molecules show a difference in their melting point, boiling point and the latent heat of evaporation. Table 2-1 shows the effect of hydrogen bonding on boiling point of solvents.

Table 2-1 : Properties of some solvents

Solvent/Substance	Molecular Weight	Boiling Point (at atmospheric pressure) [°C]	Latent Heat of Vaporization [Kcal/kg)
Water	18	100	535
Formic acid	46	101	120
Acetic acid	60	118	97
Methyl Formate	60	32	112
Ethylene Oxide	44	13.5	139
Ethyl Alcohol	46	78.4	204
Glycerin	92	290	250

Comparison of the molecular structure of acetic acid that has the same molecular formula but different structure compared to methyl formate reveals the difference caused by hydrogen bonding.

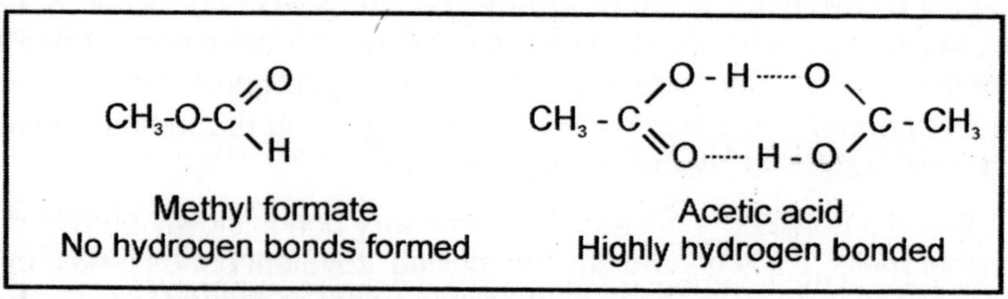

Fig. 2.1

In the case of acetic acid, hydrogen bonding causes the molecule to behave like a dimer resulting into doubling of molecular weight, and the physical properties show a marked change. When a solvent is heated, it first shows an increase in temperature and then boils. Further heating evaporates the solvent. At boiling, enough energy is supplied for the secondary bonds to break and the molecules are released free. The amount of energy required for separating the molecule increases with increasing strength and concentration of secondary bonds.

Latent heat of evaporation is a sum total of all these forces. As the solvent is evaporated, we do an additional work of pushing the atmosphere away equal to the volume of the vapor generated. Thus the net energy required to break the bonds is given by the difference of total energy supplied (Latent heat of.evaporation) and the energy spent on displacing atmosphere (RT, where R is gas constant and T absolute temperature) or L-RT. This commodity is useful to define solubility parameter. L-RT is the measure of cohesive energy. Solubility parameter is defined as square root of cohesive energy density or L-RT/molar volume. If the molecular weight ofthe solvent is M, and D is its density then the solubility parameter is given by following expression.

$$\delta = \sqrt{\frac{L-RT}{M/D}}$$

The solubility parameter is further divided in three components, hydrogen bonding (h), dispersion (d) forces and dipole forces (p) and are given by the expression:

$$\delta^2_{sp} = \delta^2_d + \delta^2_p + \delta^2_h$$

or

$$\delta_{sp} = \sqrt{\delta^2_d + \delta^2_p + \delta^2_h}$$

The values of δ_d, δ_p and δ_h are obtainable from literature(I).

For calculation of δ_{sp}, the structure of a solvent or Polymer is broken down to small fragments called groups and the cumulative effect is calculated by adding the contribution made by individual components.

Solubility parameters of some solvents and polymers are given in Table 2-1 and Table 2-2.

Once we have a quantitative idea of the solubility parameter of a solvent and a polymer, we can understand their interaction. Thus, if a polymer is added to a solvent, following three possibilities exist:

- The polymer dissolves in the solvent
- The polymer swells, but does not dissolve
- Nothing happens

The first case arises when the solubility parameter of the solvent is nearly equal to that of the polymer (difference of about 1-2 units). All the secondary bonds present in the polymer are about the same order of magnitude as the bonds formed between solvent molecules. Thus, a new bond between solvent and polymer should be capable of forming without heat effects, if a solution of polymer should result.

Table 2.2
Solubility Parameter for some polymers (1)

	dsp	**dn**	**dd**
Cellulose acetate	12.7	6.33	7.60
Cellulose acetate propionate	12.9	6.92	7.68
Ethyl cellulose	11.5	5.78	7.23
Cellulose	24.1	11.85	7.36
Nylon 6	12.4	6.69	8.45
Poly acrylic acid	14.0	7.02	8.89
Polyvinyl alcohol	19.1	11.68	7.82
Polyethylene	8.6	0	8.32
Polystyrene	10.6	0	8.88
Polyvinyl chloride	11.0	1.45	8.65
Polymethyl methacrylate	9.9	4.4	8.08
Polyethylene glycol -	9.4	4.14	7.5
Polypropylene glycol	8.7	3.48	7.18
Polyacrylonitrile	14.4	3.65	8.51
Polyvinyl formal	11.2	4.07	6.61
Polyvinyl acetal	10.3	3.71	7.48
Polyvinyl butyral	9.8	3.25	7.67

dsp- Overall solubility parameter
dn - Solubility parameter due to hydrogen bonding
dd - Soublity parameter due to dispersion forces

Table 2.3

Solubility Parameter of important Paint Solvents

	δ **Solubility parameter**	δ_n	δ_n
Acetone	10.0	9.7	2.9
n-Butyl acetate	8.5	8.8	1.9
n-Butyl alcohol	11.4	18.7	1.7
n-Butyl formate	8.7	7.5	1.9
Carbon tetrachloride	8.6	0.0	0.0
Chloroform	9.3	1.5	1.2
Cyclohexanone	9.7	11.7	2.7
Dibutyl ether	7.1	11.0	1.2
Diethyl ether	7.4	13.0	1.2
N ,N-Dimethylacetamide	10.8	12.3	2.0
Dipentene	8.5	1.5	0.0
Ethyl acetate	9.91	8.4	1.8
Ethyl alcohol	12.7	18.7	1.7
Ethylene glycol	14.2	20.6	2.3
Ethylene glycol monoethyl ether	9.9	13.0	1.6
2-Ethyl hexanol	9.5	18.7	1.7
Isobutyl acetate	8.3	8.8	1.9
Isopropyl acetate	8.4	8.6	1.9
Methyl acetate	9.6	8.4	1.7
Methyl alcohol	14.5	18.7	1.7
MIBK	8.4	7.7	2.7
Methylene chloride	9.7	1.5	1.5
Nitrbenzene	10.0	2.8	4.3
n-Propyl acetate	8.8	8.6	1.9
Pyridine	10.7	18.1	2.2
Toluene	8.9	4.5	0.4
Trichloroethane (1,1,2)	9.6	1.5	1.2
Xylene (mixed)	8.8	4.5	0.4
Solvent naphtha	7.6	0.0	0.0

If the polymer is cross-linked, then it cannot form a solution but it would only swell when dipped in a solvent. If the polymer is not cross-linked, but still only swells in a solvent, then the forces holding the polymer molecule together are stronger than the forces between solvent molecules. That results in only swelling of polymer. If the forces holding polymer together are stronger than solvent forces, the polymer resists dissolution.

As a rule, for a polymer to form a solution in a solvent, its solubility parameter should be very close to that of the polymer. If at all, there could be a difference of 1-2 units.

If the solubility parameter of the solvent is lower than that of the polymer,. the internal bonds of the polymer are stronger than the solvent can break. In such a case, the polymer would only swell in the solvent.

If the polymer is cross-linked, any solvent with any solubility parameter would neither be able to swell this polymer nor would it be able to dissolve it. Strong chemicals that may be able to break the primary (covalent bonds in most polymers) would destroy the polymer. Any efforts to recover the polymer would be futile. Cellulose if treated with 70% sulfuric acid completely

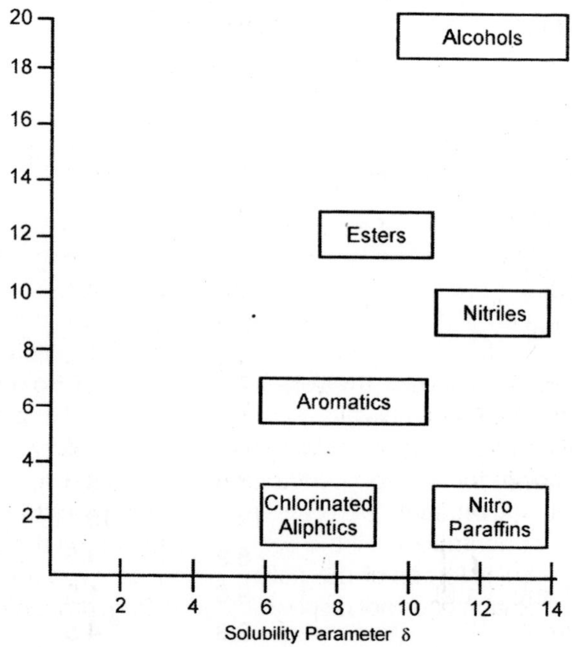

Fig. 2.2 Solubility paramter

dissolves. This dissolution occurs due to cleavage of the ether links of cellulose that degrades it to glucose. Regeneration of cellulose from the resulting solution is not possible.

Solubility parameter of several solvents as a function of hydrogen bonding is given in Fig 2-2

Of the three components of cohesive forces, hydrogen bonding has the highest contribution. Other forces that significantly contribute to solubility parameter are polar forces. This is evidenced for nitroparaffins, which, due to their high degree of polarity, have a high solubility parameter without corresponding high hydrogen bonding.

Purpose of solvent in a paint

The solvent serves two major purposes in a coating: ease of processing, and ease of application.

The viscosity of 100% resins is high. In many cases these are solids and can not be applied as films. To be able to process these materials easily, these are processed as resin solutions. Similarly, for a smooth thin coat that spreads evenly, produces good glossy films, wets the surface adequately and adheres well to the surface, solvents are necessary. If the solvent or solvent mixture is not correct, it can ruin all film properties. Depending on the hydrogen bonding and boiling point, different components of the solvent leave the film at different rates. A solvent must contain members from different classes of compounds for the purposes of economy, availability and overall film performance. .

The components of a solvent can be divided in three parts.

True solvent

This is the material whose solubility parameter is very close or higher than the solubility parameter of the polymer. This solvent is truly able to completely stretch open the polymeric chains away from each other and can satisfy the intermolecular forces by associating with polymer chains. The polymer forms a clear, free-flowing solution in this solvent without aggregation. The viscosity for a given concentration is highest as the chains are fully extended and entangle with each other causing resistance in motion. Since the solvent neutralizes all the secondary forces on the polymer chain, the inter-molecular forces of the polymer-polymer type are minimum and the polymer solution does not display deviation from properties of true solutions.

Latent solvent or secondary solvent or co solvent

These are substances whose solubility parameter is 3-5 units lower than that of the polymer. Thus, these cannot dissolve a polymer. If a polymer is put in a solvent of this nature, it would only swell. If a latent solvent is added to a solution of a polymer in a true solvent, it continues to remain a solution and would tolerate latent solvent to an extent. This action may be accompanied by rise in viscosity, even though the solids are reducing, development of turbidity and deviation from properties of a true solution such as non-linear change in viscosity with shear forces.

Non-solvent/Diluent

These are substances whose solubility parameter is quite different from that of the polymer. If the non-solvent or diluent is added to a polymer solution in true solvent, it is tolerated to a certain extent. Excessive addition leads first to rise in viscosity followed by sudden drop in viscosity. This can be explained by considering the possibility of the polymer chains interacting with each other due to reduced concentration of true solvent; this leads to the increase in viscosity. When the non-solvent concentration increases much more, polymer chains contract and exude the solvent mixture out. This is a state of aggregation. The polymer is no longer in a solution form and, the particles tend to separate out. If addition of non-solvent is continued, the polymer particles come out of phase and precipitate out. In fact, this procedure is used for separation of polymers from solutions and is termed as solvent non-solvent precipitation.

As can be understood, all polymers can not dissolve in all solvents. Therefore, it is not possible to classify solvents as true solvents, latent solvents and diluents. These will depend on the nature of the polymer. A true solvent for one polymer may be a diluent or non-solvent to another and vice versa. From the above discussion, following rules emerge.

If a coating composition contains a mixture of resins, one solvent must be a true solvent to all the resins.

During drying, the order in that the solvents leave the film must be: Non-solvent - First; Diluent - Next; and True solvent - Last.

Invariably, true solvents are the most expensive ones. The need to use a combination of solvents is purely economic. By choosing a solvent mixture that meets the criteria defined above, one ensures that the polymer remains in a true solution form for good wetting of the substrate, good flow and levelling and high gloss. A typical profile of loss of solvents as a function of time would be as shown in Fig 2-3.

First identifying the components and then comparing their evaporation rates can help selection of the solvent combination. The evaporation rate and its numerical values are discussed later in the section on testing of solvents. One way to choose solvents in different categories is from the information in literature. Another way is by experimenting.

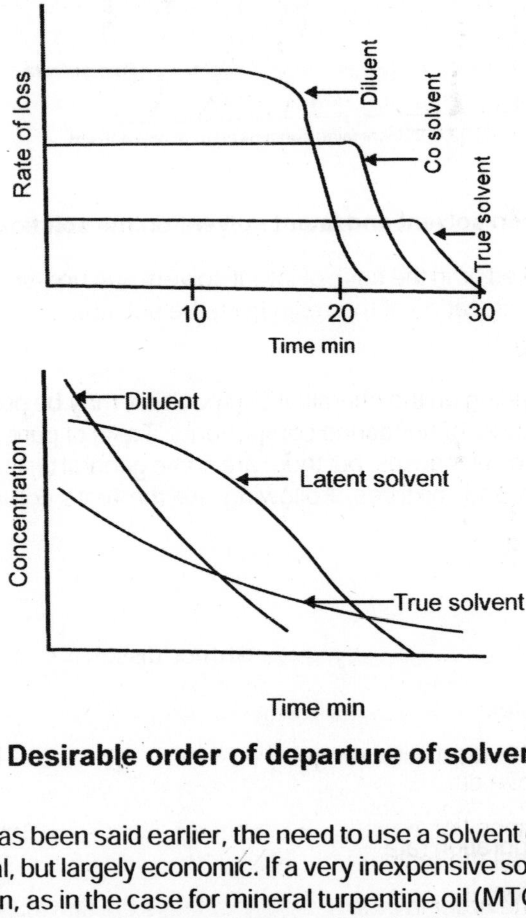

Fig. 2.3 Desirable order of departure of solvents from the film

As has been said earlier, the need to use a solvent combination is partly functional, but largely economic. If a very inexpensive solvent is a true solvent for a resin, as in the case for mineral turpentine oil (MTO) for long oil alkyds, one does not need to look further. Only in the case of difficulty soluble resins, does the need for a combination of solvents arise.

The solubility behaviour of the polymer is different for a solvent, latent solvent and diluent. If any of these is added continuously to a solution of polymers, depending on the nature of the solvent, the solution responds in the manner as shown in Fig 2-4.

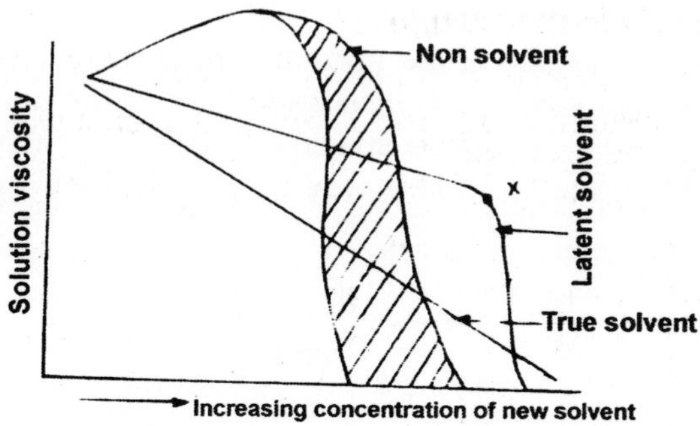

Fig. 2.4 Effects of non solvent and latent solvent on the solution viscosity

The points marked 'x' in the case of latent solvent and non-solvent effect are the points of precipitation of the resin from the solution.

Testing of solvents

Solvents, depending on the chemical composition, may be pure organic components or mixtures of undefined components. Tests of pure chemicals are applicable to pure substances, but there are some general tests applicable to pure compounds and mixtures. Following are the tests common to all solvents.

Physical tests

- Density
- Colour
- Refractive index
- Boiling point, or distillation range
- Aniline points
- Relative Evaporation rate
- Surface tension
- Purity by GC/HPLC

Chemical tests

- Copper strip corrosion
- KB value

A few of these are discussed here.

Boiling point or distillation range

If the solvent substance is a pure component, it has a defined boiling point. If it were a mixture of several compounds then it would not have a boiling point, but a boiling range. To find out the boiling range a 100 ml distillation flask is connected to a condenser, and a thermometer pocket to measure temperature of the vapors that are just about to meet the condenser. A measuring cylinder is connected to the other end of the condenser to collect the distilled solvent.

There are three measurements to be made: Temperature when the first drop condenses; Distillation range; and Dry point.

After the liquid starts boiling, the temperature at which the first drop of the liquid condenses in the container is recorded as the starting point of distillation. The distillation range is recorded as the temperature for every 10 ml. liquid collected. If the compound is substantially pure, the range may be just about a few degrees centigrade. For mixtures of hydrocarbons such as MTO or kerosene, this may extend from 180 to 270° c. The temperature at which the container becomes dry is called the 'dry point'.

Aniline point and mixed aniline point

These tests are applied to solvent mixtures to get an estimate of their aromatic content. Aniline mixes with aromatic solvents at room temperature in all proportions. It is, however, immiscible with aliphatic hydrocarbons such as hexane or heptane. If a mixture of aniline and hydrocarbon solvent that is not miscible is heated, at a certain temperature, it becomes homogeneous. Higher the temperature required for the two phases to mix, lower is the aromatic content of the solvent mixture. For determining aniline point, distilled aniline is mixed in 1: 1 proportion with the pre-dried solvent. The mixture must stay in two phases. This is then heated with continuous mixing. The temperature at which an uniform solution results is recorded (T_1). The mixture is now slowly cooled while mixing it continuously. The temperature at which slight turbidity appears is recorded (T_2)' The aniline point is average of the two temperatures $(T_1 + T_2)/2$.

If by mixing 1: 1 mixture of aniline and the solvent a solution results at room temperature,. a diluent such as n-hexane or n-heptane is added to increase the aniline point. A mixture of 1: 1: 1 of aniline solvent and n-hexane is taken for the test. This must stay in two layers. The aniline point is reported as 'mixed aniline point'.

Relative evaporation rate

The evaporation rate of a solvent is a function of its molecular weight, its latent heat of evaporation and the boiling point. The rate of evaporation also depends on the local factors such as direction and velocity of air, ambient temperature and surface area per unit weight. Since it is not possible to have a strict control on the condition of the surroundings, it is preferred to report these figures as relative evaporation rate using some pure components as standards. For very fast evaporating solvents, it is compared with diethyl ether, whereas for slow evaporating solvents it is compared with butyl acetate.

For determination of relative evaporation rate of solvents, petri dishes of exactly same diameter with absolutely flat surface are used. The area of the surface is measured. Known weights of liquids are filled in and are allowed to evaporate and the weight loss in recorded as a function of time. Precautions are taken to ensure that there is no vapour build up and there is no excessive breeze. It is advisable to keep the petri dishes in a mildly ventilated fuming cupboard. The temperature of the surroundings is recorded and evaporation rate is recorded as gm solvent/dm^2/hr at x°C or any other suitable units. If relative evaporation rate is to be reported, it is obtained by dividing evaporation rate of solvent by evaporation rate of diethyl ether or butyl acetate, as the case may be. Data on evaporation rate of selected solvents is listed in Table No. 2.4.

Table 2.4 :
Relative evaporation rates of solvents at 25°C(2)

Solvent	Relative evaporation rate
Acetone	1365
Methyl acetate	1250
Ethyl acetate	590
Methyl ethyl ketone	400
Ethyl alcohol	308
Toluene	266
see-Butyl acetate	172-208
Isopropyl alcohol/acetate	159
Ethylene dichloride	104.5
n-Butyl acetate	100

see-Amyl acetate	96
n-Amyl acetate	59
Methyl cellosolve	56.7
Ethyl carbitol	51.5
n-Butyl alcohol	38.5
Amyl alcohol (mixed isomers)	35
Methyl cellosolve acetate	34.1
Ethyl cello solve acetate	25
Butyl cellosolve	8

(Compared to Butyl acetate = 100)

Copper strip corrosion

Solvents used in protective and decorative coatings should not contain any components, that may cause corrosion. Some such materials are sulfur bearing organic chemicals or carboxylic acids. These can be detected in very small concentration by boiling the solvent with a bright copper strip. Sulfur compounds cause darkening of the surface and fatty acids, mineral acids cause formation of salts, that are coloured.

Boiling for a period ranging from 6-24 hours can result in darkening of the strip or its corrosion may form coloured salts that colour the solvent itself.

Most industrial solvents should not cause any corrosion of copper strip and the brightness of the copper strip should be maintained even with extended boiling in the solvent. Typically a copper strip admeasuring 1 cm x 15 cm about 0.1 cm thick is first cleaned with inhibited acid, rinsed with water, dried and then dipped in the solvent. The contents of the container are boiled for prolonged period. The brightness of the untreated strip is compared with the treated strip.

KB value

This is one of the oldest procedures used for determining suitability of solvents for lacquer application. This test uses a resin; ordinarily not found in our country, and based on an American resin Gum Kauri. It may be possible to adopt this procedure for Indian conditions using glycerol ester of rosin. The procedure is applicable to hydrocarbon solvents.

In this process, gum kauri (25%) is dissolved in n-butanol and filled in a tall glass tube with flat bottom. From the top, hydrocarbon solvent is added with a burette. As the solvent is added, the solution develops turbidity. A point at which letters written on a white paper with black ink become invisible is treated as the KB value.

Types of solvents

There are two main classes of solvents - organic (hydrocarbons, terpenes, oxygenates) and inorganic (CO_2, CCl_4, CS_2, H_2O). These are further subdivided into various classes depending on their chemical constitution.

Hydrocarbon solvents

Hydrocarbons are by far the largest volume solvents used by the paint industry. This is primarily because they can readily be used as primary solvents for most of the air-drying and stoving finishes and are probably cheapest, next only to water, for household or industrial paints. In fact, the economies are so much in favour of use of hydrocarbon solvents that at times this is a constraint posed to the resin chemist while designing his product. Whereas use of other true solvents such as alcohols, ether alcohols or esters may be permissible, the cumulative concentration is not expected to exceed 20% of total solvent mix. Only in special cases of difficult, high-performance resin products (such as PVC copolymers that do not dissolve in plain hydrocarbons) can one use more than 20% of oxygenated solvents. Hydrocarbons play the role of co-solvents and diluents in such situations.

Hydrocarbons are derived from naturally occurring mineral oils that are refined in refineries. As produced these are mixtures of several compounds that can not be identified by sheer chemical nature and are classified by their generic structure such as paraffins, naphthenes (cycloaliphatics) and aromatics. One more class of compounds formed during cracking of mineral oils is olefins that may be converted to paraffins or cycloparaffins by hydrogenation. These mixtures are fractionated into various components by distillation and/or extraction, and are classified as:

- Benzene, Toluene, Xylene (BTX)
- Petroleum ethers
- Solvent naphthas (light, medium and heavy)
- Mineral Turpentine or white spirit
- Biended solvents with varying degree of aromaticity and boiling range
- Kerosene
- Aromatic polyalkylates, predominantly C_9 aromatics known as CIX.

Benzene, Toluene, Xylene (BTX)

Of the three aromatics, benzene is narcotic and toxic, and its use as a solvent in paints and coating application has been discontinued. Its next homologue, toluene is considered safe and is extensively used as a solvent. Toluene (MW 92) is a colourless liquid, less dangerous and toxic in comparison to benzene. It is soluble in alcohol and petroleum hydrocarbons and is the most widely used hydrocarbon diluent in lacquers. It is a good solvent for alkyds, rosin derivatives and other varnishes. However, the high ambient temperature in our continent makes its use difficult in parts of the year, as the solvent tends to evaporate rather too fast. It is used in lacquers applied outdoors, that need to dry fast to minimise dust collection.

The next homologue, xylene, with two methyl substituents, is a more common solvent. Due to the large requirement of p- xylene for production of synthetic fibres, the availability of mixed xylenes has increased considerably. Produced by reformed C_8 naphtha, several byproducts such as toluene, ethyl benzene and C_9 (CIX) fraction also become available in large quantity. The international installed capacity for p-xylene is about 20 million tons, mostly for manufacture of synthetic fibres. Co-products, 0- and m-xylene have relatively smaller uses and are either used for preparation of phthalic and isophthalic acids or are recycled to the process of re-isomerization. Both re-isomerization and trans-alkylation reactions produce byproducts - toluene and trimethylben zenes - that are readily available for solvent use. The physical properties of the three isomers are quite identical as solvents and there is no need to use a pure component (0, m- or p-) xylene as a solvent.

Some properties of the three isomers of xylene are as shown below:

	o-Xylene	m-Xylene	p-Xylene
Specific gravity @ 20°C	0.881	0.866	0.861
Boiling Point, °C	144.1	139	138
Melting Point, °C	-28	-54	15

As can be seen, p-xylene has the highest melting point and m-xylene the lowest. Any p-xylene producer is willing to sell the raffinate after p-xylene extraction at a price comparable to p-xylene for solvent use. The melting point of the raffinate is low enough not to cause undue difficulties of crystallization and solidification of the solvent components in winter. The commercial product, called mixed xylenes, contains predominantly the m-isomer, with smaller quantities of toluene, ethyl benzene and pseudocumene (trimethylbenzene isomers), since the more valuable o-xylene and pxylene have been removed.

Solvent power of aromatics decreases as the size and number of substituents on the ring increases. Addition of alcohols (n-butanol) or alcohol ethers (cellosolve) increases the power, even when added in small proportion. As the number of substituents increase, the boiling point goes up, the evaporation rate reduces and solvent power also reduces. The next member of aromatics called CIX (C_9) fraction shows much more inferior solvent properties compared to xylenes. CIX is a mixture of mono-, diand tri-substituted benzenes.

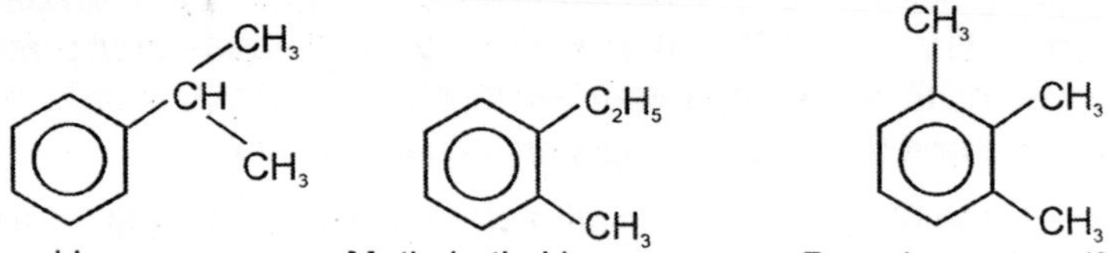

Isopropyl benzene or cumene | Methyl ethyl benzene (3 isomers) | Pseudocumene (3 isomers) (1,2,3; 1,3,4 & 1,3,5)

Fig. 2.5

These are byproducts from p-xylene production and are relatively cheaper than other aromatic compounds. Due to a large base of petroleum reforming capacity for manufacture of p-xylene, the availability of CIX is quite good and is likely to improve in future as refining capacity is increased.

The next higher members in the aromatic solvent range are a raffinate obtained from p-xylene production. It is generally polyalkylated aromatic in the range of C_{10} to C_{12}. The contents of the mixture may be low aromatic or high aromatic. It is not possible to specify the size or number of substituents on the benzene ring. Only a boiling range is defined. It is likely that the benzene ring may be substituted in 3, 4,5 or all six positions.

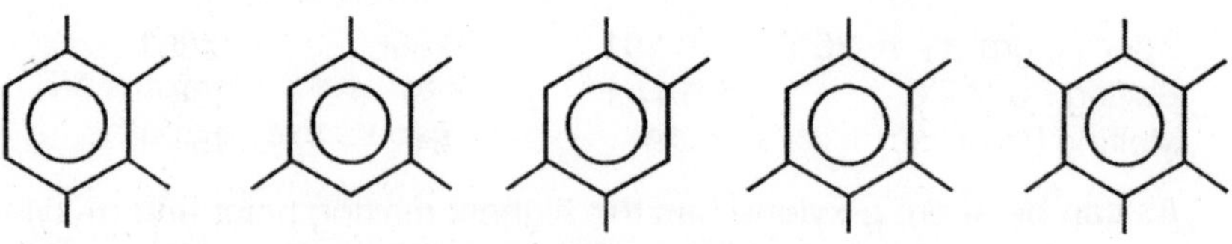

Possible substitution of benzene, With alkyl groups of 1,2 or 3 carbons

Availability of this solvent is likely to be about 150,000 MT, with the commissioning of the Jamnagar refinery of Reliance Petroleum. Since the boiling range is high and solvent power is low, it may be a likely substitute to mineral turpentine like products in long- and medium-oil alkyds that need slow-evaporating solvents for industrial use in hot conditions.

Solvent Naphtha

Naphtha is an old term (low, medium and high flash) referring to the volatile material obtained from bitumen. This term was used by chemists to describe volatile, low viscosity clear liquids that were inflammable. This product appears in several grades. The lighter fractions are a mixture of toluene, isomers of xylene, ethylbenzene, propylbenzene; heavier mixtures include products up to mesitylene, pseudocumene, durene, ethyl p-xylene, indene, cumerone and even alkyl naphthalene hydrocarbons.

The low flash naphtha has a boiling range 110-160° C and is a sol vent for natural and synthetic resins, vegetable oils, alkyds, bitumen, rubber, cellulose ethers, rosin/ phenolic derivatives. They are also diluents to polyester and polyvinyl formal resin varnishes for wire enamels. They are highly preferred where stringent specifications are not required. Closely cut fractions are used for NC lacquers, ethylcellulose-based printing inks, flat paints, industrial primers, surfacers and top-coats. Their presence in the solvent mixture adds to the solvency.

The high flash naphtha solvents have higher boiling range and lower evaporation rates. Members such as coumarone, indene, styrene, methyl naphthalene may be present in varying proportions if it is derived from coal tar. Petroleum products generally do not contain naphthalene derivatives.

Mineral spirit

It is a petroleum distillate that is a colourless liquid. It has an unpleasant odor due to aromatic and sulfur content. It has a flash point of about 36°C and a good evaporation rate at 25-30°C. It is used in brushable paints of air drying type. The petroleum characteristic odor is masked by vegetable turpentine in 1-5% concentration. It is also used as a solvent for reducing driers of cobalt, lead, manganese calcium and zinc as their octoates.

Typical properties are:

- Boiling range: 90% below 200°C
- Specific gravity: 0.77 to 0.81
- Refractive Index: 1.42-1.45

Kerosene

Kerosene is a cut above mineral turpentine with aromatic content up to 20%. It is added to paints to retard solvent evaporation, improve penetration and easy brushing. It is used in slow drying paints and primers.

Following are the typical properties.

Specific gravity:	0.81 to 0.82
Flash point:	70°C
Distillation range:	150-270°C

In addition, there are several products available from coal tar industry. India has five large steel plants that operate coke ovens (Durgapur Steel, Tata Steel, Bhilai Steel, Vishakhapattanam Steel and Rourkela Steel). Coke oven by-products are sold as mixed hydrocarbon solvents for paint and lacquer application.

More often these are sold in large bulk to solvent manufacturers (such as Ganga Rasayanee) who refractionate and blend them with other solvents to standard products. There are by-products available from some industries that are good hydrocarbons for solvent use. Producers of isobutylbenzene get a by-product ~ n-butyl benzene that is a useful solvent, available quite cheap, as it does not have many identified uses.

Turpentine

This is obtained as a co-product in the production of rosin from the sap of pine trees. Oils from different countries contain varying proportion of the constituents, depending on the geographical condition. It is a mobile liquid, slightly coloured, with pleasant odor. The common molecular formula ($C_{10}H_{16}$) allows for following isomeric compounds

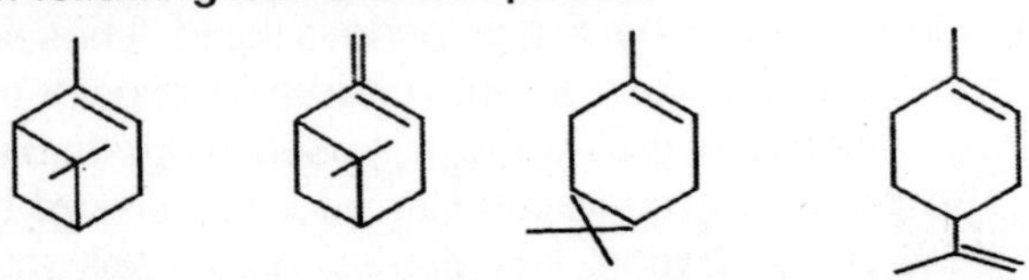

α – pinene β – pinene Δ^3- Carene dipentine

Fig. 2.7

In addition, small amounts of terpineols ($C_{10}H_{18}O$) may also be found

α-terpineol terpeneol

Fig. 2.8

The composition of a typical turpentine may vary with the source: α-Pinene 81%; Δ^3-Carene -14%; and High boilers - 5% or α-pinene - 60-70%; Δ^3 Carenes15-20%; and High boilers -7-8%.

Turpentine is also obtained by distillation of pine wood chips. The composition can vary significantly as the wood ages. The aging of wood causes the terpenes to polymerize. The components that are more susceptible to polymerization thus reduce in concentration. The difference is illustrated in Table 2.5.

Table 2.5

Composition of vegetable turpentine (3)

	Wood terpentine	Gum Terpentine
a-Pinene	80%	58-65%
b-Pinene	—	30%
Dipentene & others	1.5	2
Alcohols	1.5	2
Phenol ethers	5	1
Easters	—	2

Following are the typical properties:

	Wood turpentine	Destructive Distillation
Appearance	Clear	Clear
Colour	Colourless to pale yellow	Colourless to pale yellow
Specific gravity (20°C_, g/cc	0.86-0.875	0.86-0.875
Refractive index	1.465-1.47	1.465-1.47
Polymerization residue (38N H_2SO_4)	< 2%	<2%
Fraction up to 170°C	90% or higher	60%
Fraction up to 180°C	—	90%

Even though a good solvent, its high cost has now limited its use only as a flow additive and the perfumery value that is useful for masking the pungent aromatic or sulfurous odors of different petroleum solvents. The association of turpentine odors with paint continues. Depending on storage and age of turpentine, it may accelerate the drying of alkyd paints that is primarily associated with its peroxide content.

The presence of two double bonds makes them suitable for manufacture of polymers. They may be polymerized as such with acidic catalysts or with other materials such as phenols or cresols with or without formaldehyde. They also undergo DielsAlder addition with maleic anhydride resulting in dibasic acids that may be useful for alkyd preparation.

Halogenated hydrocarbons

Several halogenated derivatives of methane, ethane, propane, benzene are commercially available. These have been more commonly used in paint strippers, oil and grease cleaners but have rarely been used in coatings as solvents. The reasons are their odors~ anesthetic nature, toxicity and at times very high solvent power that precludes their use in subsequent coats as they are very likely to strip the under-coats and primers. They are preferred in applications when fire hazards are the most important consideration. Of late, the environmental damage these products are likely to cause has forced their withdrawal from the paint industry. Halogenated hydrocarbons, which are likely to degrade in the stratosphere and diminish the ozone layer, need to be phased out by 2010 under the Montreal Protocol of which India is also a signatory. Most of these solvents have a density greater than one, which is a disadvantage since they are bought by weight and sold by volume.

Products in this category that are considered as solvents to bitumen, oils, and waxes are methylene chloride, ethylene dichloride, trichloromethane, trichloroethane, carbon tetrachloride, tetrachloroethane, trichloroethylene, perchloroethylene, pentaand hexa-chloroethane. Chloroform and ethylene dibromide are highly toxic and can not be used in the paint industry. Aromatic chloro compounds such as monochlorobenzene and dichlorobenzene are strong, cheap solvents but due their objectionable odor and toxicity do not find place as solvents for paints.

Montreal Protocol

It is an international understanding between participating nations to curb use of ozone-depleting substances. Ozone reacts with elemental chlorine very rapidly forming chlorine oxide that reacts with ozone to produce chlorine. Thus, the reaction sequence can be written as

$$Cl_2 + 2O_3 \rightarrow 2ClO + 2O_3$$
$$2ClO + 2O_2 \rightarrow Cl_2 + 4O_2$$

The chlorine oxide produced in the first reaction can react with further quantity of ozone to regenerate chlorine. The sequence of first reaction is thus repeated and can be repeated several million times.

In the early fifties, halocarbons, several of them chloro and fluoro derivatives of C_1, C_2 and C_3 compounds, were used as propellants, refrigerants and in aerosols. In most of the cases the chlorofluorocarbons were lost to atmosphere. As a result, the ozone layer above the Antarctic region was depleted in ozone and a hole was detected in the stratosphere. The ozone layer is helpful in filtering harmful UV radiations. Some of the UV radiation is also used up in converting oxygen to ozone.

$$CO_2 \xrightarrow{h\upsilon} 2O_3$$

Thus the reaction is self-sustaining. The ozone layer is present in the atmosphere from about 16 km onwards. Sunlight consists of a wide spectrum of electromagnetic radiation of which about 2% is in the form of UV radiation. This is further classified in UVA, UVB, and UVC based on the wavelength (see section on UV and Light Stabilizers under Chapter 2, Paint Additives). The entire range of UV is capable of breaking bonds (C-C, C-N, C-O, C-S, -C = C-, -C ≡ C- etc.), that are the primary bonds of all living beings. The amount of UV received by any part of the globe depends upon the position~of the sun above the horizon, ozone content in the atmosphere, shielding by pollutants and clouds. This may be maximum during August to October, particularly in the northern parts of the world. UVB is particularly harmful to living objects, and small exposure causes sunburns. Extensive exposure causes darkening of skin and even skin cancer.

Since the 1960's, ozone loss has been monitored over different parts of the world. It was 5% in mid 60's over Europe, North America, and Australia. Since the late 1970's the ozone hole has been spotted above Antarctica each year during Sep.-Oct., with as much as 60% of the ozone depleted as a result of excessive release of chlorine and bromine derivatives of hydrocarbons. As a result, an international agreement (The United Nations Montreal Protocol on Substances that Deplete the Ozone Layer) was drafted. The progress has been continuously monitored with production of the most damaging compounds banned by 1996. Rapid developments have led to the replacement of several ozone layer depleting chemicals by environmentally safe products. This includes aerosols, solvent and refrigerants. The developed countries have curtailed emissions, and with the trend expected to continue it is expected that the original ozone levels will be restored by the middle of the 21st century. The recovery would be gradual since the CFCs require a long time to be removed from the atmosphere.

In the light of the forgoing, it is most advisable for the paint industry to use only readily biodegradable, preferably water-soluble or even plain water as a solvent in as many coatings as possible.

Oxygenated hydrocarbon

This is the single largest category of organic chemicals and is the backbone of the solvent industry. Even though, most often oxygenated hydrocarbons are used in combination with mineral spirits or aromatics, these impart most desirable properties to the paint system.

The important members of this class of solvents are:

- Alcohols - Methyl, ethyl, isopropyl, n-butyl, isobutyl, amyl, 2-ethylhexyl, etc.; cyclohexanol
- Esters - Methyl, ethyl, butyl, isobutyl, and 2-ethylhexyl acetate; dimethyl esters of dicarboxylic acids (C_3, C_5, C_6)
- Ethers - Diethyl ether, diisopropyl ether .
- Hydroxy ethers - Ethyl/methyl/butyl ethers of ethylene glycol, diethylene glycol, etc.

  Ether esters - Acetates of ethyl/methyl /butyl ethers of ethylene glycol, diethylene glycol, etc.
- Ketones - Acetone, methyl ethyl ketone, methyl isobutyl ketone, methyl isoamyl lactone, cyclohexanone
- Phenols - Phenol, cresols, xylenols, cresote oils, coal tar distillates.

Alcohols

The first four to five members of the homologous series make the most important class of solvents. These are highly polar and hence have high solubility in water; metha-nol,ethanol, isopropanol and t-butanol have infinite solubility in water. Sec-butanol and isobutanol are also substantially water-soluble (+20%), whereas n-butanol dissolves only about 7-8% in water. Solubility of water in butanol is also limited to about 7-8%.

Alcohols are readily biodegraded, but have different toxicity for mammals; Methanol is most poisonous of all- I ml taken internally can render a person permanently blind, and just 5 ml can kill. Ethyl alcohol is intoxicating and if taken in large volume can cause death.

Alcohols, particularly the lower ones, are very cheap solvents and are commonly used for wood finishes and several printing inks where they are either sole solvents or used in combination.

Esters

Most of the esters used are acetates. Exceptions are lactates (methyl lactate), pivalates and -diesters of dibasic acids (C_3, C_4, C_5 and C_6) most often produced from byproduct dibasic acids from caprolactam production. They are good primary solvents for a good range of resins such as nitrocellulose, acrylics and are good co-solvents for vinyls and chloro rubber. As a class of compounds esters have pleasant fruity odor with good acceptability with users. Lower members such as methyl and ethyl acetate are unduly low boiling (58°C and 77°C respectively). Intermediate boiling products (isopropyl acetate, butyl acetate) are common solvents for NC lacquers, acrylic lacquers and some stoving finishes. The high boiling diesters (Estasol) that is a mixture of malonic, succinic, glutaric and adipic acid dimethyl esters have a boiling range of 170-210°C. These are classified as environmentally friendly solvents and are being promoted for superior quality paints, usually in automotive finishing and coil coatings.

The solvent power of ester solvents depends on their structure. Small alcohol acetates have high solvent power, but are low boiling and highly volatile. As the chain length increases, the boiling point also increases (77°C for C_2 alcohol 'to 127°C for butyl acetate and 199°C for 2-ethylhexyl acetate). Two other properties seriously affecting utilization are: Solvent properties and Hydrolytic stability.

Both the properties get seriously affected by branching of the alcohol chain. Branched alcohol esters (acetates). are progressively poorer, their water solubility and also solubility of water in them is higher compared to their n-counter parts. The boiling points are also lower as shown ip the following examples.

Solvent	**Boiling Point °C**
n-Propyl acetate	102
Isopropyl acetate	89
n-Butyl acetate	172
Isobutyl acetate	117
Sec-Butyl acetate	112
t-Butyl acetate	97.8

Evaporation rate, which is a composite function of hydrogen bonding and molecular weight, is also significantly affected by chain branching. The evaporation rate of ester solvents increases considerably with chain branching.

Branched alcohol esters are more susceptible to hydrolysis. If adequate amount of water is present, the product acid can self-catalyze the hydrolysis reaction leading to unacceptably high levels of free acidity. By and large, esters are pleasant solvents and pose no environmental problems of degradation or ozone destruction. Their use must be encouraged. Several ofthe products (ethyl, n-butyl and amyl acetate) can be derived from renewable resources such as alcohol, almost completely. Thus they represent members of "green" solvents that can be produced from inexhaustible natural resources.

The solubility of some esters in water and that of water in them is shown below:

Ester	Solubility of ester in water, Wt %	Solubility of water in ester, Wt %
Methyl acetate	25	8.2
Ethyl acetate	8.7	3.3
IP acetate	2.3	2.6
N-Propyl acetate	0.7	1.1
Sec-Butyl acetate	0.8	3.6
Isobutyl acetate	0.7	1.1
N-Butyl acetate	0.7	1.2
Amyl acetate	0.5	0.001
2-ethyl hexyl acetate	0.03	<0.03

In India, methyl acetate is primarily produced as a by-product of polyvinyl alcohol manufacture or from p-xylene oxidation to terephthalic acid, that is carried out in acetic acid medium. Part of acetic acid produces methanol that emerges as methyl acetate with the off gases.

$$CH_3COOH + O_2 \rightarrow \underset{\text{(peracetic acid)}}{CH_3\,CO\text{-}O\text{-}OH} \rightarrow CH_3OH + CO_2$$

Methyl acetate from polyvinyl alcohol is a mixture of methanol and methyl acetate. This mixture is used as such for preparation of shellac and rosin varnishes.

Ethyl acetate is produced in our country mainly from alcohol. Ethyl alcohol is oxidized to acetaldehyde and acetic acid and is esterified with alcohol.

$$CH_3\text{-}CH_2OH \rightarrow CH_3CHO \rightarrow CH_3\text{-}COOH$$

$$+CH_3CH_2OH$$

$$CH_3\text{-}CH_2\text{-}O\text{-}\overset{\overset{\displaystyle O}{||}}{C}\text{-}CH_3 + H_2O$$

Thus, the reaction is a four-step process. The yield at every stage may go down to 95%; thus the overall yield is about 80%. Thus there is incentive to cut the number of steps.

A recent innovation is successful implementation of Tishchenko condensation where two molecules of acetaldehyde condense to produce ethyl acetate.

If acetaldehyde is derived from a petrochemical route by oxidation of ethylene, the overall cost is significantly lower.

$$2CH_3CHO \xrightarrow[Al(C_3H_7O)_3]{} CH_3\text{-}CH2\text{-}O\text{-}\overset{\overset{\displaystyle O}{||}}{C}\text{-}CH_3$$

Esters are popularly used for their low toxicity, ready availability and stable prices. They are important constituents ofNC lacquers, vinyl resin lacquers, nail polishes and industrial finishes.

These are the reaction products of carboxylic acids and alcohols and are formed by removal of a water molecule. Esters are one of the most important group of solvents. As a class, these products have sweet fruity odor and by and large are not objectionable in any composition. The properties such as boiling point and freezing point are a function of their molecular weight and structure. In most of the coating compositions, water content is the limiting reactant. The ease of hydrolysis is a function of the structure of the acid and alcohols. Thus, acids that have the carboxylic acid attached to a straight chain and esterified with alcohols that have the hydroxyl group attached to a straight chain (n-n) are the most stable and most useful products. Iso and neo alcohols produce less stable products. Thus, butyl acetate is a good solvent with good stability and solvent power. Ethyl acetate is too low boiling and is suitable in fast drying compositions such as liquid inks. n-Propyl acetate, amyl acetate, hexyl acetate and 2ethylhexyl acetate are too expensive and are used only when the conditions demand.

Esters of other acids are relatively less important. Most of the formic esters (methyl, ethyl) are too low boiling, hydrolyze easily and are poisonous. These are almost never used in coatings. Esters of secondary alcohols such as isopropanol, sec- and t-butanol are more water-soluble and solubility of water in them is also high. The hydrolytic stability is also limited and therefore they are not preferred products for coatings. Recently Eastman (USA) have introduced new product from their oxochemistry isopivalyl isopivalate that is a C_{10} molecule which is reported to have a good combination of boiling point, evaporation rate and solvent power.

Amides

Amongst the amides, there are. three important solvents that deserve mention formamide, dimethyl formamide and dimethyl acetamide. These are water miscible in all proportions, and have strong solvent power. Presently their prices have also come down considerably and these can be considered in the coating compositions, particularly the water reducible or water dispersible type coatings. Their boiling points are high (155-220°C) and evaporation rate is low. These can be used only for stoving finishes.

Ketones

There are only a few ketones used in the coating industry as solvent. Use of ketones as basic raw material such as for preparation of bisphenol-A, MEK oxime, MEK peroxide, benzophenone derivatives for UV stabilization is also known to coatings industry.

The important members of this class of products are: Acetone, methyl ethyl ketone (MEK), diacetone alcohol (DAA), methyl isobutyl ketone (MIBK), cyclohexanone and isophorone. Of these, acetone is freely water miscible and very low boiling. It is highly reactive under alkaline conditions with itself or formaldehyde. The aldol products are highly coloured and therefore, the use of acetone or any ketone under alkaline conditions must be resisted. Due to its fast evaporating nature and excellent solvency for a large number of resins, acetone is commonly used for preparations such as nail polishes. Use of acetone in humid atmosphere results into a defect called blushing. It may be used in smaller quantities in liquid inks in combination with ethyl acetate and methyl ethyl ketone.

The most common solvent of the ketone family continues to be MEK, produced by dehydrogenation of see-butanol. It is the most common solvent for vinyl copolymers. Liquid inks for polyester substrate are formulated with ethyl acetate and MEK as primary solvents and toluene as a diluent. Press speeds of as high as 180 mlsec and the small oven length (1.5-2 m) reduce the residence time below 0.3 sec., and the oven temperatures are not very high too. Thus, the coating must become completely solvent-free during this time to be recoated by other colours. The excellent release characteristics of MEK with PVC resins make this possible.

MIBK, DAA and cyclohexanone are the preferred solvents for vinyl resins used in protective coating applications. Cyclohexanone can also dissolve PVC homopolymer and is used, in combination with diluents, as an adhesive for joining PVC pipes. These products have a characteristic odor that is not acceptable in most indoor applications, and their use is thus restricted to outdoor application.

Cyclohexanone is also used as a raw material for the manufacture of cyclohexanone formaldehyde resins - also called ketonic resins by alkaline condensation. These are non-functional or hydroxy functional resins, thermoplastic and have limited applications in cosmetics and inks.

3

Pigments

Pigments are defined as inorganic or organic solids, that are insoluble or substantially insoluble in water or the organic medium with that they are used as dispersions. They impart colour, opacity, mechanical rigidity and reinforcement to the continuous phase in that these are dispersed. Inorganic pigments that do not impart colour and opacity but exhibit all other properties are termed as extenders.

In nature, we find a large number of solids. All of them are not pigments. The organic chemists synthesize a large number of coloured products in their laboratories. Not all of them develop into pigments. (There are at last 1000 unsuccessful compounds for every successful product). To qualify as a pigment, a substance must meet a series of properties not covered by the definition alone.

These are divided in 4 categories:

(a) Physical properties

(b) Chemical properties

(c) Commercial aspects

(d) Environmental and safety issues.

Physical Properties

(a) Solubility

This is the most undesirable character in a solid to quality as a pigment. The medium in that we disperse the pigment is the binder, that holds the pigmentary particles together in useful paint films. If the pigment is soluble in any commonly found liquids that are likely to come in direct contact with the painted object, the pigment might leach out. If it was coloured, it might disfigure the surroundings. Worst of all, when it dissolves, it leaves behind porosity in the film. A porous film can not protect, since it would allow corrosive ions a free passage up to the substrate. The substance should be typically insoluble in water and all the organic solvents and resins commonly used in paint and related products.

(b) Water solubles

Just as the pigment should be insoluble, its other constituents and impurities should also be water insoluble. The water-soluble components are restricted to a few parts per million. Typically, the natural solubility of the substance itself should be of the order of 30-50 mg/l in water.

(c) Should be either white or coloured

When a light is incident upon a pigment, it can act in three ways:

i. Reflect the entire radiation

ii. Reflect part of the radiation and absorb another part

iii. Completely absorb the incident light.

When all the radiation is reflected from white light, we see the object white. When the light is partially reflected from a white light, we see the object coloured. The colour is the one, that is not absorbed from the components of white light(VIBGY OR). When all the components of light are absorbed we see the object black. For a pigmentary substance, it is expected to completely reflect a particular band of light while completely absorbing others. If this is incomplete, then the shades produced are not clean and are termed as "Dirty". Dirty shades have limited use due to their poor aesthetic appeal. Similarly, if it absorbs the light completely, it must do so completely. If a black pigment reflects part of the light, it is not seen as a perfect black but either appears reddish black or bluish black. Mixed colours are undesirable in coloured pigments. We call this as clean shades.

Particle size

Fine particles are desirable for all pigmentary applications. These must not be uniform but should have a wide size distribution. This helps them to pack better. If there is a certain weight fraction of a particular size, the next size should be such that it packs between the space created by the particles of the first size. The third fraction should comprise particles, that would occupy the space created by contact ofthe particles of the first two fraction. It can be imagined that the number of particles in the first fraction would be the lowest and they would be highest in the last fraction but since the size of first particles is an order of magnitude larger than the last fraction, the weight fraction oflargest size would be highest. This is known as poly dispersity and is highly desirable for protective character of the pigment. When we look at coloured pigments being used for colouration of the film, these are used in a small concentration except for the solid shades. These are generally preferred in their finest particle size so as to increase the surface area and hence the colour strength. It is mainly the extender that is required in the highest proportion in most of the primers, under coats, architectural finishes and other protective coatings. It is preferable to have extenders in a poly dispersed particle size, primary pigments and colouring pigments in uniform particle size for best performance. As we have discussed earlier, except minerals, all other pigments that are precipitated in a fine particle form need to be flocculated, filtered and granulated for ease of packing, ease of handling transportation and storage. In the process of conversion of fine particles into agglomerates, the fine particle size should not be irreversibly lost. For this, the pigments are surface treated. Depending on the density of the pigment, the surface treatment may be from 1-10% by weight that would mean from 2-20% by volume. Some newer grades of titanium dioxide have a core of an inert pigmentary material up to 10% by volume, another 8-10% by weight of surface treatment, thus reducing the purity of TiO_2 to just about 80%. The lower concentration of TiO_2 does not in any way reduce the value of the pigment but only enhances the physical properties such as hiding, ease of dispersion and dispersion stability.

Hiding pigments should be uniform in particle size and can be diluted with extenders of identical particle size. The wetting and dispersing agent requirement of the pigment depends upon the surface area, increasing proportionately with reducing diameter and reducing density of the pigment. It is expected that the entire surface of the pigment be covered with a monomolecular layer of the surface-active agent so as to change the surface electrical character of the pigment. Thus, an anionic surfactant imparts -ve charge to the surface, a cationic surfactant imparts +ve charge to the surface and a non ionic surfactant insulates any charge held by the surface and makes it neutral. Addition of surface-active agent beyond monolayer is not beneficial and could actually be harmful since most of these compounds are water sensitive. Excess could lead to water liking properties to the resultant product.

Refractive index

One of the main functions of a pigment is to hide the defects of the surface. This is possible only when the surface is not visible, that is either no light should reach the substrate and any light reflected by the surface should not be allowed to be transmitted back to the viewer as shown in Fig. 3-1

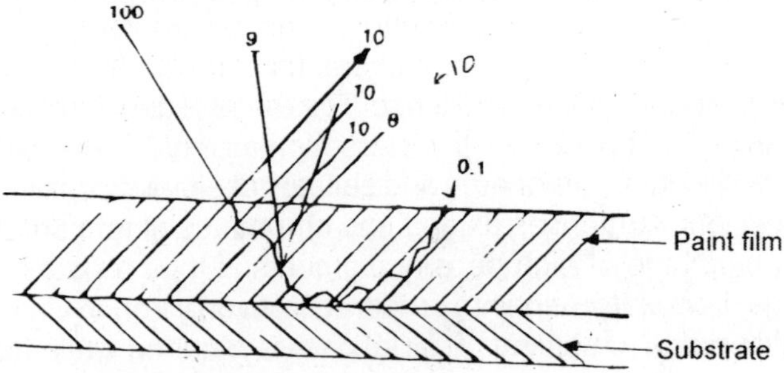

Fig. 3.1 Reflection of light from a painted surface

Thus, a large proportion of the light received by the surface should be reflected and nearly no light reflected by the substrate should be returned back to the viewer. This is possible in three ways.

i. The entire light received by the surface is reflected.

ii. All the light received is partially absorbed and partially transmitted.

iii. Certain wave lengths oflight are fully absorbed and others are transmitted or reflected.

Case I: When entire incident light is reflected from the surface, the substrate appears opaque white with all the defects of the surface totally hidden.

Case II: Certain wavelengths get fully absorbed and others are fully reflected. This situation leads to complete obliteration of the surface with intense colouration.

Case III: When certain wavelengths are fully absorbed and others are only partially reflected back. This allows some part of the light to reach up to the substrate and is received back by the viewer. The coating thus appears to only partially hide the surface.

From the above discussion, it is clear that the hiding and colouration are two distinct properties provided by pigment. Of these, the first one arises by total internal reflection. Total internal reflections at a large number of surfaces coated by fine particles helps in complete returning of the light back to the viewer. When the light passes through the pigmentary particle, certain wavelengths may get absorbed. This leads to colouration. The combination of reflection with absorption resul:s into hiding with colouration where as only absorption results into transparent colouration. For the best hiding performance, the refractive index should be high (>2). When the refractive index difference between the medium and pigment is high, the hiding is good. If the medium is air, the hiding is very good but then there is no binding.

Density

Most inorganic substances are dense. The range of density of compounds varies from as low as about 2.2. g/cc to as high as 8 g/cc. The lower end of the products is silicates, carbonates and sulfates of alumina, calcium, barium etc. The higher end comprises oxides and chromates of iron and lead. The greatest disadvantage of high-density pigments is their tendency to settle during storage. For example paints prepared from only iron oxide or red lead are very highly prone to settling. Special care is required while formulating such paints. The particle size needs to be reduced considerably to reduce the force due to gravity and increase specific area to increase the viscous drag. The rate of settling of particles depends directly upon the mass of the particle and inversely with its perimeter and viscosity of the medium in that it has been put. Thus dense particles will settle fast but if the shape has large perimeter and viscosity of medium is high, it would reduce the settling rate. Additives, that build up viscosity on storage (thixotropic), higher viscosity of medium and fine particle size, may be necessary to prevent settling of dense pigments. It is desirable that the density of pigments be in the range of 2-3 glee. If it is more, the over all density may have to be reduced by addition of other low density extenders so that even if settling occurs, it is soft and readily redispersible.

Colour, shade and strength

It is expected that the colour of the pigment should be pure. There are three opposing pairs of colours, that are mutually exclusive (can not exist together). These are black - white, Red-green and yellow-blue. These can be put at the opposite ends of x, y & z co-ordinates. It is desirable that one should get a colour or x-x, y-y & z-z axis where the values of the other two should be zero. Such colours would be pure black, white, red, green, yellow and blue. There may be slight deviation on other sides. It may be possible to use such colours without much addition of other colours. It is also expected that the strength of the colours should be high. Thus, a small concentration may be necessary to attain a particular shade.

Porosity

The pigmentary particles must be totally solid. A particle can be porous in two ways:

(a) Open porosity

(b) Closed porosity

Open porosity is the one in that all the pores are inter-connected and a penitrant such as a liquid of low viscosity and good wetting character can conveniently penetrate the pores and fill up the space. Since all the pores

are inter-connected, a penitrant can fill up the entire volume easily. Such porosity is totally undesirable in a pigmentary material. If such a material were added to the composition, the binder and solvent would enter the fine pores of the pigment thus making the binder unavailable for the purpose it has been added to the composition. The PVC of the composition would shift to the higher value thus changing the performance properties of the pigment. For this reason, the pigment must be dense. There are special situations however, when porosity in the pigments or extenders can be made use of. Thus, for water based paints using emulsion binders, porous extenders such as silica or alumina that have pores much finer (30-100°A) than the particle size of the emulsion (5000-7000°A) significantly contribute to hiding since most of this hiding is dry hiding. The pores are filled with only water till the paint film dries. On drying, the pores are filled with air thus causing considerably large difference in the refractive index between pigment and air. By using silica or alumina, it is possible to reduce TiO_2 content of the emulsion paint considerably. This introduces some defects in the film such as chalking tendency, poor stain resistance and poor washability and a careful balance is required.

Closed porosity results form a structure like a hollow sphere. This is helpful in reducing the density of a pigment but is very difficult to incorporate. Hollow spheres of glass are manufactured by very special patented technology (3 M). These spheres can be obtained in very low-density (0.125 *g/cc)* and are helpful in reducing the bulk density of products such as sol sealers, vinyl compounds and fillers. These help in reducing settling tendency of pigments. This property is not yet commercially incorporated in any pigmentary substance. If present by chance, it is not an objectionable trait. It would reduce the density of the particle, that must remain more than the binder system to avoid floating of the particles on the surface of the film.

Melting point and thermal stability

Melting point and thermal stability of most of the inorganic pigments should be higher than the highest service temperature of the products in which these are used or a temperature to that these are likely to be exposed. It is not a serious issue for most inorganic pigments that inherently melt or dissociate at reasonably high-temperature (with exception of yellow iron oxide, for which maximum temperature of use is 170-180°C), it is the organic products that must be carefully designed and selected. Phthalocyanine pigments are exceptionally heat stable. Metallic pigments have limitations depending on the melting point of the metal itself. Further, since the metals are in the finely divided form, they are susceptible to oxidation at a temperature much lower than their melting point. In fact, certain metals are pyrrophoric at higher temperature. They may appear very inert at low-temperature but can not be used in coatings that may have to be exposed to high-temperature. Titanium metal is one such material. Aluminum, that has a melting point of 600°C, can not be used above 500°C in coatings since most of the metal will be burnt before coating reaches the melting temperature of the metal.

Chemical Properties

Purity

Most of the inorganic pigments are processed minerals. The purity requirement for most of the pigments are high. The impurities, particularly the coloured ones should not be present more than a few parts per million, (PPM) particularly if they are coloured or produce coloured complexes with the chief ingredient. Invariably, transition metals produce colour. Thus, Fe, Mn, Co, Cu, Ni, Cr that produce coloured oxides and salts should not be present in PPM levels. Other impurities that may substantially affect stability in acidic/basic conditions, chemical reactivity to sulfur (lead, cadmium, tin, antimony, bismuth, mercury, arsenic, copper, that form coloured sulfides from black to orange) should be absent. The manufacturing process must ensure complete freedom from the coloured elements as well as the potentially colouring elements. The specifications of the product must mention the limits for these substances. The product chosen as a pigment must be based on raw materials, that are continuously available. No industry can depend on limited resources.

Resistance to acids, alkalies and chemicals

Paints, printing inks and coatings are all likely to be exposed to acids, alkalies, solvents and chemicals. A good pigment must display adequate resistance to all of them. For example, a printing ink used for manufacture of soap wrappers must be able to display adequate resistance to the alkaline environment in the soap cake with which it would be in intimate contact. Not just during the period it is packed in it but also during use since some users are likely to store used soap in the same wrapper. Or, there may be accidental spillage of water on packed soap, that should not alter the printing

on the package. Similarly, several paints are used in industrial environment. Fumes. of acids should not discolour, dissolve or affect the pigment in any other manner. Colour codes are conventionally used on pipelines to distinguish them. If the colours change in the industrial environment, it can lead to confusion. The pigments, along with the paint get exposed to industrial environment. They will also receive their due share of acids, alkalies other chemicals and must be able to resist them and retain the colour and other properties for the entire life of the coating. Very often we find selective fading of one colour that disfigures the entire product.

Typical example is fading of the red band on petroleum tankers, discolouration of portions of buildings, that are preferentially exposed to sun. These are caused by improper pigments, that are not stable to light.

Resistance to degradation due to oxidation

Oxidation is the most common mechanism of film formation. During the initial drying of the paint film, the environment around the pigment is highly oxidizing due to the presence of free radicals, hydroperoxides and the activated catalyst. The situation is more serious with stoving finishes that may be baked from 120 to 180°C for extended periods of 40-30 minutes (in that order). In exceptional cases very high temperature for a short time may be employed to cure the coatings. For example, PVDF coatings are cured at 250°C for 2-3 minutes and coatings on steel in continuous lines are cured at 300°C to 350°C for just 30-50 seconds. In all these operations high temperature coupled with oxidative conditions cause polymerization of the medium. The pigment must not take part in any of these reactions and should come our-totally unconverted in the process without change of shade or crystal forms. Either of these could lead to film defects.

Pigments should have no ion exchange properties

The acidic or alkaline ion exchange sites in a pigment can chemisorb some of the essential components from solution from the paint. Thus, the desired effect can not be attained due to reduced concentration in the solution. Thus, various driers, that are metallic soaps of fatty acids, may exchange the cobalt or lead with a pigment containing exchangeable ions. Similarly, wetting and dispersing agents containing zinc or calcium soaps of fatty acids may exchange zinc or calcium with the pigment. In both these cases, the activity of the important ingredient is lost. The metals, that catalyze drying, are lead and cobalt. Both of them must be available in solution. On ion exchange they become out of phase and would not be able to perform their expected duty. The drying properties of the paint will seriously suffer. Similarly, if zinc and calcium are removed, the dispersion stability would suffer and the pigment might flocculate.

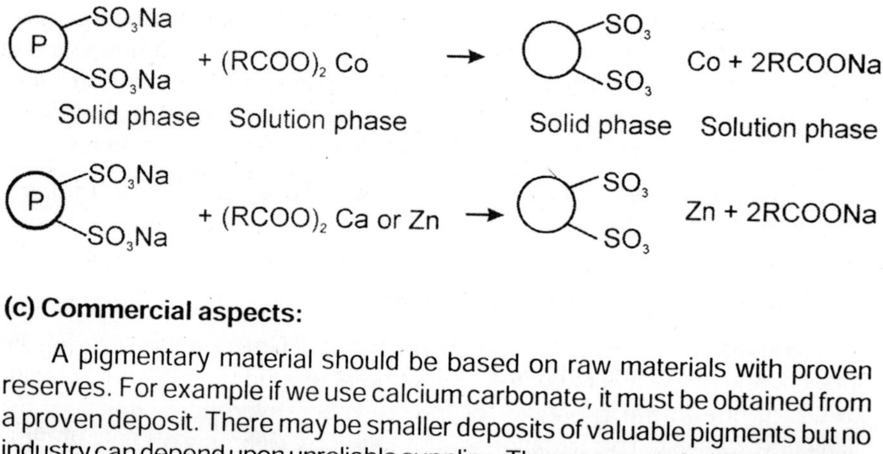

(c) Commercial aspects:

A pigmentary material should be based on raw materials with proven reserves. For example if we use calcium carbonate, it must be obtained from a proven deposit. There may be smaller deposits of valuable pigments but no industry can depend upon unreliable supplies. The process technology involving purification, reprocessing should be well established: The manufacturing process should have no steps, that are hazardous or environmentally unsafe. This is from the point of view that the pigment should be continuously available. If there are some environmental issues, that might force closure of the industry, the supply chain breaks and the user has to hurriedly look for alternatives. This may involve precious time or loss of business. Alternate supplies may be inferior, not proven, or expensive. The manufacturer may run the risk of basing his product with no dependable experience.

Toxicity and environment issues

Coated objects come in physical contact of the human body. The paint or coating must not contain any pigment with toxic effects. Toys, particularly with attractive colours such as bright yellow and red are highly prone to be chewed by children. They may ingest a part of the pigment. There are reported cases of lead poisoning due to chewing of PVC based products that contained lead stabilizer. Nail paints, that are constantly in contact of the mouth of the user, used lead based pearlscent pigments in the early days. These have been replaced with mica coated with titanium dioxide or iron oxide type of effect pigments. Mercury, cadmium, bismuth, antimony were used as special components of pigments at one time. No pigments any more contain mercury. Antimony is still used in fire retardant finishes. Lead a major component of paint in the form of white lead has been completely replaced by TiO_2 and ZnO.

One big gap still remains and that is yellows. To date, there is no economic alternative to lead chromate pigments. The hiding, the purity of tone, the permanence of colour and the low cost offered by these pigments is unmatched by any other organic or inorganic substitutes. There have been some developments in the form of cerium sulfide, that has only about half the colour strength, and three to four times the cost of lead chromates, but by and large it has been a non starter. There has been some local initiative to replace lead chromes by iron yellow on automotives but has remained restricted to the lower end of three wheelers for public transport. The yellow band on these vehicles, that used to be bright yellow at one time, has been replaced by dull looking iron oxide yellow. This problem presents one of the best opportunities for researchers to develop substitutes for lead chromate. Iron yellow is a promising line to tow with structural modification to obtain the desired shade. It appears iron can do it.

Characterization and physical relationships

Most of the organic or inorganic pigments are sold in powder form. For special applications such as colouring plastics and plastisols, these may be supplied as pre dispersed in a plastic or a suitable medium. We have discussed the commercial requirement of converting the primary particles into aggregates and agglomerates in the section on paint additives and it is understood that all the pigments are supplied in the aggregate form or even agglomerated form for ease of packing, handling storage and transport on either side - the manufacture and the user.

A good commercial pigment should be surface treated so that the redispersion is easy. It is now possible to almost completely eliminate the sand milling operation from manufacture of water-based wall paints and even synthetic enamels using high quality pigments.

Pigmentary solids are either amorphous or crystalline in nature. Amorphous solids may take, whatever shape possible. Crystals have well defined shapes such as needle, cubes, rhombus, etc. Crystal shapes determine colour, reactivity and stability of a pigment. Inter-conversions are always possible since these are thermodynamic functions. Stabilization of a crystal in a specific form and preventing it from any significant change over is very important. All other properties remaining same, change of crystal shape can completely alter colour and hue, stability of paint and colour strength of a pigment. That is why we prefer to use materials, that are completely insoluble in water, solvents or the media in that we put it. If there is any finite solubility in the solvent, water or media, the crystal reformation is aided. If by chance the crystal form being used is not the most stable form, the change over process starts soon after the pigment has been dispersed. This process can continue till the continuous medium is removed as may happen only during and after paint application. This poses problems of change of shade, most common to inadequately stabilized copper phthalocyanine pigments. The α and β forms have different undertones and different mass tones. The inter-conversions do take place conveniently. To understand this, we should look at the nature's example of white and black marble. Both are calcium carbonate of same purity. The black colour is not an effect of any impurity but it is just the difference in the crystal form. Preservation of the crystal form is therefore very necessary.

Particle size and surface area

The wettability of the pigmentary particle is a function of its surface behaviour. It is most desirable that the surface area for a given particle sizes should be minimum. Spherical shape has the lowest area to volume ratio. Additionally spherical particles, of uniform size can only make point contact with each other. Thus perfectly spherical particles of same size would generally flocculate to the minimum level. Though most desirable no commercial pigment is found in perfectly spherical shape.

The particles should resemble spherical shape as much as possible. This is done by incorporation of additives during precipitation process. Products that are ionic in nature and can replace one of the components of ionic species forming pigment can get co-adsorbed on the surface of a growing particle and change the crystal habit. This puts an end to a point of growth. More such species getting adsorbed on the surface convert it into a surface that can grow no more thus limiting the size and shape of the particle. These products are known as crystal growth inhibitors/modifiers and are used at a very low concentration so that they do not attain a contaminant level in the final product. Pigments treated in this way produce more stable dispersions and produce better over all performance in the system.

The relationship between particle size and surface area has been demonstrated. It considers only spherical particles. If one looks at pigmentary particles under a microscope, virtually all shapes except spheres may be found. We also know that the surface area of spheres is lowest for a given volume. This mean that surface area of pigments in reality is much more than what can be calculated from their particle size. Flatter surfaces can interact on a larger area and thus tend to flocculate more.

The surface area is important from the standpoint of surface-active agent demand. Larger surfaces require extra surface-active agent for adsorption and equilibrium with the vehicle around them.

For coloured pigments, large surface area means better colour strength. A coloured pigment appears coloured because of its capability to absorb a particular part of the visible spectrum and reflect the balance. More the surface available for reflection, better is the colour strength. Finer particles generate more surfaces, that add to the colour strength. When reversal of this process takes place, that is, when the pigments flocculate, the colour strength reduces. If the flocculation is not very strong, the flocks may break off with mild shear typically applied by a brush, and the film produced has non-uniform colour. A good wetting and dispersing agent takes care of this problem. Depending on pigment, proper selection of wetting and dispersing agent must be made.

Application problems

Arising out of the surface behaviour of the pigmentary particles, some application problems are as follows:

Thixotropy

Settling

Flocculation

Bronzing

Recrystallisation

Important Members

Pigments is a separate subject matter for two books. An attempt is made here to list the important members.

Pigments can be broadly classified in three categories:

(i) Primary Pigments (Inorganic)

(ii) Organic Pigments
(iii) Extenders.

(i) Primary Pigments (Inorganic)

These are inorganic compounds that are either minerals or processed minerals with high purity, fine particle size and clear tones. These are available in a range of colours.

(a) White

- Titanium Di oxide (TiO_2)
- Zinc oxide (ZnO)
- Lithopone ($BaSO_4.ZnS$)

(b) Red

- Iron oxide red (Fe_2O_3)

(c) Yellow

- Lead chromate:

This has several varieties. Depending on the composition, the colour varies from lemon yellow to dark orange. When Molybdenum is incorporated, the. darker shades of orange are obtained. As a rule, more the lead content the colour is more towards red. When a composite portion of lead sulfate is present, the colour tends,to become lighter yellow.

- Iron Yellow (FeO.OH)

  This is a natural as well as synthetic yellow pigment.

- Cadmium sulfide (CdS)
- Light fast, H_2S resistant suitable for exterior non-fading used in ceramic/ glass colouration.

(d) Black

- Carbon black

The main use of carbon black is in car tyres, printing inks and plastics. Paints barely consume 2% of carbon black. There are several grades ranging from low to very high surface area. These differ on the basis of the starting material (Furnace oil, Acetylene, Methane), process conditions (Residence time and process temperature, oxygen content, particle size).

- Iron black (FeO).

- Manganese Di oxide (MnO)

FeO and MnO_2 have limited use due to their low colour strength and reactivity with binders, instability. MnO_2 is used in ceramic applications. :

(d) Blue

- Iron blue (Fe(NH4) $(Fe(CN)_6)$
- Ultramarine Blue
- Copper Aluminate
- Cobalt Aluminate

(e) Green

- Chrome oxide green
- Nickel Aluminate

Problems with blue and green pigments is their poor strength. These are now used for high temperature requirements where organic pigments can not be used.

Organic Pigments

Organic pigments are more versatile in their colour, range, hue, depth and strength compared to inorganic pigments. Their limitations are resistance to high temperature, natural degradation and solubility in solvents and resins. With structural variations, it is possible to get a range of colours in a specific class. There are several thousand coloured organic materials of which quite a large number qualifies as pigments. These pigments meet a wide range of applications and fulfill diametrically opposite expectations in properties. In addition to pigments, there are several dyes that are used as colourants in solvents, water and resins, some of which are also converted in their insoluble form by complexing them with polyvalent metals such as aluminum, calcium or barium. Malshe and Bendale 1 have recently reported dyed crosslinked fine polymeric particles suitable for pigment application. New colourants are being constantly developed and it takes approximately 10 years for a new class of pigments to emerge. We have azoics, phthalocyanines, anthraquinones quinacridones and pyrrolopyrole pigments that appeared in market by about 10 years gap.

Presently we intend to only provide a list of class of pigments with representative structures.

(1) Azopigments

These are produced by diazotization of aromatic amines followed by coupling with phenols. There is extensive variation in the properties, colour, hue, light fastness and depth of colour depending on the structure of the pigments

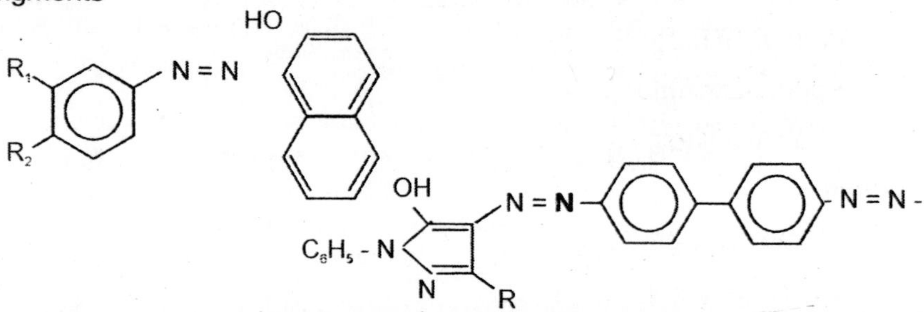

Diazo condensation pigments are obtained by reacting the carboxylic acid present on the β-Naphthol (BON acid) with aliphatic or aromatic diamine. Condensation with aliphatic or aromatic diamine considerably reduces the bleeding tendency of the pigments in solvents and resins.

The structure of azo pigments is modified on either or both the sides of the aromatic rings i.e. either the amine is modified or the phenol is modified. All changes lead to change of hue and pigmentary properties. This increases molecular weight that has positive effect on the "melting point, insolubility, exterior durability and chemical resistance of the resultant pigments.

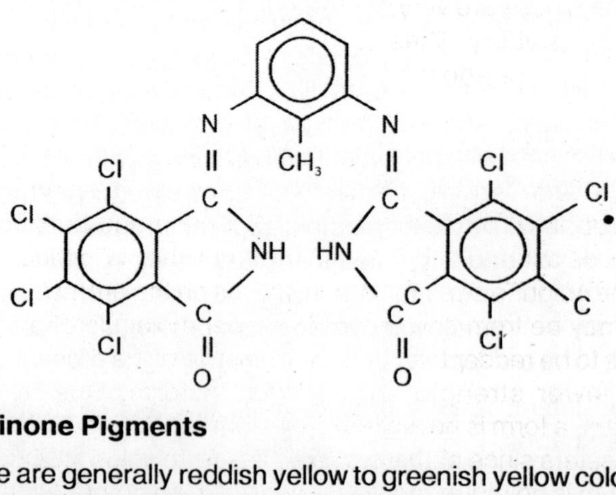

Iso indolinone Pigments

These are generally reddish yellow to greenish yellow coloured products. Suitable for plastics, industrial and automotive paints and are stable to high temperature (upto 260°C).

Metal complex pigments

These are formed by complexing organic molecules with transition elements such as iron, copper and nickel. The metals contribute their characteristic colour to the pigments but there are several surprises. For example, we expect copper to produce blue colour and nickel to produce green colour in complexed form. When complexed with salicylaldehyde and 2-hydroxy-4-phenyl aniline, copper produces a yellow pigment (pigment yellow 117) with the following formula

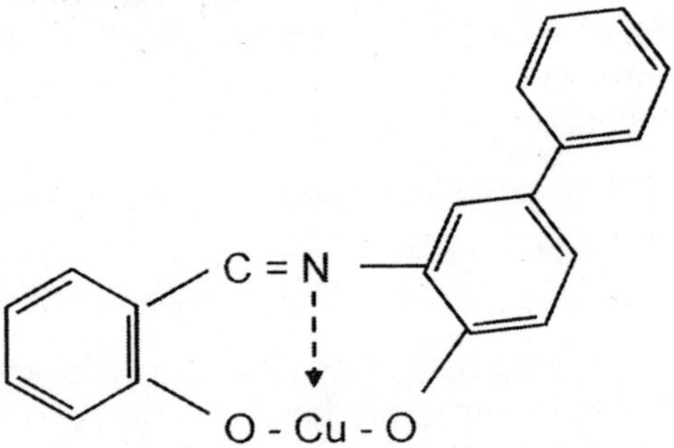

Copper phthalocyanine

Probably the most important organic pigments that have been able to displace all their competitors such as iron blue, Prussian blue, copper phthalocyanine. These are very popular due to their very high colour strength, very good colour stability. These can be crystallized in five forms (α, β, γ, δ, and ε). Of these only a and β have been commercially important.

Q form has red under tone and is relatively unstable. β form has green undertone and is more stable. The type of solvent, type of surfactant and degree of dispersion facilitate the inter-conversions. The pigments are used extensively in paints, printing inks, textile printing and bulk colouration of plastics, soaps, detergent cakes etc. Q form that is difficult to stabilize contains some chlorine or sulfonic acid groups on the aromatic nucleus. The substitution may be from one to 2 chlorine per molecule of phthalocyanine and continues to be redder than the β form in spite of the presence of chlorine. a form has lower strength compared to β form. Due to problem of recrystallisation, a form is not suited for system containing aromatic solvents, ketones and esters since phthalocyanine has finite solubility in these solvent and the medium is helpful in recrystallisation of the pigment. Phthalocyanines are suitable in all plastics and withstand high temperature up to 300°C encountered in processing of certain plastics.

Phthalocyanine Green

When nearly 13-14 hydrogen atoms present on the nuclei ofphthalocyanine molecule are replaced by chlorine, the product becomes phtahlocyanine green. The chlorination is carried out in molten eutectic obtained from aluminium trichloride and sodium chlroride. Bromination of some of the hydrogen produces brighter green shade. Excessive bromination reduces colour strength due to increased molecular weight. The strength of these pigments is so high that no other pigment in able to compete with phthalo green and it is almost the only green pigment used in inks, paints and plastics, only a minor proportion coming from chrome oxide and some anthraquinone pigments.

Derivatives of cobalt in place of copper are also important for their hue and colour strength.

Quinacridone

Pigment Red 122 and pigment violet 19 are two most important members of this family. Even though these are low molecular weight products, they have exceptiona colour stability, and strength. All automobiles that contain solid shades of red have Quinacridone pigments. These have lasted 10-15 years in Indian exposure condition. Cars produced in late 80's have retained their colours intact well after the end of last century. These are used for their permanence, clean hue, and excellent heat stability.

These are used in colouration of plastics, for high performance inks and dope dying of polypropylene fibres. These can withstand high temperature (255°C) for 2-3 hrs in air without change.

Pigment violet 23

The most unstable organic colours are violet. In fact, it has taken years of research to find a light stable violet pigment. Violet 23, also known as Dioxazine violet or carbazole violet has excellent light fastness. Invariably, violet is used for tinting of white to make it appear whiter. If the light fastness of the violet is not good, the extra whiteness of the paint or ink tends to be only temporary. Pigment violet 23 shows very good light fastness properties even at a low concentration of as low as 20-30 ppm (parts per million). It is also stable to high temperature but has relatively poor alkali resistance. Can be conveniently used at melting temperature of plastic and in stoving paints.

The newer variety of pigments belongs to anthroquinone,

Diketopyrrolopyrrol, that are characterized by their light fastness and high tinctorial strength. A great deal of exploration of the chemical structures seems to have been done by the pigment industry and a new product emerges every 10 years. Presently the pace seems to have slowed down and no entirely new class of pigments appears in sight.

4

How To Formulate a Paint

Before attempting any formulation following information is necessary.

- Specifications with methods of testing (% solids,. wt/l, gloss, drying time, viscosity, hardness, flexibility, acid, alkali, water resistance, hiding, covering wt/l, any other desired by the buyer)
- Expected performance
- Conditions and method of application
- Conditions of use
- Expected packing, price etc.

Specifications: Specifications are a set of parameters, that completely define a product. Once a set of parameters is agreed, between a seller and a buyer, it is easy to manufacture and sell. All disputes can be resolved by referring to the agreed specifications. All care is essential while formulating specifications. More care is necessary when the buyer is equipped with testing facilities and you are not. Understanding the implication of each and every test to be conducted is also necessary. Some of the elements of specifications have far reaching implications. This must be analyzed in every possible detail along with test methods. These should be read with the specification of all the bought out raw materials to ensure there is no dispute after supplies are affected. Disputes cause loss, loss of all types. Times, business, goodwill and money. I will clarify this with an example.

A small manufacturer agreed to supply a white paint to a large buyer tq his specifications. Among other things the buyer specified TiO_2 content of the paint as 30%. The small manufacturer was not equipped to test TiO_2 content of the pigment. He, therefore, based his costing on commercial TiO_2 at 30% level. A batch of few thousand liters was offered for inspection.

When the buyer's laboratory analyzed the TiO_2 content, the best value was found to be about 25% and the lot was rejected. The manufacturer had used one of the best brands and had actually put 30% TiO_2 (as bought) in his formulation. When repeated sampling after stirring etc. failed to meet the specification, he rushed for external help. Since I work as a university professor, he met me and explained his problem. I asked him for the specifications of TiO_2 he was using. He did not have a copy. I, then showed him specifications of some of the best grades of the world that read TiO_2 content 82-88%, with balance being surface treatment comprising silica, alumina and some other metal oxides. When he had put 30% of TiO_2 as bought, he was actually putting 82-88% of 30% as Ti02 i.e. 24.8-26.4% TiO_2. Since the buyer was equipped to analyze Ti02, the matter could not be resolved. Further, to bring TiO_2 level to 30% he would have required *30/0.88* = 35-36% commercial TiO_2, being most expensive component of formulation, would make the product unviable. His efforts to convince the buyer that commercial TiO_2 purity it self is less than 90% failed completely. In view of future business, he had to supply a paint with much more TiO_2 than required for a *good* formulation. The technological advantage the TiO_2 manufacturer had built in his product became a non-issue. Had the manufacturer read buyers specifications with TiO_2 supplier's specification such a situation could have been avoided.

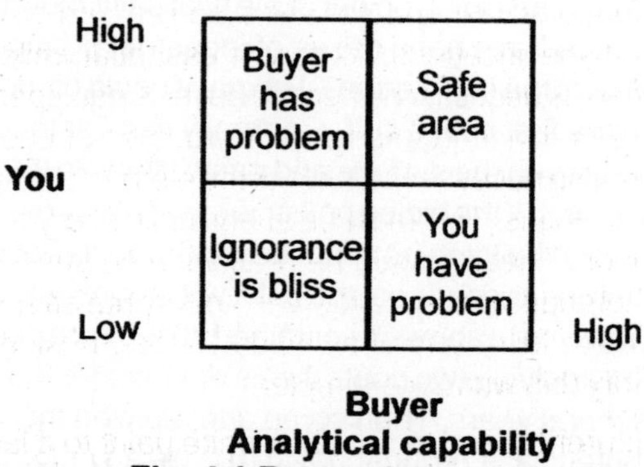

Fig. 4.1 Recognize your position

The next step is to decide PVC. The properties in a paint are completely decided by PVC. Whether you need a glossy paint, semi glossy or matt would decide the PVC level.

Following table is an indicator:

	% PVC
Glossy	17-20
Semi-glossy	25-35
Non-glossy	45 and above
Matt, Water based	50+

Other properties that also dictate a certain level of PVC are film flexibility and impact strength.

Having chosen a PVC level, the composition of the dry film in terms of pigment and binder gets fixed. Now, depending on the hiding required one can fragment the pigment constituents into hiding pigments and extenders. The ratio of the volume of pigment to volume of binder in the terms of PVC is given by

(PVC is expressed as < 1 as a fraction and not %) P and B are volume fractions of pigment and binder respectively.

Depending on shade, the colour pigments can be decided. Sometimes, only or ganic pigments need to be used for getting specific solid colours. These have to be chosen as pèr the specified shade.

In the case of ready mixed whites or dark shades an additional factor should be considered. The hiding power of the final paint must be lower than its covering power. There have been cases of industrial products where these were reversed. What is the implication? The paint could completely or almost completely hide in the first coat it self. Generally two coats are preferred for obliterating any defects on the surface and paste fillers do this. A subsequent coat, therefore, is a must. If the hiding power is lower than covering power, one does not waste paint in building up a film beyond what is necessary. If this is reverse then by applying second coat the paint will be wasted. In the case of the industrial product referred to above, it contained 30% hiding pigment by weight. It was found that by applying two coats it was doing more than required. This had gone on for several years. Then some one realized the mistake and the hiding pigment content was brought down to 23% and the balance 7% was replaced by an extender without affecting the performance of the product. It may be a consolation to think that big profits may have been made by considerably reducing the raw material cost (RMC) but the lower margins on a volume product produced for several years can also not be lost sight of.

As a rule of thumb, hiding power should be approximately half of the covering power, assuming two coats will be provided for the complete job.

The next step is to choose pigments and extenders and their relative ratios. If there is no special req~irement of chemical resistance of the coatings, TiO_2 is the best hiding pigment, 1-2%. Zinc oxide can be included to improve UV resistance provided the medium does not have a high acid value. (Serious problems of livering, bitting and premature gelling may occur if ZnO reacts with medium). The amount of TiO_2 required can be calculated from the technical literature of the product that provides data on hiding power/kg of pigment at a given PVC in white paints. Pure shades do not require TiO_2.

All primers and even undercoats should preferably be formulated with cheaper hiding pigments such as yellow iron oxide and zinc oxide. The concentration of individual components can be worked out approximately. After selecting the pigments, the next important step is to find out the optimum surfactant demand. It is also necessary to ensure that the same surfactant is suitable for all the pigments. This information is available with pigment or dispersing agent supplier.

Optimization of surfactant by Daniel flow point method

This is a very simple technique to optimize the surfactant demand. Following is the procedure:

Step (1): Take 6 equal weights of the pigment mixture (that would form part of 100 ml of final paint) in a 200 ml container.

Step (2): Prepare solution of the surfactant or their mixture in 1 to 5% concentra tion in a 6% resin solution or water for water based paint.

Step (3): Add the surfactant solution drop by drop, mixing each drop carefully, with a rod abut 8mm in diameter and about 20-25 cm. long. Flow point is attained when a drop of mixture leaves the rod when it is withdrawn from the mixture.

Step (4): Take one reading using only the solution or water without any surfactant in it.

Step (5): Tabulate the volume of the solution required to attain flow point against concentration as follows.

	Soln. conc. %	**Vol.**
1	0	30
2	1	17
3	2	13

4	3	12.5
5	4	15
6	5	18

Step (6): Plot the data on a graph. A curve with minima is obtained as shown in Fig 4-2.

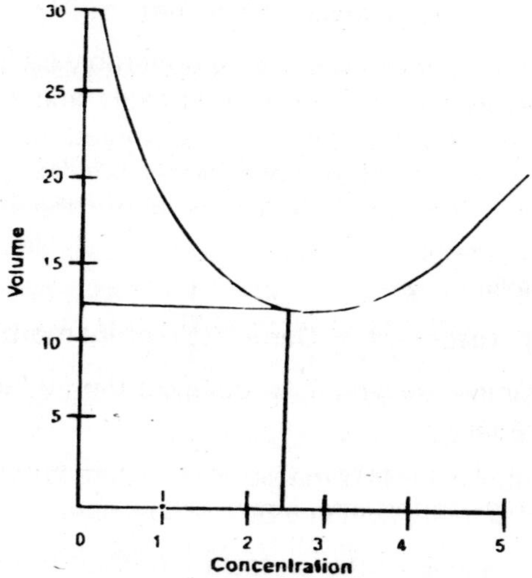

Fig. 4.2 Minimum surfactant demand for pigment mixtures

From the graph, the lowest surfactant requirement is found out to be 12 cc of 2.9% solution for the quantity of the pigment taken. Since we have started with pigment quantity adequate for 100 ml paint, we would need 120 cc of 2.9% solution or 0.35% by weight of paint.

Now most of the components of our trial paint formula have been fixed

(1) Pigment mixture — Hiding pigment, Extenders, Colouring pigment

(2) Resin solids
(3) Solvent
(4) Dispersing agent

The next step is to tryout a formulation by grinding the pigment mixture and make the paint. Other additives such as driers flow additives, thixotropic agents, anti skining agents, additive for mar resistance etc.may be added. Adjustments may be required for

- Gloss - that can be adjusted by flow additive, change of solvent and lor PVC
- Hiding can be adjusted by increasing hiding pigments and removing extenders
- Slow drying by increasing driers
- Cost reduction by using cheaper ingredients that may be within specifications.

If the above course of action is used there would be very little requirement for repeated experimentation. There are certain precautions to be taken while formulating paint.

Start with the cheapest possible ingredients first so that you are not out priced by competition at the tender stage. A case of a tender is worth mentioning here. For a large tender two manufacturers submitted samples with quotations. Both the samples passed. When bids were opened, the larger of the two suppliers was surprised to see a very low price quoted by the other. It was later learnt that where as former had used expensive organic pigment to match the shade, the latter managed with synthetic red iron oxide that was only a fraction of the cost of the red organic pigment.

Never use too many surfactants. Least of all, never ever try to adjust a defect caused by an additive by putting in another additive. In place, try to overcome the defect by adjusting the dose of the first additive. In case of difficulty, contact the supplier who is obliged to resolve your difficulty.

Be careful while choosing solvent combinations. The non-solvent, the diluent and true solvent must leave the film in that order.

Non-solvents and diluents are added to the paint to reduce cost and achieve lower solids at high viscosity. They have a definite role to play in control of film properties and rheology of the paint film. As the film is applied, it contains all the solvents. The film must get enough time to flow out and level to get best gloss and DOL The flow is best when true solvent for the resin is present in highest concentration. For this reason, the non-solvent should evaporate first of all. The diluent should leave next and the last to evaporate should be the true solvent. This is more necessary in the case of lacquers or non-convertible coatings since the resin viscosity would be higher in comparison to convertible coatings.

Use minimum essential components. I was once requested by a friend to help him reduce the raw material cost of a white enamel. When I looked at his formulation it contained about 24 ingredients. Nowadays, so many good' quality raw materials are available that the need for additives is minimized in quantity as well as numbers. I could suggest him a good formulation with just 7 ingredients (TiO_2, extender, alkyd, MTO, Dispersing agent, drier and a flow additive) that gave excellent performance. Apart from complicating the production, large number of ingredients cause problems of carrying too many items of inventory.

Look for unwanted interactions between ingredients. For example cationic and anionic substances can react and destroy each other. Calcium containing extenders can completely precipitate phosphate type of dispersing agents as $Ca_3/PO_4)_2$ and cause dispersion reversal or flocculation in water based system. Alkaline pigments can react with acidic portion of binder. An oxidizing agent can react with a reducing agent. If these combinations must be used together, they might require high imagination to keep these items separate that is like keeping fire and water together.

Understand the limitations of the ingredients used. It is not possible to expect more than their capacity. For example if a heat resisting paint is required, it is unreasonable to expect an alkyd to perform the duty beyond 200 dc. The organic components are susceptible to air oxidation and can not be stable in air above this temperature for too long. Silicone resins are a must for such a situation. If excellent corrosion resistance is expected in exterior environment, urethanes with acrylics may be the only answer. It would be a waste of time trying to meet these requirements with rosin, alkyd or styrene based products.

A mixture of surface-active agent, one suitable for one pigment and another for the other is best avoided. In a solution so dilute it is unreasonable to assume that each pigment would receive the surfactant it prefers. It may be better to separately disperse the pigments in the same binder but with different surface active agents and then mix them to the requirement.

For water based systems, several pigments, particularly organic pigments tend to flocculate when dispersed with only one dispersing agents. This may happen due to very vast difference in the surface tension of the pigment and water. Making up this difference may not be possible with just one surfactant. Mixing of surfactants is not a good idea as discussed earlier. The best way is to slowly change the surface character. The situation is similar to painting a black wall with white paint. One can either apply three or four coats of white paint one over another or slowly change the colour *from* black to gray to yellow and then white. The colour consumption in the setond case would be much lower. Similarly, the pigment may first be coated with a surfactant with HLB about 5-8. (Depending on molecular weight of the surfactant and how it is adsorbed on the pigment surface, its area of cross section, about 2-5 mg surfactant is required area of the pigment. Typically, a pigment may have 20-25 m^2 area/g i.e. about 10% surfactant by weight of pigment may be required. For pigments with finer particle size and lower density this may be still higher. With products such as carbon black with 500 m^2/g surface area, surfactant requirement may be up to 250 % of their weight). This is best done on a machine like a triple roller mill. The surfactant should be thoroughly mixed till the pigment tends to become flaky. After this stage is reached, about same weight (10% of pigment) next surfactant should be added on the surface with HLB in the range of 8-14. The last coat of the surfactant should have HLB in the range of 2025.It is not possible to get the same degree of dispersion and stability by just a physical mixture of the three surfactant. It is unreasonable to expect the surfactants to simply fall in order.

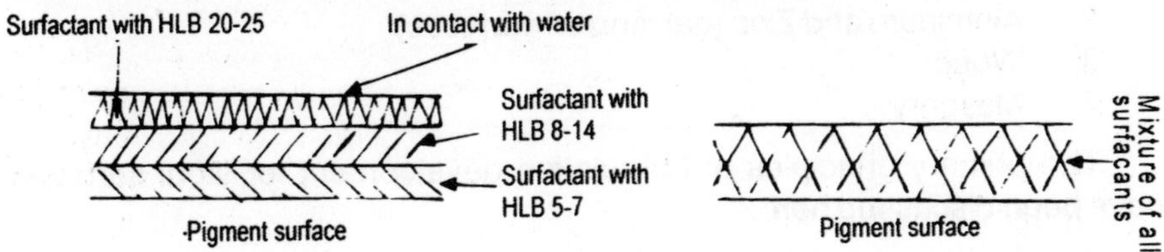

Fig. 4.3 : Decomposition of layer of surfactants and form a mixture.

The information on HLB and surface coverage should be obtained from the surfactant suppliers..

Formulating guidelines

PRIMERS

Primers, as indicated by their generic name are the products, that make a surface ready for accepting a paint. While doing so, they hide the defects of the surface, provide good adhesion, and form a protective layer that is not permeable to moisture, oxygen and other substances that may cause or promote corrosion. Invariably, these are only protective coats and may have no decorative value. The shade, gloss, finish, flow and level therefore, take a back seat.

Following are the requirements of a good primer:

(a) It must have high hiding (except for wood finishes)

(b) It must be impervious to

i) Corrosive ions
ii) Water
iii) Oxygen

(c) It must be able to prepare surface to receive the intended paint.

(d) It must resist solvents, over bake from the subsequent coats without loss of any of the properties.

(e) Corrosion protection ingredients may be present that may migrate toward the substrate and protect the surface from a likely damage in the event of ingress of liquid water.

The requirement of different surfaces are different and hence the composition of the primer needs to be developed independently in each case. The following surfaces are most commonly encountered.

1. Steel
2. Aluminum and Zinc (galvanized surfaces)
3. Wood
4.. Masonry

The primary principles of formulation development for steel surfaces have been discussed here.

Steel

For steel, different primers have been developed. The type of primer depends upon the type of product and its application, environment of use etc. Following are the types of products well developed and commercialized for steel applications.

1. Solvent based steel primers for various applications.
2. Zinc rich primers (organic binders)
3. Zinc ethyl silicate coatings
4. Primers for Electro deposition
5. Automotive refinishing
6. Convertible coatings
7. Primers for pro!ection of reinforcement

Primers for Steel

Most of the industrial surface requiring protection and decoration are made of steel. By it self, iron is a métal with grayish colour and can be polished to get a lustrous surface. This surface is not able to resist oxidation and gets rapidly air oxidized and forms four oxides. The oxidation products are coloured and opaque. Worse, the colours change from yellow-orange to black to dirty red as tte oxidation state of the metal changes. Further, there is increase in weight due to oxygen pick up and also increase in volume due to reduction in density of the metal oxide from metal. Following table will illustrate the difference more perceptibly.

Component	Density	Weightlg mole Fe in g	Volume lg mole in cc	% Change over metal
Fe	7.8-8	58	7.25 -7.43	
FeO	5.6	71.8	12.82	183
$FeO.Fe_2O_3$	5.28	77.13	15.426	221
$FeO\ O_2$	3.81	88.8	23.3	334
Fe_2O_3	5.6	79.8	14.25	204

The oxidation products formed on the surface have been listed in the order these are formed. Thus we notice that the volume of metal lost by corrosion increases by as much as 334% (i.e.3.34 times) that of the metal. .What is worse is, the volume decreases after oxidation of $FeO.O_2$ to Fe_2O_3. A close inspection of a corroded surface reveals a cracked surface with an out ward push from the metal surface.

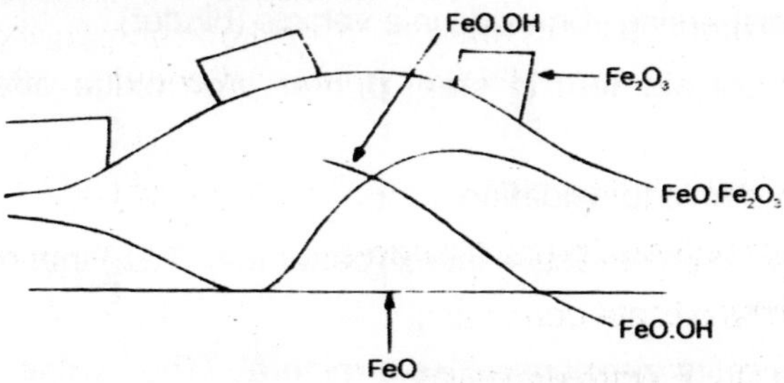

Fig. 4.4. Surfgce of a cracked exterior due to corrision

Due to this phenomenon, a steel surface can not protect it self and is always exposed to further corrosion. The corrosion products become porous and allow ingress of corrosive elements up to the substrate and the corrosion continues.

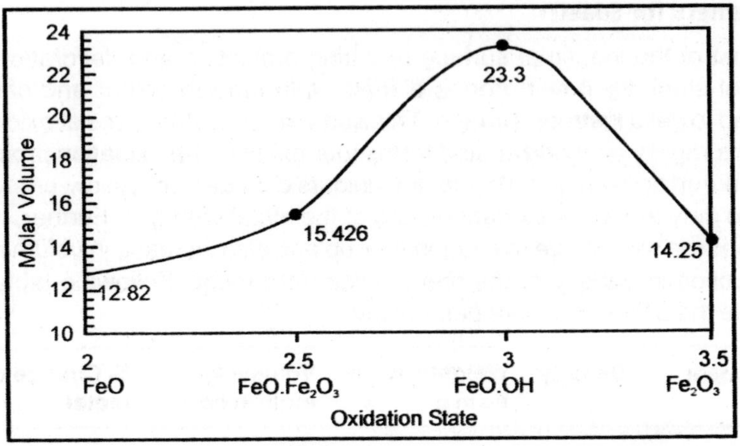

Fig. 4.5 Change of molar volume of oxides of iron with change in valency

This is the reason why many a times we find a product painted only from one side can be completely corroded from the other side, that is not painted. This happens more often with products where the unpainted side is out of sight.

From the plot above we notice that Fe_20_3 is volume stable. This can not get oxidized further, will not expand or shrink. This, therefore, becomes the most suitable material for preparation of primers. The main draw back in the scenario presented in Fig. (4.4) is the presence of porosity and absence of adhesion of the oxide film on the mild steel surface. Both these can be overcome by dispersing iron oxide in a vehicle (binder).

As a primary pigment in steel primer, iron oxide offers following advantages.

(a) It is stable to oxidation.

(b) It has high refractive index (better than TiO_2) that provides good hiding.

(c) It is quite inexpensive as a mineral. (The synthetic grades are expensive due to their pure hue and chemical composition. These are not used for primers)

(d) They have adequate resistance to degradation, dilute alkali and mild acids, are opaque to UV and do not permeate oxygen and water.

The major disadvantages are:

(a) These are very hard to grind. Grinding requires machines such as ball mill.

These equipment are noisy and have low productivity due to long process time.

(b) The density of Fe_2O_3 is high (5.6 g/cc). The compositions tend to rapidly settle if not adequately stabilized. Both the above limit the amount of iron oxide that can be incorporated in the composition even though one would like to maximize the usage due to its low cost. Further limitation arises due to specifications on the weight per litre of the finished product. High density of Fe_20_3 causes rapid rise of the weight per litre beyond acceptable levels.

(c) Fe_20_3 is soluble in concentrated mineral acids and is readily attacked in reducing atmosphere. It can not be used in chemical resisting paints.

Primers can be formulated from a variety of media. The most expensive ingredient of the primer is the binder. Therefore, the decision as to what binder to use, primarily depends on the end use. Following media are commonly used in declining order of preference.

(i) CNSL resin

(ii) Cooked oil varnishes (iii) Long/Medium oil alkyds (iv) Vinyl resins

(v) Epoxy and urethane.

General Principles of Formulation

Typical specifications of primers (Density 1.4-1.6 kg/l, % solids -60%, pye 40+ %, Fe_2O_2 content ~ 40% by weight) can be met by a range of compositions where mineral fillers such as Talc and Calcite are added to reduce the settling tendency, thixotropic agents are added to prevent settling. Mineral turpentine is the most preferred solvent for its low cost. CNSL formaldehyde condensate is one of the cheapest binders for primers. Polymeric residue from distillation of cardanol is used as such or with further condensation with formaldehyde. Cooked oil/oleoresinous varnishes, long and medium oil alkyds dry fairly rapidly with only through driers. Surface driers are not required and are avoided due to their high cost. Since the binder content of the coating is low, only through driers suffice for the drying.

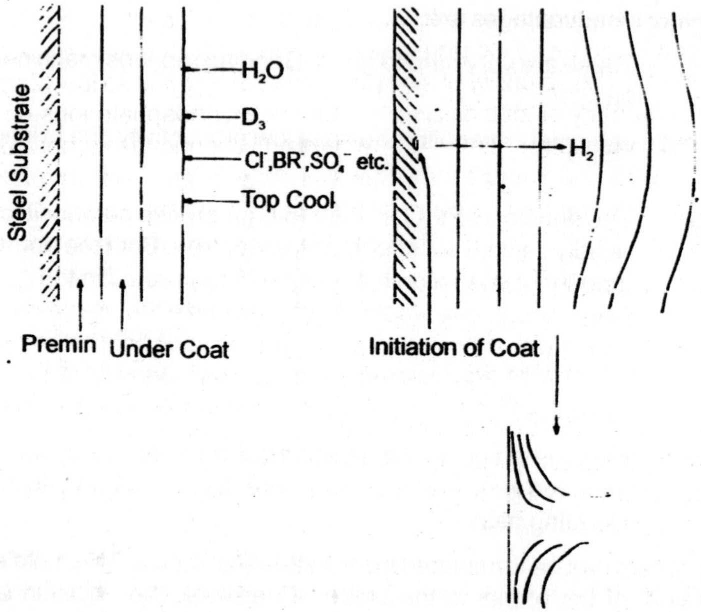

Fig. 4.6 Expansion of corrosion products exposing the substrate for further corrosion

Additives for enhancement of performance

Three components are required to cause corrosion. Steel water and oxygen. If any of the three is excluded, corrosion does not take place. Obviously, steel can not be excluded. The formulator makes all efforts to reduce permeability of the paint film to prevent corrosion. The corrosion process is self-propagating since it causes destruction of the preventive efforts as seen in the diagram below.

One way to prevent corrosion in spite of permeation of oxygen and water is to put corrosion inhibitors as integral part of the film. These are of several types but can be broadly classified in two categories.

Inorganic or organic products, that are partially water soluble, dissolve in the diffusing water and get adsorbed on the steel surface to prevent corrosion. These products could be chromates, nitrates, molybdates, tung states phosphates of zinc, calcium or barium. All these are oxidizers and promote passivation by increasing electrical potential of iron. Chromate is an excellent corrosion inhibitor. Its usage is being phased out from several applications due to its toxicity and it may be banned in future. Application in paints where the solubility is low and possibility of leaching is rather less, usage may continue. Zinc phosphate entered the industry with very great expectations. The solubility of zinc phosphate in water is so low (2 ppm) that adequate quantity of zinc or zinc phosphate as phosphate ions do not get transported across the film. The corrosion prevention is rather poor. The newer materials containing molybdenum and tungsten are currently under surveillance. Good results have been reported (1) for water borne epoxy paints where 15% of total pigmentation at 25% PVC was zinc phosphate.

Organic Corrosion Inhibitors

When added to the primer composition, these preferentially migrate to the steel surface and are adsorbed. They create a monomolecular film on the surface, that resists migration of corrosive ions to the metal surface. They have polar properties in the molecular structure that help the molecules to orient themselves along the metal surface. These are compounds containing nitrogen, sulfur, hydroxyl or keto functionalities. For corrosion inhibition, the size of the molecules must be small to be able to diffuse readily. Other important factors are orientation, shape and electrical charge distribution. Glycin derivatives, aromatic sulfonates, acetophenone and its derivatives,-alk,yl imidazolein are some of the compounds suitable for this application.

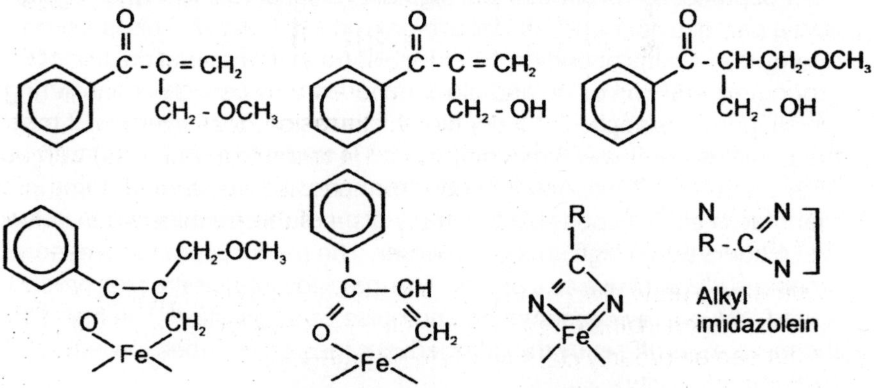

Alkyl imidazolein

Acetophenone adsorbed in iron surface

Imidazolein adsorbed in iron surface

The additives described above function by any of the following mechanisms:

- Passivate the surface by chemical reaction.
- Protect the surface by adsorption.

- Scavenge oxygen and prevent corrosion.

As we have discussed earlier in Additives section, all additives have side effects. In the case of organic corrosion inhibitors two major side effects must be guarded against.

- Loss of adhesion of primer
- Discoloration of subsequent coats

Since most of these compounds are coloured, their migration to surface coats can lead to discoloration. Excessive addition can result into complete loss of adhesion since most of the additives have surface active properties. It needs to be ensured that the additive concentration is low enough to maintain one of its ends in the film while the other is adsorbed on the metal side. The requirement of the additive to form a monomolecular layer on the metal surface depends on its molecular weight. For a typical molecular weight of about 300, this may amount to only 2-3 mg/m_2. Thus if the primer has a covering power of about 20 m_2l, the content of corrosion inhibitor may have to be restricted to about 100-500 mg/l or that order of magnitude. The higher concentration is provided to account for high surface area provided by the surface irregularities of the surface.

For production of primers, the pigments extenders and dispersing agents with a part of binder and solvent are ground in a ball mill. This is a time and energy consuming operation. For those starting new operation, use of finely ground mineral iron oxide and other minerals may be worth considering. A typical primer is applied at a dry film thickness of 25-35 microns. If most of the particles are below 6 micron (about 1,4 th the film thickness) with up to 95% particles < 2 microns as seen from product literature of some of the manufacturers, it is possible to simply disperse these minerals in solvents and binders with a high speed disperser. The products produce reasonably smooth surface for use as a primer. The main advantages are high production speed, low energy consumption and noise free operation. The high cost of the minerals is off set by the other advantages of low labor, low energy and higher productivity.

Consideration of cost is always fore most in the mind of manufacturer. In the process of cost reduction, sometime even elementary ethics of business are forgotten. One such example is addition of water to solvent-based formulation. Some surfactant manufacturers with traders are promoting the idea of adding 2-3% surfactant and 10% water to an oil based primer formulation.

The promoters claim about 5-6% cost reduction after accounting for the cost of emulsifiers. They also claim that this does not affect the performance properties of the primers. This claim is very unlikely to be valid. To best of our information, no systematic study is available to substantiate the claim. Following is our conjecture.

Effect of water on solvent based paint properties

Presence of two unwanted components in the primer can cause following side effects:

Additional surfactant would leave film more water sensitive. The primer film is supposed to be as water-resistant as possible. This ingredient to the tune of 1-2 on volume (0.5% on solids) is too high a concentration to leave the film unaffected.

The hiding power of the paint would reduce by 14% as water does not aid hiding. If tested by cryptometer, there may not be a perceptible change that would be due to the hiding produced by emulsion particles. This is a temporary effect and would last only till the paint is dried.

We must also look at the fate of water. This, most likely, would leave the film well after all the solvent has evaporated, and the film has partially dried. When water droplets evaporate from the surface, they would leave behind cavities and a continuous porosity with highly hydrophilic surface. This would defeat the very purpose of applying a primer to the surface.

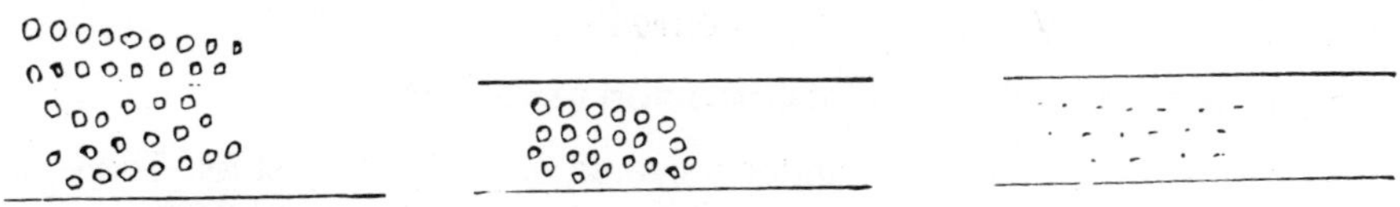

Stage 1 Fresh primer film — Stage 2 All solvent has left the film — Stage 3 All water has left the film

Fig. 4.7 Cross section of the film containing water in emulsified form

	Stage 1 Composition		Stage 2 Composition		Stage 3 composition	
	% by/wt	% by/vol.	% by/wt	% by/vol.	% by/wt	% by/vol.
Water	10	14	15.59	34.36	0	0
SA	0.3	0.62	0.46	1.02	0.55	1.57
Solvent	35.88	59.19	0	0	0	0
Resin & Pigment	53.82	26.36	83.95	64.63	99.45	98.42

Assumption		
Primer PVC	48%	
Weight/l	1.36 kg/l	
Composition	Fe_2O_3	36
	Talc	12
	Binder	12
	Solvent	40
	Total	100

When 0.3% Surface Active agent and 10% water are added, the Specific gravity reduces to 1.323 kg/l (1.36 x 0.897 + 0.103)

From the above model we see that

- The dried film contains voids, that are coated with surfactant from inside. This makes the coating highly water susceptible.
- The hiding of the liquid paint may appear unaffected in wet condition. This is a deceptive phenomenon. If actually worked out on dry basis, the hiding must be proportionately lower.
- The performance of the product would be inferior to the one, that has not been adulterated with surfactants and water.

In our opinion, addition of water to any oil based paint is cheating the clients and must not be resorted to even as a measure of cost reduction. It is better to educate the user and prevent the misuse of chemicals and manufacture of under performing chemicals.

Zinc rich primers (Sacrificial corrosion inhibitors)

These are metals with higher galvanic potential than steel. There are several methods of using these metals such as hot dip galvanizing, electroplating, flame spraying of zinc metal, electrically connecting an ingot of zinc metal that is buried underground and application of impressed current. While using the last two techniques, it is not possible to extend them to object already in existence unless the total structure is electrically connected. The results of flame spraying are not equivalent to those of hot dip galvanizing. Paints prepared from metal powders are able to overcome these draw backs to some extent. For example, it is possible to coat a bare metal object by painting rather than flame spraying. In order to get an electrical continuity, the coatings are formulated at PVC very near CPVC so that the particles remain in physical contact with each other without electrical barrier. Most of the binders used are electrical insulators. These have to be used at the lowest possible concentration. The most commonly used metal powder is zinc. It is converted in fine particle form by techniques such as flame spraying or plasma spraying.

Molten metal is sprayed at the top of a tall tower with inert gas. As the particles fall down, they acquire spherical shape and cool down in the same form. Microscopically, these particles are perfect spheres with a wide particle size distribution (5-50 micron diameter). The voidage between particles is minimal and the true density of spheres is quite high (8g/cc). Therefore, in a typical composition with CPVC of about 70%, the composition, by weight may contain up to 90% Zinc, binder and solvents constituting just about 10%.

It is quite logical to use the best available binder when such a small amount is required to be used. In industry zinc rich primers are formulated by only two binders:

- Epoxy
- Ethyl silicate.

In the case of epoxy, the hardener selected is polyamide. The zinc powder is dispersed in resin and solvent. The hardener forms the second component. Typically, the two components are mixed prior to application. Application may be by brush or spray. In the case of ethyl silicate, the binder is partially hydrolyzed and prepolymerized.

The ethyl silicate based paints dry by polycondensation of silanols by elimination of water. The final coats are very hard, adhere well and are highly chemical resistant (except strong alkalies, acids and HF). Typical coatings with *50-70/l* dry film thickness are able to produce up to 5000 hrs salt spray resistance. This is due to formation of impervious glass on the surface of zinc particles. Thicker coats tend to peel off due to higher cohesive forces.

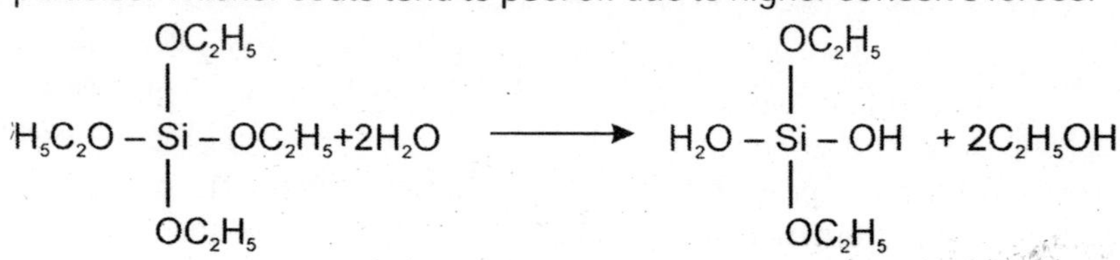

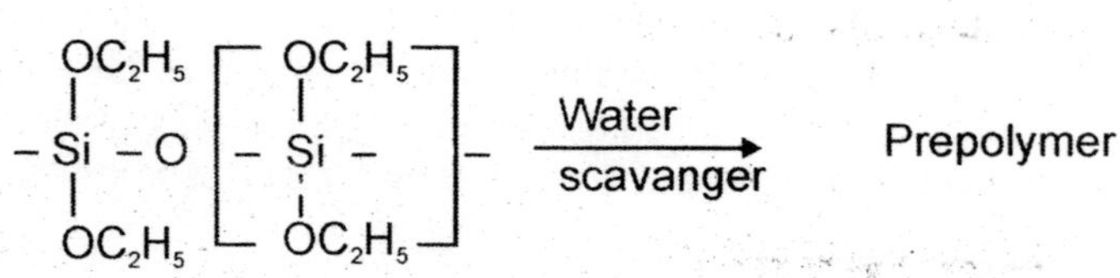

As can be seen, a small amount of water leads to hydrolysis and polymerization of silica. If the reaction is required to be stopped at a certain viscosity, the residual water is removed by water scavenger such as CaO or molecular sieves. Zinc metal is dispersed in the prepolymer with product alcohol acting as a solvent.

These products may be supplied as one pack or two packs. In the case of two pack systems, the second component may be diluent with regulated quantity of water and the polycondensation catalyst. The single pack products can be formulated with prepolymer, zinc metal powder, extenders, condensation catalyst and solvent. When the composition is sprayed, it cures with hydrolysis of ethyl silicate. The product alcohol evaporates allowing further condensation of the silanol groups. The process of cure proceeds in three steps.

- Formation of film as a loose structure
- Intermediate dried film
- Complete condensation

As the solvent evaporates and a small amount of moisture penetrates, it leads to a loose film formation. This film has neither mechanical properties nor solvent resistance for a few hours. As the moisture penetrates further, it causes condensation of the silicone atoms. This process it self retards the permeation of moisture across the film. The moderately cured film covers the uncured ethyl silicate. The diffusivity of water across the top surface is so low that adequate amount of moisture is not permeated across the film surface. The reverse diffusion of the product alcohol is also difficult. Thus the reaction does not readily go to completion. The final cure of the film may take from several days to months and thick films may take several years.

Pure ethyl silicate based zinc rich coatings in their final form are totally inorganic. The metallic zinc is covered by pure silicon dioxide coating that is amorphous and polymeric in nature. The stepwise condensation of ethyl silicate provides it this character. The physical property of glassy silicon dioxide makes it inflexible and brittle. To improve this property, addition of polymeric diols or polyols helps by incorporating some organic part in the structure, that becomes a permanent part of the silicate polymer.

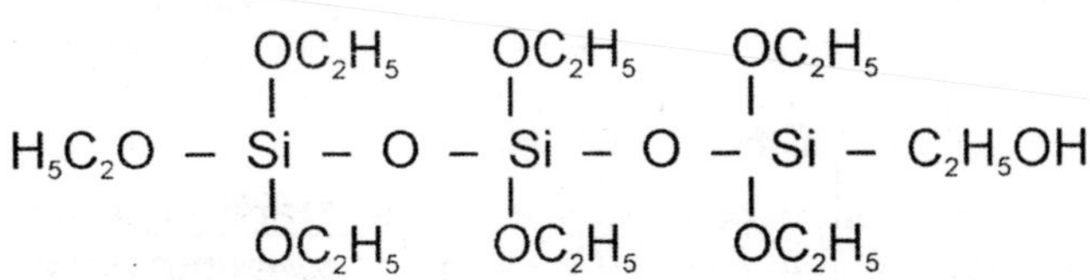

$$H_5C_2O-\underset{OC_2H_5}{\overset{OC_2H_5}{Si}}-OC_2H_5 + H_2O \xrightarrow[(HCl)]{H^+} H_5C_2O-\underset{OH}{\overset{OC_2H_5}{Si}}-OH + C_2H_5OH$$

The silicic acid formed is too weak to react with metallic zinc and displace hydrogen. In all likelihood the polycondensation of silicic acid may lead to increase in viscosity of the resin phase. A controlled amount of water is therefore required.

The water formed in the polycondensation reaction continues to hydrolyze more ethyl silicate till all of it is converted into alcohol.

The diols react by transesterification reaction or ester interchange reaction.

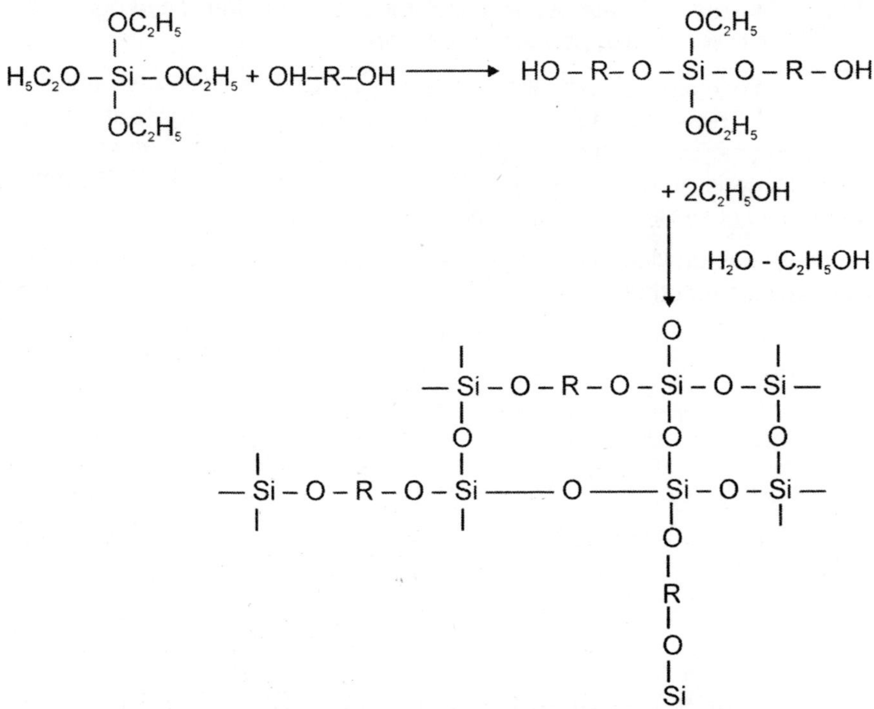

Various modifications of ethyl silicate coatings are suggested in literature. (2). For general use, one-pack ethyl silicate coatings are preferred but they pose problems of storage due to formation of hydrogen gas. This is more

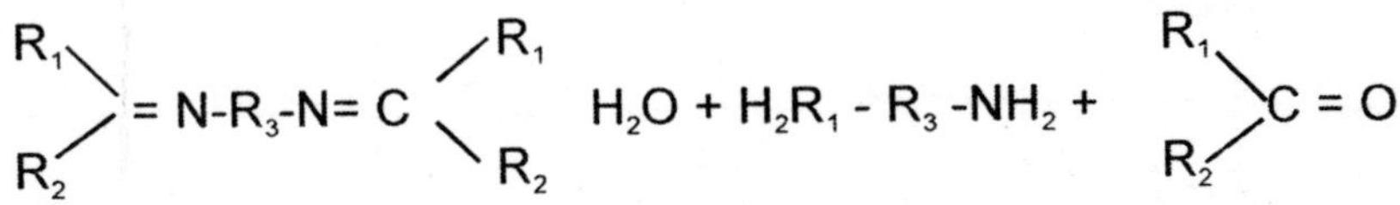

likely to be formed by the reaction of large surface area zinc with alcohols,

$$Zn + 2C_2H_5OH \rightarrow Zn(-OC_2H_5)_2 + H_2$$

or due to residual acidity/alkalinity from the hydrolysis reaction of ethyl silicate. Addition of zinc chloride improves the hardness by incorporation of zinc in the silicate polymer matrix.

$$\text{-Si-OH} + ZnCl_2 \rightarrow \text{-Si-O-Zn-O-Si}$$

Several amines as their ketemine derivatives are useful as curing agents. When these react with atmospheric moisture, they generate a hydrogen atom on amine, that can take part in the reaction.

Polymeric diols or triols that remain as a part of the film after cure are also used. These impart superior wetting properties to the substrate. These being polymeric in nature also prevent cracking of the film if these are too thick. In general, two pack systems are preferred to single pack due to superiority of storage stability, application properties and reliability.

This was an illustration of how to formulate primers. Similar principles can be used for other coats.

5

Inhibitive Primers for Metal

CORROSION is usually referred to as the degradation of the metal by chemical or electrochemical reaction with its environment. When considered broadly, corrosion may be looked upon as the tendency of the metal to revert to its natural state similar to the oxide from which it was originally smelted.

The actual mechanism in the corrosion of iron and steel is extremely complex and embraces the fields of chemistry and electro-chemistry. Iron will corrode only in the presence of both water and oxygen. This process is, in fact, two-fold involving a chemical change of iron to iron oxide and an electrical process of current flow. A simplified process of what takes place when a piece of iron corrodes is described in the following equation:

4Fe	$\rightarrow$	**4Fe^{++}**	+	**8e$^-$**	(anodic reaction)
Iron		Ferrous Iron		Electrons	

This is an oxidation reaction or anodic process, where the iron metal is converted to ferrous ions with the resultant electrons being conductive to the cathodic area.

$4H_2O$	+	$8e^-$	+	$2O_2$	$\rightarrow$	$8(OH)^-$
Water molecule		Electrones		Oxygen atom		Hydroxyl ions

The above step that follows the first step is a reduction reaction or cathodic process where the free electrons are used up. The products of the two reactions then combine to form ferrous hydroxide.

4Fa	+	$4H_2$	+	$2O_2$	$\rightarrow$	$4F_2(OH^2)$
						Red ferrous hydroxide

The iron hydroxide reacts further with air to form hydrated ferric oxide - rust.

$$4Fe(OH^2) \quad + \quad O_2 \quad \rightarrow \quad 2FE_2O_3H_2O \quad + \quad 2H_2O$$

The rate of corrosion of steel occur at varying rates on prevailing conditions and depends on the current flow between the anodic and cathodic areas. The presence of ions in water from salt or acids, enhance the flow of electrical current and increase the corrosion reaction rate. Therefore unprotected steel rusts far quicker along the seacoast or around industrial & chemical plants than in a dry environment.

Corrosion protection of steel is based on the premise that steel will always corrode. To simplify, steel in the presence of water and oxygen will corrode. To inhibit corrosion, it is therefore necessary to stop or at least reduce this flow of current. This can be accomplished by suppressing either the reaction at the cathode or at the anode by inserting a high resistance between these electrodes.

There are three main methods of using coatings to control the corrosion of steel and ferrous substrates. They are:

- Barrier protection that provides high resistance to the diffusion of water, ions, and oxygen through the coatings film to the substrate,
- Cathodic protection, usually achieved by pigmenting the coating using spherical, high purity zinc dust, which acts as a sacrificial anode in direct contact with the steel substrate as the cathode, and
- Inhibitive protection where, by pigmenting the coating using specific compounds such as anti-corrosive pigments that chemically changes the environment at the primer/substrate interface.

This article will discuss design and formulating strategies for coatings that provide corrosion protection of steel using the third method - Inhibitive protection.

Fundamental considerations

Inhibitive mechanisms involve the formation and maintenance of some type of passivating film at the anodic or cathodic sites on the metal. Inhibitive primers rely on corrosion control for the modification of the interfacial environment at the metal surface beneath the coating, so that the surface is passivated or electrochemically enabled in some manner. They deliberately modify the environment immediately adjacent to the metal beneath the primer. This modification is achieved by incorporating inhibitive compounds into the primer as a part of the pigmentation process. By including the inhibiting compounds, such as chromates, phosphates, etc., as pigments in the primer films that are applied to these metals, the films act to suppress corrosion of the metal.

It was mentioned earlier that the rate of corrosion is dependent on the type of the environment. Adding soluble chlorides and modifying the electrolyte, in which corrosion occurs, would increase the rate of attack. Addition of passivating agents facilitates the formation of polarizing films, thereby diminishing the rate of attack. Or removing from the electrolyte an element needed in the corrosion process may control the rate of attack.

Passivity may be defined as the loss of corrosivity of a metal with' its environment under specific electrolytic situation. The rapid increase in the rate of corrosion, caused by the increased oxidizing power ofthe electrolyte, results in the formation of an ultra-thin film of tightly adherent ferric oxide on the metal surface. This passive film is more insoluble and less permeable than the oxide film that naturally forms in air. The role of the inhibitor is to facilitate the formation of this oxide film.

For any interfacial modification to take place, inhibitive species must be conveyed from the primer film to the metal. To do this, the primer must be somewhat permeable to water, and the inhibitive compounds soluble in water to a certain degree. However, to avoid the depassivating effects of corrosive salts, like chlorides and sulphates, from the environment, the primer should not be permeable to these external ionic materials. It is also necessary to balance the inhibitor dissolution to enable only sufficient inhibitive ions are carried from the film to the interface and at a rate that is sufficient to sustain this process. It becomes important to control film permeability to that level that is most suited to the solubility of the inhibitor being used.

Careful balancing of PVC/CPVC ratio of the primer during its formulation becomes very important so that just sufficient moisture reaches the pigment to dissolve adequate inhibitor that will maintain the passive film for as long as possible. And it must do this without being permeable to external depassivating ions. PVC selection and the PVC/CPVC ratio are very critical in the design of inhibitive primers for metal.

Discussion on some of the specific corrosion-inhibiting pigments within the primer formulation that provide inhibitive protection follows.

Oxidizing inhibitors.

Not until pH levels exceed 10 is it possible to control the corrosion of steel solely by the amount of oxygen dissolved in the water. To increase the oxidizing power of an electrolyte and achieve passivity under atmospheric conditions at lower pH, it is necessary to use materials that will increase the oxidizing power of the electrolyte.

The most effective class of materials to do this are the chromate salts of different metals, such as zinc chromate and strontium chromate. Chromate pigments contain the chromate ion {CrO_4}, that is a powerful oxidizing agent. Because of this, a thin oxide layer forms on the metal substrate that readily passivates steel even in the absence of oxygen. Nitrates & nitrites and plumbates also act as oxidizing inhibitors. Molybdates are also known to act similarly.

Chromates are, perhaps the most effective inhibitors and constitute one of the major inhibitors in use currently in the most demanding situations. Due to their toxicity, however, their use in protective coatings is declining.

Non-oxidizing inhibitors

Somewhat less effective inhibitors are phosphates, borates, and silicates. They are not oxidizing inhibitors, and will only inhibit steel in the presence of oxygen. These ions do not form an anode film. Their function is more confined to plugging the normally defective natural oxide film. They perform better under alkaline conditions.

Molybdates functions by a mechanism that is comparable to that of chromates, and forms ferric molybdate oxide or ferric molybdates at the anode.

Another family of non-oxidizing inhibitors is the borates, generally available as salts of calcium, zinc, and barium. High levels of calcium borosilicate when used in an alkyd system will produce very hard films.

Commercially, phosphates and especially zinc phosphate is the most successful non-oxidizing inhibitive pigment. To improve the performance of zinc phosphate, a range of modified zinc phosphates have been introduced. Phosphates, polyphosphates and phosphosilicates of calcium, aluminum, barium, and strontium have also found commercial success as nonoxidizing inhibitive pigments, and have been incorporated into many coatings formulations. Calcium phosphates are similar to zinc phosphates and provide a source of phosphate ion that can be carried to the metal substrate by moisture as it permeates the paint film. This forms a protective layer at the metal interface, impeding the corrosion process.

Aluminum triphosphate is another alternative to zinc phosphate. Its effectiveness comes from the superior chelating power of triphosphate with iron as compared to other phosphates. However, this inhibitive pigment also tends to be binder specific. This has resulted in its modifications with other pigments like silica or zinc to provide a range of options for formulators.

Modified polyphosphates provide improved electrochemical activity and match the performance of chromates where modified zinc phosphates have not been able. Modified polyphosphates tend to be binder specific.

Phosphosilicates were specially developed as alternatives to zinc and strontium chromates. They are usually reacted with metals like calcium, barium and strontium. Because oftheir low water solubility and near neutral pH, they are compatible with a wide range of binder systems.

Pigment solubility

Pigment selection is to be made with the binder in mind, because pigment solubility and the permeability of the binder will markedly influence primer design. An inhibitor that releases its ions too quickly would provide an adequate level of inhibition over the short term. On the other side, an insoluble inhibitor whose ionic release is meager may not produce ions quickly to establish passivity.

The moisture vapour transmission of the binder and adjustments to the ratio of PVC to CPVC may be utilized to compensate for pigment solubility. The selection of the inhibitive pigment combination to optimize the composition in any specific binder becomes an important exercise in the design of the primer.

The pH of the environment would also significantly affect the solubility of the inhibitor. Under acidic conditions of general industrial service, zinc phosphate is soluble and hence effective. On the other hand under high pH salt spray.environment, the pigment remains insoluble and hence ineffective.

Primer design is further complicated because ions like chlorides and sulphates compete with inhibitive ions for adsorption onto the anode. At high concentratiohs they would depassivate the metal entirely, destroying the anode film or not allowing its formation. Increase in the level of depassivators, more than an equivalent level of inhibitor ions is required to maintain the passive film. In case of improper cleaning of steel where the steel bears depassivating chloride or other ionic species beneath the film and where the primer itself is contaminated with these depassivating ions, passivation with coatings would become difficult if not impossible. The inhibitive ions are derived from within the coating film, while the depassivators are derived from external environment. Because of this, it is not difficult to formulate a product that would provide a favourable ratio of passivating and depassivating ions.

Design strategies

Now that lead-based compositions are no more in use and with diminishing use of chromate-based primers, designing of inhibitive primers for metal have become a challenging and a demanding exercise. The traditional inhibitors were so effective that low volume loadings of lead and especially chromate pigments would provide to the formulation a reasonably assured protection, irrespective ofthe other aspects of pigmentation.

Although chromate pigments like yellow zinc chromate, strontium chromate and zinc tetroxychromate are still used mainly in applications that require optimum performance levels, other pigments having lower toxicity are genetally preferred for more practical services.

It is possible to formulate effective high performance primers for metal without the use of either lead and chromate pigments. Such formulation techniques are more challenging, materials used and their quantities have to be more specific and the result more specific to the service for which the system being designed.

Pigments for the inhibitive primer

The pigment composition consists of four different components:

- The prime pigment component,
- The inhibitor system,
- The extender component, and
- Any pigmentary thixotropes.

Each of the components may include more than one pigment.

Prime pigment component

Generally, selecting prime pigments depends on the required colour of the inhibitive primer. Colour in a primer may be of secondary importance, as it would inevitably be overcoated. Opacity is also not a critical consideration, unless the primed metal is to be stored for prolonged periods. Prime pigments also tend to be the most expensive item in many formulations. Prime pigment levels, and especially when using strong synthetic red oxides, could be reduced to an exact level that produces complete opacity at the minimum required film thickness. This also helps in proper application, as the applicator will apply only that quantity, which produces full opacity, thus indirectly controlling the desired dft.

Prime pigments are also the first line of defense against failures caused by light-induced weathering. Where such pigmentation is deficient, UV-induced changes in the binder would weaken the protective properties of the film. In chlorinated rubbers and PVA systems, inadequate pigmenta tion of the primer could induce corrosion failure by UV-induced dehydrochlorination of the binder and subsequent attack from acids on the substrate beneath the primer film.

Some of the range of prime pigments used in inhibitive primers is given below:

In the case of lead, they function by thickening the natural oxide layer. However, it is not fully established as yet the nature of inhibition with borates, molybdates, silicates and phosphates.

It is felt that molybdates set like chromates and are more resistant to

Pigment	Opacity	Oil Absorption	Sp. Gravity	Performance
Natural Red Oxide	Good	11	4.5	Excellent
Micronized Syn. Red Oxide	Excellent	28	5	Very Good
Micronized Syn. Black Oxide	Excellent	21	4.6	Good
Lampblack	Excellent	72	1.8	Good
Chromium Oxide Green	Very Good	11	5.2	Very Good
Micronized Syn. Yellow Oxide	Good	30 - 38	4.1	Good
Titanium Dioxide	Fair	20	4	Very Good

(Source: Coatings World, May 2000. Page # 60)

Most metal primers use one type or another of iron oxides, mostly the synthetic varieties. While there have been claims that red oxides have improved the performance of inhibitive primers, there are published reports that, except for lead-based pigments like medium chrome yellow and molybdate orange, non of the other prime pigments significantly upgrade the performance of primers.

Where epoxies and other two-pack primers are used and require accurate mixing of the two components in the field, pigmenting both the components in different colours may be used. A third colour is obtained when both the components are mixed in the field. Such an arrangement, not only identifies the respective components, but also establishes a colour standard for the correctly mixed product making easy verification of accurate mixing of the two components.

Inhibitive pigments

Inhibitive pigments are much more critical to corrosion resistance in all inhibitive primers. Different types of inhibitive pigments have specific mechanims. by which they suppress corrosion. It is known that chromate inhibition is direct and is dependent on the solubility of the chromate ion.

In the case of lead, they function by thickening the natural oxide layer. However, it is not fully established as yet the nature of inhibition with borates, molybdates, silicates and phosphates.

It is felt that molybdates set like chromates and are more resistant to chloride ion depassivation than with chromate inhibition. Borates, on the other hand, are more basic pigments and suppress corrosion through pH shift. They form soaps with acidic binders, because of which borate's efficiency in alkyd systems are relevant. Phosphates, phosphosilicates and polyphosphates of zinc, calcium, barium, strontium, iron and aluminum are all used in inhibitive primers.

For many years it has been customary for the formulators to use a blend of two or more inhibitive pigments as a part of the inhibitive package. The basis of this approach, in many cases, has been a deliberate manipulation of ionic release rates. The suppliers of inhibitive pigments have also supported these techniques by introducing a variety of inhibitor blends as well as chemical and physical modifications. All have served to upgrade the performance of the inhibitive pigments. Some of the modifications of the more widely used zinc phosphate inhibitive pigment are

- Re-engineered particle shape and size increases efficiency through increased surface area,
- Disproportionate stoichometry results in increased basicity,
- Co-precipitation increases efficiency by introduction of barium cation,
- Co-precipitation increases efficiency by introduction of molyb date anion,
- Co-precipitation increases efficiency by introduction of iron cation,

It is noteworthy that surface treatment, even after modification, has become common. Fine particle sized pigments, because of their increased surface area have enhanced efficiency, higher oil absorption and, therefore, lower CPVc. Surface treatment that lowers oil absorption and increases CPVC allows for higher pigmentation where they are necessary for higher performance.

Provided below is the utility of some phosphate & chromate pigments for inhibitive metal primers.

Extender package

Next to the inhibitor pigments, in terms of overall contribution to performance, is the extender package. They serve the primer in ways that

Inhibitive Pigment	Solvent based Alkyd	Epoxy Ester	2K Epoxy	2K Polyurethane
Fine Particle Size Zinc Phosphate	*****			
Basic Zinc Phosphate	*****			++++++
Iron Cation Modified Zinc Phosphate	*****		++++++	*****
Barium Cation Modified Zinc Phosphate			++++++	
Zinc Potassium Chromate	*****	*****	*****	*****
Strontium Chromate		++++++	++++++	++++++
Zinc Tetroxy Chromate	*****	++++++	++++++	
Zinc Borophosphate	++++++	++++++	++++++	

Keys

***** denote pigment that may be used in this binder system

++++++ denote pigment highly recommended for this binder system.

*(Source : Laporte * Phsguard*Pigments)*

are secondary to inhibition. Flat, platy extenders such as mica, chlorite and certain talcs used in lieu of silica, whiting, barytes, etc. act to reduce film permeability. They thus provide an additional device with which to modify the rate of water ingress without the need to alter binder levels. However, it should be noted that for all platy pigments, particle shape and increased surface area tends to diminish CPVC and this requires adjustments to the PVC. The second consequence of high surface area is an increase in viscosity. Therefore, excessive use of highly oil absorbent extenders like mica can also result in excessive flocculation.

Platy pigments also provide significant benefits in film reinforcement, counteracting the tendency of the film to crack while in service. It should also be noted that lextenders are totally transparent to Ultraviolet and offer no protection to the binder. Acicular pigments are also used as reinforcements, but are less efficient than the platy extenders. Fibrous pigments also reinforce the film, efficiently. But they are very oil absorbent and increase thixotropy of the formulation.

Pigmentary thixotropes

Thixotropes make up the smallest portion of pigmentation, but exert substantial properties to the performance of the formulation. Thixotropes may also be considered as rheological additives as well as a pigment. They are responsible for the control of pigment sedimentation, film build, sag resistance, flow and leveling. In protective coatings, film thickness is critical to enhanced protection. In thermosetting coatings that are often the basis of protective coatings, excessive film thickness may increase internal stress. A balanced thixotrope level in combination with a prudent level of prime pigments goes a long way in the application within the desired levels of film thickness.

Design considerations

We have discussed earlier that a degree of permeability is necessary for a proper functioning of the inhibitive primer. For long-term protection, permeability however, requires to be closely controlled without unduly depleting the reserves of inhibitive pigments. Binders that show best results under these circumstances should be hydrophilic instead of hydrophobic and impermeable. But, the binders should not be soluble or hydrolytically unstable to cathodic alkali that may dissolve in service. The favoured binders have been alkyds, epoxy esters, phenolics, and epoxies and urethanes that are extensively used today.

Optimizing PVC/CPVC

Once pigments have been selected, the next action in primer design is to determine the optimum combinations, especially the levels of the inhibitors and other functional pigments, thixotropes, etc. All ofthese pigments have the maximum influence on performance of the formulation. Optimal loadings of pigments are dictated by PVC, more appropriately the PVC/CPVC ratio and permeability. The PVC/CPVC ratio is the correct mathematical expression that represents the volumetric condition of the film matrix. An optimal level of pigmentation and that includes prime pigments, inhibitors, extenders, and thixotropes, will change from binder to binder. An optimized PVC/CPVC ratio for one binder system would require changes when the same pigmentation is used in another binder that has different wetting characteristic and water permeability. It is therefore best to design each primer formulation from scratch.

The ratio of PVC/CPVC is most critical to performance in inhibitive primers. The effect of PVC/CPVC ratio on film integrity may be summarized as

- At a PVC/CPVC ratio of less than 1, there is excess resin and the pigment is totally encapsulated. The paint film tends to be glossy and impermeable.

- At a PVC/CPVC ratio that is equal to 1 , the pigment is just encapsulated and is covered by a layer of resin. The spaces between pigment particles at the point of closest packing are filled with resin. The paint film is matte but cohesive.
- At a PVC/CPVC ratio that is greater than 1 , there is insufficient resin to coat the pigment particles entirely and fill the gaps between them. This results in a porous film with reduced cohesion.

PVC/CPVC adjustments are not the universal answer. We are aware that, should we approach CPVC too closely, the general corrosion resistance of the primer will fall rather steeply. Under these circumstances, the binder could get depleted so quickly that capillaries develop. Because of which, the film becomes so porous that it allows aggressive, depassivating ionic materials to enter from the outside too quickly.

Primers that use the more watersoluble pigments suffer increased blistering tendencies at lower PVC. At higher levels of PVC, blistering becomes less serious, as the permeability of the film to water and oxygen increases. As the PVC comes close to CPVC, the permeability opens up further and underfilm corrosion increases significantly. Thus there exists for, an inhibitive primer a PVC/CPVC window for optimized formulation. This window varies with the type of inhibitor being used, the nature and the permeability of the binder as also the oil absorption, surface treatment, particle size and shape and particle size distribution, wetting, dispersion, and degree of flocculation of all the pigments in use. The formulator may use two inhibitors of different solubility, with one providing high levels of shortterm protection and the other a slower, longer-lasting release like mica, Mio, etc. or those that increase efficiency of the inhibitor system like zinc oxide and wollastonite. Further complications can result on multi-pigment usage. These complications require compensatory modification of PVC for maintaining the desired PVC/CPVC ratio.

It therefore becomes necessary to test and evaluate the performance of a primer over a range of PVCs, for each change of pigmentation. It also becomes necessary to test the performance of a primer for any change in pigments used and that too over a range of PVC. Any change in CPVC would also change the PVC/CPVC ratio, like it does with changes in PVC. Once the optimum PVC/CPVC ratio is established, exchanging some extenders with or without some prime pigments with additional inhibitor and evaluating performance at the optimum PVC would be the next step. Any changes in CPVC at this time would be only marginal and may be adjusted in the tests themselves.

Chromate pigmentation tolerates significant loading flexibility. The newly introduced non-toxic inhibitors allow far less latitude in formulation. They require optimum selection of the inhibitive pigments along with extenders, prime pigments, thixotropes, etc.

Finally, the optimal performing system should be evaluated for application properties, flow & levelling and appearance of the dried film.

6

Paints for Ships

WHY do ships have Feminine names? Because it costs so much to keep one in paint and powder. The joke contains a kernel of truth. The upkeep of ships makes diverse and exacting demands on paints technologists. From its fowest keel and the topmost mast to the decks and inside cabins and galleys, the type of paints required for a ship are numerous.

The most important of these are the underwater anticorrosive and antifouling paints. Then there are anti-skid deck paints; fire-retardant paints for bulkhead, decks and ordnance stores; anti-condensation paints for humid areas of the ship; and various types of tank coatings.

We shall dwell on maintenances of ship by painting, and not for the new structures.

Main structures of the ship can be defined as follows:

External

1) Ship bottom (Included stern Area).

2) Boot Topping area

3) Top side

Internal

1) Engine rooms

2) A) Boiler rooms (Internal)

B) Boiler rooms (External)

3) Cargoholds

4) Deck

5) Masts

6) Cabins

7) Funnels

Seawater is complex biochemical broth covering almost 70% of the earth surface. Its primary constituents are Sodium chloride or common salt (about 2.9%) and 0.4% Magnesium sulphate. But traces of every element one can imagine are present in it. In addition, it is a living medium harbouring millions of different animals and plant species (zoo plankton and phytoplankton) life support systems for our marine food resource. The sea also harbors pests like foulers and borers, which wreak havoc on the immersed portions of the ships as well as 'on offshore structures.

Many of the species are quite happy to be carried away by currents but others need hard surface to attach themselves to multiply. Every available space in this environment is, therefore, contested and is covered also by a variety of barnacles, algae and bacteria. This phenomenon called fouling involves some four to five thousand species.

Fouling is also more severe in tropical seas. There is a wider variety of fouling organisms, which also grow much faster. Fouling leads to a roughening of the submerged part of the ship's surface. The net effect is increase in fuel consumption by as much as 50% over the period of 6 months.

Fuel savings are very important in an economic shipping trade. Much depends on the selection of underwater coatings, in addition to the strict adherence to the quality parameters so that the hull roughness is maintained at very low levels. To keep the hull roughness at minimal levels utmost care must be taken to preserve the steel surfaces at various stages of hull construction. Application of high performance zinc rich coatings and preservation with Epoxy MIO holding primers at the block stage and application of heavy duty underwater coatings with airless spray are the essential pre-requisites to ensure that the hull roughness is kept at minimum levels. In addition to this, the surface preparation must be minimum Sa2.5 standards both at the secondary surface preparation stage, which would help in keeping the hull roughness at minimum levels along with proper application of heavy-duty coatings.

Self-polishing copolymer type of antifouling paints must be used widely as this would not only control the marine fouling but also help in maintaining the hull in a appropriate condition for achieving substantial fuel savings.

Selection of underwater coating system

Selection of the underwater coating system can be classified into two categories; they are:

A) Anti corrosive composition

B) Antifouling compositions.

These coatings are applied as a total system with each of the two categories performing different roles, as far as their performance is concerned. However, the objectives of coating scientist is to ensure that they have common goal in keeping the underwater areas in an extremely smooth condition for fairly longer periods.

Anticorrosive compositions

The best-known, long lasting anticorrosive composition is either coaltar epoxy (CTE) or Rubber based coaltar coatings.

Coaltar to rubber blending ratio (50:35). After surface is blasted to Sa 2.5 standard one coat of Epoxy Zinc phosphate (50micron) is applied followed by a coaltar / Rubber based epoxy of 150 microns.

Antifouling compositions

Basically there are three different types of antifouling compositions. They are based on

a) Soluble matrix antifouling

b) Insoluble matrix antifouling

c) Self polishing antifouling paint

In all the types toxin is incorporated in the paint formulation in such a way that it is released through the paint film and ensuring that the surfaces are in foul free condition. Although the objective of the anti fouling is same in all the three types, the release mechanism is different in the three types.

Soluble and insoluble matrix type

The toxin, mainly cuprous oxide is physically mixed with the binder which is resin based in the case of soluble matrix and cyclised rubber in the case of insoluble matrix type. While in the former the binder gets dissolved in seawater, in the latter the toxin is released through the insoluble binder.

Typical formulation

1) Soluble matrix antifouling composition

	% by weight
Cuprous oxide	24.0
Zinc oxide	5.0
Tributyltin oxide	2.0
Red iron oxide	8.0
Paris white	9.0
Talc (10 microns)	6.0
Bentone 38	0.3
N Butanol	0.1
Limed rosin/boiled linseed oil, 3: 1 , 60% in naphtha	41.0
White spirit	4.6
	100.0

Insoluble matrix antifouling composition

Cyclised rubber	8.9
Tritolyl phosphate	3.2
Gum rosin w/w	0.6
Coumarone resin (95-105C)	4.5
Zinc oxide	6.3
Copper oxide	43.8
Trimethyl benzene	24.5
MTO	8.2
	100

The main difference between the above two classes of antifouling and S.P.C.A.F. is that in the case of latter the toxin is chemically mixed with the binder. In this case the binder is nothing but a polymer having highly active toxin groups and the moment these groups come in contact with seawater, the toxin is released uniformly by a polishing mechanism rather than the diffusion mechanism seen in the case of the conventional antifouling paints. The toxin employed for this purpose is generally based on tri-organo-tin derivatives. While in the case of conventional antifouling paints the leaching rate is proportional to log OFT. of the paint in the case of SPC it is directly proportional to OFT of the paint. This unique property has been taken as a major advantage in predicting the performance of underwater antifouling paint.

COATING CHART OF THE SHIP PAINTING

S.No.	Items	No. of Coats	DFT in microns per coat	Theoretical covering capacity M.sq./ltr.	Practical covering capacity M.sq./ltr.	Price/ltr. incl. Ex. duty in 20 ltr./Pack	Price/. sq.mtr./ coat	Area sq.m.	Value in Rupees
1.	Epoxy redoxide Zinc phosphate primer (2 pack)	1	30	14.28	11.42	Rs.127.25	Rs. 11.14	1681	Rs.182726.34
2.	Epoxy High build Coal Tar brown	1	150	4	3.2	Rs. 107.69	Rs. 33.65	1681	Rs. 56565.65
3.	Eopxy high build coat Tar black	1	150	4	3.2	Rs. 107.69	Rs. 33.65	1681	Rs. 56565.65
4.	Cyclised Rubber aluminium sealer coat	1	50	8	6.4	Rs.120.00	Rs. 18.75	1681	Rs.31518.75
5.	Cyclised rubber antifouling red Grade I	1	75	8	6.4	Rs. 480.00	Rs. 75.00	1681	Rs. 126075.00
6.	Cyclised rubber antifouling red Grade II	2	80	7.5	6	Rs. 266.60	Rs. 44.43	1681	Rs. 74686.83
	total INCL. GRADE I	5	455				Rs.172.19		Rs. 289451.39
	INCL. GRADE II	6	460				Rs.141.62		Rs.238063.00
TOP SIDE AREA									
1.	Epoxy red oxide zinc phosphate primer	1	30	14.28	11.42	Rs. 127.25	Rs. 11.14	312	Rs. 3475.68
2.	Epoxy high build coal tar black	1	100	6	4.8	Rs. 107.69	Rs. 22.43	312	Rs.6998.16
3.	Epoxy high build coat tar black	1	100	6	4.8	Rs. 107.69	Rs. 22.43	312	Rs. 6998.16

Cont. COATING CHART OF THE SHIP PAINTING

S.No.	Items	No. of Coats	DFT in microns per coat	Theoretical covering capacity M.sq./ltr.	Practical covering capacity M.sq./ltr	Price/ltr. incl. Ex. duty in 20 ltr./Pack	Price/. sq.mtr./ coat	Area sq.m.	Value in Rupees
4.	Cyclised rubber aluminium sealer coat	1	50	8	6.4	Rs. 120.00	Rs. 18.75	312	Rs. 5850.00
5.	Cyclised rubber finish coat	1	50	7	5.6	Rs. 145.00	Rs. 25.89	312	Rs.8077.68
	blue total	5	330				Rs. 100.64		Rs. 31399.68
FOR DECK AREA & HATCH TOP									
1.	Epoxy redoxide zinc phosphate primer	1	30	14.28	11.42	Rs. 127.25	Rs. 11.17	1134	Rs. 12632.76
2.	Epoxy micaceous ironoxide coat	2	2X100	4/COAT	3.2/COAT	Rs. 120.00	2XRs. 37.50	1134	Rs. 85050.00
			280				Rs. 86.14		Rs. 98682.76
EXTERNAL ACCOMMODATION									
1.	cyclised rubber high build zinc phosphate primer	1	50	8	6.4	Rs. 108.0	Rs. 16.87	712	Rs. 12011.40
2.	cyclised rubber finish paint light buff/white	2	2x40	4.37	3.5	Rs. 93.85	Rs. 26.80	712	Rs 19087.70
			130				Rs. 43.67		Rs. 31099.10
TOTAL GRADE I									Rs. 4,49,631.00
TOTAL GRADE II									Rs. 3,98,243.00

Tie coat / sealer coat:

The antifouling paint is not directly applied on coaltar epoxy/ cyclised rubber surfaces; it is applied on sealer coat. The best-known tie *coat!* sealer coat is vinyl tar epoxy. The objective of this coating is to ensure that it has compatibility with anti corrosive compositions on the other, as direct application of antifouling paint on anti corrosive is somewhat detrimental to the properties of the former. Thus ideal painting scheme for the under water areas blasted to Sa 2.5 standards would be,

Epoxy zinc phosphate Blast primer	50 Microns
Coaltar epoxy/cyclised rubber black	150 Microns
Coaltar epoxy/cyclised rubber brown	150 Microns
SPC antifouling paint	450 Microns

The above scheme would offer a performance life not less than 4 years from both anti corrosive and antifouling properties point of view.

Boottoppings

As distinct from the traditional boottoppings mentioned previously (table) high -performance composition for the area based essentially on the same binders as the topside paints. In this category the cyclised rubber perform very well because of their excellent intercoat adhesion.

This is particularly important because of the damage to the paint system from abrasion and impact with fenders and quays, and the consequent need for frequent repainting. With VLCCs, iouling can also be a major problem in the boottopping area, and it is common practice to use an anti- fouling composition as the finishing paint. Thus it is usual to employ the same anti fouling as is used on the bottom.

Cyclised rubber undercoat -white

	% By weight
Titanium dioxide (e.g. Tioxide R-CR2)	16.0
Blanc fixe	14.0
Zinc oxide	1.0
Thixatrol S T (thixotropic agent)	1.0
Cyclised rubber	14.0
Cerechlor	70
(chlorinated plasticizer) Cerechlor	42

(chlorinated plasticizer)	7.0
Propylene oxide (stabilizer)	0.1
Xylene	29.9
Solvesso 100	10.0
	100.0

Cyclised rubber topcoat - white

Titanium dioxide (e,g Tioxide R-CR2)	18.0
Blanc fixe	2.0
Zinc oxide	1.0
Bentone 38 (thixotropic agent)	1.0
N Butanol (Swelling Agent)	0.5
Cyclised rubber	16.0
Cerechlor 70	12.0
Cerechlor 42	4.0
Propylene oxide	0.1
Xylene	30.4
Solvesso 100	15.0
	100.0

Top side area and superstructure (recommended system)

1) Primer (quick drying) Linseed alkyd	Medium oil length 2 coasts (55-60% O.L)		50 microns
2) Undercoat	medium oil length Linseed alkyd (50-55% O.L.)	1 Coat	50 microns
3) Enamel	Long oil length Soya alkyd (65% O.L.)	1-2 coats	30-50microns

7

Drying and Curing Additives

Introduction

ALL coatings whether used to provide good aesthetic appearance, corrosion protection or any other functional need will contain a film forming material or binder. This material may be organic or , inorganic. After drying/ curing of the film the binder forms a continuous film that may vary from hard and impervious to soft and porous or combinations in-between these. The principal mechanisms by which binders form a film are evaporation of solvent, reaction with oxygen from air and/or cross linking by chemical reaction. Thus the drying process can be specified as physical drying and chemical drying. In case of physical drying there is no chemical change during the drying process whereas chemical drying implies that there is a chemical change in the structure of the binder. Depending on the mechanism the coating film can be termed either thermoplastic or thermosetting. Initially, the wet film is a solution of polymer molecules in a suitable solvent or blend of solvents. In both the cases the first step of drying process is solvent evaporation. The solvent evaporation occurs at the surface of the wet film and since the polymer molecules always have higher specific gravity than solvent, the surface of the wet film becomes enriched in polymer and is denser than the bulk of the film. This denser layer sinks and is replaced by dilute polymer solution (which has lower specific gravity) from undemeath. In this way uniform solvent evaporation is maintained from the film surface. If a thicker film is applied then this motion is hindered and solvent rich material is trapped under the drying film leading to a non-uniform surface. The retained solvent molecules can nucleate within the film or at interfaces within the film and cause voids or blisters. The solvent release, in this situation is not determined by the vapour pressure of the solvent(s) used but by the ability of the solvent molecules to diffuse through the network of swollen polymer molecules. Too

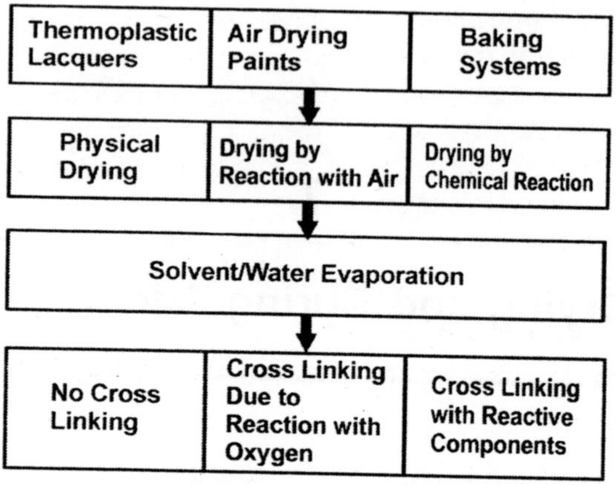

Fig. 7.1 : Film Formation

slow solvent diffusion usually leads to solvent retention in the dried film. In the subsequent stage of drying the polymer molecules get much closer to each other and the film begins to gel. The film formation mechanism of various types of coatings is illustrated in *Fig.* 7.1.

Almost all desirable properties of a coating film depend on the quality and integrity of the film which in turn depends on the polymer chemistry, formulation variables, the Tg of the dried film and the surface characteristics of the substrate. The following coating properties are generally influenced by film formation process - adhesion, hardness, chemical resistance, mechanical properties, dirt pickup, flow, gloss, sagging, surface flow and film blisters etc. The development of these properties is controlled by a number of chemical and physical factors such as: molecular weight, cross linking density, glass transition temperature, binder chemistry, viscosity, curing schedule and formulation variables among others.

Physically drying systems

The physically drying films are usually single pack. They show rapid rate of drying, thermoplastic nature and are readily swollen by true solvents. Examples of physically drying coating are pigmented and clear nitrocellulose lacquers, shellac varnishes and some of vinyl coating systems. The drying rate is mostly dependent on the evaporation rate of solvent, hydrogen bonding and physical interaction between solvent and polymer molecules. The evaporation rate of solvent(s) from the drying film depends on its volatility, ratio of surface area to volume of the film and external conditions such as air circulation/flow, temperature, and relative humidity. In physically drying systems, the cohesive strength of the final dried film is determined by the nature of the polymer and interaction between polymer chains. This property is governed by weak Van der Waal forces, the strength of which is determined by the presence of dipoles or hydrogen bonding groups in the polymer chains. Moreover longer the polymer chains, greater the interaction and higher the final cohesive strength. Due to this reason high molecular weight polymers are generally used in physical drying coatings. This however necessitates use of more quantity of solvent to achieve workable consistency that results in lower solid content and consequently lower film build.

Chemical drying/curing systems

The initial stages of chemical drying process are similar to the physical drying mechanism, until the polymer molecules get close to each other. At this stage chemical reaction starts between adjacent molecules through functional groups located along the chain leading to cross-linking. Since part of the polymerization process takes place after application of the coating on the substrate it is not necessary to use high molecular weight resins, as required in physical drying systems. This results in much higher non-volatiles in the wet coating. The increase in curing temperature encourages higher rotation of the polymer chains that in turn increases the probability of contact between reactive groups from adjacent chains. This interaction leads to faster curing rates and increased cross-linking density. As a coating film cross-links its solubility and flow reduces where as glass transition temperature increases. The chemical resistance of the final dried systems is governed by the weakest of the chemical bonds making up the polymer. These bonds are usually those that were present in the binder or were generated during the drying or curing process. For example oils and oil-modified polymers contain a variety of chemical bonds but the weakest of these is the ester link, which is susceptible to alkali hydrolysis. The drying rate of chemical drying process is temperature dependent. A broad comparison between attributes of physical and chemical drying films is shown in *Table* 7.1.

The chemical drying/curing systems can be broadly divided in two categories

- Based on drying oils and oil-modified polymers. These are dried/ cured with the help of driers (siccatives).
- Based on polymers containing reactive groups. These are cured either with the help of cross-linking polymers, catalysts, thermal initiators and photo initiators.

Table 7.1

Property	Physically Drying	Chemical Drying
Cuted Film	Thermoplastic	Thermosetting
MW prior to application	High	Low
MW of dried film	High	Very High
VOC	High	Low
Cross linking density	None-very Low	Moderate very high
Solvent resistance	Poor-good	Excellent
Chemical resistance	Poor-excellent	Moderate-excellent
Hardness	Poor-good	Moderate -excellent
Water permeability	Low-high	Very low
Gloss	Low-high	High-very low
Recoat ability	Good	Poor-good

Driers for air-drying systems

The simplest solvent-based coatings are drying oils and their pigmented version- paints. Drying oils, obtained chiefly from vegetable sources, are those oils that absorb oxygen and solidify within a usable time when exposed to the air in thin films. Linseed oil is the most common. Because the polymer is formed from small liquid molecules after application, these paints take a

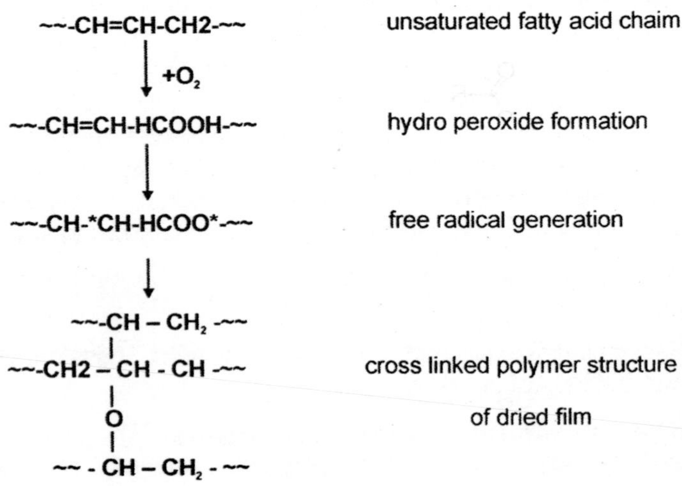

Fig. 7.2 : Oxidative polymerization

long time to dry and to cure completely. The process can be somewhat speeded up by pre-polymerizing the oil by heating it to produce so-called "bodied" oil. Because of some pre-polymerization they dry faster than untreated oils. Oleo resinous binders are made by polymerization of drying oils and solid resins. Because the binder is already partly polymerized, solvent is required to thin it to application consistency. They dry faster than bodied oils. The chemical hardening of oil based/modified binders such as cooked oils, oleo resinous binders, alkyds and epoxy esters etc. that contain adequate concentration of active double bonds takes place by reaction with atmospheric oxygen and is generally described as drying. The film formation by oxidative drying is based on molecular entanglement and crosslinking initiated by oxidative process. The resultant polymer molecules have a lattice structure and form insoluble and infusible films. Drying by this process can be broken down in following stages

- Induction period.
- Oxygen absorption.
- Peroxide formation.
- Peroxide decomposition to form free radicals and,
- Free radical polymerization at unsaturation.

The induction period occurs because most oils contain natural anti oxidants the effect of which must be over come before the drying process can start. Oxygen is then absorbed from air at unsaturation sites in the oil

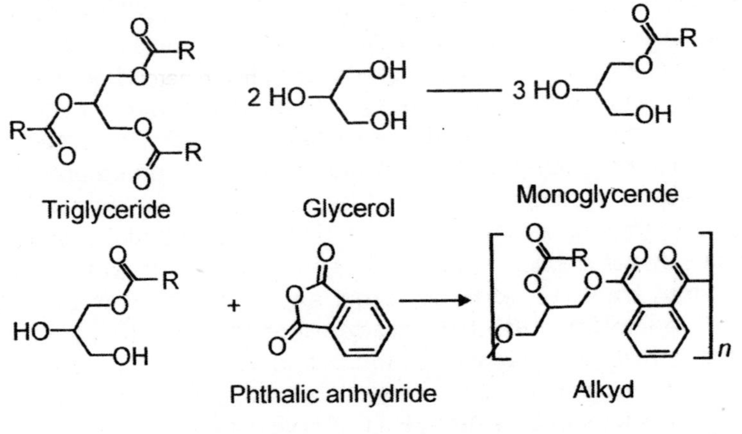

Fig 7.3 : Alkyd resin

molecule to form hydro peroxides, these peroxides decompose to form free radicals that act as catalyst for cross linking, *Fig.* 7.2. Driers catalyze or accelerate the drying/curing of drying oils and drying oil based polymers. Driers are catalytic in nature and do not chemically react with the polymeric material. The cobalt drier being most effective for oxygen absorption/hydro peroxide formation and manganese drier for hydro peroxide decomposition/ free radical generation. The final cross-linked film is assumed to contain a combination of covalent linkages formed by autoxidation process and covalent and co-ordination linkages.

Alkyd resins can be regarded as mixed esters of dicarboxylic acids, mono-functional carboxylic acids and polyols, *Fig.* 7.3. Alkyd resins based on unsaturated fatty acids are able to cross-link while in contact with air and can form more resistant films than straight oil based films. Air drying alkyds fall into two categories; nonconjugated drying oil and conjugated drying oil based. The drying speed is related to the number of unsaturated groups present per molecule. Generally if this number is less than 2.2 it is termed as semidrying oil and if over 2.2 it is called a drying oil.

Soaps and organic complexes of some of the metals such as lead, manganese, cobalt, calcium, zinc, zirconium, barium, iron, aluminium and cerium etc. when used in relatively small quantities can catalyze and accelerate the oxidation and/or polymerization of drying oils. Driers are used either for ambient dry conditions or for forced drying and according to their application in various binder systems the driers can be classified for use in either solvent or water borne compositions. Driers for solvent/water-based coatings are mainly metal salts of mono carboxylic acids such as - octoic, naphthenic, linoleic and C6-C'8 synthetic fatty acids, usually dissolved in white spirit. The choice of acid does not seem to have a noticeable effect on drying. The metal ions in the drier are active ingredients; the organic portion of the molecule makes the drier soluble in aliphatic hydrocarbon solvent as well as act as a compatibilizer and helps in molecular distribution of the metal ions throughout the binder. Insoluble salts such as acetates and chlorides do not function as a drier. The early driers were simple disoaps, of metals that are in +2 oxidation stage; excess of acid was often used to reduce the viscosity of the drier solution. Normally driers possess significant surface activity with pigments/binder and water (in alkyd emulsions). Adsorption on pigment or binder inter~ face may cause a significant drop in their efficiency that can lead to loss of drying as well as defects such as seeding, pigment settling and surface defects. Drier levels are always expressed as percent metal on solid resin.

Driers are usually classified in following groups:

Primary driers - Soaps of metals, which exist in several oxidation states and therefore undergo a reduction reaction. These include Cobalt, Lead, Manganese, Vanadium and Cerium etc.

Secondary driers - Soaps of metals that exist in a single oxidation state and which have a catalytic effect when used in conjunction with primary driers. These include Calcium, Zinc, Barium and Lithium etc.

Co-ordinate driers- Soaps of Zirconium and Aluminium. They enhance the drying action of other driers by reaction with hydroxyl and carboxyl groups in the binder. The activity of these driers is explained by a reaction with carboxylic acids that results in formation of alkoxy radicals, hydroxyl ions and a metal ion in a higher oxidative state, e.g. Co^{+2} to CO^{+3}. Co^{+3} can further react with a carboxylic group to form an additional peroxy radical, a proton, and a cobalt ion in the initial oxidative state CO^{+3} the metal ion itself is unchanged and acts as a catalyst.

When a primary drier is used in conjunction with a secondary drier it gives a "synergetic" effect. None of the single metal soap can give suffiCiently fast through dry films. For this reason either the coating manufacturer uses his own combination of driers to suit requirements of individual binder or a formulated combination that contains an optimal combination of individual driers. A number of theories have been proposed when more than one metal is present. The secondary driers are assumed to maintain an optimal pH balance, work as a leg and donor, alter the electrostatic field that creates better conditions for generation of hydro peroxides and consequent chain transfer or activate the captured oxygen molecule jointly with primary drier. Cobalt drier is used most extensively. Cobalt drier is called surface or top driers because of its tendency to migrate to the surface and enhance surface drying. Care must be taken because excess cobalt causes wrinkling, colour change in light coloured paints and gelation in some varnishes. For this reason it is combined with other metals such as lead, manganese, zirconium and calcium etc. The wrinkling property of cobalt is utilized for producing oil/ alkyd based wrinkle finishes. Manganese is also an active drier and is a potent oxidizer as well. It promotes polymerization to a greater extent than cobalt. It is often used alone in certain baking finishes. In air dry systems it is used along with auxiliary driers; however its dark colour can limit its use. Lithium improves the efficiency of other driers and is a preferred esterification catalyst in alkyd manufacture. Zinc is an auxiliary drier and gives a harder film when used in conjunction with cobalt. It retards the surface drying in order to prevent wrinkling and allows free access to oxygen, thus permitting hardening through the entire film. Zinc naphthanate is a good wetting agent and often improves gloss. Lead and zirconium driers catalyze drying throughout the film and are called through driers. Calcium cannot undergo oxidation reactions and it is thought that calcium acts by its affinity to adsorb on pigment surface thereby minimizing the adsorption of other metal ions that are available to function as driers. Aluminium offers outstanding polymerization and yellowing resistance without viscosity instability. Neodymium is a recent replacement for calcium and zirconium in vac compliant resins. Probably the most common drier combination used until recently has been cobalt/lead/calcium; but since the use of lead has been restricted on health grounds there has been a move towards lead free systems. This combination has been replaced by cobalt/zirconium/calcium combination, although in some cases the drying performance is inferior to that obtained from lead system. In such cases lithium has been found to be particularly useful in combination with cobalt and calcium driers. High solid air-drying coatings are based on low viscosity and therefore low molecular weight alkyd resins. Consequently part of resin polymerization that was previously done during resin cooking has to take place during the drying of film. This results in considerable increases in the drying time. At times optimization of conventional drier combination/content is not sufficient to give the required drying speed in such systems. Incorporation of certain aluminium organic compounds based on ethyl acetoacetate has been found to improve the drying speed of coatings based on high solid /low viscosity alkyds. The aluminium drier appears to provide a secondary source of cross linking by interaction of aluminium organic compound with carboxyl and hydroxyl groups present in the polymer chain.

Driers for water borne systems

Water borne alkyd systems follow the same drying mechanism as solvent borne alkyds. Initial physical drying takes place by evaporation of water, co solvent and neutralizing agents followed by oxidative polymerization. However, water borne systems show distinct differences due to presence of neutralizing agents such as amines and ammonia, surface active agents, and characteristic properties of water. Triethyl amine is known to provide better stability than ammonia. Water borne air-dry systems usually show slower drying time, poor through drying and hardness and loss of drying. Water can slow the oxygen uptake of the binder thereby slowing the autoxidation process. It may hydrolyze the binder that may result in loss of dry. Water also affects the stability of the driers. Moreover water is one of the strongest complexing agents with metal ions, such as Co^{3+}, Mn^{3+} and Ca^{2+}. In presence of water Cobalt forms hexahydrocobalt, $(Co\ (HP)\ 6)^{3+}$. The catalytic action of Co^{3+} is inhibited by this complex formation. The CO (HP) 6) $^{3+}$ complex has a weaker oxidation potential. This complex is unstable and is almost spontaneously hydrolyzed; this inhibits the catalytic activity of Cobalt metal ions. The sensitivity of metal ions to hydrolysis increases in the following order $Na+ < Ba^{2+} < Ca^{2+} < Mn^{2+} < Fe^{2+} < Zn^{2+} < Bi^{3+}$ and $< Zr^{4+}$. The binders *for* air-drying water borne paints include; water soluble alkyds, alkyd resin emulsions and self-emulsifiable alkyd resins. The water-soluble alkyds can be true or colloidal solutions of alkyd resins with a high acid value that have been neutralized with amines or ammonia. The acid value, of alkyd solution in water increases due to hydrolysis. The effectiveness and solubility of drier may be affected by salt formation. Further more amines or ammonia can *form* metal complex ions with cobalt or manganese that have lesser catalytic action. Cobalt is influenced to a greater degree by ammonia and manganese by amines. The alkyd emulsions mostly contain non ionic emulsifiers and are stabilized with protective colloids. High emulsifier content impairs the drying properties. The drying rate and hard ness are significantly impaired by nonylphenol ethoxylates (nonionic) but are hardly affected by ammonium alkyl sulphate (anionic). Self-emulsifying alkyds generally contain polyethylene glycol hydrophobic groups that can emulsify without incorporation of additional emulsifiers. These groups have an adverse effect on drying rate similar to that shown by non ionic emulsifiers. The loss of drier catalyst through hydration can be compensated to a certain extent by using higher levels of primary driers such as cobalt and manganese. However a marked improvement can be achieved by using pre-complexed primary driers normally pre dissolved in ethers of glycol or diethylene glycol or propylene glycol. Ligands have been used *for* precomplexing and increasing the activity of these driers. Ligands affect the spin multiplicity of electron distribution in the metal; both thermodynamic (stability) and kinetic (drying rate) are influenced by legends. Ligands such as O-phenanthroline or 2,2 bipyridyl have been conventionally used as drier activators for traditional solvent based coatings also.

The general structure of this class of driers is shown below:

$$\{Me\ (Lig.)^{\cdot}\ n)\ m\ (A)_m$$

Where
Me - Metal Cation
Lig. - Ligand
n - Valency (usually 1, 2, 3 or 4)
m - Valency of metal ion

A - Acid Anion (usually $RCOOH^-$, RPO^-_3, RSO^-_3, $R2PO^-_4$, etc. where R is hydrocarbon segment)

Selecting the right ligand for the drier metal ion can increase the effectiveness of pre-complexed drier. For example (Co (phen) $_3$) $^{3+}$ is reduced more rapidly than (Co (NH^3) ^{6}) $^{3+}$or (Co (ethylene amine) 3) $^{3+}$. Pre-complexed driers are available both as water emusifiable as well as non-emulsifiable versions. The emulsifiability in water is introduced through polarity of the ligand or presence of emulsifiers. Some of the potential problems with water borne air dry systems are incompatibility between the resin and the drier, potential for seeding and resin discolouration. Drier stabilizers are often used to prevent drier absorption or dissipation that may result in loss of catalytic power of driers.

Catalysts for chemical curing systems

Catalysts are incorporated in coating formulations to accelerate curing reaction in a number of binder chemistries such as

- Short oil alkyd and amino resin systems,
- Polyhydroxy acrylic, polyester and polyether/ polyurethane systems,
- UV/radiation cure systems,
- Unsaturated polyester systems,
- Saturated polyester and blocked polyurethane powder coating systems, etc.

The typical requirements for the catalysts selection are - binder chemistry, compatibility with the binder system in paint as well as during curing stages, catalyst efficiency, minimal interaction with pigments and other ingredients in the coating formulation. Most of the baking paint systems are based on hydroxyl-functional alkyd, polyester, epoxy, and acrylic resins in combination with amino resins based on melamine, urea, benzoguanamine and glycolurils. In these coating systems, the curing schedule - curing temperature/ time and the reactivity of the amino component are the most important parameter for achieving optimum cross-link density. The reaction of the backbone resin with an amino cross linker can be greatly enhanced by addition of appropriate catalyst. Acid or blocked acid catalysts are used to get acceptable cure rates at 70-80 deg. C or even at ambient temperatures. Proper selection of catalyst can improve cured film hardness, mechanical properties, humidity and corrosion resistance. Acid catalysts can affect and certain impurities can act as a catalyst or interact with catalysts and deactivate them. Catalyst deactivation can also be a function of water content or acid number of the

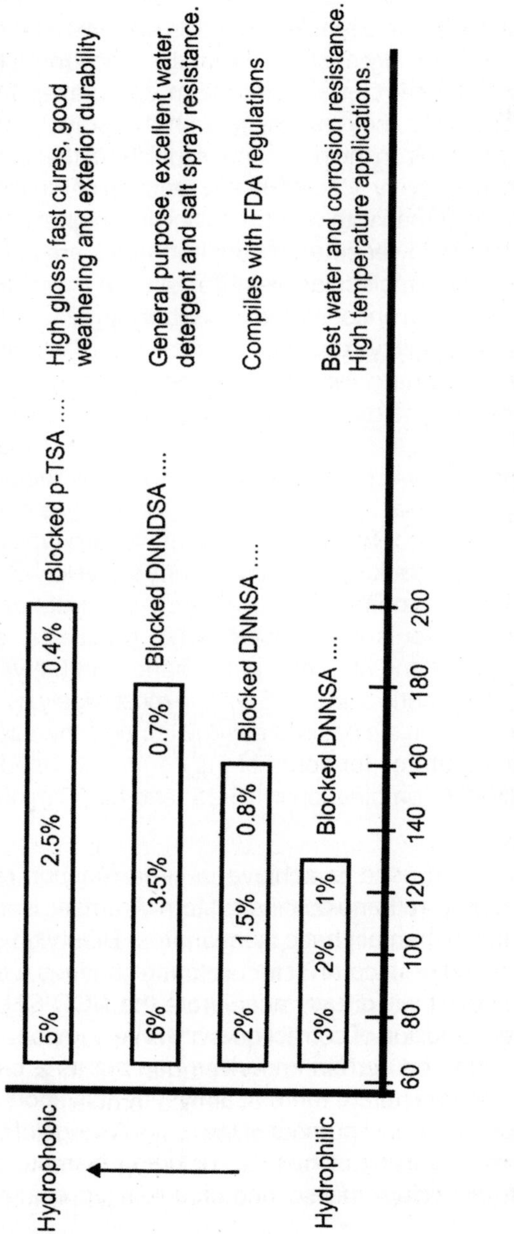

p-TSA-p-Tolune sulfonic acid (40% active). DNNDSA - Dinonylnaphthanelene Disulfonic acid (55% active), DDBSA-Dodecycle Benzene Sulfonic acid (70% active) and DNNSA- Dinonylnaphthelene Sulfonic acid (50% active)

Fig.7.4 Blocked acid catalysts

resin. A range of organotin-free catalysts based on a variety of metals, including bismuth (bismuth carboxylate), aluminum (aluminum chelate) and zirconium (zirconium chelate) have been developed. Lewis acid type catalysts, such as dibutyltin dilaurate, initially associate with the isocyanate to form a more electrophilic reactive site. Certain zirconium complexes follow the insertion catalysis mechanism; they associate with the polyol component and activate the hydroxyl groups. In the presence of moisture, these zirconium catalysts are claimed to selectively accelerate the reaction of the isocyanate with the polyol hydroxyl rather than with water resulting in a higher percentage of urethane linkages. Usually lower catalyst concentrations are used in low-solids systems that use high molecular-weight resins. As with any other catalyst, certain problems can be encountered with dibutyltin dilaurate catalyst also such as balance of stability-reactivity, hydrolysis of ester groups, catalysis of the water/isocyanate reaction and environmental concerns (presence of organo tin) etc. The resins in low solid systems can form films with quite low cross-linking while the excess solvent contributes to maintaining acceptable pot life. High solid/low molecular weight systems require exten. sive cross linking and molecular weight increase to achieve cured films package stability in some cases. Blocked acid catalysts are typically used in systems that require longer package stability as they show lower reactivity with the binder system at storage temperatures. Acid catalysts are main)y based on sulfonic and disulfonic acids (methylene, p-toluene, dodecyle benzene and dinonylnaphthalene etc.) and phosphoric acid (alkyl/aryl acid phosphates, hexafluorophosphoric acid). PTSA is the most widely used strong acid. The use level is decided on the basis of desired curing schedule. Typical use levels and cure temperatures for some of the commonly used blocked catalysts in an alkydlHMMM combination in 75/25 ratio for 30 minutes cure is shown in *Fig.* 7.4.

Metal catalysts are often used to achieve desired reaction rates and cured film properties in a polyurethane coating system. Aromatic isocyanates are generally more reactive than aliphatic isocyanates. Dibutyltin difaurate is considered to be the workhorse catalyst for urethane coatings. Low levels of dibutyltin dilaurate catalyst will greatly accelerate the NCO/OH reaction rate; hence measurement/addition of correct quantity is very important. Often resins, additives, pigments and certain impurities can act as a catalyst or interact with catalysts and deactivate them. Catalyst deactivation can also be a function of water content or acid number of the resin. A range of organotin free catalysts based on a variety of metals, including bismuth (bismuth carboxylate), aluminium (aluminium chelate) and zirconium (zirconium chelate) have been developed. Lewis acid type catalysts such as dibutyltin, dilaurate, initially associate with the isocyanate to from a more electrophilic reactive site. Certain zirconium complexes follow the insertion catalysis mechanism; they associate with the polyol component and activate the hydroxyl groups. In the presence of moisture, these zirconium catalysts are claimed to selectively accelerate the reaction of the isocyanate with the polyol hydroxyl rather than with water resulting in a higher precentage of urethane linkages. Usually lower catalyst concentrations are used in low solids systems that use high molecular-weight resins. As with any other catalyst, certain problems can be encountered with dibutylin diaurate catalyst also such as balance of stability-reactivity, hydrolysis of ester groups, catalysis of the water/isocynate reaction and environmental concerns (presence of organo tin) etc. The resins low solid systems can form films with quite low cross linking white the excess solvent contributes to maintaining acceptable pot life. High solid/low molecular weight systems require extensive cross linking and molecular weight increase to achieve cured film.

Gloss and cure rate variation are the most frequently encountered problem with catalyzed polyurethane systems. The gloss variation is often related to inconsistent moisture content in the formulation. Moisture can be incorporated into the system with solvents, pigments or the surrounding atmosphere. Gloss can also be affected by the formation of insoluble reaction products (primarily hydrolysis products from the catalyst). In many systems, particularly aqueous systems, the gloss can decrease as the paint is aged after the two components have been combined. Loss of cure on aging can be due to solubility of the catalyst, catalyst deactivation by acid groups, phosphate anions, pigment interaction and hydrolysis. These effects may not be initially evident but can occur over a period of days or weeks after adding the catalyst to the polyol component. Catalyst deactivation can also occur if an excess of acid functional groups present is present. These acid groups can partially or completely displace ligands on the metal complex forming inactive salts. Deactivation of a high acid value system, where zirconium and aluminum catalysts have been used, can be prevented by tertiary amine ego Dimethylethanol amine. The impurities left from the manufacturing process of polyol resins can also accelerate or inhibit the cross linking reaction. In some of the polyether polyol formulations phosphate anions are employed to neutralize the residual catalyst that is added during the resin manufacturing process, these ions can also deactivate systems containing zirconium catalysts. This problem can usually be resolved by adding calcium octoate or zirconium octoate in the formulation. In case of pigmented polyurethane coatings the polyol component can be contaminated by metal impurities from the grinding equipment. Pot life of twocomponent isocyanate systems can be increased without sacrificing cure response by using volatile chelating agents such as 2, 4-pentanedione ($CH_3COCH_2COCH_3$). 2,4pentanedione will complex with the tin compound and inhibit the metal catalyst from accelerating the isocyanate reaction whilst it is in the container, When the coating is applied pentanedione evaporates with the solvent the catalytic activity of the metal will be restored. Polyhydroxy resins that have some secondary hydroxyls say from hydroxy propyl methacrylate (HPMA) will have slower reaction rates as compared to resins made with hydroxy ethylmethacrylate (HEMA) that has primary hydroxyls.

Photo initiators

Radiation cure coatings are reactive, low-viscosity and usually solventfree, coating compositions that can be applied to a substrate by any of the conventional application methods such as spray, roller coating, screen, litho, flexo and even gravure and then polymerized or cured by exposure to a high-energy radiation such as ultraviolet or an electron beam. The UV curing uses high intensity ultra violet light rather than thermal energy. These coatings can be cured by two fundamental mechanisms; free radical and cationic polymerization. Free radical mechanism is more common and the curing reaction takes place through unsaturation sites on oligomers and monomers. The basic reaction consists of a chain reaction with four primary steps, Free radical formulation, Initiation, Propagation and Termination. In case of free radical cure the photo initiator, on exposure to UV light, decomposes into free radicals with unpaired electrons and starts a chain reaction with monomers. During the propagation step the active sites react with more monomer molecules to build up desired molecular weight. This reaction stops by termination. UV light alone will not usually have sufficient energy to interact with reactive groups in a molecule and generate free radicals, hence a photo initiator is used in the formulation, which when exposed to UV of a specific wavelength, absorbs the UV light and produces free radicals in a free radical polymerization system or cations in a cationic system to start the cross linking process leading to virtually instant polymerization. The choice of photo initiator depends on - resin system used in the formulation, radiation source, required speed of curing and the coating film thickness etc. To be effective the absorption band of a photo initiator should overlap the emission spectra of the light source that is between 200 and 450 nm; shorter wavelengths are absorbed by air. The photo initiator should be molecularly distributed in the monomer (should be truly soluble in the coating composition).

There are two general classes of photo initiators - those that undergo direct photo fragmentation on exposure to UV light irradiation and produce active free radical and those that undergo electron transfer followed by proton transfer to generate free radicals. Commercial photo initiators of radical polymerization for unsaturated oligoacrylates, oilgoesters and corresponding co monomers are mainly various benzoil derivatives. Benzoil moiety that absorbs in the UV and UV visible part of the spectrum is the chromophoric group in most of such photo initiators. Senzo phenone is one of the most commonly used photo initiator. *(Fig.* 7.5).

Cationic polymerization is ionic polymerization involving highly reactive positively charged polymeric centers. Generally epoxy resins are used ir'l cationic cure systems as they show superior adhesion even on difficult substrates. Typically aryl sulfonium salts and iodonium salts with a variety of counter ions are used as photo initiators e.g. Mixed aryl sulfonium hexafluoro antimonite and mixed aryl sulfonium hexafluoro phosphate etc. On irradiation with ultraviolet light these photo initiators generate strong acids. The over all curing reaction of cycloaliphatic epoxy and polyol consists of four steps: initiation, propagation, chain transfer, and termination. The initiation step involves two reactions: the formation of super-acid, and the addition of the super-acid to the monomer molecules to produce the chain initiating species and subsequent propagation of successive epoxy molecules. Nucleophiles such as water or alcohol, if present, will lead to both chain transfer or termination reactions. The propagation step of cationic UVcurable coatings occurs after UV-exposure. This phenomenon is called "dark-cure" and represents a significant part of the overall process. Darkcure is due to 'living' cationic species.

Photo fragmentation type photo initiators - alkyl ethers of benzoin, benzil dimethyl ketal, 2- benzyl-2-N, N-dimethylamino-1- (4-morpholinophenyl) butanone, 2,2-diethoxyacetophenone, 2-hydroxy-2-methylphenol-1-propanone, halogenated acetophenone derivatives, acylphosphine oxides and bis-acyl phosphine oxides, sulfonyl chlorides of aromatic compounds and benzimidazoles etc.

Electron transfer type photo initiators - benzophenone, diphenoxy benzophenone, anthraquinone derivatives, fluorenone derivatives, halogenated and amino functional benzophenones, zanthone derivatives, thioxanthone derivatives and camphorquinone etc.

Fig. 7.5 Photo Initiators

Dark cure contributes to improvement in good through cure, adhesion, low shrinkage and high chemical and solvent resistance. The toughness of the overall film can be varied as a function of the molecular weight of the polyol. Cationic cure mechanism is not affected by oxygen inhibition but affected by high ambient humidity, amines and other basic materials and pigments such as Rhoda mines and some times to substrate characteristics. Bases such as amines, urethanes, basic pigments or fillers should not be used. Since water acts as a chain transfer agent it is necessary to control humidity.

Initiators

Initiators are organic compounds that are stable at room temperature and unstable at elevated temperature or in presence of certain catalysts. They produce unstable free radicals on decomposition which are capable to initiate chain polymerization/copolymerization of unsaturated monomers and resin such as unsaturated polyester and acrylic resins. Organic peroxides and hydro peroxides are widely used for this purpose in two component coating compositions whose film formation is based on polymerization of unsaturated resins or their copolymerization with monomers. Methyl ethyl ketone peroxide, benzoyl peroxide, cyclohexane peroxide, cumene peroxide and cumene hydro peroxide are commonly used for curing unsaturated polyester, acrylic and silicone resins and their combinations with unsaturated monomers such as styrene and various acrylates. They are frequently combined with cobalt drier and tertiary amines to accelerate curing and to avoid oxygen inhibition.

Higher the concentration of initiator molecules more active centers are created in the composition due to their decomposition in a unit time. Due to this more number of unsaturated groups are involved in the polymerization process and therefore, the curing rate is simply proportional to the quantity of initiator used. Crystalline initiators such as benzoyl peroxide are normally used as solution in organic solvents and plasticizers.

8

Light Stabilizers

Introduction

POLYMERIC materials, primarily those of an "organic" nature, are susceptible to degradation from high-energy radiations. To a large extent the composition and structure of a polymer matrix determines as to how much ultraviolet radiations the material will absorb and hence its susceptibility to photo-oxidative degradation. These radiations coupled with moisture and various other air pollutants such as acid rain can quickly degrade an unprotected film. Certain polymers contain chromophores as a part of their chemical structure that readily absorb radiations. The presence of extraneous matter such as catalysts, residues from polymer processing, additives and certain other components added during coating manufacture can introduce chromophore groups. Sun emits very strong radiations throughout the ultraviolet region. The ultraviolet region of the electromagnetic spectrum extends from about 100 to 400 nanometers and consists of following regions

Ultraviolet A: 320 to 400 nanometers.

Ultraviolet B: 280 to 320 nanometers.

Ultraviolet C: below 280 nanometers.

Visible light itself is not sufficiently enrergetic to break chemical bonds. Though only a portion of the total energy reaches the earth the ultraviolet radiation from sunlight is the most common initiator of polymeric photo-oxidation reaction. As the wavelength of the radiation decreases, its intensity increases. The initial visual changes caused by ultraviolet radiations are primarily aesthetic such as yellowing, colour change, fading and chalking. Mechanical properties can also change after non homogeneous, photo-oxidative crosslin king on the surface. These may manifest in fine crazing and microfine checking of the surface as the internal stresses builds up and lead to further deterioration such as cracking and delamination as the exposure advances and the film ages. The prominent light induced changes in the film are shown below

AESTHETIC

- Colour change and fading.
- Yellowing.
- Loss of gloss.
- Loss of D.O.I. (Distinctness of Image).
- Chalking.

MECHANICAL

- Embrittlement and change in flexibility.
- Increase in hardness.
- Increase in internal stresses.
- Reduction in elongation.
- Change in abrasion resistance.
- Change in coefficient of friction.

CHEMICAL

- Oxidation
- Increase in wettability.
- Change in cross linking density.
- Change in glass transition temperature.
- Change in surface polarity.

PERFORMANCE

- Cracking, crazing and checking.
- Delamination form substrate or between coats.
- Loss of film thickness.
- Increased transmission through the film.

Degradation mechanism

The degradation of binder in a coating film by ultraviolet light is a multi stage process and involves initiation, propagation and termination steps however, to initiate the degradation process the radiations must first be absorbed by the binder. The polymers that do not absorb ultraviolet radiations in the harmful range are less prone to degradation. Materials such as all aliphatic polyesters, urethanes and acrylics exhibit much greater weathering resistance as compared to aromatic urethanes, epoxies and styrene-butadiene copolymers etc; that have light absorbing chromophores. The chro mophore groups are typified by - C = C - linkage of unsaturated polymers and aromatic groups found in epoxies, phenolics and aromatic urethanes. Materials such as cross linking agents, catalysts, catalyst residues, pigments, fillers, extenders, biocides, flow control agents and some other ingredients pr~sent in the coating composition canabsorb radiations and lead to..degradation. These impurities can radically alter and accelerate the rate of photochemical degradation. Ketones and aldehydes break down in presence of oxygen to form peroxides that lead to rapid degradation. As the chromophoric groups present in the coating film absorb incident radiations the electronic energy of the molecule increases. In this state, the excited molecule may undergo bond cleavage and generate free radicals. These highly reactive species then react with oxygen, producing peroxy free radicals. The peroxy radicals, in turn, attack the binder, abstracting hydrogen atoms from the polymer and forming hydroperoxides along with a new active radical. Hydroperoxides themselves are chromophoric and very unstable. They readily undergo photolysis, breaking down to form alkoxy and hydroxy free radicals. These very active species will themselves abstract hydrogen atoms from the polymer molecule with the formation of still more peroxy radicals. In this way, the degradation process proceeds. Termination may occur as any two free radical species in neighboring chains combine to form crosslinks. The alkoxy radicals formed by the breakdown of the hydroperoxides can also induce cleavage in the polymer chain. The abstraction of hydrogen atoms from the polymer by alkoxy and hydroxyl free radicals may be enhanced or reduced by the chemical structure of adjacent groups on the polymer. Certain functional groups such as amines, ethers, tertiary alkoxy groups, benzene rings, and double bonds usually increase the vulnerability of the hydrogen atom on adjacent methylene groups on the polymer. Wherever possible, these groups should be minimized for maximum ultraviolet resistance. On the other hand, hydrogen is not readily abstracted from methyl groups attached to silicon atoms on the highly oxidation resistant silicone resins. Both aromatic urethanesand epoxies are vulnerable because of the electronegative hetero atom attached to the aromatic ring. These structures are directly responsible for the excessive yellowing of the urethane and the high chalking tendency of the epoxy resins when exposed to sunlight.

In case of oxidizing systems such as oils, alkyds, phenolic oleo resinous varnishes, epoxy esters. and oil-modified urethanes the initial degradation attack involves oxidation at energized unsaturated bonds in the oil chain.

This oxidation reaction produces peroxides, ketones, and free radicals. These latter species then attack other sites on the molecule, such as glycerol phthalate esters in alkyds and phenolic hydroxyls in oleoresinous varnishes. In many aspects the initial oxidation and crosslinking mechanism is identical to the oxidative film forming process of coatings based on these binders. Driers which are used to accelerate the oxidative cure of these types of coatings will also increase the rate of oxidative degradation in the dry film. In view of this drier loading must be reduced tolevels necessary to obtain optimum drying and maximum ultraviolet resistance. The chemical changes - oxidation, crosslin king, depolymerization, chain scission, and volatilization of short chained terminal fragments are accompanied by typical physical changes such as increase followed by reduction of tensile strength and progressive reduction in elongation at break. These changes are eventually followed by loss of gloss, bronzing, yellowing, checking, cracking, embrittlement, and loss of adhesion. Paint films based on hydroxyl containing acrylics cross linked with melamine resins are subject to degradation involving the melamine resins used for cross linking and the bridge between the cross linker and the acrylic resin. The structure, type and nature of the melamine resin used can have a marked effect on degradation process. Free radical attack on melamine cured acrylic produces hydro peroxides that result in chain scission and generation of carbonyl groups. Similar degradation is noted in case of melamine cured polyesters also, however as a result of photo oxidation that produces ketones and acid groups the chain scission and oxidative crosslinking may occur more readily as compared to acrylics.

The epoxy coatings are known for poor weathering. They yellow; lose gloss. and chalk when used in exterior applications. Virtually all epoxies used as protective coatings are based on the diglycidyl ether of bisphenol - A, which is a highly chromophoric molecule. Additional chromophoric groups may develop due to phenoxy radical formation during chain scission that occurs as a result of the aging process and ultraviolet exposure. Dehydration at the hydroxyl groups generated after an epoxy ring opening will produce unsaturation. This will result in additional sensitivity to free radical attack and oxidation. The changes in weathering resistance due to curing agent may vary from structure to structure in a given chemical family. The polyamide and amid amine curing agents are known to be more weather-resistant than the amines.

Binders based on acrylic monomers whether they are thermoplastic lac quers, latex systems, or thermosetting acrylics are among the most ultraviolet stable coating systems. They are largely transparent to ultraviolet radiations and visual light and for the most part, their degradation is probably initiated by free radical species derived from the radiation induced breakdown. In case of methyl acrylates the photodegradation may occur due to chain scission in either the ester group or the back bone chain. This will generally be associated with cross linking reactions. Such reactions are more likely as temperatures increase. they are less common in polymers based on short chain monomers such as methyl and ethyl methacrylates as compared to polymers based on longer chain monomers such as butyl and amyl methacrylates. Polymers such polyisobutyl methacrylate and polyisoamyl methacrylate contain tertiary hydrogen in the side chains, which makes them more prone to cross linking than polymers based on the short chain acrylics. Copolymerization of monomers is said to result in maximum durability when a balance is achieved between a tendency to undergo chain scission and the tendency to crosslink. The two processes seem to occur simultaneously and their cumulative effect on mechanical properties seems to result from one process canceling out the other.

As with most other polymers, in case of polyurethanes also the reaction pathways and rates are dictated largely by the nature of the monomeric building blocks used in the polymer synthesis. Systems based on acrylic polyols are far more light-resistant as compared to those based on polyesters. However; the presence of certain monomers often used to get specific properties may reduce the performance of even the acrylic systems. Thus styrene often used as a co-monomer in the synthesis of acrylic polyols, is counterproductive to optimum light stability. The additional light induced cross linking in systems containing styrene results in earlier embrittlement/cracking as compared to systems without styrene. Meth acrylate monomer based polyols, on the other hand, are more vulnerable to chain scission. In pure acrylic systems, the principal chromophoric groups are found at the end of the acrylic chains. The presence of these groups depends largely on the type of initiator and polymerization medium used to manufacture the binder resin. Peroxy based initiators are less conducive to good light stability in the finished polymer than are azo based initiators. Aromatic solvents are preferred to ketones as a reaction medium for acrylic polymerization. Both peroxides and ketones favour production of higher levels of hydro peroxide, this increases the photosensitivity of the polymer in the early stages of weathering. Large amounts of hydro peroxide will result in free radical attack on the urethane cross links, eventually leading to chain scission.

Light stabilizers

A range of specially designed organic light stabilizers are used to prevent one or more of the various reactions that are part of the overall photo degradation process. They are categorized in terms of their respective roles as ultraviolet absorbers,' excited state quenchers and hindered amine light stabilizers. Their use may be specific to a particular formulation, but often it is necessary to use combinations of these additives to get optimum results.

Ultraviolet absorbers

Ultraviolet stabilizers are chemical compounds that protect the pigmented and unpigmented coating films from photo degradation. They absorb the ultraviolet light radiations, reducing the amount of ultraviolet light available for absorption by the resin. To be effective, the absorber must take up ultraviolet radiations in the same wavelength region as the binder or other absorptive component of the film. The absorber should not absorb visible light as this may lead to production of colour bodies within the film. The presence of catalyst residue in the polymer or other chromophores coming from polymerization and processing can also initiate degradation process due to light absorption. Incorporation of ultraviolet absorbers in the formulation can reduce this degradation. In practice sufficiently high concentration of ultraviolet absorbers and adequate film thickness are required before enough absorption can take place to effectively retard photo degradation. Ultraviolet absorbers function by absorbing ultraviolet light and converting the ultraviolet energy into molecular vibrations. This absorption mechanism follows Beer - Lambert law; hence the path length of travel (coating thickness) and additive concentration are important parameters to obtain desired protection. The Beer-Lambert law is the linear relationship between absorbance and concentration of an absorbing species and is usually written as:

$\log 1/1_0 = -\varepsilon.\text{l}.C$ or $\log I/I_0 = e^{-\varepsilon.\text{l}.c.}$

Where

1_0 = Light energy of monochromatic incident source

I = Light energy transmitted through the material

l = optical length (m) c = concentration of absorbing species (mole/liter)

ε = Molar extinction coefficient of absorbing species (liter/mole-m)

Log 1/lo is also called Absorbance or optical density

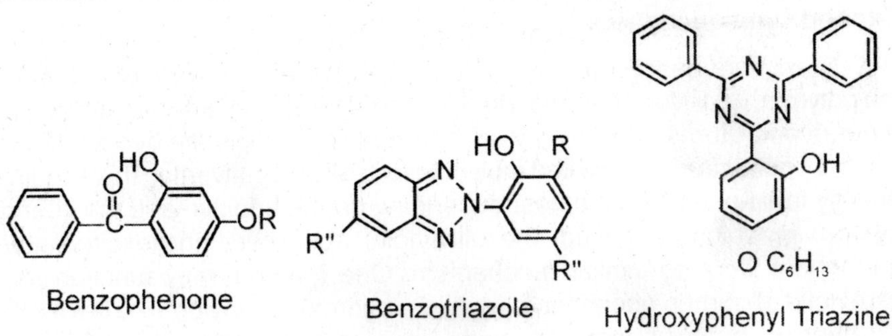

Fig. 8.1

Early Ultraviolet absorbers were the aryl salicylates; these were followed by hydroxy benzophenones and 2 - hydrcxy-phenylbenzotriazole derivatives. Presently benzophenone, benzotriazol~ and hydroxyphenyl triazine (Fig. 8.1) are the most commonly used ultraviolet absorbers.

Different substituents in the benzotriazole group affect various properties such as - physical condition, maximum absorption levels, volatility, polarity, and compatibility etc. Typical ultraviolet absorption spectra of benzotriazoles show strong absorption in the ultraviolet range between 295 and 400 nm and very low absorption in the visible range above 400 nm. The ultraviolet absorbers convert the energy absorbed from ultraviolet light into heat, via a mechanism called keto-enol tautomerism. This heat is dissipated through the substrate. Due to this cyclic mechanism the ultraviolet absorber can remain active during the lifetime of the coating (Fig. 8.2).

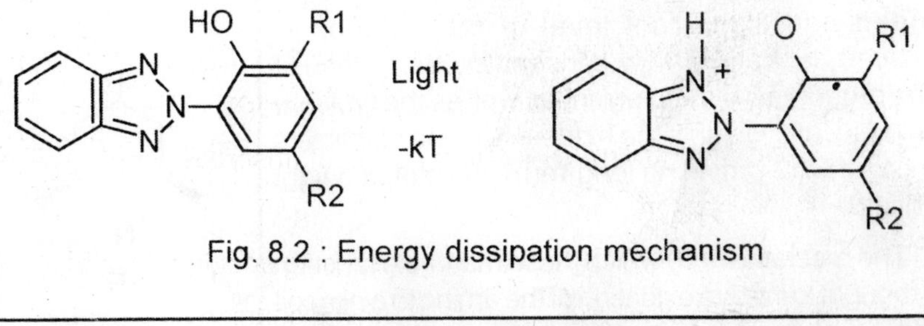

Fig. 8.2 : Energy dissipation mechanism

Excited state quenchers

Quenchers deactivate the photo chemically excited moiety present in the polymer, additives or as impurities etc; before the free radical is generated. A quencher returns the moiety to a non-excited ground state by transferring excess energy from the excited molecule to itself and converting this acquired energy into heat. Many a times, depending on the additive and the coating system in which it is used, the ultraviolet absorbers and excited state quenchers work by similar mechanism. One material may function as a ultraviolet absorber, quencher, or both. 2 - hydroxy-phenylbenzotriazole and 2 - hydroxy-benzophenones provide ultraviolet absorption as well as the quenching of photo-excited chromophores in several types of polymers. Nickel chelates are said to be very effective at quenching the excited state of carbonyl groups that are often found as impurities in many coatings based on polymers otherwise insensitive to ultraviolet radiations.

Hindered amine light stabilizers

The hindered amine light stabilizers reduce degradation of polymers by scavenging any free radicals that are formed by exposure to ultraviolet radiations. They are generally used in conjunction with ultraviolet absorbers. The ultraviolet absorbers alone are not able to absorb all the ultraviolet radiations that fall on the coating surface hence some of the ultra violet light will penetrate the hindered amine light stabilizers are incorporated in the coating to prevent degradation due to this.

The hindered amine light stabilizers do not absorb ultraviolet radiations instead they slow down the photo chemically initiated degradation reaction in a way similar to functioning of antioxidants. They are regenerated rather than consumed during the stabilization process. One significant advantage of the hindered amine light stabilizers is that no specific layer thickness or concentration limit is needed and significant level of stabilization is achieved at relatively low concentrations. Because of the regenerative mechanism as well as the typically high molecular weights the hindered amine stabilizers are capable of providing long-term thermal and light stability.

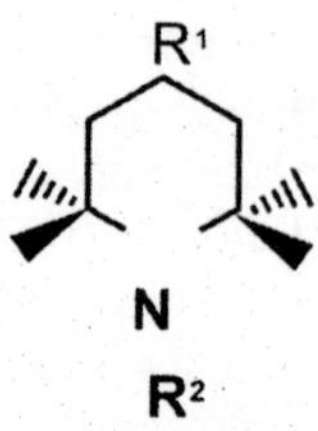

Fig. 8.3

The mechanism by which these materials function are thought to involve oxidation of the amine to a nitroxyl radical. The radical can in turn react with the hydroxy and alkoxy radicals derived from the initial degradation

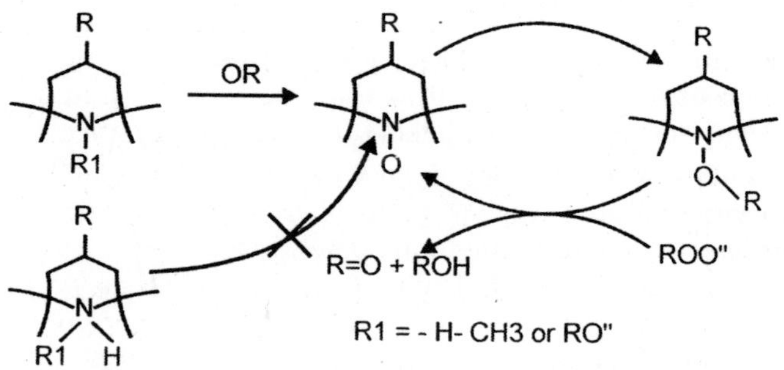

Fig. 8.4

of the light-sensitive binder or impurity etc. This reaction produces an amine ether capable of terminating peroxy radicals formed in the auto-oxidation process during these reactions the nitroxy radical is regenerated. This radical can take up new free radicals to form ether. This cycle continues virtually without end (Fig. 8.4).

Commercially, hindered amines are available in a wide range of structures and molecular weights that determine their solubility, volatility, and effectiveness in a broad spectrum of polymers. Hindered amines are typically based on 2, 2, 6, 6 - tetra methyl piperidine and are extremely efficient stabilizers against light induced degradation of most polymers. Bis (1,2,2,6,6, - penta methyl - 4 - piperidinyl) sebacate is a typical hindered amine light stab~lizer. HALS with different molecular weights and volatilities are available. The lower molecular weight additives are liquid; the higher molecular weight materials are solid. As anti-oxidants, HALS additives may retard the cure of oxidizing coatings that use metal carboxylate drier systems. As amines, HALS may also slow the rate of cure of acid-catalyzed systems. Cure retardation may be more extreme with fully alkylated melamines and the glycoluril crosslinkers. This is especially true where strong catalysts such as paratoluene sulfonic acid, didodecyl naphthalene disulfonic acid, and dinonyl naphthalene disulfonic acid are used. Alternatively, an amineblocked catalyst may be used instead of the straight acid. The reaction products of the same stabilizers (especially those based on secondary amines) with acid catalysts may also lead to seeding. While selecting a hindered amine light stabilizer care must be taken regarding the basicity of the compound. A basic hindered amine light stabilizer can react with acid catalyst, metal catalysts and even some organic pigments and retard the curing rate or affect the stability. For this type of coating systems non-basic hindered amines such as hindered amino ether can be used.

A new class of non-interacting hindered amine light stabilizers has a reactive hydroxyl functionality that enables them to co-condense with melamine and isocyanate cross-linkers. As a result they are claimed to have improved compatibility and migration resistance in many coatings systems. This new class of products offers many advantages; they react quickly, are non-interacting, and exhibit outstanding solubility, thermal permanence and light stabilizing effectiveness. Their migration resistance property makes them attractive for use in wet-on-wet-on-wet applications, where the primer, base coat and topcoat are layered one on top of the other and then cured with a single bake.

The absorbers should be soluble in the resin of the clear film and should be as non-fugitive as possible. They should not absorb visible light as this can lead to production of colour bodies within the film. Even a slow depletion of absorbers from the film can be harmful. Since the effectiveness of the ultraviolet absorber will depend on the path length of the light transmission through the film the usage levels are decided considering the anticipated film thickness. Thick films have greater opportunity to absorb a given quantum of ultraviulet radiations than thin films. The thin film will therefore require a higher degree of absorber. Loss of absorber can occur by migration, volatilization, leaching, or chemical changes that deplete the dosage overtime. In single coat systems on metal, the stabilizers appear to migrate toward the surface of the film. There, they can leave the film by evaporation or dissipation into the environment. In multi-coat systems, migration appears to favor motion across the intercoat interface. The migrations of UV absorbers from the lower coats or in some cases onto substrates such as plastic have been noted. Migration is accelerated in cases where solvents from a newly applied finish can penetrate and swell the existing primer or base coat. High-temperature curing can result in higher migration and necessitate an increase in the dosage of ultraviolet absorber in the finish coat. Migration is slower in the later stages of cure and afterwards during service life of the coating. Exudation of the ultraviolet absorber either shortly after application or during the later service can also occur, especially where very high loadings are required. Most ultraviolet absorbers have good compatibility with most of the polymers however poor compatibility may result in increased exudation. For example, some of the solid benzotriazoles have poor compatibility with nitrocellulose. This poor compatibility may increase exudation rate. The absorber may also be slowly leached from the film by water or other environmental agents, slowly volatilize from the coating, or may deteriorate chemically by free radical attack. Although most stabilizers have low vapour pressure, loss by volatilization may occur where long service life (such as automotive coatings) is required or where high bake temperatures (such as epoxy powder coatings) are required during curing. Higher molecular weight stabilizers with still lower vapour pressures will be less susceptible. These may be oligomeric materials or have functional groups such as hydroxyl groups that can react in isocyanate and melamine cured systems, reducing the possibilities of loss by solvent leaching and of migration effects induced by high temperature.

Pigments are, in fact, often the primary defense against the ultraviolet degradation of coating films. Light absorbing pigments can preferentially absorb ultraviolet light and shield the light sensitive substrates. They convert the absorbed energy of the radiation in to heat instead of chemical energy and act as a preferential sink. Light impermeable metallic flakes such as leafing aluminum and stainless steel flakes reflect almost all of the ultraviolet at the surface of the film. Not all pigments are good ultraviolet absorbers. In fact, the extenders as a group are quite transparent to ultraviolet as well as to visual light and hence afford little ultraviolet protection. Most colored inorganic pigments, such as red iron oxide and chromium green oxide are excellent ultraviolet absorbers. Transparent iron oxides that are not opaque to visible light have effective ultraviolet absorption properties. Sub-micron size titanium dioxide (TiO) particles exhibit good ultraviolet absorption and Zinc oxide strongly absorbs radiation in the near ultraviolet region between about 360 and 400 nm. Carbon black is one of the most effective ultraviolet absorber. The' carbon black has phenolic and aromatic species that are generated from burning of its petroleum-based raw material stock, attaches on to the surface. These species absorb. ultraviolet very well and are, in some circumstances, anti-oxidants. Antioxidants terminate the highly activeiree radicals generated by ultraviolet light before they can attack the polymer.

9

Foam Control Additives

Introduction

Foam can be described as a thermodynamic unstable two-phase system or alternatively a dispersion of gaseous substance in a solid or liquid medium. This definition covers both rigid and elastic foams. In most cases foam consists of a relatively large volume of aggregates of air/gas bubbles usually entrapped in a small volume of liquid or solid material. Although this is desirable in certain industries such as flotation process for ore extraction, processing of foam articles etc, in most industries the foam needs to be suppressed. More recently applications have been discussed where foam formation is intentionally induced. One of these is using foam formation as a pigment substitute, where in the occluded air forms solid foam in the cured coating film, the difference in the refractive indices of paint and air makes the film opaque even in absence or substantially less quantity of pigments. Another example is pigmentation of paint with hollow spheres with reduced quantity of titanium dioxide. Air has low specific gravity and is an excellent insulator of heat. In intumescent fire retardant coatings, foam is generated by the flame induced degradation of specific components present in the cured coating. The high flame temperatures volatilize the designated compounds and create an insulating layer of charred foam between the flame and the substrate that needs protection.

A characteristic feature of liquid foam encountered in coating industry is the extremely large interface between a gas; usually air, and the liquid coating that separates the gas bubbles from one another like a lamella. If an air stream is introduced in a liquid, the bubbles so produced will assume a spherical shape and migrate to the surface because their density is lower than that of the liquid. For energy reasons every liquid tries to keep its surface (interface with gas), as small as possible and it cannot exist without any foam stabilizing effect. According to Stake's law

$$V \sim r2/\eta$$

where V is the rate of ascend, r is the radius of the bubble and rt is the viscosity of the liquid.

This shows that the rate at which the bubble rises depends on the radius of the bubble and the viscosity of the liquid. Once the bubble has reached the surface, liquid flows downwards out of the thin film of liquid (lamella) surrounding the gas bubble. As the lamella becomes thinner and thinner and reduces below 10 nm it ruptures and the foam bubble bursts. This process is called drainage effect. This process however, takes place only for pure liquids and therefore pure liquids do not foam. For formation of stable foam the liquid phase must contain foam-stabilizing substances. These foam-stabilizing substances are generally surfactants/surface active agents that contain hydrophobic and hydrophilic groups. Because of this structure they align themselves at the liquid/gas inter-phase, thereby reduce surface tension and provide conditions for formation of stable foam.

Foam formation

Foaming may occur at various stages of paint manufacturing and/or application. Foam can be incorporated during pumping, mixing, dissolving and dispersion stages of manufacturing; airbubbles can also form as a result of chemical reaction during curing (typically urethanes), hydrogen gas generation in metallic (aluminum/ zinc) pigmented systems or can be captured during high-speed application of paint such as curtain coating, coil coating, as well as application of high viscosity paints by air less spray and during application on porous substrate (wood and concrete etc). All coating formulations whether water based, solvent based or solvent free contain a variety of surface active substances of widely varying chemistry that makes any coating system susceptible to foaming. These may be emulsifiers, pigment dispersants, wetting agents, some of the rheology modifying additives and other additives and/or surface-active agents etc. All surfactants are composed of a polar segment, which is hydrophilic and a hydrocarbon chain segment, which is hydrophobic. In case of simple anionic surfactant conventionally used in water based systems, the surfactant molecule will be adsorbed at the air/ water interface with its polar group, such as carboxyl group, in the aqueous phase and the hydrocarbon chain in the air. This results in distribution of negatively charged carboxyl groups in the water inside the bubble lamella. A positive charge accumulates next to it, forming a double layer. This leads to an electrolytic repulsion. This repulsion prevents the bubble wall from thinning by opposing the approach of the two charged surfaces. The presence of surfactant functions in a number of ways to retard the drainage of water in the lamella and thereby stabilize the foam. Further more, water being a dipole, is attracted and bound to the carboxyl groups, and is prevented from draining that is necessary for rupture of a bubble. Immediately after it is formed, foam still contains relatively large quantity of liquid and is therefore called a wet foam. The foam bubbles are spherical at this stage and have little influence on each other. As the bubble rises the liquid drains out ofthe lamellae (also termed as drainage effect), the lamellae becomes thinner and the bubbles shift closer to each other and deform into a multi su(faced structure known as polyhedral or dry foam.

High levels of foam may occur during grinding process and defoamers are often used as an additive in the grinding paste. Due to the activity of some surfactants at the air/water interface foam is often created and stabilized in premixing and milling chambers of dispersion equipment. Foam slows down the dispersion process. Foaming can occur during application process also. For example, air entrapment can occur in air less spray, curtain coating carries entrapped foam air continuously around in the system. Spray application in relatively low humidity or high temperature conditions can increase the tendency of foam entrapment. This can however be somewhat controlled by optimizing the settings on the spray gun and by adjusting the viscosity/solids of the formulation. Latex paints are stabilized with surfactants that easily generate foam under agitation. In some systems densely packed micro foamcan form on the surface and remain there even after the film has cured. In 19wer solid films that dry quickly the viscosity of coating increases quickly. As this is happening the small micro bubbles are still rising to the surface but at a slower rate. If the rising bubbles penetrate the surface the restricted flow may lead to pinhole formation. At times the rising bubbles cannot penetrate the surface, but they push a very thin viscous layer of the coating to the surface. This layer will remain on the surface after curing and show as spherical blisters.

The life cycle of foam can be described in three steps - formation, stabilization and destruction. In coating industry foam formation can be observed both during the manufacturing process where vigorous mechanical agitation is used that entraps air in the coating formulation and during application of a coating (spraying, roller or brushing) where high shear stress of up to 10000 sec; favour incorporation of air bubbles. Foam can lead to crater formation and other undesirable surface defects in the cured film. In general the foam encountered in coating industry can be described as microfoam or macrofoam. In both cases air is distributed in the coating material, the main difference being the location of the distributed air. In case of macrofoam the air forms foam bubbles at the surface of the coating material where as microfoam is formed by air entrapment within the coating material. After drying microfoam gives very small pinholes that are seen as indentations where as macrofoam produces large and perfectly round blisters having raised edges. As the micro bubbles rise to the air/liquid interface they coalesce to form large bubbles. At the air interface the bubbles burst due to the effect of defoamer. Foam is stabilized by several mechanisms

(a) When the foam lamella is thinner as compared to those formed by pure liquids ,this slows the draining out of liquid and thereby stabilizes the foam.

(b) When ionic surfactant molecules present on the surface create electrostatic repulsion - this prevents coalescing of bubbles, and

(c) When the foam lamella exhibits higher elasticity due to a stretching effect caused by the presence of surfactant molecules. This effect is explained by Gibbs elasticity theory. According to this theory additional stabilizing effect is provided by the elasticity of the foam lamella. When the lamella is stretched there is a reduction in the concentration of surface-active substance at the interface, since the same volume of liquid displays a larger interface area to which the surfactant molecules must orient. However lower concentration of surfactant leads to higher surface tension. In its effort to achieve the lowest possible surface tension, the stretched film contracts and remains intact, thus the foam is stabilized (*Figure* 9.1).

The current theory on foam formation makes a distinction between antifoam and deaerators/air release additives, but it is not possible to make a clear differentiation between the two. Antifoam agents are employed to prevent foam formation and/ or to rapidly destroy foam that has already been formed. They work by direct destruction of macro foam at the air interface by preventing air entrapment. These are mainly . used in paint production, particularly for water-based pain:t:s. Deaerator/air release additives function during and after film application by increasing the rising speed of the foam bubble to the surface. They also draw together the neighboring bubbles within the coating, which join together and form larger bubbles. By Stokes law large bubbles rise faster to the surface. Antifoams are also active against micro foam to a certain degree. Antifoams are low surface tension liquids with following properties. They are insoluble in the liquid to be defoamed. They

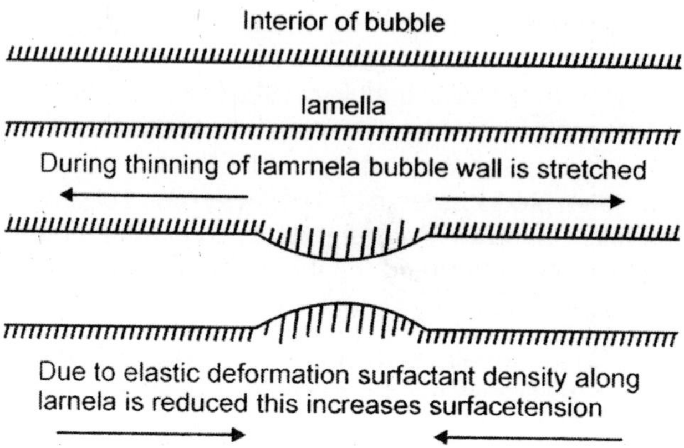

Fig. 9.1

have positive spreading coefficient and entering coefficient. Have desired solubility and compatibility with the coating composition.

The antifoaming agent should have a desired balance of compatibility. If it is too compatible it will migrate in to the coating binder system rather than into the foam lamella and loose defoaming properties. On the other hand too incompatible antifoam may lead to defects such as craters or haze on the film. Due to this reason a specific antifoaming additive cannot be effective in a variety of formulations that are based on different chemistries.

To be effective antifoams should possess very low solubility, high molecular mobility and they should be very easily dispersible into fine droplets in the foaming material. Furthermore they should be able to enter the bubble spontaneously and spread across it causing the bubble to break. To achieve this they must have a positive entering coefficient (E) and spreading coefficient (S) that can be expressed as follows

$$S = \gamma F - \gamma EF - \gamma E$$

$$S = \gamma F - \gamma EF - \gamma E$$

Where γF - is the surface tension of the foaming liquid, yEF - is the interfacial tension between liquid and the antifoam and yE is the surface tension of the antifoam additive.

Since $E - S = 2\ \gamma EF$, positive value of the spreading coefficient is more critical for the defoaming efficiency than the entering coefficient. Normally individual defoamers do not exhibit spreading coefficient greater than zero,

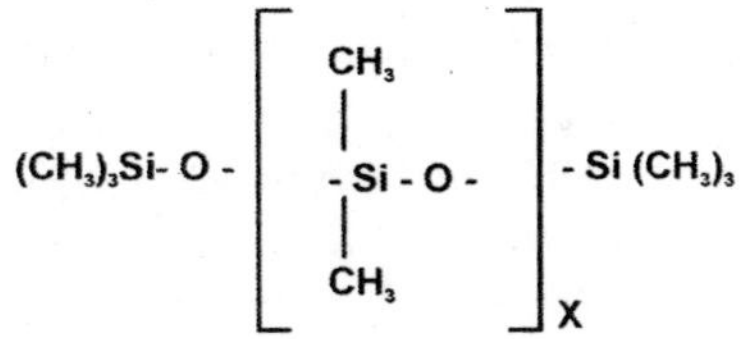

The value of x is approximately 180 repeating units

Fig. 9.2

but this can be achieved by blending with specific surfactants and/or co-solvents.

Composition of foam control additives

The foam control additives are quite often proprietary blends of various ingredients such as mineral oils, organic solids, fatty oils, alcohols, esters, surface active compounds and silica derivatives. They are usually made up of three major components - primary/carrier fluid, surface-active agents and active substances. The carrier fluid serves as a defoamer by itself as well as acts as a carrier to transfer the active substances uniformly to the site of their function. This liquid must be insoluble in water, have a low surface tension and a high interfacial tension in the foaming medium. Some of the carrier fluids are silicone oils, mineral oils, vegetable oils, glycols, glycol ethers, alcohols and selected organic liquids among others. The surface active agent controls the emulsification of active substance in the foaming medium and concentrates the defoaming activity at the air/medium interface by bringing the hydrophobic active matter in contact with the stabilized foam structure. They determine the rate of entering into the lamella and spreading rate at the liquid/air interface. For the obvious reasons the surfaceactive agent must not be a foam stabilizer by itself. The choice of active substances depends on the nature of the medium to be defoamed. In general they include fatty acids, coupling agents, esters, amides and other hydrophobic materials, waxes, hydrophobic fumed silica or organic urea derivatives etc.

The defoamers can be classified in Following groups

- Mineral oil based defoamers.
- Silicone based defoamers and
- Silicone free defoamers.

Mineral oil defoamers are primarily used in flat or semiglossy emulsion paints. They are not used in full gloss emulsion paints and water based industrial coating formulations, as they are likely to cause gloss reduction and other surface defects. They are not suitable for solvent-based systems also due to their relatively low spreading efficiency. Mineral oil defoamers usually consist of approximately 80% mineral oil carrier and 5% emulsifier, remaining 15% is made up with hydrophobic particles. Usually aliphatic mineral oil is proffered as a carrier as aromatic oils may lead to undesirable film yellowing. The emulsifier used in this type of defoamers should disperse the hydrophobic particles in the carrier oil as well as help in incorporation of the defoamer in the coating composition. Nonylphenol ethoxylates are usually used as emulsifiers in this range of defoamers.

Silicone based defoamers contain poly dimethyl siloxane as active ingredient *Fig.* 9.2 Poly dimethyl siloxanes of progressively increasing molecular weight/chain length are used as flow and leveling agents, surface slip additives, antifoams and hammer finish additive *Fig.* 9.3. The suitability of a particular polysiloxane as a foam control additive depends on its compatibility and solubility with the coating, as only selectively incompatible and insoluble polysiloxanes are effective as a defoamer. Low molecular weight poly dimethyl siloxanes that are used as surface control additive are more compatible. They usually lead to foam stabilization rather than function as a defoamer. High molecular weight siloxanes that are used in hammer finish are completely incompatible that makes them unsuitable for antifoam application. The compatibility of the silicone antifoam additives can be controlled in the desired range by introduction of organic side chains in the silicone backbone. Replacement of the second methyl group by polyether/ alkyl or acrylic side chains increases hydrophilic segment and therefore increases compatibility in polar coating systems. The siloxane block contributes to interfacial activity whereas the nature of polyether block determines compatibility. Modification of polysiloxanes with perfluro organic compounds results in very low surface tension that confers strong defoaming properties. Emulsified hydrophobic silicone oils are used as defoamers in aqueous systems.

The silicone oil, alcohol and mineral oil based defoamers are many a times combined with fine hydrophobic fumed silica, hydrophobic particles based on aliphatic polyureas and ethylene bis-stearamide wax etc., to improve dispersibility and their performance as a defoamer. Typically the hydrophobe particles are dispersed into the carrier fluid (silicone oil/mineral oil) with small amount of selected emulsifiers. This emulsifier also facilitates the

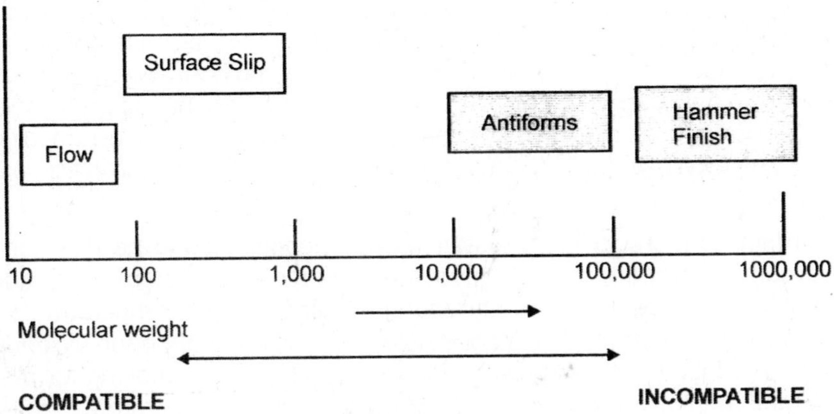

Fig. 9.3 Poly Dimethylsiloxanes

incorporation of the hydrophobe into the foaming paint, but it should not contribute to foam stabilization. The finely divided hydrophobe particles are carried into the lamella by the carrier fluid, where they absorb the surfactant and starve the lamella of its electrostatic field. Thus the foam is destabilized. These particles also displace water themselves as well as repel water due to their hydrophobic nature. The optimum particle size of fumed silica particles ranges from 0.01 - 10 microns. At times, on prolonged standing, these particles may settle in the defoamer liquid that may necessitate homogenization prior to use.

The silicone free defoamer range consists of organic phosphates, polyacrylates, polyalkaline glycols, fatty acid esters and imides etc. Certain solvents having high water immiscibility such as odor less minerai spirit, pine oil, dibutyl phthalate and octyl alcohol show defoaming properties of their own in water based formulations, but none of them is as effective as a formulated defoamer.

As mentioned earlier deaerators/air release additives function by increasing the velocity at which the air bubble rises to the surface of a liquid coating. Small air bubbles/ micro bubbles rise slowly and some times (high viscosity systems) may not rise at all. Deaerators are usually non-polar compounds with specific incompatibility in the liquid coating. This leads to the concentration of the deaeration additive in the air bubble at the liquid/air interface. The airbubbles are thus covered with a nonpolar layer of deaerator. When two such bubbles come together they coalesce to form a larger bubble. This increases the velocity of rise to the surface and consequently release of air from the coating system. Air release additives are based on a variety of chemical substances such as - poly dimethylsiloxanes, alkyl/-aryl modified poly dimethylsiloxanes fluorinated silicone oils, polyethers and polyacrylates etc.

Foam control agents are system/formula dependent and the selection of appropriate antifoam additive is governed by the nature of foaming liquid, foaming tendency, the solubility and concentration, pH, temperature and viscosity of the system. The laboratory evaluation is usually done by adding various defoamers to a known volume of paint sample, shaking for a set time and then measuring the height of the foam that is generated.

Inappropriate selection of defoamer can lead to gloss reduction, inferior intercoat adhesion, crater formation and haziness in clear coats.

10

Additives for Powder Coatings

Introduction

COATING powders are finely divided particles of organic polymers that generally contain pigments, extenders and additives. The concept of applying an organic polymer in powder form dates back to 1950s. These powders were essentially based on thermoplastic resins and flame-sprayed on metallic substrates. All the components used In the manufacture of the coating powders are solids and the simplest way to process is to physically blend solid resins, hardeners. pigments and other materials and grind them to {i suitable particle size powder. However this material will stili be considerably heterogenous. Other early methods to produce powder coatings were hot-melt compounding on a heated twin-roller millor a heated sigma mixer followed by dry grinding. These methods could give marginal Improvement but had low output; additionally the sigma mixers needed extensive cleanup after each batch. The next step was blending of ingredients, extrusion followed by milling/ sieving to produce a powder with narrow particle size range. A typical coating powder formulation contains following ingredients

Binder (resin+ curing agent)	-50-65%
Pigments and fillers	- 25-50%
Additives	-3-5%

The finished powder Is a ready to use product. The nature of production process does not allow adjustment of colour or modification of the composition as done in case of liquid coatings; however the surface properties or the curing behavior of the finished powder can be modified to a limited extent by post blending special additives. In view of this limitation following parameters are taken Into account while formulating a coating powder.

- Physical, chemical and mechanical properties of the finished coating film.
- Colour and surface appearance - gloss and texture.
- Physical and chemical properties of the substrate to be coated.
- Curing schedule.
- Parameters of the application installatlon, and
- Shape of the object to be coated.

The basic properties of a coating powder are predominantly dependent on the binder system. The binder in this case Is a combination of resln(s) and curing agent. Currently following binder chemistries are used In powder formulations.

- **Pure epoxy** - Majority of pure epoxy powders are based a type 2 or type 3 blsphenol - A epoxy resins (epoxy equivalent in the range 680 to 750). Dicyandiamlde (DICY) Is most commonly used as curing agent.

- **Epoxy/polyester hybrid** - These are commonly based on 50:50, 60:40, and 70:30 combinations of carboxyl polyesters and type 2 or type 3 blsphenol - A epoxy resin. The acid number of carboxyl polyester determines polyester/epoxy ratio. Imldazoles are used as curlng agents for hybrid powders.
- **Polyester/ urethane** - These are also called polyurethane systems and are based on hydroxyl polyesters and blocked Iso phorone dllsocyanate (IPDI) with 80:20 to 84:16 ratios. The hydroxyl number of polyester determines the polyes ter/blocked IPDI ratio. IPDI is generally blocked by E - caprolactone, or triazole.
- **Polyester/triglycldal iso-cyanurate (TGIC)** - These systems are based on carboxyl polyester and TGIC with a 93:7 resin: curing agent ratio. The acid number of polyester determines the polyester/TGICratio. Toxicity tests conducted by some laboratories have determined TGIC to be slightly mutagenic to rats and mice hence Polyester/ TGIC combination is being replaced by Polyester/ß-hydroxyalkylamide (HAA) chemistry.
- **Polyester/glycourlls** - Polyester/ Glycouril systems are based on hydroxyl polyesters with a 96:4 resin: curing agent ratio. Glycourils are amino-plast type curing agents. They have a tendency to considerably lower the Tg of formulated powder; hence polyesters of higher Tg generally above 60 deg. Care selected for use with glycourils.
- **Epoxy/acrylic hybrid** - Epoxy/Carboxyl acrylic hybrids are formulated

in the same way as polyester/epoxy systems. They show much higher chemical resistance and somewhat improved exterior durability as compared to regular epoxy/polyester hybrids.

- **Glycldyl methacrylate (GMA) acrylic** - GMA acrylic resins are formulated with acrylic resins having acrylic and epoxy dual functionality. They are used in free radical UV cured powder formulations.
- **UV curable epoxy** - These are based on UV curable epoxy resins system and use cationic cure initiators.

Curing agents

The curing agents used in coating powders should be free flowing solid materials with sufficiently high melting point (so as not to block). They should have low reactivity powder processing temperature but high reactivity at curing temperature. The final coating properties depend on the choice of curing agent used in the formulation. Various curing agents used for epoxy, polyester and acrylic chemistries are shown below

Resin Chemistry	Curing Agent
Epoxy resins	
Epoxy-amine reaction	Dicyanidiamide (DICY), Substituted Dicyandiamide, Substituted Imidazola and Cyclic Amidine salts
Epoxy-phenolic reaction	Solid phenolic resins.
Epoxy-anhydride reaction	Used mainly as adducts.
Epoxy-carboxyl reaction	Carboxyl polyesters.
Polyester resins	
Carboxyl functional	Triglycidal iso-cyanurate (TGIC), b-hydroxylkylamide (HAA)
Hydroxyl functional	Blocked IPDI
Acrylic resins	
Hydroxyl functional	Decane and Dodecane di caroxylic acids.

Additives

In addition to matting, flow control; degassing agents and texturing agents other classes of additives such as tribocharging additives, antioxidants, and light stabilizers etc are frequently used in powder coatings.

Low gloss or matt finishes can be achieved by creating incompatibility during the curing process by way of two curing reactions that occur at different rates. This can be, done in two ways - by blending two powders of different reactivity or by use of special additives/curing agents during powder manufacturing process. Polycarboxylic salts of cyclic amidines and SMA resins (styrene maleic anhydride polymers and their partial esters) are commonly used for the latter purpose. SMA resins can be added during extrusion, grinding or dry blended. The matting effect of SMA resins is a function of the reactivity of the system leading to formation of micro texture on the surface that causes scattering of reflected light and makes the surface less glossy.

- Flow control additives are incorporated in the formulation to prevent cratering and to improve the appearance of the cured film. Most flow additives are low molecular weight acrylic polymers such as Ethyl acrylate-2-ethylhexyl acrylate copolymer; they act by altering the surface tension of the coating system during the melt stage. Flow control agents are high viscosity liquids and are supplied as a master batch in one of the main resins or absorbed on finely divided silica. Both types are added in the premixing stage.

- Degassing additives solvate the resin-curing agent mix during the liquid phase of the cure cycle and thus assist the evaporation of volatile products trapped at the surface boundary between the powder film and air and prevent pin holing. Some of them are surfactant like while others are wax like, but both affect surface tension to promote degassing. The most widely used degassing and anti pin holing additive is benzoin.

- Texturing agents are basically anti flow or anti leveling additives and can give a finish ranging from a coarse wrinkle finish, fine wrinkle finish to a smooth texture. Most of them act by creating micro craters or by placing non-melting particles such as PTFE or high melting polypropylene in the film. Another method of preparing a texture finish is post blending a surfactant in the powder. During the baking cycle, surfactant particles distributed throughout the curing film melt and create areas of low surface tension. Molten coating material flows away from these areas and accumulates in the space between them to form a texture finish.

- Presently coating powders are applied by two techniques - corona process and tribo process. In corona charging process the sprayed powder particles are forced through an electrical field to become negatively charged. The charged particles are attracted and deposited on the grounded metallic object. In case of tribo charging process the particles are forced through a Teflon tube and are charged positively by friction with the tube walls. Depending on their composition, tribo-static powders require additives to improve their chargeability. Certain hindered amine light stabilizers (HALS) improve tribo-charging in addition to their light stabilization properties.

- Heat and processing stabilizers are commonly included in powder coating formulations. They should be thermally stable and not volatilize during high temperature powder extrusion and curing processes. Various classes of antioxidants have different thermal stabilization mechanisms. High-molecularweight hindered-phenolic type antioxidants are effective as oxygen radical scavenger, but are prone to darkening in the presence of combustion gases like NOx, which can be found in gas oven exhaust. The phosphite type antioxidants act as a decomposer of hydro peroxides and provide protection during high temperature processing and/or curing cycles. Th~ new lactone antioxidant functions as a carbon or oxygen scavenger and inhibits auto oxidation.

- High resistance against UV degradation is necessary in all exterior applications. This is achieved through a combination of UV absorbers and Hindered Amine Light Stabilizers (HALS). Among the UV absorbers benzotriazole ultraviolet absorbers such as hydroxyphenyl benzotriazole and 2-(2Hbenzotriazol-2-yl)-4,6-EL V(1-methyl-1-phenylethyl)phenol are used most commonly. These UV absorbers show a synergistic effect when used in combination with hindered amine light stabilizers. The UV absorbers preferentially absorb the harmful UV radiation and, through a process known as "keto-enol" tautomerism, harmlessly dissipate it as heat. This process is regenerative. UV absorbers are incorporated at 1 - 3% level based on binder solids. The number of free radicals formed due to photo-oxidation can be minimized by the use of UV absorbers, but they cannot absorb 100% of the incident UV radiations. Hindered Amine Light Stabilizers (HALS) can effectively control the radicals that are still formed or that may be present in the coating raw materials or formed through heat.

  HALS "defuses" free radicals by way of several mechanisms, an important one being the termination of the high-energy peroxy radicals. Similar to UV absorbers hindered amine light stabilizers are also regenerative.

- The best performing anticorrosive, hexavalent chromate, is regarded as carcinogenic and is being replaced gradually. New organic corrosion inhibitors such as 1(Benzothiazol-2-ylthio) succinic acid have been developed for Use in protective coatings for metal surfaces.

Catalysts

The curing temperature is mainly dependent on the resin system used. The typical cure temperature of various systems is, Epoxy - 115 to 150°C, Epoxy/Polyester hybrid - 135 to 150°C, pure polyester - around 135°C and Polyurethane - around 150°C. The cure time varies between 10 to 30 minutes. The curing rate of powder coatings is dependent on several factors that include resins, cross linkers, catalysts, manufacturing method and the formulation. Catalysts and accelerators are added to the powder formulations to accelerate cure rate, to lower cure temperature or to improve physical and chemical properties. They are generally predispersed in the main resin in the form of a master batch to have a good dispersion in the finished composition. Some of the commonly used catalysts are -

UV curable powders

Curing of powder coatings with UV light instead of thermal energy has opened up new possibilities for powder coatings in a wider range of applications. The fast curing cycles and low temperature requirements of UV powders offer multiple benefits, including time, space and energy savings, high productivity and the possibility to coat on heat-sensitive substrates.

During application the UV powder coating is generally melted by exposure to IR light. This process takes only 1-2 minutes with a required final temperature of 90-140°C, depending on the selected UV powder system. Because of this relatively low temperature it is possible to cure heat sensitive substrates such as Medium Density Fiberboard (MDF), plastic, glass and pre-assembled parts that combine metal and heat sensitive materials, with UV powder. UV powder can also be applied on metal, with the main advantage

Resin system	Catalyst
Epoxy/amine, epoxy/phenolic and epoxy/polyester systems	Imidazoles 2-methyl imidazole, 2-propyl imidazole
Epoxy/amine, and epoxy/ polyester system.	Cyclic Amidines. (Also used as a curing agent)
Epoxy/polyester system.	Alkyl (Aryl ammonium halides. (most common is tetra butyl ammonium bromide)
Polyester/blocked IPDI system	Stannous octoate, Dibutyl in dilaurate, Di butyl tin oxide and Dibutyl tin acetate.
Polyester, acrylic /isocrynate Systems	Zinc alkyl/aryl thiocrbamates.

that the metal does not have to be heated to such high temperatures, or for as much time as required with thermal curing powder coatings. Cross-linking of the melted UV powder occurs by exposure to UV light for few seconds that gives a total curin~ time of 1-3 minutes

UV curable powder coatings are based on resins developed specifically for this purpose. The curing of complex shapeslhidden parts can be a problem and there might be limitations in the choice of shades that can be cured with UV light. For instance, it is known that yellow pigments can interfere with efficient curing. Resins containing (meth) acrylic double bonds are used in UV powder systems. In addition to the usual additives used in powder coating system these coatings contain a photoinitiator for initiating cross-linking process. No separate hardener is required. *a* -hydroxyacetophenone photoinitiators give best results in clear coatings and among them (1-hydroxycyclohexyl) phenyl methanone and 2-hydroxy-1- (4-(2hydroxyethoxy)-phenyl)-2-methyl-1propanone (HHPMP) are most popular. The latter offers the advantage of very low volatility at extrusion and film formation temperature of UV curable powders. The low volatility is attributed to a polar hydroxyethoxy substituent in the para position of the benzoyl group. More recently introduced bis-acyl-phosphinoxide (BAPO) photoinitiators are useful in powder coatings containing light absorbing components. They absorb light at the borderline between the visible and the near UV spectral range and form radical species that are transparent to this radiation. This property enables them to cure very opaque white and coloured coatings as well as clear coatings containing UV absorbers that function as light stabilizer. Among this range bis (2,4, 6-tri methyl be nzoyl) -phenyl phosphineoxide (BTPPO) gives best over all performance. Combinations of UV absorbers and hindered amine light stabilizers are incorporated in clear powder coating formulations to provide exterior durability. The concept of light stabilization appears to contradict the criteria for a UV cure system as the UV absorber may compete with the photo initiator for the available light and reduce the amount of initiating radicals that are formed, while the activated HALS compound, which is a radical in nature, may scavenge photoinitiator and growing chain radicals. This filtering effect of UV absorber can be partly overcome by a careful selection of UV absorber and photoinitiator combination. A suitable UV absorber should exhibit a steep transmission cutoff at a wavelength just long enough to provide UV protection in the required range. Newly developed hydroxyphenyl-s-triazines meet this requirement. BAPO initiators such as BTPPO overcome the filtration effect of hydroxyphenyl-—triazines and can cure a coating eontaining UV stabilizers without sig,nificant loss of reactivity.

11

Calcium Aluminium Silicate and Magnesium Aluminium Silicate

Introduction

Hiding by spacing of TiO_2 pigment particles

The concept of spacing is basically rather easy: If it happens, that two or more titanium dioxide pigment particles are not completely dispersed but still have contacts with each other, it can be calculated that the theoretical maximum of white pigment efficiency is not reached. As the scattering volumes are larger than the particles themselves the volumes will overlap, influence each other and are all together decreased therefore.

If it is possible to place an inert filler particle just between these agglomerated titanium dioxide particles, the pigments are pushed apart so that the scattering volumes are free again. Scattering power recovers to 100% of the theoretical maximum value. Due to the increased efficiency of the pigment the titanium dioxide loading can be reduced respectively.

Calcium aluminum silicate ($CaAl_2Sip_8$) and magnesium aluminum silicate ($MgAl_2Si_2O_8$) have potential to replace rutile or anatase TiO_2 partially for solvent based and water based paints respectively. It has been reported that calcium aluminum silicate liberate calcium ions in water based coatings resulting in gradual increase in viscosity of the paint hence it is used only for solvent based paints [4] Both the extenders are synthesized from naturally occurring mineral "Actinolite".

Present work

In the present work enamels, primers were prepared using calcium aluminum Silicate with different percent replacement (5% to 25%) of titanium dioxide. These two coatings of low and high PVC respectively enabled the study of different PVC on performance properties of coatings. Similarly magnesium aluminum silicate was used in water based coating systems namely premium interior emulsion paint and acrylic washable distemper. The effect on properties of water-based paint was studied by replacement ranging from 1 % to 18% of Rutile TiO_2 with magnesium aluminum silicate. The coatings prepared were studied with coating based entirely on titanium dioxide and their properties evaluated.

Experimental

Materials

Both calcium aluminum silicate and magnesium aluminum silicate provide better whiteness, opacity and coverage with significant cost reduction. As compared to other functional fillers both calcium and magnesium aluminum silicate have better wet hiding properties. Their use does not reduce any gloss in the final products due to its lower oil absorption values. These are the prime reasons why it is considered as a better additive to titanium dioxide. The detailed properties of both these fillers are shown in the *Table:* 11.1

Their properties were compared with convential fillers and extenders like Calcined Clay, Calcium Carbonate, Kaolin, Talcum, Barytes and Zeolite and are shown in *Table:* 11.2.

Structural and morphological study:

The shape of the functional fillers is plate like needle structure. It is used for giving "spacing effect" between two TiO_2 particles. The particle size of TiO_2 pigment is 0.2 microns. Thus spacing effect enables to form aggregates betweenthe two TiO_2 particles.

Figure 11.1 and Figure 11.2 show particle shape of calcium aluminium silicate and magnesium aluminium silicate functional fillers.

The raw material used for this study are long oil (P) soya alkyd (60%), TiO_2 rutile RC - 822, calcium aluminum silicate, various wetting and dispersing agent, metallic driers, mineral turpentine oil (MTO), various fillers and extenders for the solvent based coatings. Similarly pure acrylic emulsion, styrene acrylic emulsion, vinyl emulsion, Ti02 rutile RC - 822, magnesium aluminum silicate, wet ground mica, talc, calcite and various additives for the water based coatings.

The alkyd resin was procured from Mis. Macro Polymers Ltd., Ahmedabad, titanium dioxide #rom KMML Ltd., Kerala, calcium aluminum silicate, magnesium aluminum silicate and various extenders, additives, solvènts and

Table 11.1 : Physical properties of calcium aluminium silicate and magnesium aluminium silicate

Properties	Calcium aluminium silicate	Magnesium aluminium silicate
Chemical Name	CaAl2Si2O8	MgAl2Si2O8
Colour	White	White
Apperance	Fine Powder	Fine Powder
Averge Particle Size	2 Microns	10 Microns
Particle size Distribution (<97%)	6 Microns	25 Microns
Refractive Index	1.75-1.9	1.75-1.9
Screen Residue on 325 mesh	<0.01%	0.01%
Specific Gravity (By Pycnometer Method)	2.4	2.1-2.4
pH (10% Suspension in Water)	7-8	7-8
Whitenss (Against Mgo Standard)	96	99
Bulk Density (ml/gm: gm/ml) (Tapped)	1.29:0. 77	3.99:0. 42
Loose Density (gm/ml)	0.51	0.51
Oil Adsorption Value (gm/100 gm of Pigment) (By Spetula Rub-out method)	21-24	35-39
Bulking Value (lb/gal : gal/lb)	19.992:0 .052	20.07 : 0.049
Hegman Grinding	7+	7+
Moisture @ 105°C	<0.1%	<0.1%

driers from Mis. Aromax Corporation, Ahmedabad. All acrylics and vinyl emulsion from Mis. Rohm & Haas Company.

Methods for preparing different paint compositions

The enamels and primers were prepared in laboratory bead mill and high speed disk disperser. The mill base was ascertained by Daniel flow poinf technique and pigment was grinded for enamel and primer to a Hegman scale of rand 5+ respectively. The white synthetic enamel is prepared by using the formula as shown in *Table:* 11.3 with different % replacement of Ti02 rutile RC 822 ranging from 1% to 10% by alcium aluminum silicate.

The interior emulsion paints and acrylic washable distempers were prepared in high speed disk disperser. The pigment was grinded to a Hegman scale of 5^+. The magnesium aluminum silicate is suitable for the water based system. The premium gloss interior emulsion paint is made using different replacement with magnesium aluminum silicate ranging from 1% to 15% of Ti02 Rutile RC - 822, and 5% to 25% of TiO_2 anatase for acrylic distemper.

Table: 11.2: Comparative physical properties of the Functional Fillers.

Extenders	**Chemical formula**	**Particle size, mean, microns,**	**Specific gravity**	**Oil absorption**	**Bulking value (Gall 100lb)**	**Whiteness Index**	**Refractive index**
Calcium Aluminum Silicate	CaAl2Si2Os	2.0	2.4	21 - 24	5.2	96	1.75 - 1.9
Magnesium Aluminum Silicate	MgAl2Sips	6.0	2.1 - 2.4	35 - 39	4.9	99	1.75 - 1.9
Calcined Clay		2-3	2.6	55 - 75	4.6	90 - 92	1.47
Calcium Carbonate	CaC03	0.05 - 1	2.65 - 2.9	20 - 45	4.4 - 4.5	96 - 98	1.5 - 1.68
Kaolin Clays	AlP3' 2Si02.2HP	2.00	2.58 - 2.65	24 - 60	4.4 - 4.6	80 - 90	1.56 - 1 .58
Talc	3MgO.4Si02.HP	2 - 45	2.7 - 2.85	23 - 52	4.2 - 4.6		1.54 - 1.59
Barytes	BaSO 4	1.5 - 4	3.8 - 4.5	6 - 18	2.7 - 2.8	70 - 98	1.61 - 1.64
Zeolites	9Nap.67Si02.12A203	0.015-0.060	1.9-2.3	90-180	-	92-96	1.46-1.55

Table 11.3 : Composition of synthetic enamel with various replacement of calcium aluminium silicate

Ingredients	100 TIO_2	1% CAS	2% CAS	3% CAS	4% CAS	5% CAS	6% CAS	7% CAS	8% CAS	9% CAS	1 0% CAS
TiO_2 Rutile RC - 822	21.00	20.79	20.58	20.37	20.16	19.95	19.74	19.53	19.32	19.11	18.90
Calcium Aluminum Silicate	—	0.21	0.42	0.63	0.84	1.05	1.26	1.47	1.68	1.89	2.1
Soya Lecithin	0.20	0.20	0.20	0.20	0.20	0.20	0.20	0.20	0.20	0.20	0.20
Zinc Naphthenate (6%)	0.30	0.30	0.30	0.30	0.30	0.30	0.30	0.30	0.30	0.30	0.30
Long Oil Soya (P) Alkyd (60%)	12.0	12.0	12.0	12.0	12.0	12.0	12.0	12.0	12.0	12.0	12.0
MTO	7.0	7.0	7.0	7.0	7.0	7.0	7.0	7.0	7.0	7.0	7.0
Long Oil Soya (P) Alkyd (60%)	3.00	3.00	3.00	3.00	3.00	3.00	3.00	3.00	3.00	3.00	3.00
MTO	2.00	2.00	2.00	2.00	2.00	2.00	2.00	2.00	2.00	2.00	2.00
Long Oil Soya (P) Alkyd (60%)	49.00	49.00	49.00	49.00	49.00	49.00	49.00	49.00	49.00	49.00	49.00
Pb Octate (18%)	1.20	1.20	1.20	1.20	1.20	1.20	1.20	1.20	1.20	1.20	1.20
Co Octate (6%)	0.30	0.30	0.30	0.30	0.30	0.30	0.30	0.30	0.30	0.30	0.30
Mn Octate (6%)	0.30	0.30	0.30	0.30	0.30	0.30	0.30	0.30	0.30	0.30	0.30
MEK Oxime	0.20	0.20	0.20	0.20	0.20	0.20	0.20	0.20	0.20	0.20	0.20
MTO	3.30	3.30	3.30	3.30	3.30	3.30	3.30	3.30	3.30	3.30	3.30
TOTAL	**100.00**	**100.00**	**100.00**	**100.00**	**100.00**	**100.00**	**100.00**	**100.00**	**100.00**	**100.00**	**100.00**

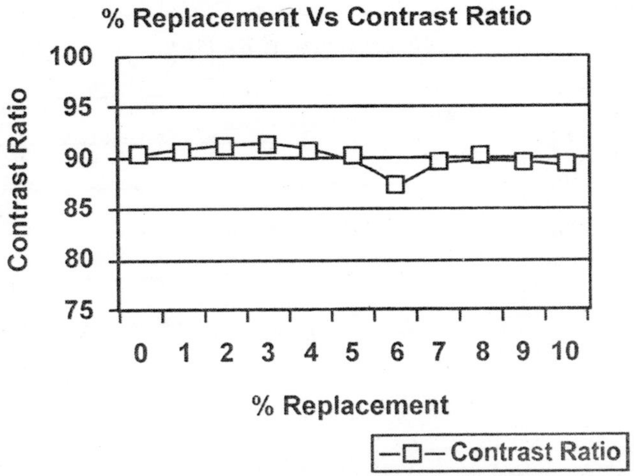

Fig. 11.3 : Effect on contrast ratio by replacement of TiO_2 with calcium aluminium silicate

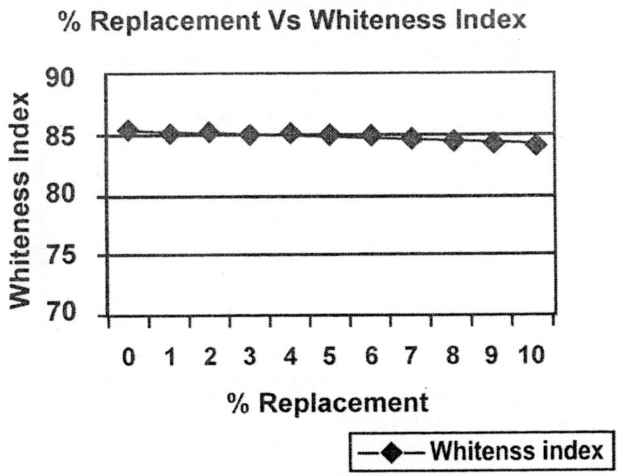

Fig. 11.4 : Effect of whiteness index by replacement of TiO_2 with calcium aluminium silicate

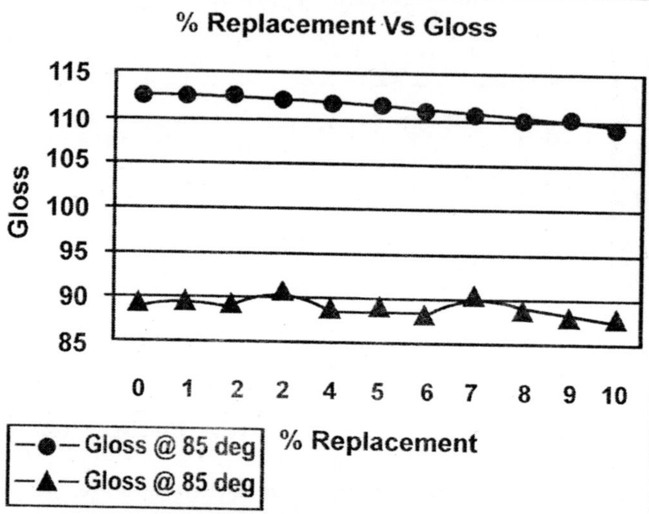

Fig. 11.5 : Effect on gloss by replacement of TiO_2 with calcium aluminium silicate

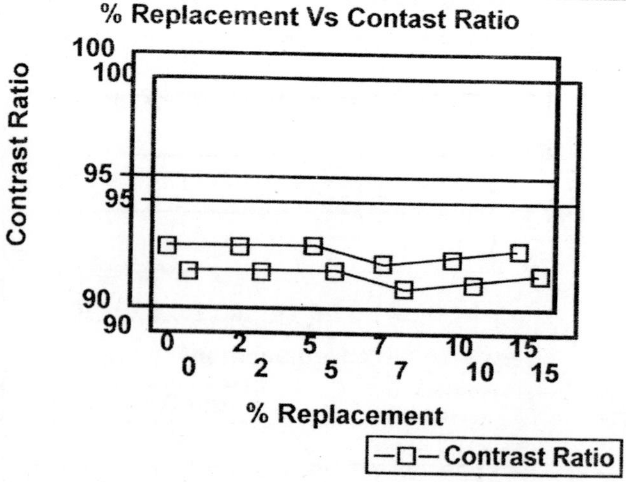

Fig. 11.6 : Effect on contrast ratio by % replacement of TiO_2 with magnesium aluminium silicate

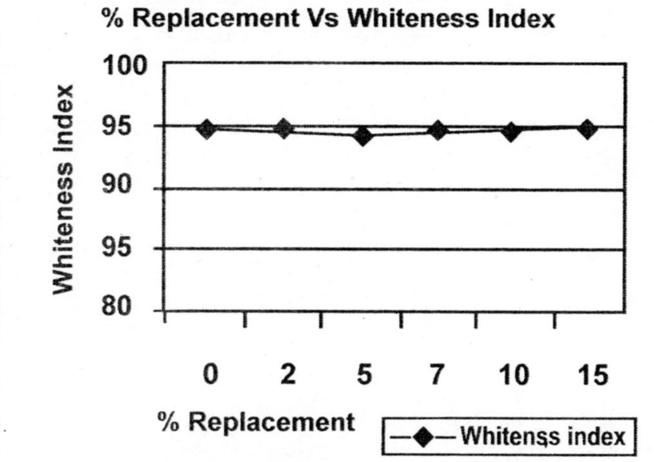

Fig. 11.7 : Effect of whiteness index by % replacement of TiO_2 with magnesium aluminium silicate

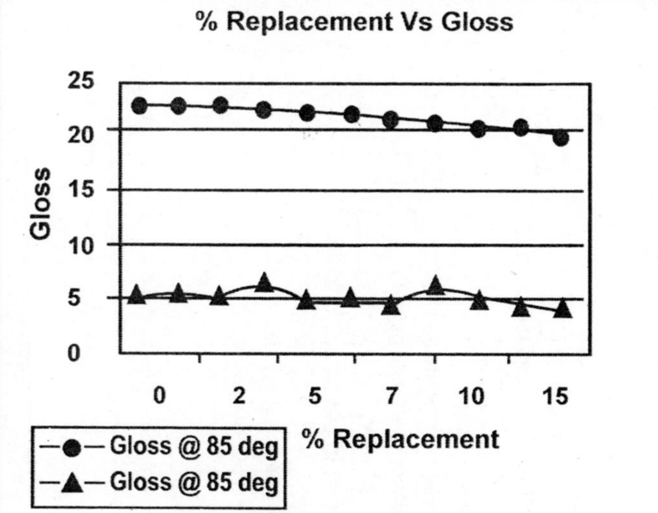

Fig. 11.8 : Effect on gloss by replacement of TiO2 with calcium aluminium silicate

Table 11.4 : Composition of high gloss premium interior emulsion paint with various replacement of magnesium aluminium silicate

Ingredients	100% TiO_2	2% MAS	5% MAS	7% MAS	10% MAS	15% MAS
Soft Water	21.00	21.00	21.00	21.00	21.00	21.00
SHMP	0.20	0.20	0.20	0.20	0.20	0.20
SPCP	0.40	0.40	0.40	0.40	0.40	0.40
Anionic Dispersing Agent (Lutron 850)	0.70	0.70	0.70	0.70	0.70	0.70
Non Ionic Dispersing Agent (Hyoxide AAO)	0.40	0.40	0.40	0.40	0.40	0.40
Deformer	0.20	0.20	0.20	0.20	0.20	0.20
Hydroxyl Ethyl Cellulose	0.50	0.50	0.50	0.50	0.50	0.50
In-Can Preservative (Kathone LXE)	0.20	0.20	0.20	0.20	0.20	0.20
Dry Film Preservative (Rocima 363)	0.70	0.70	0.70	0.70	0.70	0.70
Ammonia (28% W/V)	0.20	0.20	0.20	0.20	0.20	0.20
Mono Ethylene Glycol	2.20	2.20	2.20	0.2.20	2.20	2.20
TiO_2 Rutile RC -822	18.00	17.64	17.10	16.64	16.20	15.30
Magnesium Aluminium Silicate	--	0.36	0.90	1.26	1.80	2.70
Calcined China Clay	5.00	5.00	5.00	5.00	5.00	5.00
Talc 5 um	9.00	9.00	9.00	9.00	9.00	9.00
Calcite 5 um	5.00	5.00	5.00	5.00	5.00	5.00
Pure Acrylic Emulsion (50%) Primal AC-261	35.00	35.00	35.00	35.00	35.00	35.00
Deformer	0.10	0.10	0.10	0.10	0.10	0.10
Ammonia	0.20	0.20	0.20	0.20	0.20	0.20
Pine Oil	1.00	1.00	1.00	1.00	1.00	1.00
Total	**100.00**	**100.00**	**100.00**	**100.00**	**100.00**	**100.00**

All the ingredients are in Parts by Weight (PBW)

Table 11.5 : Composition Acrylic washable distemper with various replacement of magnesium aluminium silicate

Ingredients	100% TiO_2	5% MAS	10% MAS	15% MAS	20% MAS	25% MAS
Sowt Water	29.00	29.00	29.00	29.00	29.00	29.00
SHMP	0.10	0.10	0.10	0.10	0.10	0.10
SPCP	0.10	0.10	0.10	0.10	0.10	0.10
Anionic Dispersing Agent (Lutron 850)	0.40	0.40	0.40	0.40	0.40	0.40
Non Ionic Dispersing Agenty (Hyoxide AAO)	0.40	0.40	0.40	0.40	0.40	0.40
Deformer	0.20	0.20	0.20	0.20	0.20	0.20
Hydroxyl Ethyl Cellulose	0.50	0.50	0.50	0.50	0.50	0.50
Ammonia	0.20	0.20	0.20	0.20	0.20	0.20
Di Ethylene Glcol	0.30	0.30	0.30	0.30	0.30	0.30
TiO2 Antase	3.00	2.85	2.70	2.55	2.40	2.25
Magnesium Aluminium Silicate	--	0.15	0.30	0.45	0.60	0.75
Calcined China Clay	10.00	10.00	10.00	10.00	10.00	10.00
Talcum 20 um	23.00	23.00	23.00	23.00	23.00	23.00
Calcite 20 um	24.00	24.00	24.00	24.00	24.00	24.00
Styrene Acrylic Emulsion (Primal AS -398)	8.00	8.00	8.00	8.00	8.00	8.00
Deformer	0.10	0.10	1.10	0.10	0.10	0.10
Ammonia	0.20	0.20	0.20	0.20	0.20	0.20
Pine Oil	0.50	0.50	0.50	0.50	0.50	0.50
Total	**100.00**	**100.00**	**100.00**	**100.00**	**100.00**	**100.00**

Al the ingredients are in Parts by Weight (PBW

PERFORMANCE DATA OF SYNTHETIC ENAMEL

Table 11.6 : Properties of Synthetic Enamel

Tests	100% TiO_2	1% CAS	%2% CAS	3% CAS	4% CAS	5% CAS
Colour	White	White	White	White	White	White
PVC	11.00	11.08	11.15	11.22	11.30	11.37
Total Resin Percentage	38.4	38.4	38.4	38.4	38.4	38.4
Skinning	Nil	Nil	Nil	Nil	Nil	Nil
Settling	Nil	Nil	Nil	Nil	Nil	Nil
Flocculation	Not Observed	Not Obserted	Not Observed	Not Observed	Not Observed	Not Observed
Viscocity in BF_4@30°C	103	102	103	104	103	104
Viscocity in BF_4@30o°C (After 96 Hrs. @ 60°C)	115	111	113	111	113	114
% Increase in Viscocity	11.65	8.88	9.70	6.73	9.70	9.61
Weight /Liter, Kg	1.105	1.105	1.103	1.106	1.104	1.105
Finish of Dispersion on (Hegmann Gauge)	7+	7+	7+	7+	7+	7+
% Non Volatile Matter	58-62	58-62	58-62	58-62	58-62	58-62
1. Surface Dry	1.2-1.3	1.2-1.3	1.2-1.3	1.2-1.3	1.2-1.3	1.2-1.3
2. Tack Free Dry	2.5	2.5	2.5	2.5	2.5	2.5
3. Hard Dry	Overnight	Overnight	Overnight	Overnight	Overnight	Overnight
Adhesion (Cross Cut)	Passes	Passes	Passes	Passes	Passes	Passes
Flexibility, 1/8* Mandrel 96 hrs	Passes	Passes	Passes	Passes	Passes	Passes
Impact, Resistance, 50 lbs inch	Passes	Passes	Passes	Passes	Passes	Passes
Hardness, After 48 Hrs.	Passes	Passes	Passes	Passes	Passes	Passes
Contast Ratio	(CIE)	90.38	90.60	91.05	91.36	90.79
Whiteness Index (CIE)	85.48	85.28	85.30	85.13	85.08	85.00
Gloss @ 20 deg.	77.90	78.10	77.80	79.00	74.70	70.80
Gloss @ 60 deg.	89.30	89.60	89.2	90.60	88.9	88.75
Gloss @ 85 deg.	112.60	112.7	112.6	112.3	111.85	111.52
Colour Strength (Tinting Strength) (Against Standard)	Reference	Lighter Less Greener Less Bluer Brighter	Lighter Less Greener Less Bluer Brighter	Lighter Less Greener Less Bluer Brighter	Lighter More Greener Less Bluer Duller	Lighter More Greener Less Bluer Duller
Ammonia Test (for Yellowing)	Comparable	Comparable	Comparable	Comparable	Comparable	Comparable

PERFORMANCE DATA OF SYNTHETIC ENAMEL

Cont. Table 11.6 : Properties of Synthetic Enamel

Tests	6% CAS	7% CAS	8% CAS	9% CAS	10% CAS
Colour	White	White	White	White	White
PVC	11.44	11.52	11.59	11.66	11.73
Total Resin Percentage	38.4	38.4	38.4	38.4	38.4
Skinning	Nil	Nil	Nil	Nil	Nil
Settling	Nil	Nil	Nil	Nil	Nil
Flocculation	Not Observed	Not Obserted	Not Observed	Not Observed	Not Observed
Viscocity in BF_4@30°C	106	107	107	110	112
Viscocity in BF_4@30o°C (After 96 Hrs. @ 60°C)	115	118	120	124	129
% Increase in Viscocity	8.49	10.28	12.14	12.72	15.17
Weight /Liter, Kg	1.106	1.107	1.107	1.109	1.109
Finish of Dispersion on (Hegmann Gauge)	7+	7+	7+	7+	7+
% Non Volatile Matter	58-62	58-62	58-62	58-62	58-62
1. Surface Dry	1.2-1.3	1.2-1.3	1.2-1.3	1.2-1.3	1.2-1.3
2. Tack Free Dry	2.5	2.5	2.5	2.5	2.5
3. Hard Dry	Overnight	Overnight	Overnight	Overnight	Overnight
Adhesion (Cross Cut)	Passes	Passes	Passes	Passes	Passes
Flexibility, 1/8* Mandrel 96 hrs	Passes	Passes	Passes	Passes	Passes
Impact, Resistance, 50 lbs inch	Passes	Passes	Passes	Passes	Passes
Hardness, After 48 Hrs.	Passes	Passes	Passes	Passes	Passes
Contast Ratio (CIE)	87.39	89.45	90.13	89.51	89.07
Whiteness Index (CIE)	85.48	85.28	85.30	85.13	85.08
Gloss @ 20 deg.	80.70	78.90	71.60	78.00	78.20
Gloss @ 60 deg.	89.30	89.60	89.2	90.60	88.9
Gloss @ 85 deg.	111.05	110.65	109.85	110.00	108.66
Colour Strength (Tinting Strength) (Against Standard)	Reference	Lighter Less Greener Less Bluer Brighter	Lighter Less Greener Less Bluer Brighter	Lighter Less Greener Less Bluer Brighter	Lighter More Greener Less Bluer Duller
Ammonia Test (for Yellowing)	Comparable	Comparable	Comparable	Comparable	Comparable

PERFORMANCE DATA OF PLASTIC EMULSION PAINT

Table 11.7 : Properties of Plastic Emulsion Paints

Ingredients	100% TiO_2	2% MAS	5% MAS	7% MAS	10% MAS	15% MAS
Colour	White	White	White	White	White	White
PVC	40.97	41.11	41.30	41.44	41.64	41.96
Total @ Binder %	17.5	17.5	17.5	17.5	17.5	17.5
Consistency	Free Flow	Free Flow	Free Flow	Free Flow	Free Flow	Free Flow
Brushability	Easy	Easy	Easy	Easy	Easy	Easy
Surface Finish	Smooth	Smooth	Smooth	Smooth	Smooth	Smooth
Thermal Stability (at 60°C for 96 hrs.)	Passes	Passes	Passes	Passes	Passes	Passes
Weight per Liter, Kg	1.381	1.381	1.381	1.383	1.382	1.381
Finish of Dispersion	5+	5+	5+	5+	5+	5+
% Non Volatile Matter	54-58	54-58	54-58	54-58	54-58	54-58
Drying Time (Minute)						
1. Surface Dry	10-12	10-12	10-12	10-12	10-12	10-12
2. Track Free Dry	25-30	25-30	25-30	25-30	25-30	25-30
3. Hard Dry	Overnight	Overnight	Overnight	Overnight	Overnight	Overnight
Contrast Ratio (CIE)	92.23	92.26	92.34	92.64	91.83	92.26
Whitenss Index (CIE)	94.83	95.04	94.53	94.88	94.67	94.88
Gloss @ 20 deg	1.30	1.30	1.40	1.40	1.20	1.30
Gloss @ 60 deg	5.80	5.96	5.76	5.65	5.90	5.60
Gloss @ 85 deg	21.90	21.85	21.85	21.76	21.65	21.00
Colour Strength (Tinting Strength) (Against Standard)	Reference	Lighter Less Greener Less Bluer Brighter	Darker More Greener More Bluer Brighter	Darker More Greener More Bluer Brighter	Darker More Greener More Bluer Brighter	Darker More Greener More Bluer Brighter

PERFORMANCE DATA OF ACRYLIC WASHABLE DISTEMPER

Table 11.8 : Properties of Acrylic Washable Distemper

Ingredients	100% TiO_2	5% MAS	10% MAS	15% MAS	20% MAS	25% MAS
Colour	White	White	White	White	White	White
PVC	74.23	74.26	74.28	74.31	74.33	74.35
Total % Binder %	4	4	4	4	4	4
Consistency	Thick Paste	Thick Paste	Thick Paste	Thick Paste	Thick Paste	Thick Paste
Brushability	Easy	Easy	Easy	Easy	Easy	Easy
Surface Finish	Smooth	Smooth	Smooth	Smooth	Smooth	Smooth
Thermal Stability (At 60° C for 96 hrs.)	Passes	Passes	Passes	Passes	Passes	Passes
Finish of Dispersion	5+	5+	5+	5+	5+	5+
% None Volatile Matter	64-67	64-67	64-67	64-67	64-67	64-67
Drying Time (minute)						
1. Surface Dry	12-15	12-15	12-15	12-15	12-15	12-15
2. Tack Free Dry	30-35	30-35	30-35	30-35	30-35	30-35
3. Hard Dry	Overnght	Overnight	Overnight	Overnight	Overnight	Overnight
Conrast Ratio (CIE)	90.08	90.96	90.41	89.65	89.42	89.11
Whiteness Index (CIE)	76-406	76.263	75.908	75.514	75.756	74.856
Colour Strength		Lighter	Darker	Darker	Darker	Darker
(Tinting Strength)		Less	More	More	More	Less
(Against Standard)	Reference	Greener	Greener	Greener	Greener	Greener
		Less Bluer	More Bluer	More Bluer	More Bluer	More Bluer
		Duller	Brighter	Duller	Brighter	Brighter

Table 11.4 & 5 shows the different formulations with magnesium aluminum silicate for interior plastic paint and distemper respectively.

Characterisation of different properties of paints

Various physical, optical and mechanical properties like contrast ratio, gloss, tinting strength, viscosity, adhesion, hardness, impact resistance, flexibility, % solids etc. of both water based and solvent based paints has been evaluated by standard methods (815 and ASTM)8 The results are given in *Table* 11.6, 7 & 8for synthetic enamel, interior plastic paint and acrylic distemper respectively.

The effect of replacement in the optical properties viz opacity (contrast ratio), whiteness index and gloss are shown in *Figure* 11.3 to *Figure* 8.

Result & discussion

The results of the performance properties shown in the *Table* 11.6 and *Table* 7 for the solvent based and water based coatings reveal the followings.

% Non volatile matter

The non volatile content in enamel, primer, interior emulsion paint and acrylic washable distemper was in perfect agreement with theoretical values.

Viscosity

The viscosity was not affected in the non-aqueous paint based on calcium aluminum silicate and aqueous coatings based in magnesium aluminum silicate, The viscosity was almost stable in the accelerated storage test. There was however a 15% increase in viscosity in enamel having 10% replacement with calcium aluminium silicate.

Finish & grinding

The comparatively large particle size of calcium aluminum silicate and magnesium aluminum silicate did not affect the degree of grinding of pigment in any of the coatings prepared based in them.

Mechanical properties:

The mechanical properties of coatings viz adhesion, flexibility, hardness and impact resistance are affected as PVC in increased, Abnormality in these properties is seen at PVC = CPvc. With the use of these functional fillers no such abnormality in these mechanical properties is seen as PVC is increased.

Opacity

The optical property of vital importance is opacity. This was studied by evaluating contrast ratio (K/S values)10, In calcium aluminum silicate based synthetic enamels it was noticed that it increase with per cent replacement at a certain point then slightly decreases at certain range of PVC value before finally increasing. This slight increase in contrast ratio at 3-5% is attributed to the spacing effect of the TiO_2 pigment particles spaced by calcium aluminum silicate extender particle. Thus we find that 8% to 9% replacement of TiO_2 with calcium aluminium silicate is possible without disturbing the contrast ratio of the paint entirely based on TiO_2

In aqueous paint there is no effect of 10% replacement with magnesium aluminium silicate of TiO_2 on the contrast ratio of paint.

Whiteness index

As revealed by whiteness index both CAS and MAS do not deter whiteness of the paint system when used as replacement of TiO_2 mentioned above.

Gloss

Gloss is not much affected in both aqueous and non aqueous paint when-either of these functional fillers are used as 8% replacement of TiO_2 for Water based paints and 5% replacement of TiO_2 for solvent based paints.

Tinting strength

Tinting strength of the paint system shows that as the % replacement increases the shade will become darker and brighter. So there is a chance of colour pigment saving in the coloured paint in both the system.

12

Paint Stainers

Introduction

THE requirement *of* universal stainers is increasing consistently due to several reasons. The colour matching by computers in colour world has certainly increased the need for more stable highly dispersible universal stainers. Secondly the painters get a fair choice to develop their own shades and formulate paint with white base in their own premises. The present day stainers are based on several synthetic resins like alkyds, acrylics, epoxies and others. The pre'sent work is aimed at developing novel base resin for stainers. Rice bran is abundantly available throughout the world at reasonable cost. The quantity *of* linolenic acid present in rice bran oil is very less so chances *of* yellowing in the final film are reduced. The malenization *of* rice .bran oil give an improved product with higher viscosity, better drying and durability characteristics. The industry is searching for renewable resources rather than petroleum based products. Use *of* vegetable oils in various finished products will to some extent promote an 'Green' ecofriendly environment. The present work on malenization, emulsification and use *of* these products in stainers is a step ahead in these objectives. We are first trying to summarize the essential characteristics *of* ideal stainers.

Characteristics *of* ideal stainers

(a) It should have highly homogenous consistency flow and compatibility with adverse vehicles like oils, alkyds epoxy acrylics and other resins.

(b) It should not adversely affect the physiochemical and film properties *of* the base resins and paints.

(c) It should have light fastness and maximum tinting strength.

(d) The pigments selected should be excellent quality having good oil absorption resistance to chemicals like acids, solvents and alkalies.

(e) The pigment selected should have excellent resistance to atmospheric conditions like rain sunlight and humidity.

(f) The pigment should have good opacity and compatibility with resins.

(g) The pigment should not have any bleeding tendency.

(h) It should be reasonably stable andshould not show separation at least for one year.

(i) It should accept in reasonable quantity organic solvents like xylene, mineral turpentine and solvents like butanol, water and alcohol.

Table 12.1: Synthesis, cooking schedule and analysis of malenized rice bran oil

(A) Synthesis of Malenized Oil.

Ingredients	Wt.
Rice Bran Oil	85.47%
Maleic Anhydride	12.84%
Sodium Bisulphate	0.42
Sodium Bisulphite	1.26

(B) Cooking schedule for Malenized Oil Synthesis.

Time (Hrs)	Temperature in ^{o}C
0	30
2	100
2	150
3	200
4	225
5	225
6	220
7	210
8	200
9	180
10	150

(C) Analysis of Raw and Malenized Rice Bran Oil.		
Property	Commercial Rice Bran Oil	Malenized Rice Bran Oil
Refractive index	1.472	-
Specific Gravity	0.92	-
Acid Value	4.81	74.62
Sap. Value	178.27	306.18
Iodine Value	104.06	84.62
Viscocity by Ford Cup No. 4 at 30°C	30	154.00

Malenized oils were the first resins used for electrodeposition 1. They are used for making water thinnable coatings 2. The synthesis of malenized oil is simple easily controllable and economically viable proposition.

Experimental

The commercial rice bran oil was thoroughly analysed for its characteristic constants and then it was converted to malenized oil in the following experimental set up.

The reactor

The preparation of malenized oil was carried out in a glass reactor. The reactor consists of two parts. A lower part of the reactor is a round bottom vessel with wide mouth, the upper part of the reactor is its lid having four necks with standard joints. A motor driven stirrer was inserted in the reactor through the central neck while another neck was used for thermometer. A condenser was fitted with the reactor through third neck. The fourth neck is used for introducing chemicals in the reactor. An electrical heating mantle having special control of temperature ±2°C has been used for heating. A regulator controls the speed of the stirrer. The reaction vessel and its lid were tided together with the help of clamps. The ratio of ingredients, cooking schedule order of addition and analysis of raw and malenized rice bran oil is given in *Table* 12.1.

Preparation of emulsion

A malenized oil emulsion has been prepared in which water-soluble and oil soluble ingredients are mixed separately and brought to a temperature of 80°c. The water phase was added slowly with constant stirring in a about 20 minutes. The stirring was continued for one hour. The organic solvents were added in last ten minutes. The emulsion was stored in a brown bottle and sealed properly. The analysis and compositions of emulsion is given in *Table* 12.2.

Preparation of stainers

Premixing: in this process a part of the pigment and resin are taken in a premixing and mixed thoroughly. It is expected that the binder must cover the pigment particles completely and a part of proper dispersion take place in this stage of premixing. The premixing operation is essential in order to avoid problems like flocculation, floatation, agglomeration etc. The mixer is rotated for around 1 - 2 hours. Then the material is subjected to grinding operations. The composition of stainers using toludene red, Phthalocynine blue and middle chrome is given in *Table* 12.3.

Table 12.2: Composition and analysis of emulsion of malenized rice bran oil

Ingredients	% By Weight
Malenized Rice Bran Oil	50.00
Poly Vinyl Alcohol	1.35
Ammonium Acrylate	1.16
Xylene	1.43
N-Butanol	2.16
Toluene	1.00
Pine Oil	1.16
Ammonia	6.65
Water	35.09

Analysis of Malenized Oil Emulsion

Acid Value	25.16
% Non Volatile	54.24
Specific Gravity	0.96
PH	7.5
Consistency	A free flowing viscous homogeneous liquid

Table 12.3: Composition of stainers based on malenized oil

Ingredients	**% By Weight**
Colour Pigment	40.0
Titanium Dioxide (Rutile)	03.0
Malenized oil emulsion (54.24% Solids)	35.0
Diethylene Glycol	05.0
Mineral Turpentine 10.0	

Xylene	04.0
n-Butanol	02.4
Tween 20	0.1
Soya lecithin	0.5

Analysis and comparative performance of stainers with commercial samples : The stainers have been analysed for physico chemical characteristics and compared with commercial samples available in market. please Table 12.4.

Effect on physiochemical and film properties or commercial white plant: The white commercial paint was stained with 10 stainers and change in charateristics were noted. table 12.5. Standard methods have been followed for analysis [3,4,5]

Separation point on dilution by solvents : Different solvents were taken in a burette and added to stainers. The separation point was recorded. See *Table* 12.6.

Results and discussion

The composition of malenized oil, cooking schedule and analysis of raw and malenized rice bran oil is given in *Table* 12.1.

The acid value, iodine value and viscosity of malenized oil indicate that substantial amount of maleic anhydride is added to the molecule of oil by dieles alder Diene addition and through active methylene group. The colour of malenized oil is also superior because of the catalysts.

The composition of emulsion based on malenized oil is given in *Table* 12.2. A small quantity of polyvinyl alcohol and ammonium acrylate has been added to promote the homogeneity, viscosity and stability of emulsion. Ammonia is used for neutralization of acidity. Small quantities of various organic solvents like xylene butanol have been added to make the stainers universally acceptable in organic solvents as well as water. Three stainers yellow, red and blue have been prepared as representative samples. The physico chemical characteristics and thinning capabilities are compared with commercial samples it has been observed that our samples are quite close to commercial sample. *(Table* 12.3)

The effect of 10% incorporation of our prepared stainers on physico chemical properties of a standard white commercial paint is given in *Table* 12.5. Drying, brush ability, scratch hardness and other film properties are not adversely affected by incorporation of our malenized oil based stainers.

Table 12.4: Comparison of prepared novel stainers with standard commercial samples

Analysis	Yellow Stainer		Red Stainer		Blue Stainer	
	Our Sample	Commercial Sample	Our Sample	Commercial Sample	Our Sample	Commercial Sample
Density	1.29	1.02	1.19	1.03	1.19	1.03
Viscocity by Ford Cup No. 4 at 30°C (in Sec.)	48	45	30	44	30	45
% Non Volatile	55	62.5	53.0	61.1	52.4	61.1
P/B Ratio	1.22: 1	Not Known	1.22: 1	Not Known	1.22: 1	Not Known
Tinting	Excellent	Excellent	Excellent	Excellent	Excellent	Excellent

The tolerance of stainers to water and other organic solvents is tested and given in Table 12.6 separation point on dilution with solvents is noted. In general we can say that our samples can tolerate 50% or more of organic solvents and water. The tolerance of commercial sample is slightly better in some instances however for practical purposes the stainers based on malenized oil can be accepted as universal stainers.

Conclusions

Table 12.5. Effect of using 10% stainers for commercial white synthetic enamel.

Test	Commercial White synthetic enamel	White enamel+ 10% Yellow Stainer	White enamel +10% Red Stainer	White enamel +10% Blue Stainer
Surface Dry (in minutes)	14	15	16	16
Tack free dry (in minutes)	60	65	65	65
Scratch Hardness	>1000 gms	> 1000 gms	> 1000 gms	> 1000 gms
Nail Hardness	Excellent	Excellent	Excellent	Excellent
Brush ability	V. Good	V. Good	V. Good	V. Good
Resistance to Water (48 Hours)	V. Good	V. Good	V. Good	Good
Hiding Power sq mt/Liter	11.0	11.7	11.2	11.1

Table 12.6: Separation point on dilution with solvents

Samples	Solvents	Our Sample	Commercial Sample
Yellow Stainer	Xylene	1: 1.5	1 : 2.5
	Mineral Turpentine	1 : 2.4	1 : 1.19
	Water	1 : 2	1 : 2.21
Red Stainer	Xylene	1 : 1.2	1 : 2.24
	Mineral Turpentine	1 : 1.8	1 : 2.21
	Water	1 : 1.6	1 : 2.22
Blue Stainer	Xylene	1 : 1.2	1 : 2.04
	Mineral Turpentine	1 : 2.2	1 : 2.25
	Water	1 : 1.8	1 : 2.30

The following conclusions stand confirmed in the light of above experimental work:

(1) Malenized rice bran oil with higher acid value, viscosity and lower iodine value can be prepared by heating the oil with novel catalyst sodium bisulphate and sodium bisulphite. The colour of the sample is improved by using this catalyst.

(2) The malenized rice bran oil is converted into an emulsion paste by neutralization with ammonia; polyvinyl alcohol and ammonium acrylate has been used in small quantity to promote the homogeneity, stability and rheology of emulsion. Small quantities of organic solvents promote the universal application of stainers in solvent and water based paints.

(3) Three stainers viz yellow, red and blue have been prepared. A systematic analysis of these stainers along with commercial samples has been undertaken. It is observed that our stainers are on par and some times better than commercial products.

(4) Considering the present market trend raw material cost of malenized oil emulsion comes to Rs.33/- per kg. This is certainly an economical price. The present day stainers are based on various resins that have certainly a higher cost and they are more based on petroleum products. Our base is of vegetable origin. This is an attractive Green Environment feature of our formulation.

(5) The tolerance of our stainers to water and other organic solvents is excellent and in practical limits *(Table 12.6)*

(6) The stainers do not adversely affect the performance of a white commercial paint when used in an amount of 10% *(Table* 12.5)

(7) The use of malenized-based emulsion for stainers compositions is economically and technically viable proposition. Pilot scale studies are essential for commercial production of these novel stainers.

13

Painting of Aircraft

Introduction

ALTHOUGH the exterior paint work for civil and military aircraft usually amounts to only 0.1-0.2 per cent of the aircraft weight and may be taken forgranted by the users, for the manufacturers the paint is a vital factor in the safety and performance of their aircraft and hence in the economics of the business. It is obvious that exterior paint work serves to enhance the decorative appeal of an aircraft. However of more importance is the fact that the coating system affords protection to the metal substrate from various damaging influences thereby ensuring adequate safety during the life of the aircraft. As we shall discuss shortly, aircraft coatings must be truly versatile. For example, they must withstand extreme conditions like temperature change from blistering tropical heat to subzero conditions within few minutes, must be resistant to abrasive effects of hailstorms, sandstorms, etc and must withstand commonly used hydraulic fluids, some of which are effective paint strippers. All these will have to be achieved by applying a few mis thick of a coating system. While doing so, the quantity of the coatings to be applied for protection has to a bare minimum as each litre of paint. added is traded against increased fuel consumption or decreased payload.

Requirements of aircraft coatings

As mentioned earlier, in addition to providing the decorative appeal, coating systems for aircraft are expected to cater to a host of different functions. In particular they must

1. Provide protection against surface corrosion, stress corrosion and filliform corrosion for the life of aircraft.

2. Afford protection against aircraft fluids and chemicals. Aircraft fluids can form very effective paint strippers. The most aggressive fluids include:
   - Hydraulic fluids like Skydrol 500B, Hijet 4
   - Deiciing fluids like ethanol, water, ethylene glycol mixture (DTD 406A)
   - Pyrolised oils
   - Battery acids which are usually sulphuric acid
   - Toilet fluids
3. Be resistant to environmental extremes like
   - Very rapid change in temp e.g from a ground Temp of 40 - 45°C in tropical climate to about - 60°C at high altitudes within few minutes.
   - High humidity which can easily lead to blistering and detachment of the paint film thereby exposing the surface to corrosion
   - Distilled water immersion as some parts of the interior of an aircraft may be subjected to near permanent immersion in distilled water from condensation.
4. Contribute to high level of decorative appearance
   - For civil aircraft, gloss and colour must be high and the colour must be retained for long periods.
   - For military aircraft, a constant level of solar heat reflection and constant sheen/colour level for camouflage needs to be maintained. In both cases, the coatings should be amen able for easy cleaning.

It should also be flexible enough to prevent cracking of the paint at skin joints and popping of paint from rivets. Both the paint failures are caused by movement of the painted surface relative to the adjacent metal surface. The cracking problem is further aggravated at the low temperatures encountered at high altitudes due to reduced flexibility of the paint film.

Types of aircraft coatings

Advent of aircraft coatings began with the first flying machine where cellulose dope was used to tighten and water proof the fabric stretched over wooden structures. Large amounts were brushed in about six thick coats. Corrosion protection became important with the introduction of metal aircraft specially the ones with jet engines. Cver the years various types of coating systems have been used and in the fcllowing we shall be discussing them briefly.

Synthetic coatings

These are basically alkyd based synthetic coatings. These coatings are inferior to the new generation coat because

- they have no resistance to the fluids used on modern aircraft in particular, hydraulic fluids.
- of relatively poor anticorrosion properties
- of cracking tendency at high altitude temp - poor durability although the initial gloss is satisfactory.

Nitrocellulose coatings

Nitrocellulose based coatings, till the introduction of new generation coatings like acrylics, polyurethanes and epoxies, has been the most common coating systems for aircraft. Presently they are being replaced by more advanced systems mainly because

- they have no resistance to the fluids used on modern aircraft specially hydraulic fluids.
- of relatively inferior anticorrosion properties
- of tendency towards cracking at high altitude
- of low initial gas.

Acrylic coatings

Development of acrylic coatings primarily to replace nitrocellulose coatings was prompted by the requirement of improved protection under increasingly stringent conditions.

These coatings provide good heat resistance and colour retention and are relatively rapid drying with good repairability and high gloss after polishing. Although noticeably better than cellulosics, acrylic coatings have drawbacks.

These are:

- acrylic systems do not have inherently good anticorrosive properties and usually have to be upgraded by the use of good epoxy primer.
- resistance to aircraft fluids are considerably inferior to that offered by epoxies and polymethanes.
- acrylic do not have abrasion resistance and flexibility thereby making

them susceptible to chipping and crazing /cracking.

Nevertheless acrylic coatings are used selectively on military aircraft replacing nitrocellulose finishes. This is particularly so as most military aircraft do not use skydrol type hydraulic fluids. Besides, being a one-pack nonconvertible coating they can be easily removed from the two-pack epoxy primers by very mild paint strippers like trichloroethylene or other solvents for maintenance purposes.

Epoxy coatings

Epoxy coatings, which are two-pack systems, are truly the first of the modern generation of aircraft coatings. These coatings provide good chemical/solvent resistance, good corrosion protection and good adhesion. As a result they are commonly used on weapons, missiles, spacecraft and for interior/exterior protection of civil and military aircraft. However as an exterior finishing coatings, epoxies suffer from several limitations such as :

- epoxies rapidly lose their gloss and chalk. This disrupts appearance on civil aircraft and spoils camouflage on military aircraft.
- the hydraulic fluid resistance of epoxy coatings is generally inferior to that of polyurethane coatings.

As a result of these limitations, epoxy coatings are used extensively as primers and for protection of aircraft interiors.

Polyurethane coatings

Polyurethane coatings, which are generally two-pack systems, are the latest major development in aircraft coatings which occurred around 1970. Initially, rigid polyurethane systems were developed and they offered significant improvement on epoxy coatings, in that they had, far superior gloss, retention, toughness, and extremely good chemical/fluid resistance, subsequently, the development of flexible polyurethane systems solved the other outstanding problem Le. the cracking of paint at skin joints and on rivets.

In light of the above outline, it is apparent that polyurethane coatings, because of their superior performance, are the most effective of the different aircraft finishes. In fact they now account for about ninety per cent of the exterior finishing market for aircraft. This is mainly because they offer extended painting intervals due to better durability, improved appearance with much higher gloss and because they are relatively easier to clean. Besides, compared to epoxies and acrylics they give better chemical resistance to hydraulic fluids, greater durability and exceptionally smooth finish.

Regarding primer coats, two pack epoxies and polyurethanes containing corrosion inhibiting pigments are extensively used. Polyurethane primers are preferred where superior fluid resistance and exceptionally smooth finishes are required.

Paint application

In addition to the right quality of paints, unless application conditions, surface preparation and the application method used are satisfactory it is difficult and sometimes even impossible to obtain an acceptable standard of fiish. Regarding general application conditions, care must be taken about adequate ventilation and control of temperature and humidity. The temperature and humidity control are of prime importance as low temperature and high humidity retard drying, whereas high temperature and high humidity cause deposition of moisture resulting in blushing. In addition, care must be taken to conduct the paint application in a clean dust-free atmosphere in order to obtain a high quality smooth finish.

Surface preparation

In internal/external painting of aircraft, various substances are encountered. It is imperative that the substrates are properly prepared for the paint application. In general, solvent cleaning by hand is seldom adequate and some form of chemical pretreatment should be adopted whenever possible. Following are the salient features regarding surface preparation of various substrates.

Aluminium and its alloys

For painting of new aircraft, preparation of aluminium and its alloy surfaces is usually carried out in two stages - degreasing and cleaning followed by chemical pretreatment or etching. In case of assembled aircraft, degreasing is done by rubbing with clean fluffles rag and solvent. For individual parts degreasing is done with chlorinated diluted with stabilizers to avoid formation of hydrochloric acid. After degreasing, cleaning is effected by treating with alkaline solutions containing surface active agents and then followed by water rinsing.

Etching is carried after cleaning on assembled aircraft by using a combination of phosphoric or choromic acids, alcohols and dampening agents. These are applied with rag, sponge, brush or gun and removed after a stipulated period with the help of one or two water rinsing. Individual parts are etched by immersion in an etching agent bath or in a sulphocromic bath of which temperature, composition, immersion time are controlled.

Alternatively, though not commonly used, aluminium substrates can be prepared by anodizing. Here, a thin film of metallic oxide is deposited on the surface by electrolysis. With this form of pretreatment it is essential that the paint is applied as soon as possible after anodising, as the anodic film is initially highly porous and will readily absorb grease and dirt. However the anodized film will harden and, if left for a few days, is likely to become impervious thus causing poor adhesion to the paint film.

Steel and magnesium alloys

Steel surfaces, whether phosphated or not, are degreased with ketonic solvents like methyl ethyl ketone. Due to risk of fatigue, use of chlorinated solvents is prohibited. On the other hand, magnesium alloys may be degreased with both M.E.K. and chlorinated solvents. Chemical etching agents are not recommended due to high risk of fatigue and of a non-adherent effect.

Composites

Composite surfaces usually fibre reinforced epoxies and polyesters, can be adequately prepared by degreasing with ethyl acetate or other solvent combinations primarily to remove the demoulding agents. If surface irregularities are present, use of a primer is recommended for improved finish.

Application methods / defects

Although various application methods are used for specialized purposes in painting of aircraft, most of the application jobs are conducted by using conventional spray. Conventional spraying is a standard application technique and the precautions to be followed while painting of aircraft are same as those to be observed for other jobs. In general the operator must ensure application of an even wet coat which will flow out smoothly, be free on the one hand from spray dust and inadequate covering due to spraying too lightly, and on the other hand from runs or sags caused by spraying too heavily. Brush application is generally not followed in aircraft painting and is resorted to only for small repair/touch up work and for surfaces where it is not possible to paint by spray.

In spite of the paint quality being as per the stipulated / specified standard, it is possible to have defects in the paint film caused by improper application. Some of the common problems are as follows:

Adhesion

Paint films properly applied to correctly pretreated surfaces should adhere satisfactorily and when thoroughly dry should not be readily removable. However, poor adhesion may result from

- inefficient cleaning and pretreatment
- inadequate stirring of liquid paint - coating at incorrect time interval - application under adverse condition

Lifting

This effect is literally lifting of the primer from the surface and is manifested as swelling and wrinkling of the film. The tendency of any primer to lift is increased if the : surface is inadequately cleaned. This may also result due to inadequate stirring of the paint before application as also owing to over-coating at incorrect time intervals.

Orange peel

This effect is usally due to high application viscocity, air pressure., or too close a distance between the gun and the job. In presence of orange peel, the paint film will appear wavy thereby adversely affecting the gloss.

Dry spray

This effect is caused by the atomized particles of paint becoming dry before reaching the surface being painted and results from low air pressure or too large a distance between the gun and the job.

Sagging/running

This happens when too much paint is applied and the film moves downwards under gravity. Usually this is caused by low application viscosity, high air pressure and inadequate gunhandling.

Blushing

This appears as a clouding or blooming of the paint film. It is caused by moisture in the airline, high humidity, draughts or sudden changes in temperature and is most commonly experienced with nitrocellulose based paints. It can be avoided by suitably adjusting the thinner.

14

Anionic Bitumen Emulsions

Introduction

AFFLUENCE can be found in effluence holds good for bitumen which is basically a 'byproduct' of crude oil distillation. This material has attracted several major industries due to its potential to be used in roads and public works, constructions, sealers and even in paint coatings. The use of bitumen as coatings has become obsolete due to several reasons except for some applications. But its relatively lower cost compared to other binder systems demands extensive research so as to make this material more feasible to be used as a coating material. Imbued by its interesting properties, this review has been done so as to make the reader 'imbibe' its importance in various fields. Starting from the basic chemistry of bitumen, this article gives an insight into the various modifications done, so as to obtain/enhance the desired properties.

Basic bitumen chemistry

Bitumen is a material obtained as a byproduct in the distillation of crude petroleum. Composition of crude depends on the source of availability of crude. Some crudes may have significant bitumen fractions and some others very little bitumen fractions. For instance, the Boscan Venezuela crude may contain up to 60 per cent of asphalt residuum and Nigeria light crude may contain as low as 1 per cent. Bitumen from different crude sources have different properties.

Bitumen is made up of polar and non-polar compounds in complex associations. It is the interaction of polar compounds which gives bitumen its structure and imparts mechanical properties. The main chemical species present in bitumen are carbon, hydrogen and 'hetero' groups such as sulphur, nitrogen and oxygen besides nickel and vanadium. The 'hetero' atoms are responsible for imparting the functionality and polarity.

Three types of molecules can essentially be found in bitumen viz., aliphatics, cyclics and aromatics. Aliphatics are linear chain molecules. Cyclics are the naphthenic ring type molecules and aromatics are unsaturated ring molecules. These molecules in the presence of 'hetero' atoms determine the magnitude of molecular interaction and hence impart specific properties to the bitumen. The characterization of bitumen by simple fractionation yields two fractions namely the asphaltenes and maltenes.

The molecular masses of asphaltenes extend over the range of 103 to 104 depending on the source of bitumen. They have a strong tendency to form 'micelles'. Asphaltenes essentially consists of highly condensed planar and heteroatom polar groups, polarisable ring systems and large amounts of hetero atom polar functional groups. They represent 10 to 30 per cent of bitumen.

The maltenes consists of two fractions, oils and resins. Oils which are in liquid form constitute about 40 to 60 per cent of the bitumen. Their molecular masses are in the range of 600 to 1000. They are non polar and contain paraffins and condensed naphthenes with some alkyl aromatics. Resins represent a transitional phase between asphaltenes and oils.

Bitumen as a coating material

Bitumen was the first anti-corrosion coating and is still in use in some applications. A comparative performance study of bituminous coatings with other binder systems will present a clear picture of bitumen as'a coating material *(Table* 14.1). The fact tl,at they can be applied on poorly finished surfaces makes them a 'surface tolerant' coating and they can be exploited 'gainfully' for rehabilitation purpose. Bitumen can also be blended with various polymers for enhancing the physical and mechanical characteristics[1].

The need to develop 'Cold Technology'

Since pure bitumen and its polymer blends are highly viscous, large amount of energy is required for heating the bitumen' so as to apply it on the surface. This gives rise to environmental and health hazards due to toxic fume emissions. A very good solution to overcome the above problem is to convert bitumen into an emulsion form. This technology is commonly referred to as 'cold technology'. This technology not only saves substantial amount of energy but also promotes surface interactions leading to better adhesion on to the substrate. The fact that bitumen in carcinogenic in nature can be

Table 14.1: Comparative performance of various binder systems

Type	Cost	Tolerance to poor surface preparation	Chemical resistance	Solvent resistance	Over-coatability after ageing
Bituminous	Low	Good	Moderate	Poor	Good with similar type
Alkyds	Low-medium	Moderate	Poor	Poor-moderate	Good
Vinyl	High	Poor	Good	Poor	Good
Epoxy	Medium-high	Very poor	Very good	Good	Poor
Urethane	High	Very poor	Very good	Good	Poor

effectively controlled and its effect can be substantially lessened by employing this technology.

Some of the advantages of this cold technology are

- Primarily saves energy
- Easier handling and storage even at room temperatures
- Safe and environmental friendly
- Low cost on-site and in-place technology
- Good compatibility with other binder systems

The 'Science' of bitumen emulsions - A brief review

A simple system of bitumen in water is called bitumen dispersion. By adding small concentrations of surfactants and stabilizers to the dispersion, an emulsion is made. The rheological properties of the bitumen emulsion are largely dependant on the interfacial film structure. The emulsifiers/ surfactants added to the bitumen dispersion determine the interfacial properties of the emulsion. When bitumen emulsions are prepared, the surfactant molecules diffuse from the water phase and arrange themselves at the bitumen-water interface. The rate of diffusion and the resulting interfacial charge depends on the structure and composition of the surfactants. A cationic emulsifier imparts a positive charge at the interface and an anionic emulsifier imparts a negative charge at the in terface. A third group of emulsifiers also exist which is called the non-ionic emulsifiers.

One of the main functions of adding emulsifiers is to avoid flocculation and coalescence of the bitumen droplets in water. However, the coalescence is important in the later stages for setting of bitumen onto the substrate as a result of chemical reaction with the substrate or gradual evaporation of water from the emulsion. The first two groups of emulsifiers act on electrostatic repulsion mechanism, that is, repulsion of like charges takes place thereby avoiding close contact of the bitumen droplets. The non-ionic emulsifier acts on 'steric repulsion' mechanism thereby avoiding close contact of the bitumen droplets. The types of emulsifiers are shown in *Fig.* 14.1.

The emulsion chemistry is based on the following reactions:

Cationic emulsifier reaction:

$R\,NHCH_2CH_2CH_2NH_2 + 2HCl$ = Insoluble neutral form

$R\,NH_2^{+}CH_2CH_2CH_2NH_2 + 2Cl.$ + acid = soluble cationic soap

Anionic emulsifier reaction:

RCOOH

Insoluble neutral form

$+ NaOH = RCOO^{-}Na^{+}$

+ alkali = soluble anionic soap

Based on the setting rates, bitumen emulsions are classified as Rapid setting (RS), Medium Setting (MS) and Slow setting (SS) emulsions. Cationic and anionic emulsions are represented as CRS, CMS, CSS and RS, MS and SS respectively, the prefix 'C' standing for cationic. The rapid and medium setting emulsions undergo a chemical reaction with the substrate by which water is expelled and cohesion develops instantly. On the other hand, in

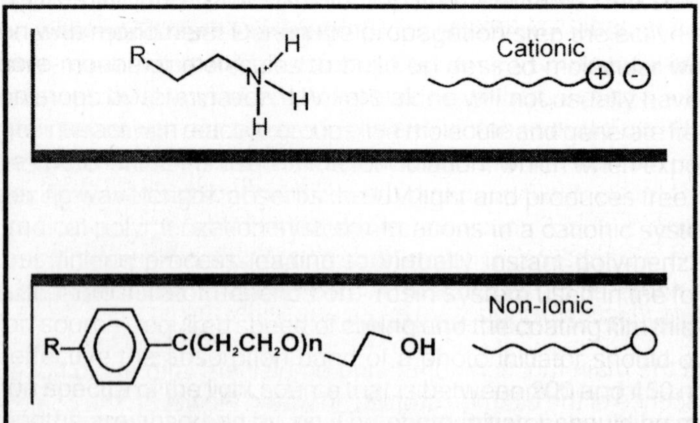

Fig. 14.1 : Types of emulsifiers

slow setting emulsions the mechanism of setting is by water evaporation and therefore cohesion develops slowly.

Significance of HLB number in emulsions

Surfactants are characterized according to the 'balance' between the hydrophilic (water-loving) and lipophilic (oil-loving) portions of their molecules. The hydrophilic-lipophilic balance (HLB) number indicates the polarity of the molecules in an arbitrary range of 1-40, with the most commonly used emulsifiers having a value between 1 and 20. The HLB number increases with increasing hydrophilicity. *Table* 14.2 some of the applications corresponding to various ranges of HLB numbers.

This quantity was first defined by Griffin. There are a number of empirical formulae to calculate the HLB number of any emulsifier6. These numbers give an idea about the stability of the system. In fact the efficiency of an emulsifier depends greatly on this number.

Table 14.2: HLB dependent applications

Range	Application
3-6	Water in oil emulsifiers
7-9	Wetting agents
8-18	Oil in water emulsifiers
13-15	Detergents
18-18	Solubilizers

The manufacturing processes, properties and the general behaviour of cationic bitumen emulsions are studied in detail elsewhere 2,3.4. The general behaviour and properties of anionic bitumen emulsions are dealt in detail in the succeeding sections.

Anionic bitumen emulsions

The first step for preparing an anionic emulsion is to prepare a suitable emulsifier. The basic raw materials for preparing an anionic emulsifier are tall oils and lignin from trees. *Fig.* 14.2 the preparation of anionic bitumen emulsifier from tree based oils. The end product obtained is amidoamines. *Fig.* 14.3 the preparation of anionic bitumen emulsifier from lignin. In this case, the end products which behave as an emulsifier are lignosulfonates or amino lignins.

For rapid setting and medium setting anionic bitumen emulsions tall oil acids are commonly used and for slow setting emulsions, lignosulfonates are used.

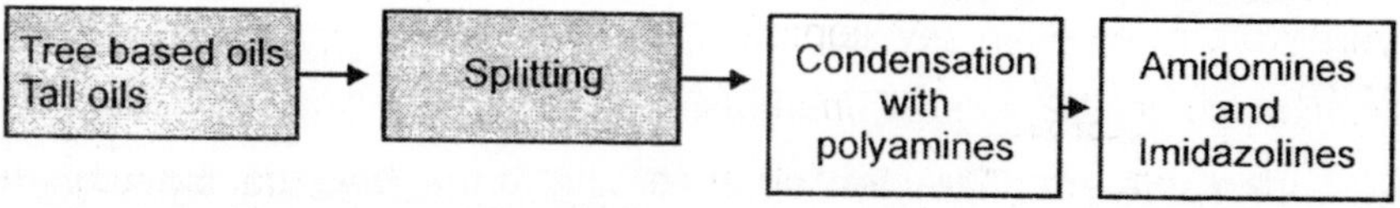

Fig. 14.2 Preparation of anionic bitumen emulsifier from tree based oils

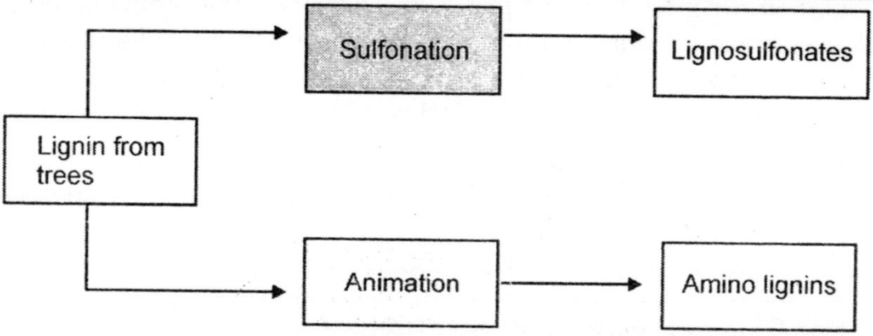

Fig. 14.3 Preparation of anionic bitumen emulsifer from lignin

Now, the next step is to prepare the anionic emulsion. A simple schematic of a batch emulsion plant is in the *Fig.* 14.4.

Colloidal mills produce colloidal suspensions and emulsions with particle or droplet size less than one micron. Typically, a colloidal mill consists of a rotor and a stator. The rotor speed is between 3000 and 15000 rpm. The suspension, consisting of particles of about 100 mesh size, is introduced through a funnel and it is thrown outwards by centrifugal action and by the action of attrition, shear and centrifugal force, size reduction is achieved.

The soap which is prepared in the soap tank is usually of the following types depending on the emulsifier used.

Anionic surfactants: soaps

A number of patents are available for manufacturing asphalt/bitumen emulsions to be coated on aggregates for pavements. The bitumen content of the emulsion can range from about 30% to about 75% by weight of the emulsion depending upon the intended use, preferably about 55% to about 65% by weight. The anionic emulsifier is present in the final emulsion in a concentration ranging from about 0.1 % to about 10.0% by weight of the emulsion, preferably about .5% to about 3.0% by weight of the emulsion. The choice of emulsifiers depends on the application aspect. Alkali hydroxides

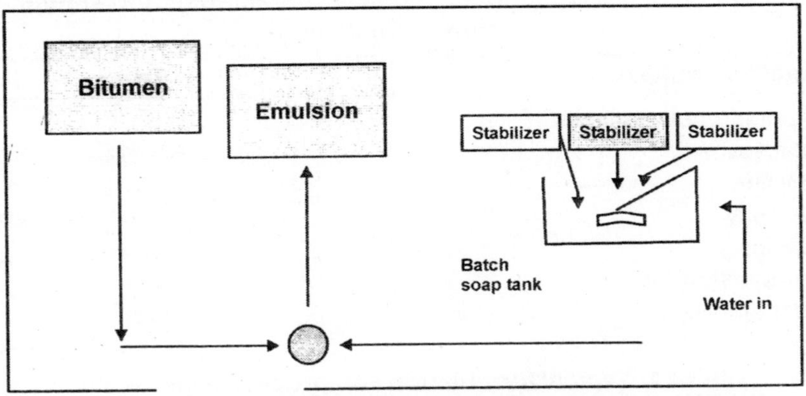

Fig. 14.4 Schematic of a batch plant for the manufacturing of anionic bitumen emulsion

were used to saponify the surface active acids naturally occurring in asphalt. The use of alkyl or alkoxy alkyl phosphoric acid as emulsifiers for asphalt is described by Conn. The use of partially desulfonated oxygenated lignosulfates and non-ionic surfactants is described by Oetroit. For quick setting anionic emulsions, a combination of aryl alkyl sulfonates and ethylene oxide adducts of alkyl phenols and of fatty alcohols is described by Ferm. A combination of sodium lignite or lignosulfonate and saponified tall oil or rosin is disclosed by Sommer and Evans". The pH for the above process is in the range of 10 to 13.

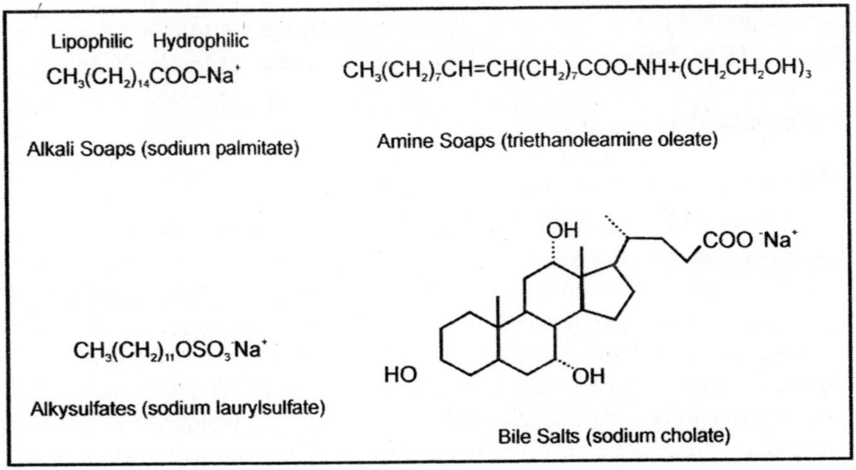

Table 14.3: Some Important physical characteristics of anionic bitumen emulsions

Physical Property	Value
Bitumen emulsion basis	B 80
Total solids	58-60%
pH value	11.5-12.5
Viscosity	5000-10000 mpa.s
Density	1.01 kg/l
Storage stability	1 year
Frost stability	Poor

Table 14.4: Typical formulation and properties of 1 K system

Ingredients	Weight %
Water 16.00 Hydroxylethylcellulose (Bermacol, Akso)	00.25
Biocide / Fungicide	00.20
Wetting aid (NP 4.5)	00.50
Antifoam (AS 33)	00.10
Butyl cellosolve	00.40
Oimethylaminoethanol (OMEA)	00.20
Talc	28.00
Synthomer 20W20 (54%)	10.00
Revacryl 123 (60%)	05.00
Antifoam (AS 33)	00.20
Bitumen emulsion (Hincol)	35.78
Synthomer 9523	00.15
OMEA / TEA / MEA	00.02
Water	03.00
Worlee Add 315	00.20
Total	**100.00**

Typical properties of 1 K Coating formulation described above:

Tensile Strength	:	4-6 kg/cm^2
Elongation	:	900 - 1000%
Recovery	:	85%
Water permeability	:	4 g/ 24 hrs.
Softening temp.	:	+70°C
Coating thickness	:	1.5-2 nm
Tack free	:	2 -3 hrs.

The main physical properties of anionic bitumen emulsions are listed in Table 14.2.

The main advantage of using anionic bitumen emulsion is its lower cost compared to its cationic counterpart. But if the substrate/aggregate is negatively charged, then the adherence to the substrate would be poor due to repulsion of the like charges. To overcome this problem, 'anti-stripping' agents or adhesion promoters are added. These are basically amines or diamines. Sometimes, the emulsifier itself acts as an adhesion promoter.

The use of anionic bitumen emulsions for construction and road building have been reported in the literature and this technology is making rapid strides in the road building industry. With an idea to exploit bitumen in all fields, 'modified' anionic bitumen emulsions could be used for coating on underground pipelines. Since bitumen has good compatibility with other binder systems, rubber modified bitumen was developed for nipping the bottlenecks of pure bitumen in the bud.

Polymer modification of bitumen emulsions

Understanding the fact that anionic bitumen emulsions have poor cohesive strength and poor film forming tendency of the matrix besides its inert behaviour, it is essential to incorporate a suitable polymeric binder to impart desired properties such as film formation combined with the ability to form high OFT coating with desired adhesion, barrier properties, chemical resistance etc., In this regard, the construction industry has made the best use of this material, formulating an effective barrier coating with water proofing characteristics by combining the Anionic bitumen emulsion with carboxylated SBR Latex and Acrylic emulsions. Range of custom designed Synthomer 20W20, SBR Latex and Revacryl-123 are the preferred grades of acrylic emulsion being offered by Synthomer for above applications. Typical formulation for 1K water proof coatings based on combination of Bitumen emulsion and polymer are shown in Table 14.3. Formulations can be :

- 1 K coating formulations with lack
- 1 K coating formulations tack free
- 2K coating formulations with cement

While making a coating formulation, care must be taken of the low shear stability of the Anionic Bitumen emulsions. Therefore typical procedure involves grinding all the pigments, fillers, extenders etc. in water using suitable wetting and dispersing aids in alkaline pH followed by slow mixing with anionic bitumen emulsion and SBR Latex and Acrylic emulsion to get a final coating formulation.

The typical properties are 1000% elongation with 80% recovery with excellent water proof properties to old and new concrete surfaces.

It is also possible to make 2K coating system by combining with Cement. In this case, the anionic bitumen emulsion+Synthomer SBR Latex is taken as the liquid component and mixed with Cement and sand at site for application. The 2K offers combined properties of cement setting while retaining all the properties of bitumen as well as polymers. Typical formulation is shown in Table 14.4 The preferred grades are Synthomer 20W20, and thickenrs like Synthomer 9523.

Preferred grades of Synthomer/Revacryl used for modification of anionic bitumen emulsions :

- Synthomer 20W20 (Carboxylated SBR Latex, Highly recommended for faster drying system).
- Synthomer 29Y41 (Carboxylated SBR Latex, Universal Type binder)
- Synthomer 28W20 (Carboxylated SBR Latex, Low temperature flexible, high elongation & low tack)
- Synthomer 9523 (Carboxylated SBR Latex Used as thickener)
- Revacryl 123 (Acrylic emulsion of infering excellent elastomeric property and light fastness)

Table 14.5: Typical composition of 2K bituminous building protection products

	Wet Component A	
85-90	pbw	bituminous
10-25	pbw	Synthomer latex
1.2	pbw	polystyrene beads
0.2	pbw	antiform agent
0.5-1.5	pbw	Synthomer 9523
	Powder Component B	
80	pbw	Quartz sand 0-0.3mm
10	pbw	OPC
10	pbw	lafarge cement

Mixing ratio : 22 pbw comp. A : 8 pbw Comp. B

Table 14.6: Peformance of Rubber modified bitumen emulsion (RMBE) coating

Test	Results	Procedures
Accelerated weathering	No film deterioration	ASTM G 155/ASTM D412
Chemical resistance	No loss of integrity	ASTM G20, 10% HCl 10% NaOH, saturated lime water
Hardness	50 Type A	ASTM C836
Salt Spray	Passed 1000 hours	ASTM B117-97
Tensile	89.6 psi	ASTM D412
Water permeability	5	ASTM E 96
Surface corrosion	No corrosion after 504 hours <03% after 1000 hours	ASTM D 610
Blistering	No blistering after 1000 hours	ASTM D714
Corrosion creepback	No corrosion creep back after 1000 hours.	ASTMD1654

Rubber modified bitumen emulsion coatings
(Commercially called as "liquid rubber")

An amazing elastomeric membrance coating using anionic bitumen emulsion modified with rubber was developed to give excellent adhesive, elastic and protective properties. This system does not require sophisticated equipment for application. It can be applied by a spray or brush at ambient tempeatures. It is a one coat system requiring minimal surface preparation. It is completely VOC free and hence no problems of health hazards. The performance of rubber modified bitumen emulsion coatings are listed in Table 14.5.

The characteristics given in Table 14.6 clearly show that RMBE coatings can be used for corrosion protection apart from its conventional use in water proofing. Apart from the above properties, it has a very good puncture, tear and abrasion resistance which is very vital for an underground pipeline coating. Added to these features, it has an excellent elongation (up to 1300%) and recovery (up to 90 per cent).

Some application of RMBE :

- Due to its superior chemical resistance, it is used for linings which ought to be chemical resistant (Fig. 14.5)
- Due to its excellent resistance to water permeation, it is used in water proofing applications (Fig. 14.6)

- Rust proofing of truck body (Fig. 14.7)
- Corrosion resistant roof lining for chemical plants such as fertilizer industries. These coatings are resistant to the off gases from the fertilizers (Fig. 14.8)
- Dam concrete protection (Fig. 14.9)
- Coatings for storage tanks (Fig. 14.10)
- And many more... RMBE is also used to coat steel structures such as pipeline and containments.

15

Rheology Modifiers in Waterborne Paints

Introduction

GALAAOMANNAN gum (Guargum) is extracted from the seed of the legumi'J nous shrub of Cyamopsis tetragonoloba. It is vertically stalked plant having height of about 3 to 6 feet and extensively grown in semiarid region in north west of India in Rajasthan, Haryana, Gujarat, Punjab etc. and Pakistan. The seeds are separated from the pods, subsequently a series of operations like crushing, shifting and grinding steps will separate valuable galactomannan gum (endosperm) from the seeds. The chemical structure of galactomannan *(see Fig.* 15.1) is a linear chain of D - mannopyranosyl units linked (1-→ 4) with single membered ∝ - D - galactopyranosyl units occurring as side chain(1). The ratio between galactose and man nose Polysaccharide is 1 : 2.

Earlier it was reported that the molecular weight of galactomannan gum was 2,20000 Dalton. But more recent results obtained with size exclusion chromatography and low - angle laser light - scattering show the average molécular weight to be in the range of 1 - 2 X 106 Daltons[3].

Hydroxyethyl galactomannan gum is prepared by reacting galactomannan gum with non-ionic ethylene oxide reagent in presence of alkaline catalyst (sodium hydroxide). The ethoxylation reaction may be illustrated by the following equation.

$$\text{Guar - OH} + \underset{\diagdown\ O\ \diagup}{CH_2 \text{---} CH_2} \xrightarrow{NaOH} \text{Guar - [O - } CH_2 \text{ - } CH_2 \text{] n OH}$$

Rheology modifiers for waterbased paints

Application properties of latex paints rely on the use of rheological additives modifiers to a greater extent than their solvent-based counterparts. Depending on the properties desired for a given end-use market, typical latex paints may contain up to four rheological additives. Typically a combination of additives is used to provide a good balance of container viscosity, application viscosity, antisettling properties, spatter resistance, flow and leveling etc. Often a combination of two or more of cellulose,polyacrylate, clay and associative thickness is used to provide the rheological profile required for a specific paint application.

In a present study the hydroxyethyl galactomannan based rheology modifiers are used in distemper, plastic emulsion paint as well as Exterior paint, and their performance properties are evaluated for the comparison with equivalent experimental sets made from polyacrylate thickeners, carboxymethyl cellulose (imported & indigenous) and hydroxyethyl cellulose (imported) thickeners.

Experimental

Materials and Methods

The rheology modifiers used in the present study, hydroxyethyl cellulose (HEe), carboxymethyl cellulose (CMe) and polyacrylate were of commercial grades, they were used as such without any further modification or purification.

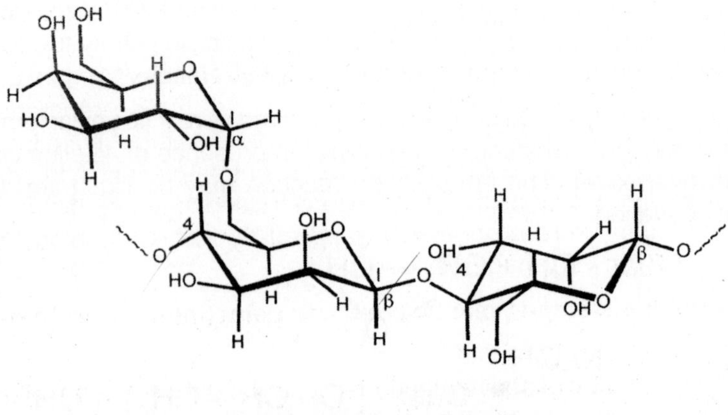

Fig. 15.1 : Structure of Galactomannan

Table 15.1 : Distemper paint formulation

Sr. No.	Ingredients	Wt.%
1.	Soft Water	6.7
2.	4% solution of CMC (Domestic & Imported). Encotech PVA -128 and Encotech PVA-908 HDS/Polyacrylate solution	14.7
3.	@ Anionic Dispersant (Indofil -850)	0.2
4.	@ Nonionic Dispersant (Aestolyne-1000)	0.3
5.	Sodium Hexameaphosphate	0.1
6.	Monthylene Glycol	0.1
7.	Sodium Penta Chlorophenate	0.2
8.	Defomer (NOPCO NDW)	1.4
9.	Soft Water	3.3
10.	TiO_2 Anatase	4.8
11.	Aluminium Silicate	1.4
12.	Calcite (20 microns)	21.9
13.	Dolomite (20 microns)	14.3
14.	China Clay (20 microns)	14.3
15.	Liq. Ammonia	0.1
16.	Emulsion (Styrene Acrylic, 50% solids)	10.0
17.	Deformer (NOPCO-NDW)	0.1
18.	Liq. Ammonia	0.1
19.	Soft Water	6.0
	Total	**100.0**

@ infofil-850-Anionic disopersant indofil chemical co. Bombay
@ Aestolyne-1000-Nonionic dispersant (HLB-13)) from Sun Chemicals Co. Bombay
*NOPCO NDW -Deformer from Henckel Germany

The rheology modifiers based on hydroxyethyl galactomannan (HEG) (Encotech PVA128 & Encotech PVA - 908) used in the preparation of waterborne paints were from Mis Encore Natural Polymers Private Limited, manufactured in a PLC (programmable logic control) plant at Ahmedabad (India). The other additives pigments, extenders and emulsion binders etc. used in the study were proprietarily supplied by Mis. Champion Paints Industries, Vallabh Vidyanagar (INDIA).

Preparation of distemper, plastic emulsion paint (interior) and exterior house paint

In the preparation of above mentioned waterbased paints, the following procedure was followed in the laboratory to make various experimental sets as per the compositions shown in *Table* 15.1, 3 and 5 for distemper, plastic emulsion paint and exterior house paints respectively.

In the process, 4 per cent solution of the thickener was prepared under highspeed disc disperser to be used for the subsequent steps. The thickener solution along with the soft water were charged into the vessel under high speed disperser. The additives dispersing agent, defoamer, sodium hexametaphosphate, monoethyleneglycol, preservative etc. were separately dissolved into the vessel kept under highspeed disperser. Mixing was carried out so as to get intimate mixture of rheology modifier and the additives.

The pigments titanium dioxide and aluminium silicate were charged into the above and dispersed to primary particle size, then subsequently extends were added in a stated sequence and dispersed to desired fineness. The content then was allowed to cool below 50°C, prior to addition of emulsion binder under slow speed mixing to give the sesired composition of distemper, plastic emulsion paints and exterior house paint based on the formulations shown in Table 15.1, 3 and 5.

Characterization of distemper, plastic emulsion paint and exterior house paint

The various experimental sets of distempers, plastic emulsion paint and

Table 15.2: Physical and performance properties of distemper

Paint properties	Thickener used in paint formulation				
	PVA-128	PVA-908 HDS	Domestic	Imported	Polyacylate
	Encotech	Encotech	CMC	CMC	
Sp. Gravity *(gm/cmJ)*	1.443	1.467	1.459	1.457	1.482
PH	8 to 9	8 to 9	8 to 9	8 to 9	8 to 9
% Non Volatiles	61.28	60.50	60.23	58.18	59.79
Ease of Application (Brushability)	Excellent	Excellent	Fair	Good	Excellent
Open Time / Wet edge	4	5	3	4	3
Contrast Ratio	75.20	75.12	75.50	74.90	74.50
Yellow Index	6.17	6.5	7.5	6.24	7.15
Scrub Resistance (Sheen Instrument)	6	13	3	4	5
Shelf Stability					
by Measuring viscosity. (25.C)					
(i) Initial	65000	45000	37000	39000	1000
(ii) After 6 days at 50.C	+0.04	+0.12	+0.8	+1.45	+0.64
(iii) After 12 days at 50.C	+0.17	+0.41	+1.2	+1.93	+2.58

* Brookfield viscometer RVT, spindle-6, rpm-20.

Table 15.3 : Distemper paint formulation

Sr. No.	Ingredients	Wt.%
1.	Soft Water	7.0
2.	HEC (Imported) Encotech PVA-128 and Encotech PVA-908 (4% solution in soft water)	7.5
3.	Anionic Dispersant (Indofil-850)	0.8
4.	Nonionic Dispersant (Aestolyne-1000)	0.4
5.	Sodium Hexametaphosphate	0.2
6.	Monoethylene Glycol (M.E.G.)	2.00
7.	@Acticide EP Paste-In Can preservative	0.2
8.	@Acticide EP Paste-In can preservative	0.2
9.	Deformer (NOPCO-NDW)	0.1
10.	Pine Oil	0.5
11.	TiO_2 Futile	20.0
12.	English China Clay	12.0
13.	Calcite (5 microns)	7.0
14.	Talcum (5 microns)	6.0
15.	Soft Water	4.2
16.	Liq. Ammonia	0.2
17.	Emulsion-Vinyl Acrylic, 50% solids)	28.0
18.	Deformer (NOPCO-NDW)	0.2
19.	Liq. Ammonia	0.2
20.	Pidicryl 4310 (Ammonia polyacrylate)	0.3
21.	Soft Water	3.3
	Total	**100.0**

@ Thor Industries U.S.A.
*Pidilite Industries, Bombay

exterior house paints were evaluated for their physical properties like % nonvolatile, sp. gravity, viscosity (Brookfield) and performance characteristics including contrast ratio, yellow index, ease of application, shelf stability and wet edge time using std. methods(8.9). The results are reported in *Table* 15.2, 4 *and* 6 for Distemper, Plastic emulsion paint and Exterior house paint respectively.

Results and discussion

The result of physical properties like % nonvolatile and specific gravity are quite in good agreement with the theoretically expected values in all the experimental sets of distemper, plastic emulsion paints and exterior paints.

The results of viscosities in distemper formulations are quite interesting. Encotech PVA-128 based composition gave the highest viscosity amongst all experimental sets. Encotech PVA-908 based paints gave lower viscosity than Encotech PV A-128 based paints but higher than CMC based (imported and indigenous) composition. This shows relative efficiency of the thickeners in the paint composition. The shelf stability studies reveal the excellent stability characteristics of the HEG based composition. Polyacrylate based paints were poor in term of viscocity buildup and also in terms of stability.

The results of contrast ratio and yellow index in all the experimental sets of distemper, plastic paint and exterior paints reveals that there was no significant effect of colour of thickeners on the colourvalue of paints. Slightly higher value of opacity in case of HEG based composition may be due to better film buildup because of higher thickening efficiency.

The results of ease of application and open time (wet edge) were alsomost comparable with the exception of CMC based compositions, which were inferior. The wet scrub resistance of Encotech PVA-908 based distemper was far better than other compositions. The Encotech PVA-128 was second highest with better performance than CMC and polyacrylate based products the Molecular weight of the polymer and its modification by the other moieties may be the responsible factors.

The findings in the present study were quite promising and confirming with the earlier studies of HEG in water based paint application [10].

Table 15.4: Physical and performance properties of emulsion paint

Paint properties	Thickener used in paint formulation		
	PVA-128	PVA-908 HDS	HEC Imported
Sp. Gravity (Gm/Cm$_2$)	1.41	1.418	1.367
PH	8 to 9	8 to 9	8 to 9
% Non Volatiles	60.05%	61.65%	59.87%
Ease of Application (Brushability)	Excellent	Excellent	Good
Open Time/Wet Edge	8	9	8
Contrast Ratio (Hiding)	82.05%	80.90%	81.50%
Yellow Index	4.05	4.25	4.5
Scrub Resistance in Strokes (Sheen Instruments)	>500	>500	>500
Shelf Stability by Measuring Viscosity* 25°C			
(i) Initial	1600	850	1380
(ii) After 6 days at 50°C	+5.0%	+1.17%	+3.58%
(iii) After 12 days at 50°C	+7.5%	+4.70%	+4.93%

*Brookshield Viscometer RVT, Spindle-6, rpm-20

Table 15.5: Exterior emulsion paint formulation

Sr. No.	Ingredient	Wt.
1.	Soft Water	4.80
2.	HEC (Imported) Encotech PVA-128 and Encotech PVA-908. (4% solution in soft water)	7.5
3.	Anionic Dispersant (Indofil-850)	0.7
4.	Nonionic Dispersant (Aestolyne-1000)	0.4
5.	Sodium Hexametaphosphate	0.2
6.	Monoethylene Glycol	2.5
7.	Acticide EP Paste - In can preservative	0.5
8.	Acticide SPX - Film Preservative	0.4
9.	Defoamer (NOPCO - NDW)	0.2
10.	Pine Oil	1.0
11.	TiO_2 Rutile	22.0
12.	Alluminium Silicate	4.0
13.	Talcum (5 microns)	8.0
14.	Mica (325#. Wet ground)	3.0
15.	Liq. Ammonia	0.2
16.	Emulsion - (Pure Acrylic. 50% solids)	42.0
17.	Defoamer - (NOPCO - NDW)	0.1
18.	Liq. Ammonia	0.2
19.	Soft Water	2.3
	Total	**100.0**

Conclusion

The above study reveals the excellent rheology control, shelf stability in HEG based product as compared to CMC (imported and domestic) as well as polyacrylate based products. HEG based products gave equivalent performance to that of HEC in both plastic emulsion paints and exterior paints. The results of scrub resistance and ease of application with minimum sag were very attracting in HEG based compositions as compared to their equivalent counterparts.

16

High Performance Coatings

Introduction

A commercial capital of UAE, Dubai is set to take off as one of the fastest growing cities in the world, in terms of new high rise structures, buildings with the modern amenities, super shopping malls, roads - infra structures, bridges, international facilities, festival cities, internet cities, various ,sports complexes, metro rails etc. The growth is phenomenal, iand present sandy area is'being covered by artificial greenery, trees, flowers, subways and number of newer projects, required in terms t)f city infrastructure.

To implement all these' projects variety of paints and coatings are used, during constructions, after completion, for interior and exterior applications The highly corrosive and saline atmosphere harsh climatic conditions 85-95% relative humidity, high temperature upto 50-55°C and strong unfiltered ultraviolet rays, along with sand storm, demands resistant coatings, for high performance. Some of these coatings have been discussed.

High performance coatings

Major developments in the Middle East-Dubai is in the field of decorative paints and coatings. The client, consultants, architect, engineers, contractor, paint manufacturers and applicators are involved, in deciding the products and performance requirements.

- Acrylic textured coatings
- Thermal insulating paints
- Anti carbonation coatings
- High build acrylic coatings for bridges
- Epoxy and polyurethane floor coatings

- Silicone - siloxane primer
- Water repellent coatings
- Heavy duty glass flake coatings
- Fire retardant and intumescent coatings
- Water proofing materials
- Anti fungal treatment coatings
- Wood preservatives
- Perlescent coatings
- Aqua acrylic coatings

Acrylic textured coatings

The major trend in the Dubai and Middle East, in the field of decorative paints for building exteriors is the use of a variety of textured and stone finishes. The application of these coatings not only gives a new aesthetic look but equally these coatings protect the exterior wall, not allowing water and saline material to penetrate. The use of pure acrylic emulsion as binder imparts non yellowing, UV resistance and weather resistance properties. The coating is responsible for light, medium or heavy texture, as also the look of traditional and antique finish. Use of specific grades of aggregates gives different designs with grooves, stone finish look. *(Table* 16.1).

Properties Requirements :

Table 16.1: Acrylic texture coating

S.No.	Properties requirements	Specification of results
1.	Resin binder	Pure acrylic emulsion, high solids
2.	Paint rheology	High solids, high viscous, thixotropic
3.	Application	Easy to apply and spread
4.	Adhesion	Should have excellent adhesion on all cementatious surfaces
5.	Antibacterial properties	Should be resistance to algicides, fungicide, inhibit mould growth
6.	Reduction in chloride ion penetration	Minimum 97% ASTM C 1202
7.	Crack bridging ability	Minimum 1 mm

Thermal insulating paint

Highrise buildings are having continuous exposure to sunlight. The solar energy has total intensity of about 0.1 kilowat per square feet at sea level, and the intensity increases with altitude. The solar energy is divided in three region of electromagnetic spectrum.

1. Ultraviolet region :- bet. 190 -360 nanometers (nm), 5°(0 energy in sunlight
2. Energy in the visible region:- bet 360-720 nanometers (nm) 45% of solar energy
3. Near infrared region bet. 720-2500 (nm), 50% of total solar energy. For reflectance of this energy, thermal insulating paint is commonly used, containing hollow ceramic microspheres, that reduces the transfer of heat. The proper use of reflective grades ofTitanium dioxide, non conductive filler controls the thermal conductivity, solar emittance (*Table* 16.2).

Anti carbonation coatings

Anticarbonation coatings are depoyed in large area of construction work. Any cementitious surface can be protected from the carbonation process, carbon dioxide permeability to save the structure, life of buildings. The pure acrylic emulsion binders or thermoplastic aliophatic acrylic high build coatings are widely used with excellent salt and alkali resistance, reduction in the chloride ion penetration, with antifungal and antibacterial properties. The use of inert filler further strengthened the dry film, preventing chalking and degradation. By selecting medium or low Tg polymer crack bridging properties are better. (*Table* 16.3).

High build acrylic coatings for bridges

The coatings applied on bridges and interchange, should have typical properties. Topcoat is based on the pure aliphatic acrylic resin, high performance water based or solvent based, pigmented system. Coating when applied in two coats. On one coat of silone - siloxane primer should have following critical properties.

- Excellent crack bridgeability
- Resistance to water
- Resistance to carbon dioxide and other air borne acids
- Should have the ability to allow the passage of water vapour from within the structure
- Excellent UV and weather resistance (*Table* 16.7).

Table 16.2: Thermal insulating paints

S.No	Properties requirements	Specifications / results
1.	Chemical nature	Pure acrylic emulsion as binder, pure sodium borosilicate hollow microsphere
2.	Breathable system	Should have moisture vapour permeability
3.	Thermal conductivity	0.019-0.025 Wmk = ASTM E 1225
4.	Solar reflectance, with exterior quality Titanium dioxide	Minimum 82% = ASTM E903
5.	Solar emittance	94% ASTM E903
6.	Heat flux equivalent	0.04 W/MIC
7.	Crack bridging ability	Minimumm 1 mm
8.	Resistance to ultra violet light	No effect, no cracking, chalking, no film degradation

Table 16.3: Anticarbonation coatings: Basement, garage area

S. No.	Properties requirements	Specification of results
1.	100% acrylic emulsion	High washability, water resistance
2.	Antibacteria system	Resistance to algicides, fungicides, inhibit mould growth
3.	Alkali resistance	Resist attack from alkali & salt
4.	Anti carbonation	To reduce coarbondioxide attack carbon dioxide permeability = R (m) 198-204
5.	Water permeability	90-105 gm/m^2/day (EN1062-2)
6.	Reduction in chloride ion penetration	minimum 97%/ASTM-C-1202
7.	Crack bridgeability	Minimum 1 mm
8.	Spread of flame	Sould meet B.S. 476 Part 6 & Part 7

Epoxy - polyurethane floor coatings = antiskids/screeds

A variety of floorings needs to be protected by application of most suitable coatings. These flooring may be of car parking area, office or residential basement, swimming poolside, industrial production area, corridor - passage area, garage, shopping malls. The quality needs will be different. However the choice of resins will be solvent based epoxy, solvent free epoxy, waterbased epoxy and water or solvent based aliphatic polyurethane coatings.

- Light duty flooring:- One coat penetrating primer - Two coats solvent / water based
- Medium duty flooring:- One coat of epoxy penetrating primer - two coats of solvent free high build epoxy
- Heavy duty coatings:- One coat of epoxy penetrating primer - one coat solvent free high build epoxy - sprinkle aggregates - one coat solvent free high build epoxy
- Heavy duty exterior coatings:- One coat epoxy penetrating primer - one coat solvent free epoxy with aggregates - one coat aliphatic PU topcoat.

The coatings should withstand heavy machineries, forklifts, tyre marks, other mechanical damages and chemical attack coatings should be impermeable to liquids, resistant to crackings and should have good elongation to take care of contraction, expansions. (*Table* 16.4)

Table 16.4: Epoxy floor coatings: Solvent free heavy duty

S.No	Properties requirements	Specifications/results
1.	System requirement (Interior application)	Epoxy primer sealer, Epoxy S.F Topcoat, with screeds or without screeds
2.	Compressive strength	62.5 *N/mm*^{2} = ASTM C 579
3.	Tensile strength	29.3 Nlmm^2 = ASTM C 307
4.	Fluxaral strength	18.6 *N/mm*^{2} = ASTM C 580
5.	Bond strength to host concrete	2.83 N *Imm*^{2} = ASTM C 884
6.	Rapid chloride permeability	1249 coulombs
7.	Impact resistance	No cracking or effect
8.	Shore a hardness	98: ASTM D 2240
9.	Flame of spread	Class A: ASTM D 1360

Table 16.5: Water Repellent Coatings

S.No	Properties requirements	Specifications/results
1.	System requirement	Silane-silixane modified polyacrylates
2.	Penetration properties	Sould penetrate in cermentitious surfaces, painted surfaces
3.	Transparency	Clear transparent, best clarity
4.	Water repellency	Should have lotus effect, when drop of water is placed over
5.	Reduction in chloride ion	Minimum 90%
6.	Water absorption	<1%
7.	Breathability to moisture vapours	Film sould be resistance to water peremeability, however should have good moisture vapour permeability

Silicone-siloxane penetrating primers

In the building and construction activities, once the structure is ready, walls are built using cementitious material, bricks, cement blocks or concrete precast. The most effective penetrati ng primer now in use is, solvent based silane-siloxane primer. The monomeric effect of silane and dimeric effect of siloxane takes care of penetration and sealing, with excellent adhesion to substrate and with good intercoat adhesion with topcoats. The primer allows moisture to evaporate and at the same time does not allow external salt or water to penetrate.

- Moisture vapour permeability - should meet specific values, depends on the system
- Reduction in chloride ion and water penetration - As required by specific projects

Water repellent coatings

Moisture protection though polymer network is, deployed for many masonry, old material structures, which protect the surface of coementitious materials for year together. Silicone based masonry water repellents currently provides the most effective protection against moisture decay and penetration of water. The silicone coating builds up an extremely stable, durable, three dimensional silicone resin network, which repels water, but the coating film

Table 16.6: Fire retardant paint

S.No	Properties requirements	Specifications/results
1.	Polymer binders	Thermoplastics solution polymer acrylic or SBS plasticized
2.	Fire resistance chemical additives	System should chemically retard the fire, prevent spreading
3.	Fire retardant BS 476	Resistance of dry film for certain period, for direct and indirect flame
4.	Minimum volume shrinkage	High solids, special aggregates for better retardation
5.	Adhesion of different substrates	Once subjected for fire test, should not loose adhesion, no peeling of

as excellent moisture vapour permeability. Coatings are flame resistant, easy to overpring, have low dirt pick up and reduces colorization of microorganisms. The well formulated water repellent coating, gives best results in context with reduction in chloride ion and water adsorption (Table 16.5).

Heavy duty glass flakes coatings

Glass flake epoxy coatings are well known as anticorrosive coatings, for protection in highly corrosive atmosphere. The nature of glass flakes, size, shape, ratio of epoxy to flakes, OFT are responsible for the highest

Table 16.7: Bridges and interchange coatings

S.No	Properties requirements	Specifications/results
1.	Chemical nature	Aliphatic acrylic high build, thermopastlic solution polymers
2.	Resistance to	Water, carbondioxide, waterborne acids
3.	Breathability	Ability to allow the passage of water vapour from within the structure
4.	Flexibility	Shall be elastomeric, flexible
5.	Reduction in water absorption ASTM C642	82% minimum after 28 days
6.	Reduction in chloride ion penetration	90% minimum after 28 days
7.	Water vapour transmission	> 13 gm/m²/day
8.	Carbon dioxide diffusion resistance	Equivalent to 500 mm of 30 N/mm² concrete

Table 16.8 : Floor coatings for ramp and car parking area

S.No	Properties requirements	Specifications/results
1.	System requirements	Epoxy primer, high solids epoxy intermediate coat, reinforced with glass flakes, topcoat high build aliphatic polyurethane
2.	Adhesion peel strength	35 : ASTM D 1000
3.	Tear Strength	28.6 N/mm = ASTM D 624
4.	Crack bridgeability	2 mm : ASTM C 836
5.	Rapid chloride permeability	488 coulombus = AASH TO T277
6.	Water permeability	Nil = DIN 1048
7.	Shore A abrasion	87 = ASTM D2240
8.	Taber abrasion	Weigh loss 0.001 = ASTM 4060
9.	Pull of strength	2.6 N/mm^2 = BS 1881

performance. The parallel orientation of platy glass flake, helps to achieve high level of moisture vapour impermeability. Also glass flakes imparts, higher hardness, chemical resistance, excellent abrasion. A flooring with antiskid properties are widely used for chemical plants, marine environment, splash zone heavy duty pathways.

Fire retardant and intumescent coatings

Whereever people and property needs to be protected from fire, paints-coatings which retards - resist fire are used when there a sudden fire breaksout, it tries to spreadout very fast. To overcome the situation, for evacuating people and limiting the structural damage, fire retardant paint that resists the flame are used, the unqiue chemicals present in the dry film prevents fire to reach directly to the surface - substrate, for certain interval of time. These paints are mainly used for high rise buildings, towers, schools, mosques, temples, churches, malls, cinema theatres, hospitals, airports, (*Table* 16.6).

Some of the projects with high performance coatings

Burj Oubai down town: 45 million sq.ft, 30,000 new homes, nine hotels, five million sq.ft retail space, 32000 sq meters of landscapes garden and 12 hector lake.

Bur; Dubai Tower: Highest tower in the world, in Burj Dubai down town, with mall, Gold souk, residential apartments and office complexes.

Dubai Mall: Situated in Burj Dubai Towerwill be ready by mid 2007.

Table 16.9 : Water proofing materials = Roof coating

S.No	Properties requirements	Specifications/results
1.	Chemical nature	Pure acrylic copolymer emulsion of aliphatic polyurethane emulsion
2.	Elongation at break	Flexible, continous membrance (20%)
3.	Ecological nature	Water based, environmental friendly
4.	Average permeability	8.8 perms per inch
5.	Adhesion strength	Not less than 8 kg f/CM2 {N/cm^2}
6.	Water vapour transmission ASTM	Not more than 600 mg/m^2-50 hrs.
7.	Ultraviolet resistance	No chalking, fading, cracking etc.
8.	Chemical resistance	As per ASTM 1308, resistance to various 27 chemicals listed.

Largest mall in the world, 4 levels bigger than Edmonton mall, Canada, more than 50 soccer pitches.

Palm }ebel Ali, Palm }umeirah, Palm Daira: Artificial islands with palm design in the deep sea water with waterfront, beaches, many five star hotels, villas.

Dubai Creek Business Bay: Near creekside on large area, business bay being created, with office complexes.

Internet City: Software and hardware hubs, offices. *Knowledge City:* University & study complexes.

City of *Arabia:* Entertainment, children amusement parks.

Falcon City of *Wonders:* Seven Wonders of the World at one place.

Park Square with Shopping Malls: Metrorail main office - status, train on surface and underground. Hanging stations, train track, parallel to shaikh zayed Road, Dubai.

Festival City Dubai Land: Permanent structure of entertainment places, worlddifferent countries pavallions, amusement park, five star hotels, restaurants.

Calf City Dubai and Cold club: Full of greenery with 6 star resorts and hotels.

The World Island: Creation of world map in the deep sea area, with residential complexes, hotels and restaurants,

waterfronts, clubs, recreation clubs.

International City: Residential complexes and malls being constructed, with different countries surroundings.

Dubai Sports Complex: Number of sports stadiums at one place, modernised facilities, one cricket stadium.

Jumeirah Beach Residences and Hotels: Number of high rise residential buildings, with 40 international hotels.

Applications of high performance coatings

* High rise buildings
* Towers
* Swimming pool
* Bridges and interchange
* Shopping malls
* Office complexes
* Health clubs
* Roads, curbstones
* Industrial floorings
* Garage, malls flooring
* Drinking water tank
* Sports stadiums, tracks
* Beach hotels
* Water fronts areas
* Subway-underground stations
* Artificial lakes
* Sports complexes
* Horse riding trails
* Squash, tennis courts
* Amusement parks
* Car show rooms
* Hospitals
* Conductive floorings
* Basement car parking

17

Bio-Diesel – Opportunities for the Coating Industry

BIO diesel has suddenly become relevant due to escalating price of crude oil. In the 1970's, the international crude oil price was about $ 2.40/ barrel. This was suddenly jacked up is US$12/barrel by the OPEC (Organization of Petroleum Exporting Countries.) From 1973 to 2005, the oil has travelled a long journey from $12 to the record price US$ 67/barrel. This has put the world economy under pressure. The availability of oil is decreasing on one end and our dependence seems to constantly increase on it.

Bio diesel is one of the most interesting initiatives in the direction of reducing dependence on petroleum fuels. The technology goes a full circle here. Diesel, the inventor of diesel engine run his first machine on vegetable oil. This was before mineral oil was discovered. Now we are reconsidering changing over to vegetable oils. Only difference is, in place of using it as a tri glyceride, it is being proposed as methyl or ethyl esters.

As proposed, bio diesel is a mixture of vegetable oil methyl or ethyl esters. Thus most of it would be methyl or ethyl stearate followed by methyl of ethyl oleate with a small proportion of limoleates palmitate and laurates. It may also contain some small amount of hydroxy or keto acid which may be formed by the air oxidation of the products. At present, the eastern world which prepared it self about 30 years ago, with the vision of what is happening today, is the primary suppliers of cheap non edible-edible oils which form the basic raw materials for manufacture of bio diesel. Considering the current selling price diesel (Rs. 37/lt, density 0.84 g/cc) and the international price of vegetable oils ($ 400/T) (Soyabear $520-530) methanol ($ 300/T) and ethanol ($ 400/T), the viability of setting up a new plant is very remote. The Rs 37/lt price includes about Rs 17-18 in the form of various taxes thus leaving very little margin for the refiner to use this mixture as an extender in refinery diesel. The sulfur content of biodiesel is near zero. This can offer the refiner some advantage in refining costs. Substantial policy changes in the import of vegetable oils would have to be implemented before bio diesel becomes a reality. Today, the best option for the manufacturers appears to be use of deodorizer distillate from vegetable oil refining industry. This is a distillate rich in free fatty acids (80%) with tochoferol, sterols and vitamin E. The vegetable oil refining capacity of the country is about 30,00,000 T/A. The deodorizer distillate is about 1 % of the processed oil. Thus, about 30,000/T of it is available annually, locally. The imports of the distillate as a commodity attracts lower duty rate. It may soon become possible for several chemical industries to use their surplus capacity to convert vegetable oils into bio diesel and glycerine. Some policy changes for the nation may go long way to reduce the pressure of the oil imports and also utilize the unused capacity of several chemical industries.

The conversion of vegetable oils to biodiesel is a very simple process. A good review is available (1) The trans sterification process is non corrosive, can be conveniently used even in mild steel vessels, is fast, can use methanol or ethanol in dry conditions. From this point of view, use of methanol is favourable. The reaction mixture is separated into bio diesel and glycerine by phase separation after the alcohol, the dissolving phase, has been distilled out. The glycerine is separated due to insolubility in the oil phase and due to its considerably higher density separates out conveniently.

There are two main products of the process.

1. Methyl esters of mixed fatty acids
2. Glycerine

We propose to discuss the opportunities for our industry with both these materials.

There are situations when the paint chemist would like to process an alkyd with zero acid value. It is almost impossible if one starts processing with vegetable oils, polyols and diacids. If a large excess of polyol is used, it is lost in several undesirable reactions such as evaporations, etherification oxidation, acetyl formation etc. Thus the option to prepare low acid value alkyds are limited to either addition or monohydric alcohols or use transesterification process by starting with methyl or ethyl esters of fatty acids and the dibasic acid. In this way, the acid value of the batch would be zero through out the reaction and several side reactions would be completely avoided. Lower reaction temperatures can also be employed. Thus the polymerization of the oil can be avoided and the drying properties of the alRyds would be superior. The loss of polyol by side reactions such as etherification, dehydration, acetal formation can be drastically reduced for the advantage of the product. The diacids must also be used as dimethyl or diethyl esters. One opportunity that opens up with this technology is incorporation of basic materials such as zinc oxide to prevent yellowing of white alkyds.

Refined vegetable oils show some acid value (0.5 -1 mg KOH/g) The bio diesel would show zero acid value. Thus mixture of bio diesel (up to 60-65% by weight), polyol such as glycol penta erythritol and di esters of dibasic acids such as diethyl or dimethyl o-phthalate could be transterified in a batch to prodtlce the alkyd would have lower viscosity at higher solids and should have better drying characteristics due to absence of thermal polymerization.

Glycerine

Where as bio diesel presents itself as the greatest opportunity of the next century in terms of employment potential for the rural poor and sick chemical industry who would be able to produce volumes they have never imagined, glycerine presents itself is the biggest problem in the growth of the bio diesel industry. The available quantities of glycerine would out strip all the requirements and the entire chemical industry would be busy finding value added outlets to this abundant "Green" raw material.

Each ton of vegetable oil would yield about one ton of bio diesel and about 100 kg of glycerol. India is expected to manufacturer 30 million T of bio diesel by year 2020. For which large scale plantation of Jatropa has been taken up on arid lands of various parts of the country. This would lead to production of about 3 million T of glycerol/year. As it is, the prices of glycerol have started falling after some vegetable oils have been converted in bio diesel in the East and Europe.(3) The quantities for chemical consumption have been coming from the.soap industries with very little coming from the synthetic routes. There are nearly 1583 reported uses of glycerine (4) which are currently met by natural glycerine. We are putting out some thoughts for utilization of glycerine, some of these may require extensive research programs to establish their usefulness.

Selective reduction to trimethylene glycol (TMG) (Propane 1-3 diol)

$$\begin{matrix} CH_2OH \\ | \\ CHOH \\ | \\ CH_2OH \end{matrix} \; + H_2 \xrightarrow[\text{Catalyst}]{\text{Selective}} \begin{matrix} CH_2OH \\ | \\ CH_2 \\ | \\ CH_2OH \end{matrix}$$

Ethylene Glycol is the essential raw material for manufacture of synthetic fibre polyethylene terephthalate which has already reached the level of 40 million tons per year. This requires about 13 million tons of ethylene glycol. This is almost entirely produced from petrochemical ethylene. (India is an exception with a small alcohol based capacity). The molecular weight of trimethylene glycol is slightly higher than ethylene glycol (62 vis 76), the requirement would be slightly higher at 15 million tons. This would come from about 20 million tons of glycerine. The world is eager to change over to trimethylene glycol to make a superior grade of fibre forming polymer PTT (Poly trimethylene terephthalate) provided adequate quantities ofTMG become available. Catalytic (chemical or bio) appears to be the only viable option for a sustainable development.

Other interesting glycol is propylene glycol which can be usd by the paint industry for preparation of polyesters for urethanes.

Eco friendly solvents

Glycerine undergoes etherification reactions with aldehydes and ketones with ease. Some examples are cited here.

1.
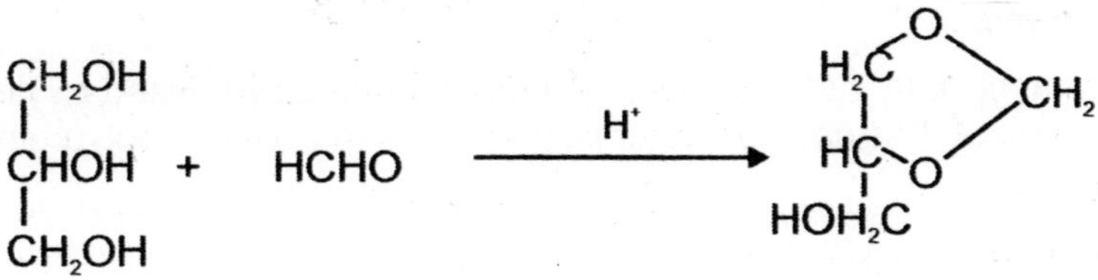

2.
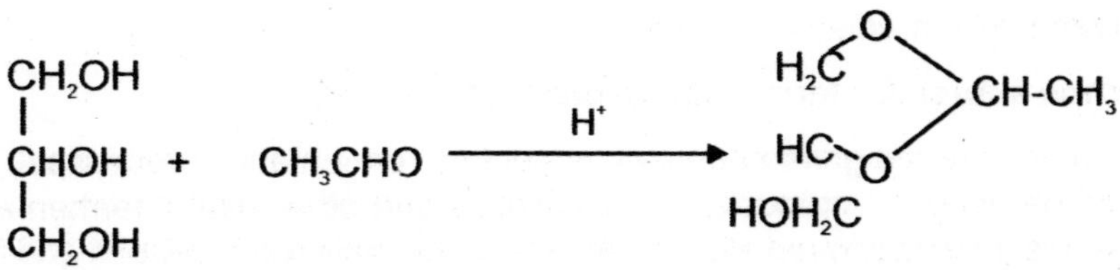

3.
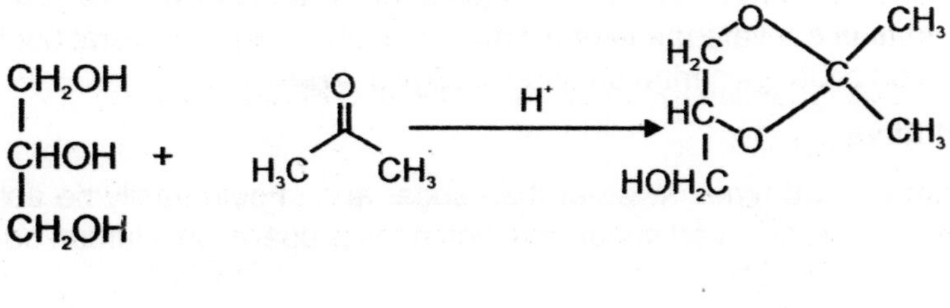

All of these are primary ether alcohols, are water soluble miscible with all the solvents used in paint industry and good solvents for resins and polymers. These are potential candidates for replacement of glycol ethers and their esters from the coatings industry. The rate at which the hydrocarbon prices are going up, we would not be surprised if they replace a part of MTO in alkyd paints also.

Epichloro hydrin, glycedol and polyglycerol

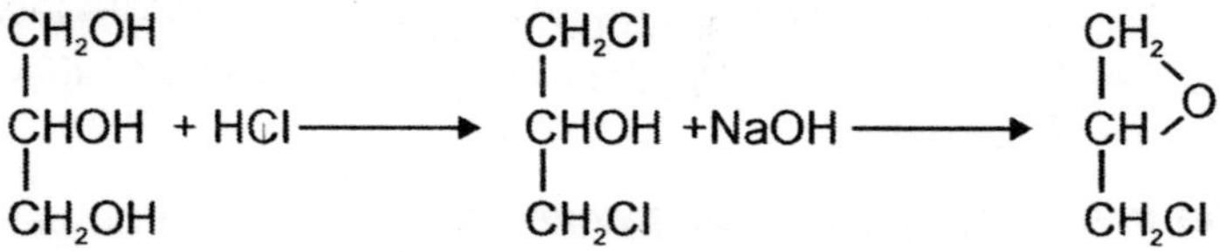

The primary reaction in all these cases would be hydro chlorination of glycerol. If the product at the first stage, glycerol mono chloro hydrin, is treated with sodium hydroxide, glycedol results. Dichlorination followed by dehydrochlorination would lead to formation of Epichloro hydrin. This is one important raw material for epoxy resins.

Poly glycerol

On heating with a strong base, glycerol can be polymerised to yield a polyether polyol. This can be further tailored for preparation of polyurethane rigid foams.

Acrolein and acrylic acid

Under special dehydrating conditions, glycerine can be dehydrated to acrolein which is well established intermediate for acrylic acid, so badly required to be produced in India.

Carbon source for fermentation product

Glycerine is a good source of nutrient for fermentation processes. This could be used for production of antibiotics and other useful fermentation products, probably even alcohol. As a feed for microbial reactions and food preparations, Glycerol is a non-toxic substance. The LDso for mice is > 25g/kg. This makes it a safe material for microbial processes. Several bacteria can thrive on dilute glycerine solutions (25g/l or lower.

Food additive

Glycerol is 1.6 times sweeter than sugar and should easily be able to substitute sugar and invert sugar from soft drink preparation. Human beings any way consume it as a part of fat. It may be possible to use some glycerine as a good substitute to liquid sugars and take away the pressure from lands for production of sugar cane.

Carbon credits

The global warming has started showing its effects. The changes in environment such as extreme cold, extreme high temperature and excessive rainfall are all being attributed to high carbon dioxide emission. The world has taken note of this and there have been international conferences and agreements to reduce fresh carbon emissions. Under the Kyoto agreement, the signatories will minimize fresh CO_2 emissions. Thus, cement, power, petroleum, automotive, fertilisers, steel, mining, non-ferrous metals, chemicals and refining industries are under pressure. A penalty of US \$ 7/ T CO_2 emission is payable for remedying the excess CO_2 emissions. The interesting part for us is that this is tradable. Anyone recycling carbon dioxide i.e. using natural products for the manufacture of industrial chemicals can trade the credits @ US \$7/T CO_2 not produced in manufacture of the corresponding petrochemicals. This is where we find huge opportunity for the paint industry. Indian paint industry has traditionally used natural raw materials such as vegetable oils, rosin and vegetable turpentine. These should be tradable with petrole.um based products such as acrylates, phthalates, other diols and polyols, derived from petroleum. The carbon dioxide produced while producing these chemicals would have to be carefully calculated and authenticated for carbon credits. For example phthalic anhydride is manufactured by oxidation of ortho xylene. The typical yield may be about 80%. Thus about 20% P-xylene is lost by complete oxidation to carbon dioxide and 200 kg o-xylene is converted to carbon dioxide.

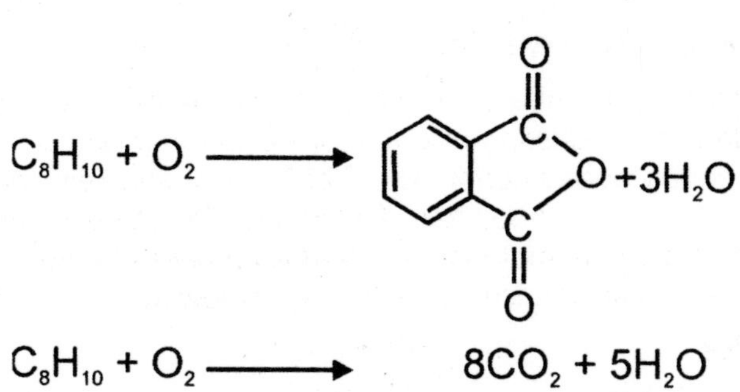

Thus for every ton of phthalic anhydride manufactured - about 0.5 tons of carbon dioxide is produced or for every ton of phthalic anhydride not used, 0.5 ton of CO_2 is not produced. Therefore, for substituting each ton of phthalic anhydride US $ 3.5 can be ~imed as carbon credits. Similar data needs to be worked ciut and authenticated for petroleum raw materials.

We see a big opportunity for Indian paint industry here because we still use a large quantity of natural products.

18

Road Marking Paints

Introduction

HOT melt thermoplastic road marking paint nowadays is most widely used for road marking. This type of paint dries quickly in less than ten minutes. It is very ideal for marking in a full traffic condition. The paint is heated at 180-200°C in a kettle with constant stirring and released from a closed system and sprayed on the road surface.

Composition of HMTP road marking paint

British Standard 3262 has been adopted in 1989 to cover the specifications for HMTP road marking paint. The same has been recommended by ministry of surface transport Govt. of India in the form of M.O.S.T. Specification. The clause 803-4 of this specification, gives the composition of the HMTP road marking paint, which is shown in *Table* 18.1 *(A)*.

The composition is just like a powder coating except that it includes glass beads. The glass beads are dispersed in the mix to impart the reflectivity to the marking. At night, under the headlamp illumination, the marking should be visible and this visibility is brought about by the inclusion of glass beads. The specification of the glass beads to be included in the mix is also mentioned in the M.O.S.T. specification under clause 803.4.3. It is given in *Table* 18.1(8). The glass beads should be transparent, colourless and free from milkiness, dark particles and excessive air inclusions.

These glass beads do not become effective until some wear has taken place. For this reason "drop on" glass beads are spread onto the surface of the marking immediately after the application to achieve immediately

Table 18.1 (A): M.O.S.T. specification for composition of hot melt thermoplastic road marking paint

Sr.No	Component	Percentage by weight	
		White paint	Yellow Paint
1	Binder	18.0 min.	18.0 min.
2	Glass beads	30-40	30-40
3	Titanium dioxide	10.0 min.	As per requirement
4	Yellow pigment	-	-- do --
5	Calcium carbonate & Inert fillers	42.0 max.	-- do --

reflectivity. The M.O.S.T. specifications for "drop on" glass beads are also given in clause 803.4.3 which is shown in *Table* 18.1 *(C)*.

Properties

The essential properties for a paint to be applied as HMTP road marking paint are also specified in the M.O.S.T. specification. They are given in *Table 18.1(D)*. The paint should have the softening point 102.5±9.5°C. It should dry within 15 minutes with minimum 65% luminance factor.

After application and proper drying, the marking stripe shall show no appreciable deformation or discoloration under traffic and under road temperature up to 60°C. The marking shall not deteriorate by contact with Sodium Chloride, Calcium Chloride or Oil dripping from traffic.

Binder for HMTP road marking paint

Hydrocarbon resins, derived 'from materials obtained by deep cracking of various streams of petroleum distillation, are generally used for the preparation of HMTP road marking paint. Some research work has also been done in Central Road Research Institute, New Delhi on this subject. They utilized hydrocarbon resins along with maleic resins and some other synthetic modified resins for this purpose.

Aim of the present investigation

The authors are interested in utilizing rosin modified Lac (RM- Lac) resins for the preparation of HMTP road marking paint. The RM-Lac resins with varying softening point have been developed by the author. These resins were found to have excellent film properties. The RM-Lac resin with softening point 95°C as chosen for the study since the was chosen for the study since the softening point of the paint as per M.O.S.T. specification should be 102.5±9.5°C.

Table 18.1 (A): M.O.S.T. specification for glass beads

(A)	Sieve size	Per cent retained
	1.18 mm	0 to 3
	850 micron	5 to 20
	425 micron	65 to 95
	180 micron	0 to 10
(B)	Roundness	70% min, true spheres
(C)	Refractive index	1.50 min.
(D)	Free flowing properties	Should pass free flow test

Experimental

The raw materials used in investigation are lac, rosin, whilting glass beads, wax and pigments. They were tested for various properties and the results are reported in Tables 18.2(A) & 2(B).

Preparation of rosin modified lac

Lac and rosin were charged in the reactor in the ratio 1:3 by weight. The charge was heated to a temperature between 200-220°C for 4 hours and the samples were withdrawn periodically to check the acid value. When no further decrease in acid value was observed, the reaction was stopped. The product obtained was tested for its acid value, softening point. Specific gravity,viscosity & colour. The results are given in *Table* 18.3.

Preparation of HMTP of marking print

Compositions : Three different compositions were selected for the preparation of HMTP road marking paint namely PA. PB & PC. In all the three compositions the quantities of the glass beads, wax and pigment were

Table 18.1 (C): M.O.S.T. specification for "drop on" glass beads

(A)	Sieve size	Per cent retained
	850 micron	0 to 5
	600 micron	5 to 20
	300 micron	30 to 75
	180 micron	10 to 30
	Below 180 micron	0 to 15
(B)	Roundness	70% min. true spheres
(C)	Refractive index	1.80 min.
(D)	Free flowing properties	Should pass free flow test

Table 18.1 (D): M.O.S.T. specification for HMTP road marking paint

Sr. No.	Properties	Requirements
1.	Luminance 6 at45°	65% min.
2.	Drying time	Not more than 15 minute
3.	Skid resistance	Not less than 45
4.	Cracking resistance at low temperature	Should show no cracks
5.	Softening point	102.5±9.5°C
6.	Flow resistance	Not more than 25%
7.	Yellowness index 10 for white paint	Not more than 0.12

kept constant as 35%, 9% and 16% respectively. The resin content varied from 25% to 35%. In composition P A, the resin was taken as 25%, while in PB & PC the resin content were 30% -and 35% respectively. The compositions are given in *Table* 18.4.

Preparation: Pigments, whiting, wax and the resin were taken in a pot and heated to make a uniform mixture by grinding and mixing in hot condition. The mixture was then cooled and' broken into chips and small pieces.These pieces were then crushed into fine powder using a grinder mixre. The fine powder thus obtained was mixed with required quantity of glass beads to get the final product.

Application and evaluation

For application, the sample was heated to melt with constant stirring in a small pot. The fluid molten paint thus obtained, was applied on cement blocks to get 5-10 mm thick uniform coating using a screed box. The coating was then evaluated for its drying time, cracking resistance, luminance factor, flow resistance, resistance to water, salt water and lubricating oil and other properties. The results are reported in Table 18.5.

Testing Methods

Free flow test : Pour 100 gms of clean dry glas beads into a clean, dry glass funnel having a 100 mm stem and 6 mm orifice. If necessary, initiate the flow by lightly tapping in thefunnels. The glass spheres should be essentially free of lumps and clusters and should flow freely through the funnel.

Flow resistance test: Cat two conical specimens of the road marking materials, so that each has an angle of nominally 60° at its apex and a verticla height of 100±5 mm. After cooling and setting for 24 hours, remove

Table 18.2 (A) : Analysis of raw material

Sr. No.	Raw Material	Result of analysis	
1.	Lac	Softening Point	94°C
		Acod Value	42.6
		Hydroxyl value	755.5
		Colour (50% Lac solution in toluene)	R=12
		By lovibond tintometer	Y=12
2.	Rosin	Softening point	73°C
		Acid Value	168.4
3.	Whiting	Oil absorption	22.6%
		Bulk density	0.833 gm/cc
4.	Paraffin wax	Melting point	75°C
		density	0.63 gm/CC

the specimen from the mould and place it, point upwards on a flat level surface in a room or box maintained at a temperature of 23±2°C for 48 hours. Measure the height of the cone before and after the conditioning period. Calculate the decrease in height of the specimen as a percentage.

Results and discussions

Rosin modified lac used in this investigation was prepared in the laboratory as per the procedure development by the authors Three different compositions were tried for HMTP road marking paint. Since the softening point of the

Table 18.2 (B) : Analysis of Glass beads

A)	Sieve size	Per cent retained
	1.18 mm	Nil
	850 micron	5.0
	425 micron	85
	180 micron	10
B)	Roundness	87% True spheres
C)	Refractive index	1.50
D)	Free flowing properties	Passed free flow test

Table 18.3 : Analysis of rosin-modified lac

Sr. No.	Properties	Result of analysis
1.	Softening point	95°C
2.	Acid value	78.2
3.	Specific gravity	0.965
4.	Viscocity (70% solid in toluene) By Ford Cup method	24 seconds
5.	Colour (50% solid in toluene) By Lovibond tintometer	R=2,Y=12

paint shoud be 102±9.5°C (as per M.O.S.t. specification) i.e. between 93°C & 12°C, the RM-Lac having softening point as 95°C was used in the investigation. For the preparation of this RM-Lac resin the Lac: Rosin ratio was taken as 1:3 by weight. the colour of RM-Lac was improved by the reaction from 12R+16Y to 2R+12Y. The composition PA contained 25% resin, while PB & PC samples were prepared with 30% & 35% binder contents respectively. As perthe M.O.S.T. specification, the glass beads content should be between 30 to 40%; therefore 35% glass beads were utilized in all the three compositions. To maintain the flexibility of the coating 9% paraffin wax was incorporated in all the three formulations. The paint was given yellow colour by using TiO_2 and yellow pigment as 15% & 1 % respectively in these compositions.

Table 18.4 shows the properties of the road marking paints. The softening points obtained were between 96-99°C. The drying time was less than 10

Table 18.4 : Composition of HMTP-Road marking paint (% by weight)

Sr. No.	Ingredients	Composition		
		PA	PB	PC
1.	Rosin modified lac	25	30	35
2.	Pigments			
	A) TiO_2	15	15	15
	B) Yellow pigment	1	1	1
3.	Glass beads	35	35	35
4.	Whiting	15	10	5
5.	Paraffin wax	9	9	9

Table 18.5 : Properties of road marking paints

Sr. No.	Ingredients	results of analysis of composition		
		PA	PB	PC
1.	Softening point	99ºC	98ºC	96ºC
2.	Drying time	8 min	8 min	8 min
3.	Luminance at 450	77.3%	78.4%	79.6%
4.	Cracking resistance at 00C (24 hours)	No crakcs	No cracks	No crcaks
5.	Flow resistance	12%	16%	19%
6.	Resistance to			
	a) Water (48 Hours)	Ex.	Ex.	Ex.
	b) Salt water (30% salt) 48 hours	Ex.	Ex.	Ex.
	c) Lubricating oil (48 hours)	Ex.	Ex.	Ex.

minutes, while luminance factors were much higher than the required values. The coated cement blocks were tested for the resistance towards water, salt water ,and lubricating oils for 48 hours and excellent results were obtained. All the three samples showed no cracking at O°C for 24 hours. All the results obtained are well within the limit required by M.O.S.T. specification.

19

Emulsions

Introduction

EXTERIOR masonry walls have long been represented as one of the most difficult maintenance challenges for the contractors and the painters. Masonry often exists as large monolithic areas that usually contain some cracks, most of the cracks are relatively small ranging from hair line thickness to not more than 1/8" in width, but they undergo remarkable fluctuations in size as much as 300% to 400% or even higher, that is experienced due to wide swings in temperature. When conventional paint experiences the stresses caused by this movement it responds by cracking. So a quality exterior paint should have crack bridging ability as well as elasticity.

Virtually all of the polymers tested by the industry into mid 1970s proved unsuccessful with respect to elasticity as they formed hard films that were too rigid to accommodate the temperature related fluctuations in the dimensions of the cracks. Recognizing that hard binders were not the answer, the industry turned to "Softer polymers" with lower glass transition temperature. These furnished excellent elasticity over a wide range of temperature. Unfortunately in solving one problem, the soft binders created another. These polymers produced tacky films that accumulated dirt, with a totally adverse effect on the appearance. The challenge is to have coating with the desired elasticity and very good dirt pick up resistance. For country like ours, dust and dirt is an issue and so are the temperature fluctuations.

The various possible binder types for flexible exterior coating are pure acrylic, styrene - acrylic and vinyl acetate - versatate copolymers.

Table 19.1 : List of the raw materials and suppliers

Emulsion Raw Materials	Suppliers
Methyl methacrylate	GSFC-Commercial grade
n-butyl Acrylate	LG-international-commercial grade
Methacrylic acid	ICI international-commercial grade
Hydroxy ethyl methacrylate	Rohm Gmbh
Potassium persulphate	E-Merck
Sodium bi carbonate	E-Merck
Hexane diol diacrylate	Sartomer
Ethyl methacrylate	Degussa
Isodecyl acrylate	Degussa
Isobornyl methacrylate	Degussa
Veova 11	Revolution B.V.
Conventional Surfactant (Alkyl Sulphonate)	Dow chemicals
Polymerisable Surfactant (Alkene Sulphonate)	Rhodia
Tert. dodecyl mercaptan	Omega Corporation
Paint Raw Materials	
Titanium dioxide, Rutile	Duopont
Calcium carbonate	Lih Hsjang Ind. Cop.
Cosolvents	Eastman Chemicals
Dispersant	Rohm and Haas
Glycol	Eastman Chemicals
Preservative	BTP (1) Lltd.
Dapro 4164	Dani Global Elementis (USA)
Cellulosic Thickener	Clariant

The most significant distinction lies in the area of the inherent elasticity, dirt resistance, hydrolysis and ultra violet stability. As per the literature pure acrylic emulsion polymers are the only type that can provide most of the properties. Styrenated - acrylic and vinyl acetate - Versatate binders are each lacking in one or more parameters. In our work we have studied, the elasticity and its retention of all these three fundamental typc of binders and selected pure acrylic and its modification for further study.

Initially it has been thought that addition of typical plasticiziers such as phthalate esters to conventional paints would give the desired elasticity but it was soon found to be operative at limited range of temperature and more it migrates to the surface and eventually out of the coatings entirely. Dirt from air tends to adhere to the oily liquid plasticizer and seriously affects the coating appearance. The migration of plasticizer from the coatings also has an adverse effect on elasticity and durability.In order to achieve optimum dirt pick up resistance along with elasticity, it is desirable to have a suitable glass transition temperature of the polymer system along with moderate chemical and surface crosslinking. It is desirable for any exterior coating

Table 19.2 : Paint formulations

Ingredients	Parts by weight
Water	9.40
Glycol	1.00
Gellulosic Thickener	0.20
Biocide	0.10
AMP 95	0.10
Incan preservative	0.10
Defoamer	0.05
Fungicide	1.00
Dispersant	0.60
Non ionic sufractant	0.15
Defoamer	0.05
Mineral Turpentine	1.00
Urethane Modified Thickener	1.00
Titanium dioxide (Rutile)	22.00
Calcium carbonate	14.00
Defoamer	0.05
Cosolvent	1.00
Liqour ammonia	0.20
Emulsion	38.00
Ropaque OP 62	10.00
Total	**100.00**

technology to aim at taking care of and protecting surface by controlling water absorption and its repellency and at the same time allowing water vapour and gas diffusion, along with crack bridging ability.

In this paper, the work carried out to study various aspects of development of emulsion for exterior coating with respect to optimum dirt pick up resistance, elasticity, its retention, and water resistance is highlighted.

Experimentation

The raw materials used and their suppliers are given in *Table* 19.1. Raw materials are used as such supplied by the supplier.

Emulsion processing

In a flask, deionised water is taken, and then surfactant is added, followed by initiator and chain transfer agent. Monomer mixture was added into this flask under stirring over a period till milky white pre-emulsion was formed.

Deionised water, surfactant, and initiator were charged in the reactor and temperature raised. Seed comonomer was added into the reactor and the temperature raised gradually to processing temperature, 80°C.

Table 19.3: Emulsion formulations with different Tg developed for exterior paint

Ingredients	**Expt.1 Tg =-20°C**	**Expt.2 Tg = -10°C**	**Expt.3 Tg = 0°C**	**Expt.4 Tg = 10°C**
Deionised water	53.08	53.08	53.08	53.08
Surfactant	1.80	1.80	1.80	1.80
Potassium per sulfate	0.12	0.12	0.12	0.12
Sodium bi carbonate	0.08	0.08	0.08	0.08
Tert.dodecyl mercaptan	0.06	0.06	0.06	0.06
Methyl meth acrylate	13.00	16.40	19.50	22.60
Butyl Acrylate	30.10	26.70	23.60	20.50
Hydroxy ethyl methacrylate	0.20	0.20	0.20	0.20
Glacial Meth acrylic acid	0.60	0.60	0.60	0.60
Tert.butyl hydro peroxide	0.02	0.02	0.02	0.02
Sodium Formaldehyde sulfoxylate	0.02	0.02	0.02	.02
Fungicide	0.10	0.10	0.10	0.10
Defoamer	0.02	0.02	0.02	0.02
Liq. Ammonia (16 %)	0.80	0.80	0.80	0.80
Total	**100.00**	**100.00**	**100.00**	**100.00**
Characterisation of emulsion developed				
Viscosity on stormer (gms)	80	79	79	80
%NVM	45.80	45.70	45.80	45.8
PH	9.30	9.20	9.30	9.20
Particle size (microns)	0.12	0.11	0.11	0.11

Table 19.4: Paint study on emulsion developed

Paint properties	**Exp.1**	**Exp.2**	**Exp. 3**	**Exp.**
Elongation after (12 days)	350%	300%	180%	60%
Tensile strength in kgf/mm2 After (12 days)	0.18	0.20	0.26	0.32
Dirt Pick up rating (10 : best)	2	5	6	8

At process temperature, the pre emulsion addition started into reactor charge at constant rate over a time period of four hours. After completion of pre-emulsion addition small dose of chaser catalysts was added and digestion carried out for 120 minutes. Batch is then cooled and preservatives, defoamer and finally neutralizing agent was added under stirring. Then the material was filtered through nylon, coagulum collected and developed aqueous polymeric dispersion used in paint for further characterization.

Paint processing

Water, propylene glycol, thickener, biocide were mixed under the highspeed mixer, and then AMP 95 added. To the jelly prepared fungicide & surfactant were added, mixed well for 15 min. Then Titanium Dioxide and calcium carbonate were charged and grinded for 30 minutes, finish was checked, - it was smooth and uniform. Then co solvent and neutralizing agent were added under stirring. In the mill base prepared, emulsion, Ropaque OP 62, water and defoamer were charged under slow stirring speed & stirring continued until uniform paint is obtained. *Table* 19.2 depicts the paint formulation used for study of the Emulsion properties.

The emulsion polymerization was carried out with variations in monomer composition resulting in various glass transition temperature

These experimental lattices were studied in paint formulation given in *Table* 19.2 and characterized for paint properties.

Characterization

The following test methods were followed for characterization of emulsion & paints:

1} *% NVM:* As per ASTM D4758-92.

2} *Viscosity on stormer:* As per ASTM D562-81.

3} *Particle size:* Through UV visible Spectrophotometer based on correlation with TEM.

4} *pH:* pH meter was calibrated at 7.0 and 9.2 pH.

5) *Water resistance:* As per ASTM D870-97.

6) *% Water absorption:* % increase in weight of film after 96 hrs immersed in water.

7} *% loss in alkali:* % loss in weight of film after 96 hrs immersed in 5% alkali solution.

8) *Water vapour transmission rate:* As per ASTM D 1653-93 .

9} *Elongation & tensile strength:* A paint film of 500 microns is applied on Lanneta release paper, and it was kept for drying in humidity chamber [maintained at 25 Deg. C. for 12 days]. A strip of width 15 mm is cut and used to check elongation & tensile strength on Lloyd Tensile Tester.

10) Dirt pickup resistance: Two coats of paint were applied on the asbestos panel. The painted panel was kept for exterior exposure for 3 months at an angle of 5 deg from the horizontal.

Results and discussion

Glass transition temperature for desired coating

The glass transition temperature (Tg) is one of the important characteristics of the coating. Dirt pick up is a major problem with coatings that are soft and tacky. If the Tg is high, the coating may exhibit excellent nonblocking characteristics, but the coating will be brittle, and have poor impact resistance. Low Tg would result in tacky film which would be of little value for decorative application. The desirable Tg for coating application is dependent on the specific characteristics of the polymer used in the coating.

Tg effects the following properties of a coating:

1. Blocking
2. Adhesion
3. Elasticity
4. Flow and Leveling
5. Viscosity
6. Tackiness (dirt pick up)
7. Impact Resistance
8. Hardness

The theoretical Tg of emulsion was calculated using Fox equation:

$$\frac{1}{T_{gp}} = \frac{W_1}{T_{g1}} + \frac{W_2}{T_{g2}} +$$

Where

W_1 : Weight fraction of monomer 1 in the copolymer

W_2 : Weight fraction of monomer 2 in the copolymer

T_{g1} : Glass transition temperature of homopolymer of monomer 1 in Kelvin

T_{g2}: Glass transition temperature of homopolymer of monomer 2 in Kelvin

T_{gp} : Glass transition temperature of gp copolymer in Kelvin

Table 19.3 depicts the emulsion formulations with varying glass transition temperature with varying comonomer composition. The glass transition temperatures studied were in the range of -20°C to 10°C.

Table 19.4 shows the comparison of the properties of Paints prepared with above emulsions.

From the above study *(Table* 19.4) it is seen that experiment 2 shows desired elasticity with optimum dirt pick up resistance through experiment 3 & 4 shows good dirt pick up resistance but do not have desired elasticity *(Table* 19.4). So Tg -1Q°c has been selected for further exploration to improve dirt pick up resistance keeping elasticity as in experiment 2 based paint.

Specialty monomer incorporation

To improve the dirt pick up resistance following specialty monomers were incorporated in the polymer backbone and studied in paint formulation.

Each of the studied monomers had their characteristics properties.

Iso bornyl methacrylate

Iso bornyl methacrylate is shown in the *Fig.* 19.1. It has Tg=11 O°c8 and recommended for reacted system. The idea is to have Tg higher than methyl methacrylate but total tg of copolymer -10°C, for improvement in DPUR with an expectation to have similar elasticity. In *Table* 19.6 , the results of paint characterization based on exp.6 indicates that though dirt pick up resistance improves the elasticity is reduced with respect to paint based on emulsion without the subject monomer.

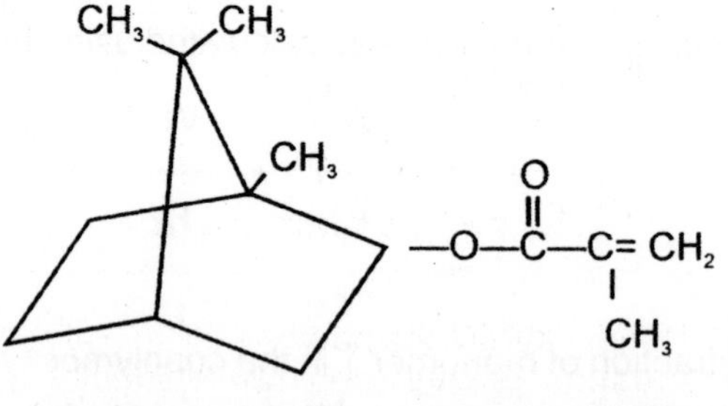

Fig. 19.1 : Iso bornyl Methacrylate

Iso decyl acrylate

Iso decyl Acrylate *(Fig.* 19.2) is a monomer with longer alkyl chain which helps in imparting the elasticity along with hardness to the paint film due to its Tg(-70°C)8. Our experiment with the monomer *(Table* 19.6) (Exp. 7) indicates that the paint based on it gives good dirt pick up resistance with reduced elasticity as compared to paint base on emulsion without Iso decyl acrylate (Exp.2).

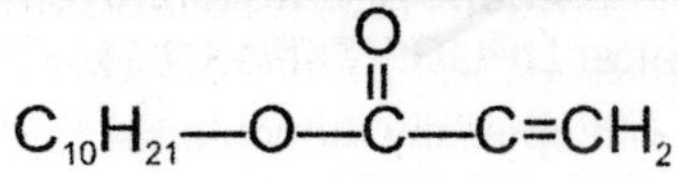

Fig. 19.2 : Iso Decyl Acrylate

Veova-11

VEOV A monomer 11 is the vinyl ester of VERSATICTM Acid 11, a synthetic saturated monocarboxylic acid of highly branched structure containing eleven carbon atoms. The glass transition temperature of its polymer is -40°C. Its structure may be represented as shown in *Fig.* 19.3. The experimental emulsion *(Table* 19.6) (Exp.8) also known as Veocryl latexes based paint gives excellent dirt pick up resistance with good alkali resistance in 5% alkali solution though elasticity gets reduced compared to experiment 2 based paint.

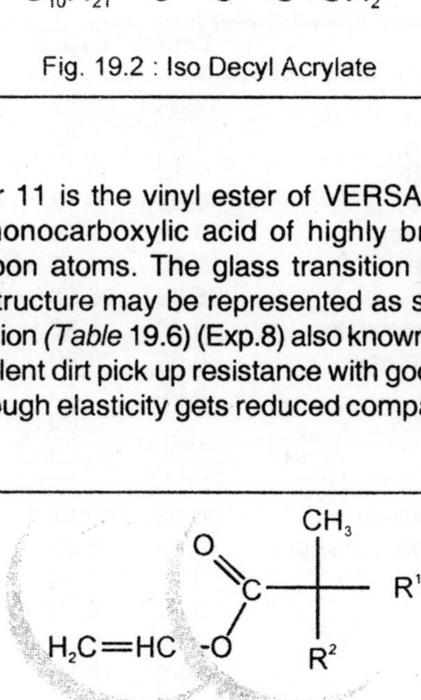

Fig. 19.3 : Veova 11

Where R^1 and R^2 are alkyl groups having chain length of 11 carbon atom. It imparts a combination of high polymer elasticity (low Tg= -40°c), hydrophobicity and UV resistance.

Ethyl methacrylate

Ethyl methacrylate is a monomer having Tg=65°c along with hydrophobic chain[8].

$$[H_2C{=}C(CH)C0_2C_2H_5]$$

With above ethyl methacrylate monomers *(Table* 19.9) experiment 5 and experiment 9 were carried out and paint based on it studied. Our study indicated that at similar glass transition temperature of polymer system MMA / BA / EMA / MAA (exp. 5 & 9) based system gives slightly better DPUR and elasticity than MMA/BN MAA (*Table* 19.4) (exp.2) polymer system. It was found that with increasing dosage of EMA improves elasticity and its retention along with relatively better DPUR. (*Table* 19.5)

Table 19.5: Emulsions with specialty monomerss

Ingredients	**Expt.5**	**Expt.6**	**Expt.7**	**Expt.8**	**Expt.9**
Deionised water	53.08	52.71	52.71	52.71	52.71
Surfactant	1.80	1.80	1.80	1.80	1.80
Potassium per sulfate	0.12	0.13	0.13	0.13	0.13
Sodium bi carbonate	0.08	0.18	0.08	0.08	0.08
Tert dodecyl mercaptan	0.06	0.06	0.06	0.06	0.06
Methyl meth acrylate	12.20	11.50	17.30	15.70	8.00
Butyl Acrylate	25.90	26.60	20.80	22.40	25.10
Hydroxyl ethyl methacrylate	0.20	0.20	0.20	0.20	0.20
Glacial meth acrylate acid	0.60	0.60	0.60	0.60	0.60
Ethyl methacrylate	5.00	.....	....	......	10.00
Iso bornyl metharylate	.....	5.00	....	.....	......
Iso decyl acrylate	.....	.....	5.00	......	......
Veova -11	.....	.....	.....	5.00	......
Tert butyl hydro peroxide	0.02	0.02	0.02	0.02	0.02
sodium formaldehyde sulfoxilate	0.02	0.02	0.02	0.02	0.02
Fungicide	0.10	0.10	0.10	0.10	0.10
Defoamer	0.02	0.02	0.02	0.02	0.02
Liq. Ammonia	0.80	0.80	0.80	0.80	0.80
Total	100.0	100.0	100.0	100.0	100.0
Characterisation of emulsion developed					
Viscosity on stormer (gms)	79	80	79	79	79
%NVM	45.80	45.80	45.70	45.80	45.80
PH	9.30	9.30	9.20	9.30	9.30
Particle size (microns)	0.12	0.12	0.11	0.11	0.12

Table 19.6: Paint Study

Paint Property	**Expt.5**	**Expt.6**	**Expt.7**	**Expt.8**	**Expt.9**
Elongation (after 12 days)	320%	100%	120%	130%	350%
Tensile strength in kgf/mm²	0.22	0.40	0.42	0.42	0.22
Dirt Pick up rating (10 : best)	5.5	6.5	6	7	6.0

Table 19.6 shows the comparison of paint properties prepared with above emulsion.

From the above study (*Table* 19.6) it is seen that incorporation of specialty monomer, isobornyl methacrylate, iso decyl acrylate and Veova11 improves DPU R but at the same time drastically reduces the elasticity. The reason may be the steric orientation of the molecule. The ethyl methacrylate is interesting exception. The MMA/BA/EMA/ MAA elasticity and dirt pick up resistance better than MMA/BA/MAA. But quite a high concentration is desired to exhibit appreciable difference. This is probably due to more favourable polymerization with butyl acrylate.

Effect of the crosslinkers

Crosslinkers can be effective in two ways: chemical reaction between polymer chains following interdiffusion and crosslinking at the interfaces of the particles. In the first case, a coherently formed film is fixed and the molecular weight if the chains present in this film is increased. In the second case, two particles are chemically bound by crosslinking during or just after film formation.

There are self-crosslinking systems where all reactive components are present and long-term storage stable. The crosslinking reaction can be triggered by the evaporation of water upon drying, a change of pH, or by curing at elevated temperature, where the crosslinking reaction is faster, or reactive groups are de-blocked.

Self crosslinking system. Ambient temperature crosslinking systems contain internal moieties that cause a crosslinking reaction to occur upon drying after the product has been applied to the substrate. In this type of system no post addition of catalyst prior to application and no thermal curing is required. Further the crosslinking reaction takes place not instantly but with time upon drying. The optimum crosslinking system reacts by loss of water via a condensation reaction as a polymer dries. Therefore faster the polymer dries, the more quickly the cross-linking will take place.

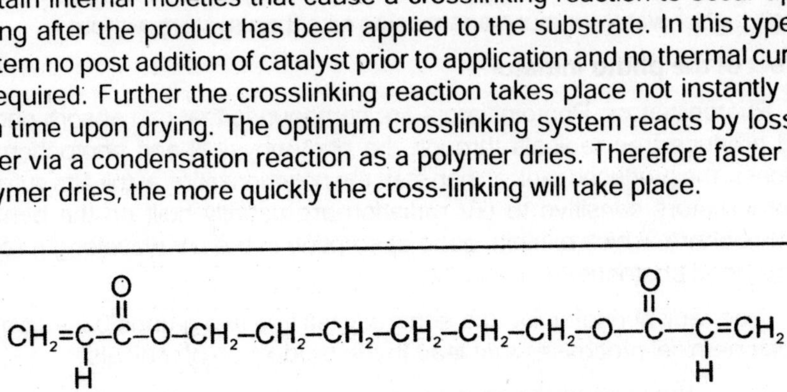

Fg. 19.4 : Structure of HDODA

Hexane Dial Diacrylate (HDODA)

Structure of HDODA is shown in Fig. 19.4. 1,6 hexanediol diacrylate is a low viscosity, fast curing monomer with low volatility, a hydrophobic backbone, and good solvency for use in free radical polymerization.

Glycidyl Metha Acrylate (GMA)

Structure of Glycidyl methacrylate is shown in *Fig.* 19.5. The epoxy linkage is being attacked by a nucleophile (OH^-) or electrophile (H^+) and forms linkages with polymer while unsaturation at the other end also forms a bond with a polymer. (Fig. 19.6)·

Aceto Acetoxyethyl Methacrylate (AAEMA)

Structure of AAEMA is shown in the Fig. 19.7 It offers room temperature crosslinking via acetoacetyl functionality. The active methylene and ketone carbonyl of AAEMA participates in numerous cross-linking reactions·

Table 19.7 depicts expeirments carried out to study the effect of crosslinker based emulsion in paint.

Table 19.8 shown the comparison of paint properties prepared above emulsions.

From the above study (Table 19.8) it is seen that experiment 10 shows significatn improvement w.r.t. DPUR and at the same time very slight reduction in the elasticity. Experiment 11 and 12 shows slight improvement in DPUR at the cost of elasticity. So exp. 10 is selected for further exploration. Water vapour transmission rat of emulsion were studied by experiment 2 and 11 (with epoxy modification as shown in Table 9 Epoxy crosslined system shows much higher water vapour transmission rate than system without it.

Effect of the photo initiator

Photoniitiators. Photoinitiators are compounds that can absorb photon and produce free radicals through the photophysical and photochemical process, the produced radical then start the polymerization at the film sufrace. Photoinitiators sensitive to UV radiation are usually built on the benzoyl chromophere, which exhibits good absorption in the UV wavelength range and a good photochemical reacitity.

Free radical photoinitiators gener*ally* fall into two groups based on the photochemical processes that lead to the production of radicals:

(1). *α-cleavage photoinitiators:* involve a cleavage that takes place at CC bonds such as benzoin ether (BME), hydroxy alkyl phenylacetophenones

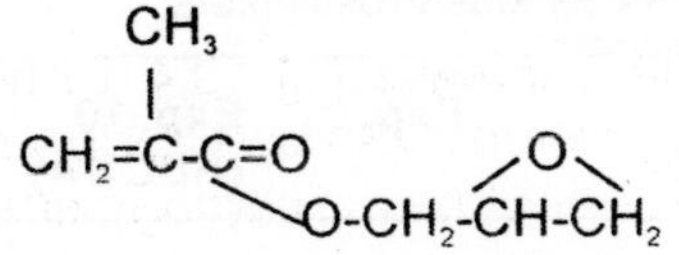

Fig. 19.5 : Structure of Glycidyl Methacrylate

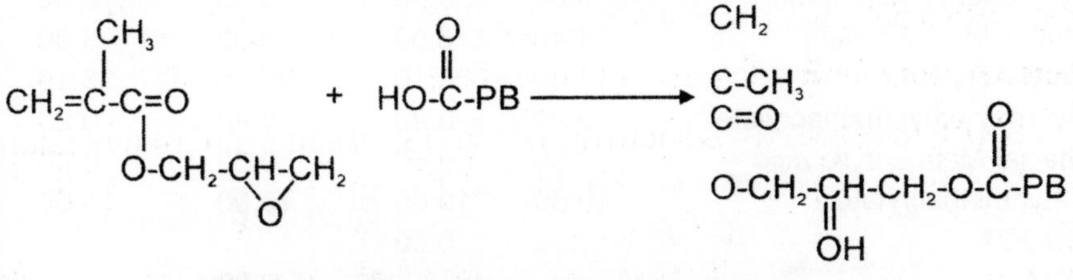

Fig. 19.6: Crosslinking through epoxy functional group

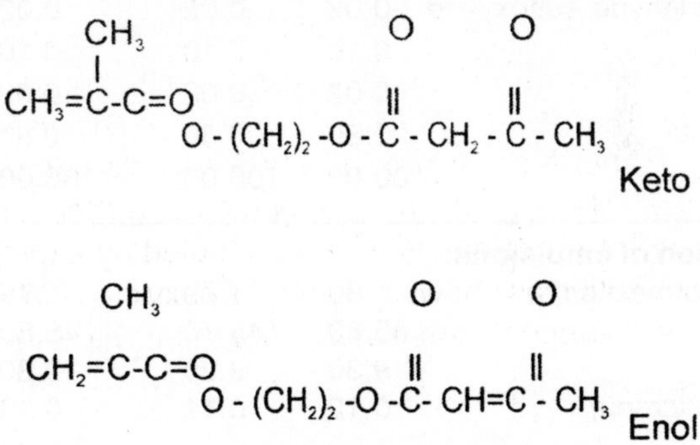

Fig. 19.7 : Structure of AAEMA

(HAP), and phosphine oxide derivatives (TPO).

(2). *Hydrogen abstraction photoinitiators:* Hydrogen abstraction photoinitiators generally consist of an initiator and a co-initiator. The co-initiator is generally an amine with an a-hydrogen and functions as the H donor. The initiator is typically based on benzophenones (BP), thioxanthones (TX), benzyls.

Two photo initiators were selected representing each of above two classes;

Table 19.7: Emulsions with various crosslinkers

Ingredients	**Exp. 9**	**Exp. 10 (HDODA)**	**Exp. 11 (GMA)**	**Exp. 12 (AAEMA)**
Deionised water	53.07	53.57	53.57	53.57
Surfactant	1.80	1.80	1.80	1.80
Potassium per sulfate	0.13	0.13	0.13	0.13
Sodium bi carbonate	0.08	0.08	0.08	0.08
Tertdodecyl mercaptan	0.06	0.06	0.06	0.06
Methyl meth Acrylate	14.40	6.00	6.00	6.00
Butyl Acrylate	18.40	26.10	26.10	26.10
Hydroxy ethyl methacrylate	0.20	0.20	0.20	0.20
Glacial Meth acrylic acid	0.60	0.60	0.60	0.60
Ethyl methacrylate	10.00	10.00	10.00	10.00
HDODA	....	0.50	......	......
GMA	....	....	0.50	....
A.A.E.M.A.	....	....	....	0.50
Tertbutyl hydro peroxide	0.02	0.02	0.02	0.02
Sodium formaldehyde sulfoxylate	0.02	0.02	0.02	.02
Fungicide	0.10	0.10	0.10	0.10
Defoamer	0.02	0.02	0.02	0.02
Ammonia (16 %)	0.80	0.80	0.80	0.80
Total	100.00	100.00	100.00	100.00
Characterization of emulsions:				
Viscosity on stormer (gms)	80	79	79	78
%NVM	45.80	45.70	45.80	45.7
PH	9.30	9.20	9.30	9.20
Particle size (microns)	0.12	0.11	0.13	0.12

Table 19.8: Paint Study

Paint Properties	**Exp. 9**	**Exp. 10**	**Exp. 11**	**Exp. 12**
Elongation (after 12 days)	350%	340%	225%	245%
Tensile strength in kgf/mm2 after (12 days)	0.22	0.28	0.32	0.32
Dirt Pick up rating (0 : best)	5.5	7	6	5.5

Table 19.9: Water vapour transmission rate of films of studied emulsions

Experiment	**Water vapour transmission (gm/m²/hr)**
Experiment 11	6.3379
Experiment 2	3.8471

2,2 dimethoxy- 2phenylacetophenone(DMPA)

Fig. 19.8 depicts the mechanism of Free radical production of DMPA:

Benzophenone derivative (BPD)

The photoinitiation process of BP derivative is as follows *(Fig.* 19.9):

The following emulsions *(Table 19.10)* (expt 13 & expt 14) were prepared with 2 different photoinitiators.

Experiment 13 is a system with photoinitiator DMPA while experiment 14 is with BPD *(Table 19.10)*. The paint based on photoinitiator shows similar elasticity to that of system without photoinitiator *(Table* 19.11). Dirt pick up resistance with photoinitiator systems were substantially better than similar system without photoinitiator. Again DMPA system was found to have better dirt pick up resistance as compared to Benzophenone based systems *(Table* 19.11) on natural exposure study of panels for 3 months.

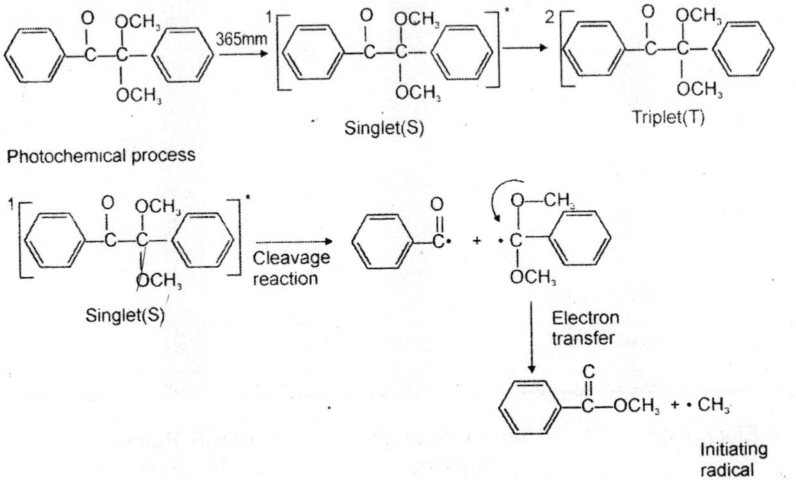

Fig. 19.8 : Scheme for free radical production of DMPA

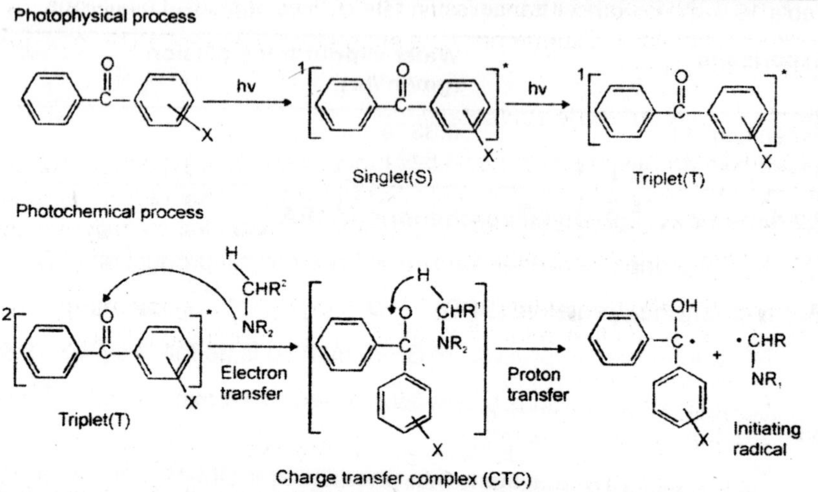

Fig. 19.9: Scheme for free radical production of BPD

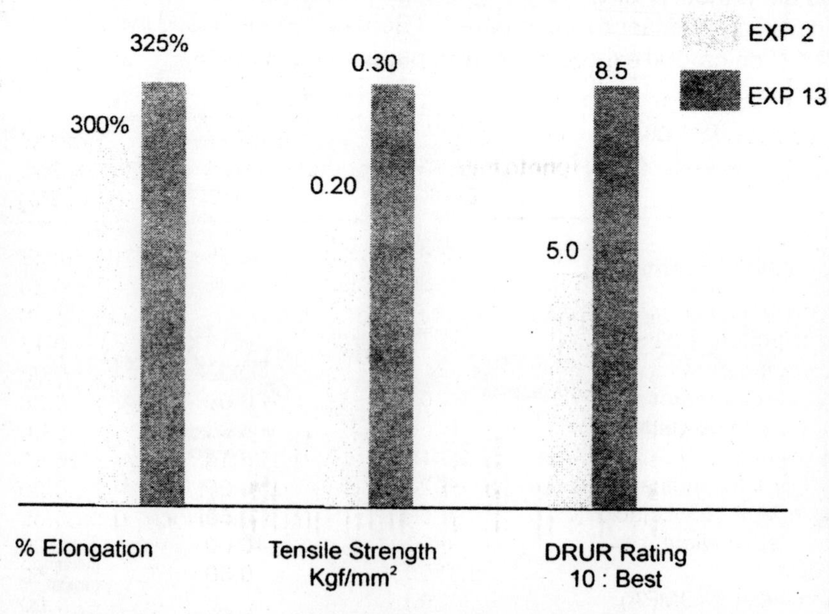

Fig. 19.10 : Comparison : Initial design (Exp 2) vs. Development design (Exp. 13)

From above comparison *(Table* 19.10) it is clear that paint based on developed emulsion Experiment 13 is substantially better DPUR, elongation and tensile strength.

Effect of polymerizable surfactant

Conventional surfactant increases moisture sensitivity, affects adhesion and appearance of the dry film. Surfactant is desired in emulsion polymerization but after polymerization it should be part of the polymer chain to reduce the negative effects of it.

Polymerizable Surfactant (alkene sulphonate) offers advantages to the latex and to the dry film in the final application through the following:

- Superior water resistance
- Superior alkali resistance
- Superior protective properties and durability of the dry film

So experiment 15 was carried out (table 10) in which 85% conventional surfactant was replaced by polymerizable surfactant. *Table* 19.12 depicts the difference in water resistance of emulsion based on the conventional surfactant and polymerizable surfactant. The experiment 15 based paint had been studied for crack bridging ability and washability too.

Table 19.10: Emulsions with different photoinitiators and with polymerizable surfactant

Ingredients	**Expt 13 (photo initiator) DMPA**	**Expt 14 (photo initiator) BPD**	**Expt. 15 (Exp. 13 with PS)**
Deionised water	52.57	52.57	52.57
Surfactant	1.80	1.80	0.50
Polymerisable surfactant (PS)	....	....	1.30
Potassium per sulfate	0.13	0.13	0.13
Sodium bi carbonate	0.08	0.08	0.08
Tert. dodecyl mercaptan	0.06	0.06	0.06
Methyl meth acrylate	6.00	6.00	6.00
Butyl Acrylate	26.10	26.10	26.10
Hydroxy ethyl methacrylate	0.20	0.20	0.20
Glacial Meth acrylic acid	0.60	0.60	0.60
Ethyl methacrylate	10.00	10.00	10.00
HDODA	0.50	0.50	0.50
Photo Initiator (DMPA)	1.00	....	1.00
Photo Initiator (BPD)	....	1.00	....

Tert.butyl hydro peroxide	0.02	0.02	0.02
Sodium Formaldehyde Sulfoxylate	0.02	0.02	0.02
Fungicide	0.10	0.10	0.10
Defoamer	0.02	0.02	0.02
Ammonia (16%)	0.80	0.80	0.80
Total	100.00	100.00	100.00
Characterization of Emulsions			
Viscosity on Stormer (in gms)	80	79	85
%NVM	45.5	45.7	45.6
PH	9.2	9.3	9.2
Particle size (microns)	0.12	0.13	0.11

Table 19.11: Paint study of emulsion of table 10

Paint Properties	Expt 13	Expt 14	Expt. 15
Elongation (after 12 days)	325%	320%	310%
Tensile strength in Kgf/mm^2 After (12 days)	0.28	0.28	0.30
Dirt pick up rating (10 : best)			

Table 19.12: Comparison of water resistance & alkali resistance.

Parameters	Conventional Surfactant Experiment 13	Polymerisable Surfactant Experiment 15
Water Resistance (% Absorption)	30	12
Alkali Resistance (% Loss in 5% soln.)	0.10	0.03

2

Silica Gels

Introduction

PRACTICALLY all man-made objects or constructions have surfaces which have been treated or coated for one purpose or another. With a few specific exceptions, the purpose of the coating is generally either decorative or protective, or has elements of both.

Alongside colour and texture, gloss is major factor determining the appearance of a surface and as a consequence of a surface and as a consequences if often a specifiied feature of the coating, which is applied to the surface as a finish. The actual gloss level chosen is largely a matter of fashion or taste and in some cases e.g. furniture or leather goods, a matt surface is regarded as characteristic of a certain elegance or luxurious appearance. On the other hand, matt surfaces also offer the practical advantage over high-gloss finishes of rendering the blemishes suffered in every-day use, such as scuffing, marking or fingerprints, Less Immediately obvious.

Any coating is a more or less complex mixture of a binder, solvent, pigments and fillers, and one or more functional additives. Matting agents belong to this latter groups of paint raw materials; they have a specific function to fulfill and should do this and preferably little else. For the formulator the ideal matting agent should:

- give cost-effective gloss reduction
- be easy to handle and incorporate
- have reproducible quality and performance
- have the minimum negative impact on other properties of the coating

- be non-toxic or non-hazardous in use.

In theory, many materials could be, and indeed are used to provide a matting effect in coatings, but in practice only a very few match the 'ideal' demanded by the formulator. Synthetic silica gel forms an ideal base material for such a product.

Mechanism of matting

In order to appreciate this, it is first necessary to understand by what mechanism matting is achieved.

The gloss of any surface depends on the way light is reflected from that surface and this in turn depends on the structure of the surface (*Fig.* 20.1). If

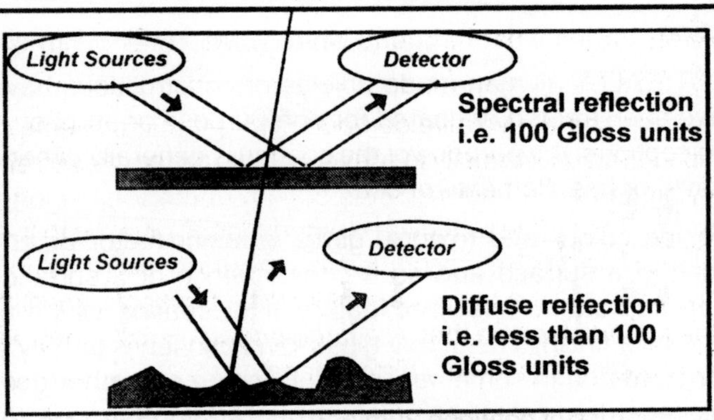

Fig. 20.1 : Gloss Measurement

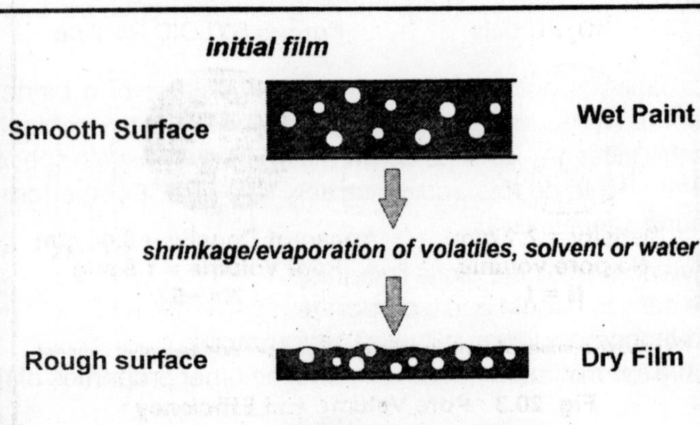

Fig. 20.2 : Mechanism of Matting

a surface is perfectly smooth all the light reflected from that surface will be reflected at an angle equal to that of the incident light, reflected images will be clearly defined and 'a gloss meter, if suitably calibrated will record a value of 100 gloss units. A structured surface on the other hand will scatter the light reflected from the surface, reflected images will be diffuse and a gloss meter will register a value less than 100 gloss units. In order to influence the reflection of light, but not be visible to the naked eye surface structures must be in the range of 0.3-1.0μm in size.

In order to get a low gloss or matt surface in a coating, it is therefore necessary to create a microrough surface, with a mean roughness of a similar order. This can be achieved by packing particles of a suitable size and number Into the coating film.

Fig. 20.2 illustrates what happens when a wet coating film containing suitable particles dries.

Most coatings contain volatile components, organic solvents or water, which are added to adjust viscosity to a level suitable for the chosen application process. Drying therefore involves evaporation of these components and the film undergoes a volume reduction or shrinkage equivalent to the original volatile content. The volume occupied by the solid particles in the film increases dramatically as a consequence of this shrinkage, and if there are enough of these particles and they are large enough In size they will create a permanent irregularity in the dry film surface.

Typically, particles of between 2μm and 20μm in diameter are sufficiently large to create the degree of microroughness necessary for gloss reduction

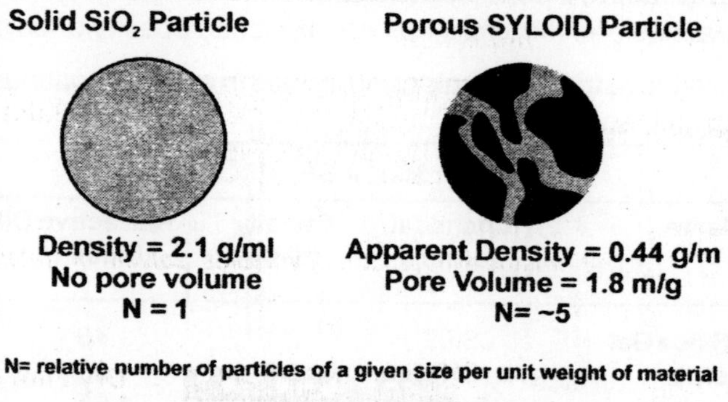

Fig. 20.3 : Pore Volume and Efficiency

or matting in most coatings.

The "ideal" base material

In order to be effective as a matting agent, a material must be capable of providing the highest possible number of particles within the prescribed size range. Clearly, low density materials with a rugged structure will be the most capable. Furthermore, the product must be easy to handle and to incorporate into the coating. A matting agent must not affect the transparency of clear, unpigmented lacquers or the colour and opacity of pigmented paints. Finally, the material must be chemically pure, stable and inert during the entire life of the wet and dry coating.

In theory, almost any particulate material could provide the necesary particles, but in practice only a few types are in common use. By far the most widely used materials are synthetic silicas, exemplified by the micronised silica gels.

The great advantage of any synthetic material over those gained from natural sources, is the controllability of the process. This allows important quality criteria and performance properties to be achieved in a reproducible and consistent manner.

Amorphous silica gel (*Table* 20.1):

- has a low density relative to many other inorganic compounds used in coatings;

- has a high level of purity, the unmodified, dry product being composed of at least 99.9% SiO_2;

- has a refractive index close to that of most resins or polymers commonly used in coatings and therefore has no Impact on opacity or colour;

- is unreactive to other components used in modern coatings and stable over a wide pH range.

TABLE 20.1: SILICA GEL PROPERTIES

Generic Name	Chemical Formula	Density (g/ml)	Refractive Index	Oil Adsorption (ml/100g)
SYLOID®Silica Gel	Si02	2.1	1.45	250-320
Calcined Clay	$Al_2(OH)Si_2O_6$	2.6	1.56	40-70
Barium Sulphate	$CaCO_3$	2.71	1.65	5.70
Titanium Dioxide	$BaSO_4$	4.35	1.64	14-18
(Rutile/Anatase)	TiO_2	4.1	2.7 /2.52	1 5-40

Silica gel technology: Features and benefits

Porosity: the key to high efficiency

Firstly, silica gel has, in addition to its low density, a clearly defined microporous structure. This porous, sponge like structure means that individual particles are much lighter than for other non-porous and/or denser materials. MIcronised silica gel can thus provide a much higher number of particles of a given size per unit weight, than other materials.

This becomes more obvious when comparing a porous silica particle, pore volume = 1.8ml/g, with a non-porous silica particle of the same dimensions (*Fig.* 20.3).

Calculating the "apparent" density of the porous particle in the example, taking Into account the "void space" provided by the porosity, reveals a value close to one-fifth of that of the nonporous particle. Consequently, any unit weight of this product will be com~sed of almost 5 times as many particles of a given size as the non-porous product. In matting terms this would equate to ca. 5 times the efficiency, since the matting effect is directly related to the number of particles of a given size present in the film.

There are two common objections raised in connection with porous silicas, thickening effect and resistance to overgrinding.

A high porosity is also associated with a high oil-adsorption, which in tum is often seen as negative since it affects properties like viscosity.

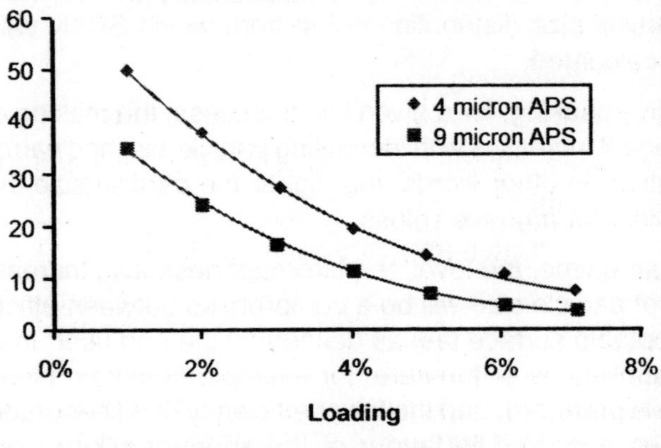

Fig. 20.4 Particle size and efficiency

However, this is more than offset by the high efficiency and the consequent low addition levels required to achieve a certain gloss level. Also, unlike fumed silicas, the high surface area of micronised silica gels is mostly inside the pores i.e. internal to the particle, thus minimising particle-particle interactions which might lead to unwanted thixotropic or pseudoplastic viscosity effects.

"Over-grinding" during dispersion is related to particle stability. In spite of their porous structure, silica gel particles have a very sturdy structure and, in contrast to precipitated or aggregated fumed silicas, are highly resistant to the shear forces needed to disperse them easily, such as are developed in a high-speed stirrer or dissolver. Even A short duration in a bead mill, (10-15 minutes) will cause no significant particle size reduction.

Particle size control: optimum gloss reduction and surface smoothness

Secondly, the most up-to-date technologies are used in milling and controlling particle sizes of micronised silica gels. The necessary particle size distribution is achieved in high-energy jet mills and controlled by laser diffraction measurement techniques. Products with a mean particle size between 3μm and 12μm are available to enable effective matting to be achieved over the range of dry film thicknesses commonly applied.

The spread of particle size distribution can be adjusted by classification, an inherent feature of jet-milling, and interpreted by SPAN values. Particle size measurement techniques normally deliver values representing the cumulative volume of particles within certain size limits. These are then plotted a particle size distribution curve from which SPAN values can be defined and calcuated.

Generally speaking, for a given film thickness, the matting efficiency of the matting agent Increases with Increasing particle size and narrower particle size distribution. In other words, the higher the particle size the lower the loading required for *any* given gloss.

At the same time, the level of microroughness also Increases and the final choice of particle size will be a compromise between efficient matting and an acceptable surface feel as defined by the end user. In coatings for household appliances or furniture, for example, a certain pleasing and/or velvet touch is preferred, and the lower efficiency of a finer grade of matting agent is often accepted In favour of the superior silky smooth touch it guarantees. On the other hand, coatings for ceilings, floors or walls do not commonly need to be so pleasing to the touch and coarser grades are often preferred, simply on the basis of their superior matting effect.

Surface modification: Stability and compatibility

Thirdly, the nature of the manufacturing process for mlcronlsed silica gels provides ample opportunity for modification of the silica surface, for example adjustment of pH or application of surface treatments, Historically, the first treatments for synthetic silica matting agents were inorganic, but these have been superseded by organic wax based materials.

The purpose of the wax treatment is to provide adequate suspension properties to the matting agent. The favourable refractive index of silica (1.45) relative to many binder types means they can be used to matt clear, unpigmented laquers and varnishes without affecting transparency. Thus, for example, the natural and aesthetically pleasing grain effect of wood substrates much desired in modern furniture does not become hidden or diminished when a low gloss finish is applied,

The silica will often be the only particulate material in the formulation and in low viscosity systems *may* tend to settle and form a hard sediment if no antisettling additive is included. The wax treatment attached to the particle surface "swells" in the organic solvents and the particles attain a certain buoyancy, which retards their tendency to settle (Figure 20.5). In the event that settling does occur, the treatment will prevent close packing of the

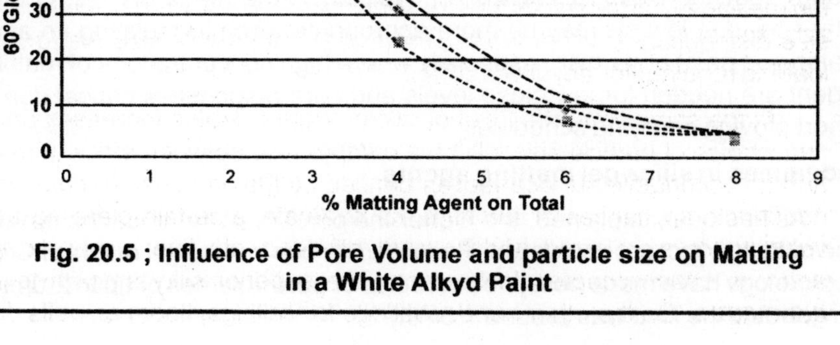

Fig. 20.5 ; Influence of Pore Volume and particle size on Matting in a White Alkyd Paint

Table 20.2 : Influence of Pore Volume on Performance in a white Alkyd Paint

Matting agent	% Matting agent to achieve 30 60ºGloss units	Amount relative to Product A	Dispersion fineness (Dissolver 10 min@3000rpm)	Viscosity (Mattler RM 180 Rheomar)
A (PV 2.0 ml/g) : AOS 9μm)	3.6	1.00	30μm	1.16 pa's
B (PV 2.0 ml/g : APS 7μm)	4.03	1.12	25μm	1.85 Pa's
C (PV 1.8 ml/g : APS 9μm)	4.33	1.20	30μm	1.21 Pa's
Unmatted Paint	n.a.	n.a.	20.25μm	1.09 Pa's

particles to form hard sediments and, at worst, a phase separation *may* occur which, can easily be re-dispersed by agitation. The suspension of the treated silica will generally look cloudy or opaque due to the difference in refractive index between the wax treatment and the solvents, but careful selection of wax treatment ensures that dry film clarity is not impaired when the solvents have evaporated,

Silica gels are stable over a wide pH range (pH 3-10) and can be produced to have acidic, neutral or alkaline character. Silica gels with a wide range of pH values are commercially available. Previously, neutral or slightly alkaline character (pH 6-8) was deemed to be the most attractive and potentially least problematic. Recent developments have seen a shift towards a more acidic character (pH 3-4).

A neutral or slightly alkaline pH will avoid Interactions with a wide range of other components used in paints. This is also more appropriate for water-borne coatings where pH levels are typically in the range pH 7-9. On the other hand, a low pH may be more appropriate when formulating an acid-catalysed paint or varnish, especially where high concentrations of matting agent are needed for low gloss levels and cure response is critical due to short stovlng or drying schedules.

Advances in silica gel matting agents

As has been explained, the higher the porosity of the silica the greater the matting effect per unit weight. Recent advances In silica gel manufacturing technology have made possible porosities or pore volumes of up to 2.0ml/g. Previously the limit was around 1.8ml/g.

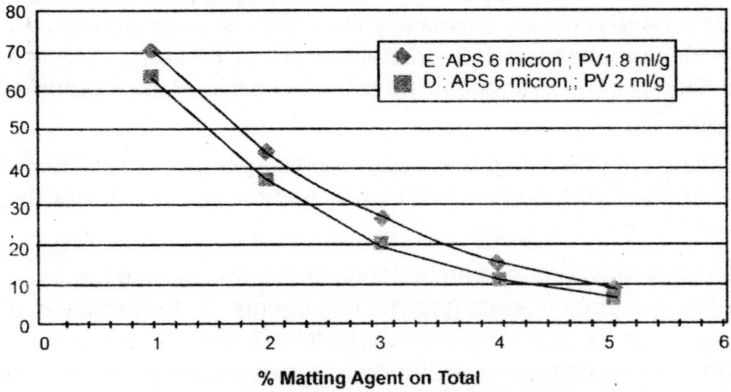

Fig. 20.6 : Influence of Pore Volume on Matting in a 2-Pack Polyurethan Clear Lacquer

Alongside advances in pore volume, milling and classification techniques have been Improved such as to minimise the spread of particle size. A narrow particle size distribution:

- ensures the maximum number of particles within the effective size range for matting;
- avoids very fine particles which con tribute little to the matting, but create unwanted thickening;
- avoids very coarse particles which create unpleasant surface feel;
- ensures a compact, uniform microroughness, which in turn leads to smooth surfaces both visually as well as to the touch.

As can the particle size spread of the new generation silica (SYLOID@ C 809 PV 2ml/g) represented by the red curve is narrower than for the previous generation grade (SYLOID@ ED 5 PV 1.8ml/g) represented by the green curve, though both have an average particle size (APS) of 91µm.

Fig. 20.6 and *Table* 20.2 show the Impact of these advances in pore volume and particle size distribution on the matting performance of mlcronised silica gel in a decorative white alkyd paint. The higher pore volume matting agent A shows a significant Improvement in efficiency compared to the lower pore volume grade B over a range of gloss levels *(Fig.* 20.6). From these curves the relative efficiency for a specific gloss level can be determined and other performance criteria compared at equal gloss level.

ample *(Table* 20.2), ca.20% more of matting agent C is required relative to A. The viscosities are practically the same and not significantly higher than In the unmatted paint. Because they are of the same particle size and give similar dispersion fineness, no differences In surface roughness will be detectable.

Matting agent B also offers a higher efficiency, but in addition will give a smoother paint surface due to Its lower particle size and lower dispersion fineness.

Similarly, advantages can be Identified for the surface treated versions of the new generation .sillca gels matting agents. As the results In a 2-pack PU lacquer, an Increase In pore volume from 1.8ml/g for product E to 2ml/g for product D, leads to an overall increase in efficiency over the whole gloss range Investigated. Due to their equivalent mean particle size no significant differences In surface smoothness will be apparent. The smooth velvety feel so highly valued In the furniture finishing industry for this type of lacquer will be maintained.

A higher efficiency translates directly Into a raw material saving and more Importantly Into an opportunity to reduce formulation cost without sacrificlng performance.

21

Emulsion Paints

Emulsion paints are characterized by the fact that the binder is present in a dispersed form in water. In contrast, in a solvent paint the binder is present in solution form. Because of this inherent physical difference, the formulation and handling of emulsion paints differ from conventional solvent systems.

Emulsion paints are composed of a pigment dispersion and a resin dispersion. The pigment dispersion is obtained by milling the pigments into water. The resin dispersion is either a latex formed by emulsion polymerization or a resin put into emulsion form. The pigment dispersion and the resin dispersion are blended to produce an emulsion paint. Surfactants and protective colloids are included to give stability to the product.

Since the binder is present in dispersed form, the external water phase controls the viscosity of the system. The molecular weight of the polymer which is in the internal phase does not affect the viscosity of the system. In a solvent system, as the molecular weight of the binder is increased, the viscosity increases, sometimes beyond practical limits of application. Usually higher molecular weight in the polymer gives better physical performance.

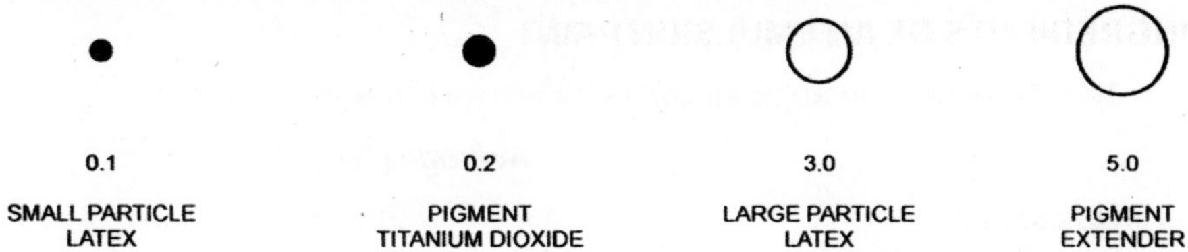

Figure 21.1 Partilce size comparison (average microns)

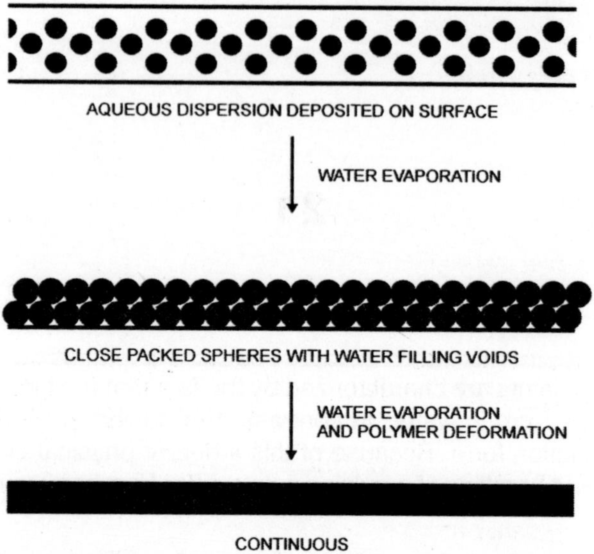

Figure 21.2 Film formation from an emulsion

Polymers with high molecular weights and improved properties can be readily utilized in emulsion systems.

The unique properties of emulsion paints which have promoted their popularity are ease of application, minimal odor, easy cleanup and outstanding performance in many applications.

The three principal latex systems used today are styrene-butadiene, polyvinyl acetate and acrylics. Resins such as alkyds, epoxies, etc., can be produced in emulsion form by post-emulsification. The size of the emulsion particles ranges from 0.1 to 10 µ.

INGREDIENTS OF AN EMULSION PAINT

The ingredients in an emulsion paint are as follows:

	Average (%)
Opaque pigment	20.0
Extender pigment	15.0
Pigment	0.3
Protective colloid Latex	1.2
Plasticizer[a]	40.0
Modifier	–

Preservative	–
Antirust agenta0.5	0.1
pH buffer	0.1
Fungicidea	0.5
Coalescing agent	2.0
Defoamer	0.5
Thickener[a]	0.5
Freeze-thaw stabilizer[a]	2.5
Water	16.8
	100.0

[a] Optional in some formulas

The pigments are ground with a dispersant and a protective colloid with the minimum amount of water. The dispersant aids in wetting the pigment and keeping particles separated. The protective colloid forms an envelope around the pigment particles. It protects the system from coagulation in the presence of an electrolyte or from excessive shear stress. It protects the system during manufacture and storing. As little as 1% protective colloid will suffice to envelope sticky polymer particles to keep them from coalescing.

The latex is then added to the pigment paste along with other ingredients such as defoamers, preservatives, buffers, fungicides, etc. A defoamer eliminates air bubbles or foam. A preservative protects the paint against microorganisms that may be present in raw materials or equipment. The buffer prevents pH drift. A fungicide protects the final paint film from attack by fungi. A coalescing agent is sometimes used to get good film fusion and in reality is a volatile plasticizer. Thickners are added to adjust viscosity. Emulsion paints are usually not stable to freezing, and materials are added to protect against freeze damage. Anti-rust agents are sometimes added to water-type paints to retard rusting of the container or, in the case of metal coatings, to prevent flash rusting on application.

Surfactants

Surfactants have multiple uses in aqueous coatings: (I) A surfactant is used as a dispersant during the grinding of the pigment by providing better wetting of the pigment particles. (2) Surfactants are required as emulsifiers to produce stable interfaces between oil and other materials and water. (3) They impart certain properties to the aqueous coating such as better wetting, flow, etc.

A surfactant is a compound which affects the surface forces of a liquid or a solid in relation to other liquids, gases or solids. The surfactant generally consists of a molecule in which one end is hydrophilic (water loving) and the other end is lipophilic (oil loving).

The sodium salts of fatty acids (i.e., ordinary soap) would be an example of a surfactant:

$$\underbrace{CH_3{-}CH_2{-}CH_2{-}CH_2{-}CH_2{-}CH_2{-}CH_2{-}CH_2{-}CH_2{-}CH_2{-}CH_2{-}CH_2}_{\text{Lipophilic}}{-}\underbrace{\overset{\overset{\displaystyle O}{\|}}{C}{-}ONa}_{\text{Hydrophilic}}$$

When a soap is added to water, it lowers the surface tension (i.e., it reduces the interfacial tension between water and air). The resulting solution foams readily and has other attributes of soap solutions. In addition the soap promotes wetting of solids, mixing of immersible liquids such as oil, etc.

Structure of Surfactants. Surfactants are compounds in which one portion of each molecule is hydrophilic (water loving) and the other portion is lipophilic (oil loving) or hydrophobic (water fearing). The hydrophilic part of the molecule may be a carboxylate, sulfate, sulfonate, alcohol or alcohol-ether. The lipophilic portion of the molecule may be a long hydrocarbon chain in fatty acids, a straight, branched or cyclic hydrocarbon of petroleum, or an aromatic hydrocarbon containing alkyl side chains.

Types of Surfactants. Surfactants may be classified as anionic, cationic, amphoteric and nonionic.

Anionic. The anionics bear a negative charge and migrate toward the anode, or positive pole, while in solution. These are the oldest and best known of surfactants.

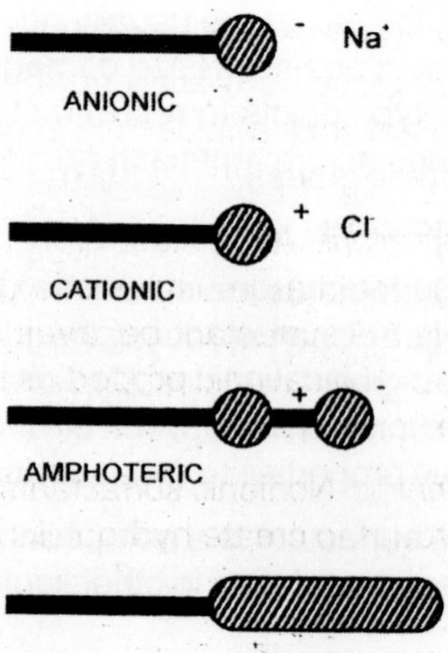

Figure 21.3 Types of Surfactants

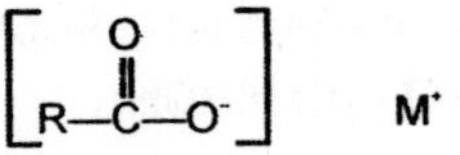

Soap

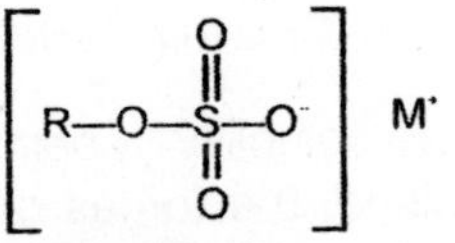

Alkyd Sulfate

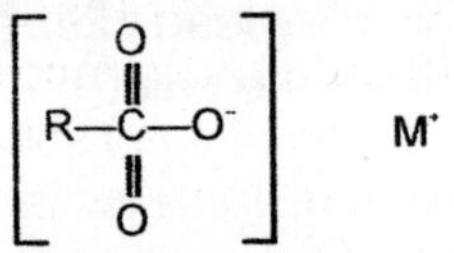

Alkyl Sulfonate

Cationic. The cationic group is the opposite of an anionic group. Its surface activity is due to the presence of a long-chain, oil-soluble cation. These are used very little in latex paints since they would neutralize the charges of an anionic surfactant which might be present and cause a break in the emulsion. Cationic surfactants are used to produce stable asphaltic emulsions. Cationic surfactants also possess germicidal anticorrosive, antistatic properties. The following is the structure of a cationic surfactants.

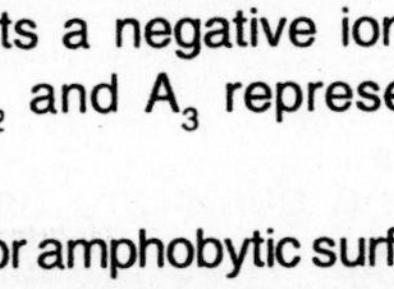

R represents a hydrophobic group such as a long-chain aliphatic or aromatic group. X represents a negative ion such as Cl, Br, I, or other monovalent ion, and A_1. A_2 and A_3 represent hydrogen, alkyl, aryl or heterocyclic groups.

Amphoteric. Amphoteric or amphobytic surfactants contain both a positive and negative charge. These charges may neutralize each other so that at a given pH the surfactant behaves as if it were nonionic. These surfactants usually exhibit cationic properties in acid solutions and anionic properties in alkaline solutions.

Nonionic. Nonionic surfactants depend chiefly upon hydroxyl groups and ether groups to create hydrophilic action.

$$RC(=O)—O—(CH_2)_n(OH)_n$$

$$RC(=O)—O—(CH_2H_4O)_nC_2H_4OH$$

These compounds achieve solubility by being hydrated in water solutions. When the temperature is raised, the forces of hydration are reduced and there is a precipitation of the surfactant lowering its effectiveness. This shows up as a turbidity or cloud. This may lead to erratic results when processing produces a higher temperature in the paint.

Behaviour of Emulsions

Lipophilic groups dissolve in the surface of the oil droplets with the hydrophilic groups oriented toward the water phase. There is an interfacial film between the water phase and the oil phase. A strong film prevents coalescence of the dispersed droplets. The charged droplets are stabilized because of repulsion between like charges.

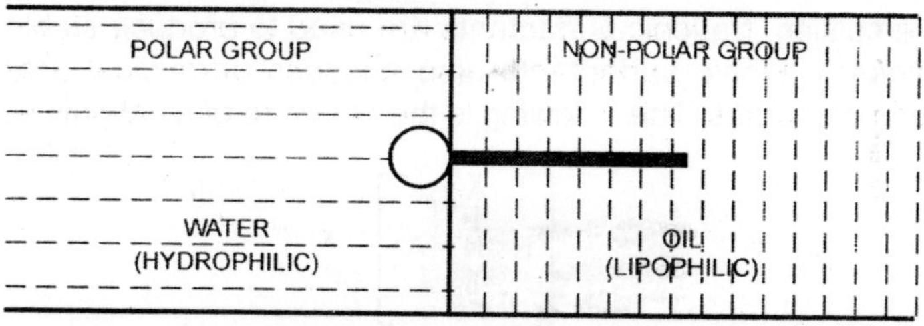

Figure : 21.4 Emulsion interface

Protective Colloid

Water-soluble resins and gums are used as protective colloids or thickeners in emulsion paints. Their presence in the water phase aids dispersion of pigment, protects the paint against coagulation and settling, and adjusts viscosity.

The hydrophilic colloids include starch, sodium alginate, methylcellulose, hydroxyethylcellulose, sodium carboxymethylcellulose, polyvinyl alcohol, ammonium caseinate, sodium polyacrylate. The materials produce high-viscosity solutions at low concentrations. As little as .1 to 1% of protective colloid is usually sufficient.

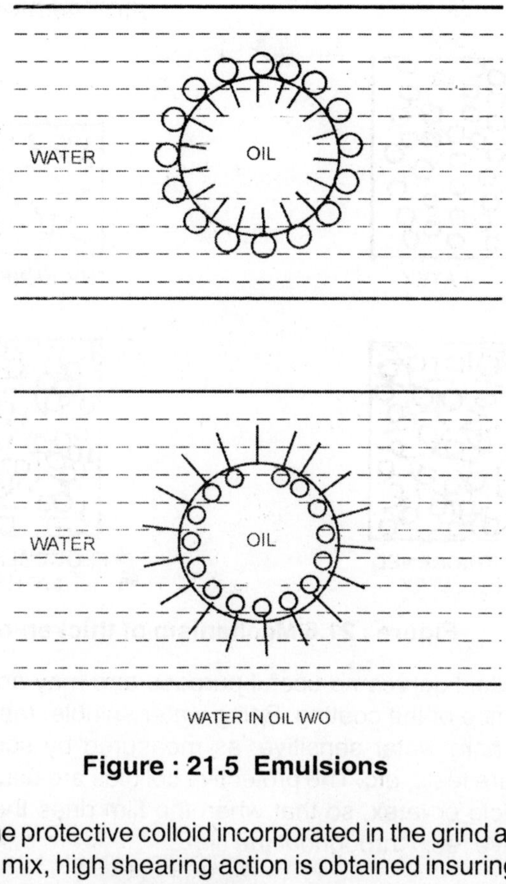

WATER IN OIL W/O

Figure : 21.5 Emulsions

A portion of the protective colloid incorporated in the grind aids dispersion. By thickening the mix, high shearing action is obtained insuring good mixing. The pigment particles are completely coated with the protective colloid which improves the stability of the paint. A protective colloid is added to an emulsion or latex in manufacture. The protective colloid, because of the increased viscosity it imparts to the water phase, reduces settling tendencies. This improves stability of the system by minimizing the tendency of the dispersed particles to stick together if subjected to stresses by mechanical means, freezing, etc. The water-soluble resin when used as a thickener produces the correct viscosity for application. The type of protective colloid used will affect the flow and leveling of the coating. For many reasons, including economy, it is advantageous to keep the amount of protective colloid to a minimum. Protective colloids are relatively high in price compared to the other ingredients used in the paint. Once the film is applied and dried, the

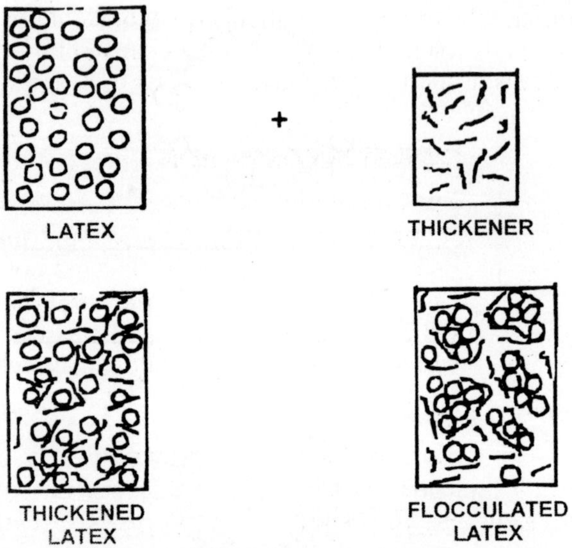

Figure : 21.6 Mechanism of thickening

protective colloid serves no useful purpose and may actually detract from the performance of the coating. Being water soluble, these materials make the coating more water sensitive, as measured by scrub tests, humidity tests, exposure tests, etc. The protective colloids are usually not compatible with the vehicle or latex, so that when the film dries there is a network of water-sensitive resin throughout the film.

pH

pH is the logarithm of the reciprocal of the hydrogen ion concentration or the hydrogen ion activity. This measure holds for aqueous systems only and has a scale from 0 (strongly acid) to 14 (strongly alkaline), with the neutral point at 7. A unit change in pH corresponds to a tenfold change in acidity.

The pH of a water paint has a profound effect on the physical properties and performance of the system. Buffers are used to maintain the pH level of the paint. Each latex system is stable in specific pH ranges. Surface agents, particularly those of the anionic type, have pH ranges in which they are the most effective. Protective colloids such as carboxymethylcellulose, casein, polyacrylates and algenates are soluble only in the alkaline range and become insoluble at low pH. High pH ranges will hydrolyze materials such as proteins. Maintenance of high pH in the package keeps certain bacteria that might cause spoilage under control. The use of permanent alkalies such as sodium hydroxide and other salts to adjust pH should be avoided if possible since water-soluble materials will be left in the film, reducing water resistance. If possible, a volatile alkali such as ammonia should be used for adjusting the pH of the paint.

EMULSION FORMATION

Resin emulsions can be prepared by two different methods: Emulsion polymerization and post-emulsification of the resin. As the term implies, emulsion polymerization is actually two processes carried out in a single operation. Post-emulsification of the resin involves the emulsification of the resin which may be obtained from natural sources or produced from synthetic materials through polymerization by addition or condensation reactions.

Emulsion Polymerization

Most commercial latices are manufactured by a technique known as emulsion polymerization. The monomer is dispersed in water in small droplets and the polymerization takes place within these droplets. Because of good heat transfer through the water phase, the heat of polymerization can be removed easily and polymerization proceeds rapidly. High molecular weight polymers are produced.

Latices in use today are derived from the free radical initiated addition polymerization of unsaturated monomers of the vinyl or maleic type. These are compounds containing the -C=C- structures, with various groups such as a chloride, acetate or benzene attached to the carbons. The polymers can be considered as substituted polyethylene; for example, vinyl chloride polymerizes as follows:

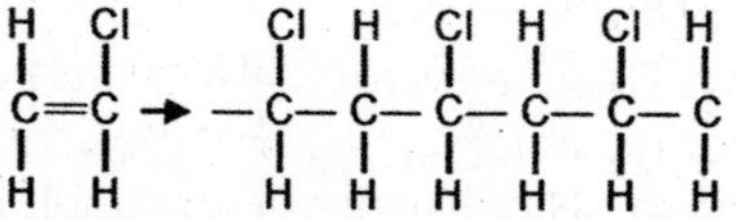

Polymerization. The polymerization process begins with the initiator dissociating into a free radical. The free radical collides with a monomer molecule to form a more complex free radical which continues to combine with additional monomer to form a long polymer chain.

The free radical is formed by the decomposition of an initiator such as benzoyl peroxide, hydrogen peroxide or potassium persulfate.

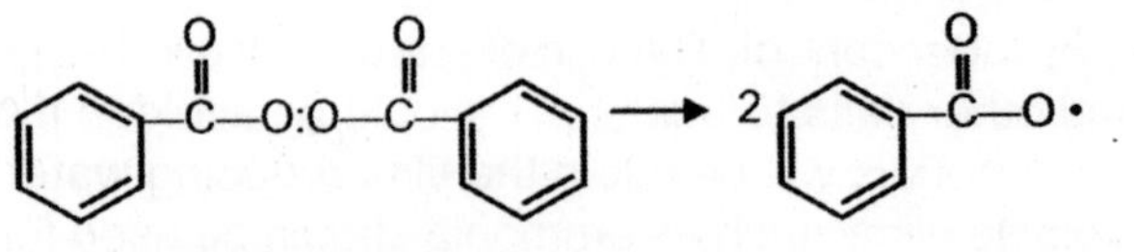

Benzoyl Peroxice

$$S_2O_8 \rightarrow 2SO_4$$

Potassium Persulfate

The second phase of the polymerization is known as propagation. The free radicals react with the monomer to open double bonds.

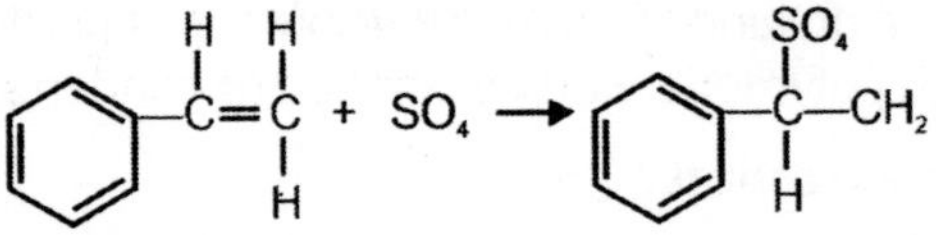

Note that the radical from the initiator actually participates in the reaction. Therefore, one end of a polymer chain is a fragment of the initiator.

The final phase of the polymerization process is termination. This may occur in several ways, such as the combination of two growing chains, combination of a growing chain and a free radical, etc.

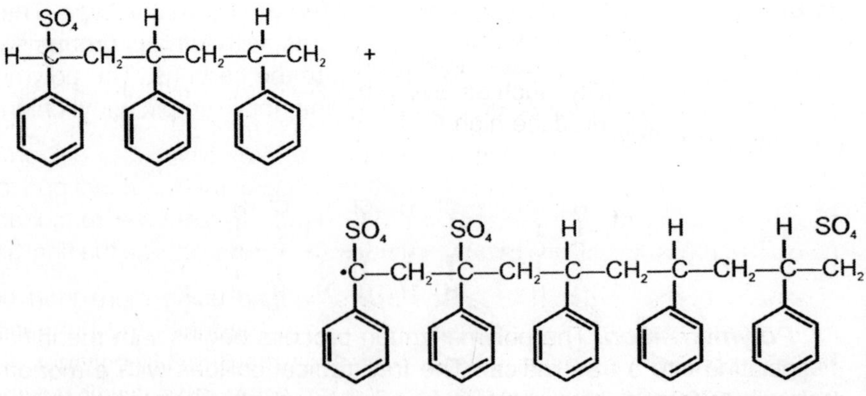

With monomers with a functionality of one (one double bond for molecule), linear polymers are formed. When a molecule with a functionality greater than one is incorporated into the system, branching and crosslinking may occur.

Linear

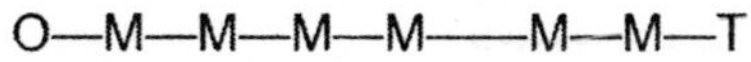

Branched :

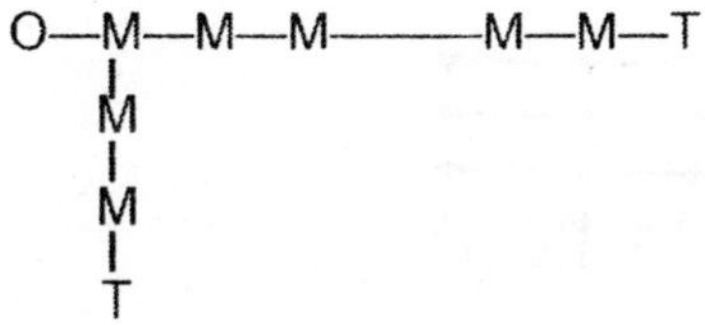

Cross linked :

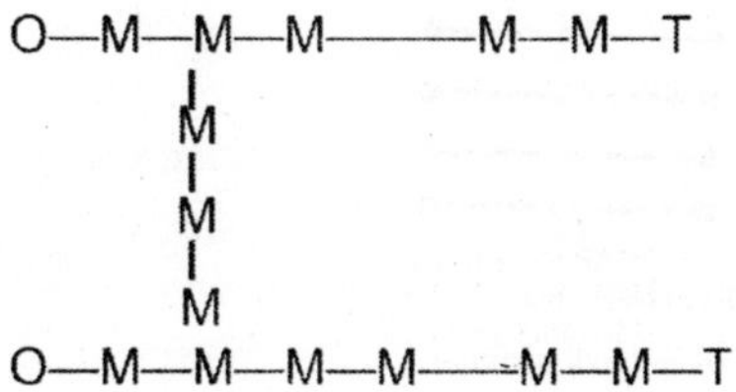

Where
O= Initiator fragment,
T = Terminator fragment,
M = monomer

Cross-linking can be accomplished by the incorporation of monomers with higher functionality, such as divinyl benzene, etc. In a solvent system, cross-linking would produce high viscosities and poor solubility and might even produce gels or insoluble polymers. In a latex which is a dispersed system, the viscosity and solubility characteristics of the individual polymer particles do not affect the viscosity of the latex. In latices a reasonable amount of cross-linking is desirable to toughen and insolubilize the final film.

Many of the commercial latices are produced using more than one monomer to attain the desired properties such as hardness and elongation. For example, vinyl acetate is itself a relatively hard, brittle polymer. It is copolymerized with dibutyl maleate to produce a softer, more elastic polymer. This is known as internal plasticization. The softening point of the polymer in a latex film is important as it controls the fusion or coalescence of the latex particles. For example, a latex that has polymer particles with a softening point above room temperature will, upon evaporation of the water, produce a powdery deposit. If the softening point is close to room temperature, the film may perform satisfactorily in warm weather but fail in cold weather.

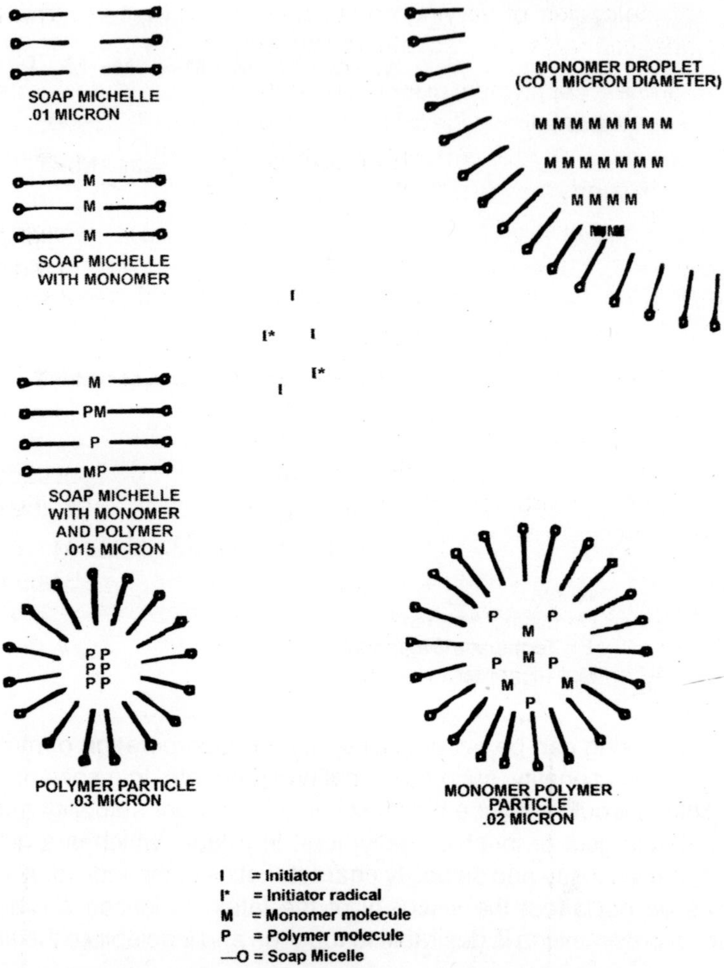

Figure : 21.7 Emulsion polymerization concept

Copolymerization. Copolymerization is any polymerization reaction in which two or more different monomers are converted into a homogeneous polymeric product. First the composition of the copolymer depends upon the concentration of the monomer at the locus of reaction. Copolymerization is further complicated by the fact that monomers polymerize at different rates. Therefore, the composition of a copolymer will vary with the degree of conversion. Thus, the polymers formed at the start of the copolymerization may contain a highér proportion of the more reactive monomers than those formed at the end of the polymerization. A latex may contain a wide range of polymer molecules of varying composition and structure. The individual polymerization rates are also affected by temperature.

To prepare copolymers of more uniform composition, various procedures may be used. Sometimes the more reactive monomer is added slowly during the polymerization. Also temperature, pressure and catalyst content may be varied during the polymerization.

One of the advantages of emulsion polymerization is that high molecular weight polymers can be obtained by this method. Increasing the molecular weight of the polymer increases toughness, scrub resistance, solvent resistance, chemical resistance, etc.

Theory. Emulsion polymerization is a complicated process. Harkins' publication did much to explain the theory of emulsion polymerization. Previously, it had been thought that the polymerization took place within the droplet during emulsion polymerization, although this was not substantiated by fact, since the droplet is many hundred times bigger than the final latex polymer particle.

According to the Harkins theory, the monomer is distributed in three different phases in the emulsion systems, i.e. dissolved to a small extent in the water phase, suspended in the form of monomer emulsion droplets, and solubilized in the surfactant micelles.

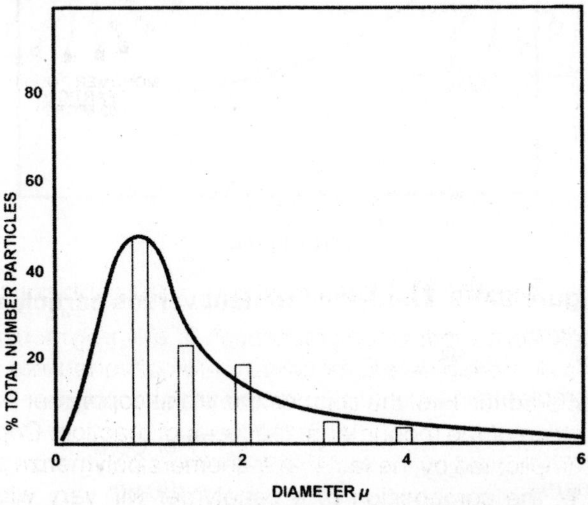

Figure : 21.8 Particle size distribution of a typical latex.

The process of initiation occurs in the aqueous phase and the monomer radical diffuses into the micelles where polymerization occurs. The monomer emulsion droplets act as a reservoir for monomer. During the polymerization, the monomer emulsion droplets become smaller and the micelles grow larger. It has been proved experimentally that the rate of polymerization is dependent on the number of particles present, which is largely dependent on the concentration of emulsifier.

The greater the amount of emulsifier present, the greater is the number of micelles present and finally the greater is the number of polymer particles which have a smaller size.

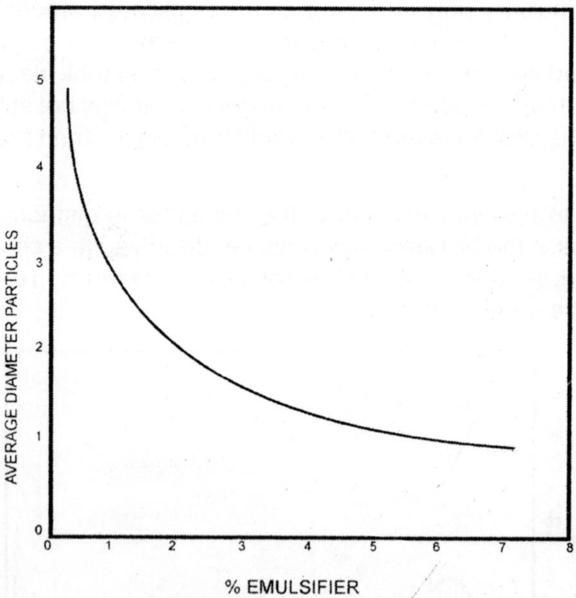

Figure : 21.9 Emulsifier content versus particle size.

Ingredients

The ingredients in an emulsion recipe are as follows:

	Per Cent
Monomers	30-50
Surface-active agents	1-3
Protective colloid	0-3
Initiator	1-3

Modifier	0-1
Buffer	0-1
Water	50-70

Reaction medium-deionized, soft or distilled water is generally used as the continuous phase in an emulsion polymerization. Sometimes small amounts of alcohol or glycols are added as antifreeze materials for lowtemperature reactions.

Monomer-one or more polymerizable materials which amount - to 45 to 55% of the overall composition of the final latex.

Initiators-these are usually water-soluble peroxides, hydroperoxides and persulfates used to initiate the polymerization reaction.

Emulsifiers-surfactants which may be anionic, cationic or nonionic and are needed to carry out the emulsion polymerization reaction. Their function is to solubilize monomer, suspend monomer droplets and suspend polymer particles.

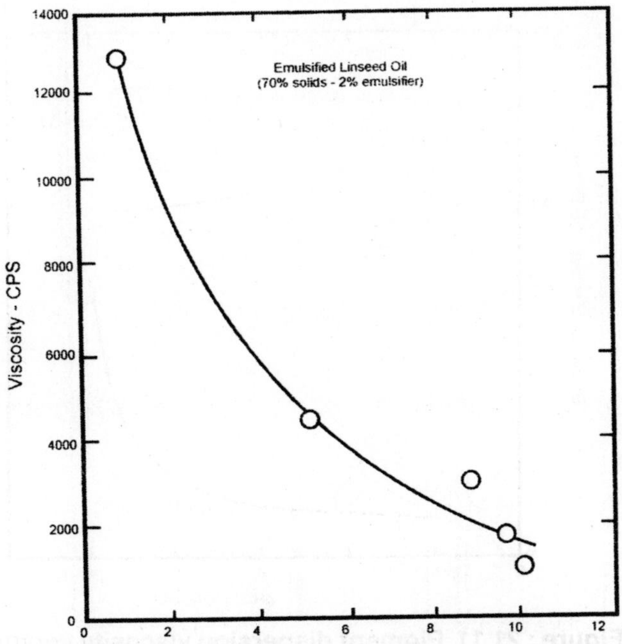

Figure : 21.10 Effects of pH on viscosity.

Modifiers-these materials which may be aldehydes, mercaptans or chlorinated hydrocarbons serve to control the polymerization reaction restricting cross-linking and controlling the molecular weight.

Protective colloids-water-soluble materials such as polyvinyl alcohol

or methylcellulose are incorporated in the batch to stabilize the final latex.

Buffer salts-the pH of an emulsion polymerization batch must be controlled very carefully as the reaction rate, particle size, etc., are effected by pH. These buffers are phosphate, citrate, acetate, carbonate salts, etc.

Post-emulsification

Oils, resin and waxes can be prepared in emulsion form by combining with a surfactant and water under proper mixing procedures.

For emulsions under normal procedure, the resin, oil or wax must be in a liquid state or converted to a liquid state by the use of heat or the addition of a solvent.

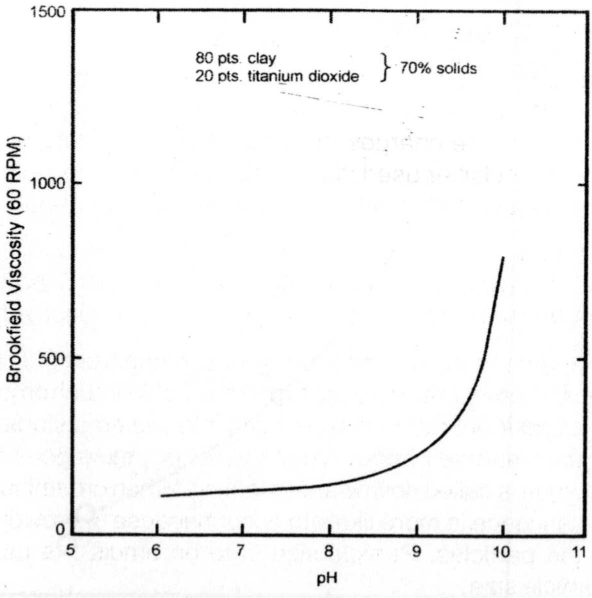

Figure : 21.11 Pigment dispersion viscosity versus pH.

There are several techniques for preparing emulsions in which the resin and water are combined by various mechanical means such as stirrers, mixers, pumps, colloid mills, etc. The techniques are as follows:

Agent in Water. The surfactant is added to the water and then oil is added slowly with agitation. This produces an oil/water emulsion directly.

Agent in Oil. The emulsifying agent is dissolved in the oil phase. This mixture is added directly to water, forming an oil/water emulsion. When water is added to the oil-surfactant mixture, a water/oil emulsion is formed first which inverts to an oil/water emulsion. This method produces fine particle size emulsions. Viscosity is at its maximum value at the inversion point.

Combination. When a combination of surfactants is used, they may be put into both phases. The lypophilic emulsifier is put into the oil phase and the hydrophilic emulsifier is put into the water phase.

In situ. In either oil/water or water/oil emulsions, the fatty acid may be dissolved in the oil and the alkali in the water. The soap then forms at the interface.

Alternate Addition. In this method, the oil and water are added alternately in small portions to the surfactant.

STABILITY OF EMULSIONS

Emulsions must have good stability. The stability depends upon the particle size, the difference in density of the two phases, the viscosity of the continuous phase, the charges on the particles, the nature, effectiveness and amount of emulsifier used, the conditions of storage including high and low temperatures, agitation, vibration and dilution or evaporation.

Since the particles of an emulsion are fully suspended in a liquid, they obey Stokes law unless they are changed. The rising and settling of the particles are termed creaming and sedimentation, respectively.

The phenomena of creaming receives its name from the common exam ple- the separation of cream to the top of the bottle in unhomogenized milk. This is not a break but rather a separation into two emulsions, one of which is richer in the disperse phase. When the richer phase goes to the bottom, the phenomenon is called downward creaming. When creaming or sedimation occurs, coalescence is more likely to occur because of crowding or physical contact of the particles. Particle size data on emulsions usually give the average particle size.

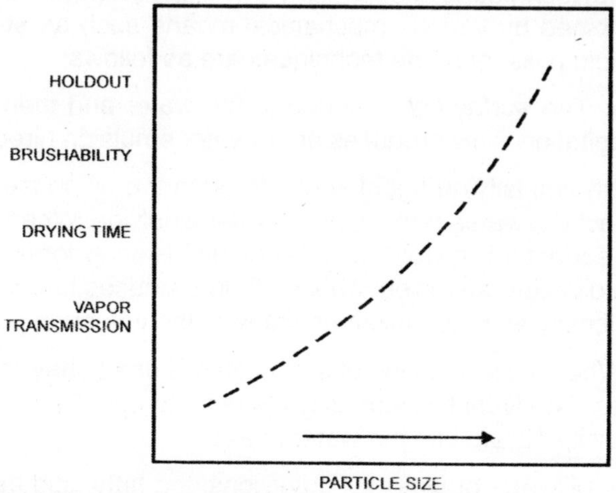

Figure : 21.12 Properties improved by increased particle size.

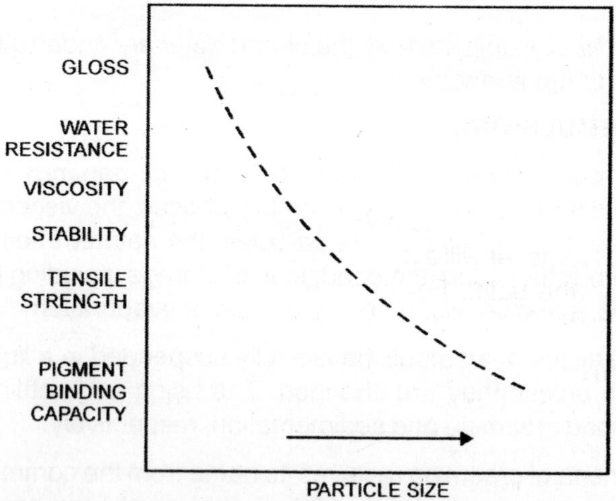

Figure : 21.13 Properties improved by decreased particle size.

Phase Volume

An emulsion consists of many spheres (internal phase) packed into a definite volume of space (external phase). According to solid geometry, an assembly of spheres of equal radius can be placed in a position of packing in two ways. In either case, the spheres occupy 74% of the total volume. Any attempt to exceed this volume will cause breaking *or* inversion.

22

Paint and Varnish Removers

As paint formulations improve, it becomes more of a problem to remove coatings in order to apply a new coat of paint. Special stripping compositions have been developed to keep up with advances in modern paint technology.

Coatings which are particularly difficult to remove are catalyzed epoxies, polyurethanes and thermosetting acrylics. The older the coating, the more difficult it is to strip.

There are two broad types of paint removers: the solvent type and the chemical type which is usually alkaline in nature.

Paint Removal

Paint and varnish removers which are usually applied by brush but can be applied by spray or other methods must contain a thickener so that the paint and varnish remover will stay on a vertical surface, such as a wall, long enough to soften the paint. For coatings that are difficult to remove, the painted part is immersed in a tank of the stripper.

The problem of removing a coating is often very complex. Some of the factors which influence the problem of a stripping operation are:

(I) Type of film former,
(2) Thickness of coating,
(3) Type of surface applied,
(4) Primer used,
(5) Type of pigment,
(6) Curing time, temperature and method,
(7) Age of coating.

Formulation

The correct paint and varnish remover for a given application is the one which does its task satisfactorily at the lowest cost. An inexpensive material which requires the use of heat, is slow acting, or takes several applications may cost more than a higher-priced remover.

When choosing a paint remover, the nature of both the coatings and the substrates must be taken into consideration. Frequently a single stripper must work on a variety of materials, whose composition is often unknown. In this case, methylene chloride strippers are generally used. However, when a paint remover is needed for a specific application such as stripping of rejects of a coating of known composition, then several considerations should be made.

Most common substrates are unaffected by solvent-based strippers. Some exceptions are plastics and certain aluminum alloys which are corroded slightly by chlorinated hydrocarbons or their decomposition products. Some of the modifiers incorporated into organic solvents may have undesirable effects. For example, amines may discolor wood or react with copper or cadmium surfaces, and acids may corrode ferrous and magnesium alloys. Aqueous strippers should not be used on wood since water raises the grain. Caustic rapidly attacks aluminum and zinc alloys.

Solvent Paint and Varnish Removers

The most popular type of paint and varnish remover is the solvent type. These removers contain a primary solvent plus a co-solvent, activator, thickener, evaporation retarder, corrosion inhibitor and emulsifier (for water rinsable type).

A number of factors must be considered in formulating a solvent-type remover. All of the desirable features may not be realized in one product, but the goals are rapidity of action, correct viscosity, nontoxicity, nonflammability, low odor, clean rinsability, noncorrosiveness and package stability.

Solvents. Since the active ingredient is the solvent, most attention is paid to its selection. By far the most popular paint remover solvent is methylene chloride. It is practically nonflammable, thus minimizing fire hazards, one of the greatest dangers in paint removal. Methylene chloride is one of the least toxic of the chlorinated hydrocarbons. It is also one of the most efficient paint removing solvents.

In general, the efficiency of a chlorinated solvent decreases as the chlorination or the chain length of the organic radical increases.

One method of rating the efficiency of a solvent for paint removal is the time required to wrinkle a standard (oleoresinous) paint film. As methylene chloride is the most effective, it is given the top rating as shown below.

Methylene chloride	100
Chloroform	69
Ethylene dichloride	45
Trichlorethylene	36
Monochlorobenzene	36
Carbon tetrachloride	24
o-Chlorobenzene	22
Propylene dichloride	15
Trichlorobenzene	10

Other solvents which will soften paint films are (in approximate decreasing order of efficiency): ketones, esters, aromatic hydrocarbons, alcohols and aliphatic hydrocarbons. Many less common solvents are useful for specific applications, but they are too costly for widespread use. Some of these are: 2-nitropropane, dimethylformamide, dimethyl sulfoxide, tetrahydrofuran and I, I ,2-trimethoxyethane.

Co-solvent. Combined with methylene chloride, methanol is one of the less expensive and most frequently used co-solvents. The general rule to follow in adding co-solvents to methylene chloride is that polar solvents reduce stripping time, nonpolar solvents do not. Small concentrations of polar solvents are more effective than large concentrations except when used on air-dried phenolic coatings and shellac.

Activators. Activators enhance penetration of the solvent into the protective coating. With a methylene chloride remover, the addition of enough water to saturate the methylene chloride will reduce the time as much as 90% for some formulations. A small amount of acetic acid (0.2%) will speed up removal further.

Amines and other alkaline ingredients are often used as activators. Some of these are ammonia, monoethylamine, morpholine, etc. Amines, however, sometimes react with chlorinated solvents and stain wood.

Thickeners. The thickener must meet four major qualifications: (1) It must impart high viscosity at low solids concentration. (2) It must be compatible with the blended composition. (3) It should maintain uniform viscosity during storage. (4) It should form a soft, nonadhering film upon drying. The thickened system should be thixotropic for easy application and nonsag properties on vertical surfaces.

A number of substances, organic and inorganic, are used as thickeners. The most important are organics such as methylcellulose, ethylcellulose, cellulose acetate and nitrocellulose. Also used as thickeners are materials such as bentonite, metallic soaps, starch, zein, casein, polyacrylate esters, etc. If surface-active agents are' used, methylcellulose is practical in a flush-off form ula. The viscosity of the thickener is influenced not only by the solvent but also by the co-solvent. The thickener in flush-off formulations should be water soluble or at least ~ter dispersible in the presence of emulsifying agents.

Penetrants. Wetting agents, primarily amines, not only promote wetting power, but also augment the penetration of the coating and make rinsing easier. Other agents used are petroleum sulfonates and ethylene glycol monobutyl ether.

Evaporation Retarders. Evaporation retarders in paint and varnish removers are waxes of petroleum origin. Upon application the wax crystallizes out to form a film on the surface, retarding the evaporation of the solvent. The concentration of wax should be kept at a minimum, as all wax must be removed from the surface before repainting since wax will soften, decrease adhesion and possibly hinder the drying of the new paint.

A typical formulation is shown in Table 22.1.

TABLE 22.1. Paint and Varnish Removers (Wash-off Type)

Methylene chloride	71	gal
Toluene	3	gal
Methanol	12	gal
Di-triisopropanolamine	9.5	gal
Water	1.5	gal
Methylcellulose (4000 cps)	13	lb
"Areskap"[a]	33	lb
Potassium oleate	22	lb
Paraffin (122-124°F, mp)	16.5	lb

[a] Registered trademark, Monsanto Co.

Chemical Removers

A boiling solution of caustic soda, at a concentration of a few pounds per gallon, is an effective and inexpensive paint remover, and is often used for general stripping purposes. Additives such as sequestering agents, surfactants and activators are added to the caustic to increase stripping rates. Gluconic acid and alkali metal gluconates are good sequestering agents in highly alkaline solutions. Sequestering agents aid in the removal of paints containing oxide pigments and keep metallic ions from precipitating in alkaline solution. The function of-the surfactant in these removers is to act as a wetting agent and to emulsify and remove the partially decomposed paint film from the surface. Surfactants that are stable in hot alkalies are sodium resinate, fatty acid soaps, sodium lignosulfonate and petroleum sulfonates. Activators such as phenols and their sodium salts are added to speed removal.

Table 22.2 shows a formula for a dry alkaline paint stripping compounds.

Nonchlorinated Solvent Paint Removers

Because of their low cost, strippers based on solvents other than chlorinated hydrocarbons are still used for removing oleoresinous finishes and less resistant finishes. They are of the lacquer solvent type containing aromatic solvents such as benzene and toluene with co-solvents such as methanol, and sometimes ketone solvents. Activators, thickeners and waxes of the same kind used with methylene chloride can be incorporated.

Table 22.2 Dry Alkaline Paint Stripper

Sodium hydroxide	85
Sodium lignosulfonate	6
Sodium Gluconae	5
Crysylic acid	3
"Nacconol"[a]	1
	100

a Registered trademark, Allied Chemical Corp. National Aniline Divison

Phenols and chloroacetic acids are highly active chemicals which are useful in specific situations. Specific materials which are commercially available at low cost are cresylic acid (mixed cresols) and a crude mixture of mono-, di- and trichloroacetic acids.

Removal of Epoxies. For the removal of epoxy coatings, acidic-type materials are particularly effective. One of the most effective strippers for this purpose is a solution of concentrated nitric acid in dimethyl sulfoxide used in the temperature range of 120 to 130°C.

Mechanism of Paint Removal

In order to understand why a particular paint remover is more effective at stripping certain types of coatings than others, it is helpful to consider how a paint remover works. Simple dissolution of the film is almost never observed except when shellac or lacquers are removed with certain solvents. Usually the coating is swelled, softened and raised so that it can be quickly removed by scraping or flushing with water. In solvent-type removers, the film is swelled by the solvent. In many types of coatings (e.g., oils or alkyds), materials such as alkali saponify or break down the ester

linkage, thereby aiding removal. The remover attacks the weakest part of the film and increases penetration.

Methods of Paint Removal. There are four basic methods used in stripping paints. A hot flow-on method is most economical for removing multiple layers of paint from large areas. The remover, usually an alkaline type, is heated to temperatures of 180 to 212°F and applied through a spray head which is a perforated pipe or rake. The runoff is collected and recirculated. A second method is a steam gun, in which an alkaline-type remover is applied at 5 to 10 pounds of pressure.

Tank stripping is applic.able where small work must be stripped. This is an excellent method for reclaiming parts in volume. Parts remain immersed until the paint is loosened. Agitation will speed paint removal. For tank immersion stripping, a welded steel tank with an overflow dam to carry away loosened paint is recommended. Where stripping is done with hot solutions, a closed steam coil or immersion-type gas burner is required. Once paint has been loosened, a high-pressure rinse effects complete removal.

Manual brushing is used when dealing with large vertical or inverted surfaces where it is not desirable to set up a hot flow on a steam gun stripping operation. The paint is removed manually by brushing on a viscous solvent-type stripper. After the paint is softened, it is loosened by steam or water pressure.

23

Spray Painting

The title "Spray Painting" is really not inclusive enough to describe all the materials and processes of atomizing liquids for protective, decorative and technical purposes. By this is meant that materials other than paints are sprayed, and special types of equipment are available to spray-apply coatings and chemical formulations.

Continuing developments in spray equipment parallel the paint and chemical industry's requirements for proper application of today's modern paints, coatings and resins. The growth of these two industries in many instances is associated with specialization resulting in precise coatings or paints for particular results. Spray equipment meets application needs with various systems.

The five systems that are extensively used for paint and coating applica tion, both in product finishing and maintenance painting, are:

(I) Conventional air spray,
(2) Airless spray,
(3) Hot spray,
(4) Dual component (catalyst spray),
(5) Electrostatic spray.

Conventional Air Spray

This is the oldest of all systems. It is the most universal and is used more than all the others.

The principle of atomizing with compressed air permits conventional equipment to be practical in outfit sizes ranging from one using only a ⅓hp compressor and low-pressure, low-volume gun to one requiring a multi horsepower compressor supplying a high-volume gun.

Most any liquid and even semiliquids can be sprayed with a conventional system. Abrasive paints and coatings with aggregates are handled and sprayed with no difficulty.

The simplest conventional system is the suction type. This setup consists of a gun with a suction air cap whose design produces a vacuum action around the center hole. The attached cup containing the paint has a vent hole in the lid. When air rushes through the cap center hole with the fluid tip centered there, the vacuum developed siphons the paint from the cup.

A suction feed hookup is limited to spraying low-viscosity paints and the volume of paint sprayed is small. This means that suction feed is used most by auto, furniture and appliance refinishers and craftsmen using materials adaptable to this setup.

For high-speed spraying, a pressure feed lineup 'of equipment is used. The paint is forced to the gun through hose from a pressure tank or pump. Gun-attached pressure cups can also be used. The name of the hookup describes the operation-paint is supplied by pressure. In the case of the pressure tank and pressure cup, air pressure is regulated into these containers to push the paint up and out the fluid tube to the gun.

In contrast to limited suction feed, pressure feed is unlimited. Extremely heavy paints and coatings can be pumped to the gun. Medium- or light-viscosity materials can be supplied from a pressure tank or pumped in volumes to meet the needs of even the highest production.

Great progress has been made in pump design and performance for supplying paints in large amounts for maintenance painting and product finishing.

Airless Spray

This system of spraying has made a big impact on the industry. While conventional spraying is still most universal, more painting contractors each year are switching to airless for large commercial work. The airless system is a simplified hookup available in air-operated pump style or electric oil motor type requiring no compressed air.

The air-operated high-ratio pump requires a compressor. The electric airless model is of a design requiring no air compressors for pumping or spraying. In either type, the requirement is to pump paint to high pressure generally beyond 1000 psi and commonly to 3000 psi.

It is evident that considerable size is necessary in the equipment itself to develop this pressure and to pump a volume of paint equal to production requirements. Size alone and high capacity somewhat preclude airless for auto, furniture and similar refinishing. At this time, conventional spraying is used for these smaller jobs.

Atomization. It is necessary to digress from our discussion of the other spray painting systems-hot spray, dual component and electrostatic-in favour of an explanation of the atomization processes in conventional and air less systems. Both of these systems are better understood and used to their fullest advantage when correctly evaluated as to how paints and coatings are atomized.

Atomization is the breaking up of a stream of paint by some source of energy into small spheres. In conventional spray, the atomization is done by air pressure. Compressed air is a source of energy. As compressed air is directed through the air cap, it is aimed at the material stream to form the droplets into a pattern which now is directed onto the surface while the gun is moved.

Not all paints atomize alike. The viscosity of the material is one factor that determines the atomizing pressure required. Heavy and viscous paints need high pressure, while low-viscosity paints will break up with low air pressure.

The other factor determining the air pressure necessary for uniform atomization is the fluid flow from the gun. For example, to atomize a 32-oz/min flow of enamel may require 70 pounds of air pressure; to atomize 16 oz/min of the same enamel only 45 pounds of pressure would be needed. Variations in air pressure affect the degree of atomization, and spray operators must exercise good judgment in selecting pressures.

The energy in airless atomization is hydraulic pressure. When paint is pumped to high pressure and then directed through the small orifice of the cap on the gun, it comes out of that orifice at extremely high velocity. The sudden release of the high velocity causes the paint stream to split apart into atomized particles. The design and angle of the orifice are determinants of pattern size.

It could be said that atomization in the conventional system is done with outside forces, i.e., by compressed air jets, whereas the atomization in airless spraying is caused by the release of the internal velocity of the paint stream.

What really happens in airless spraying is that the material tears itself

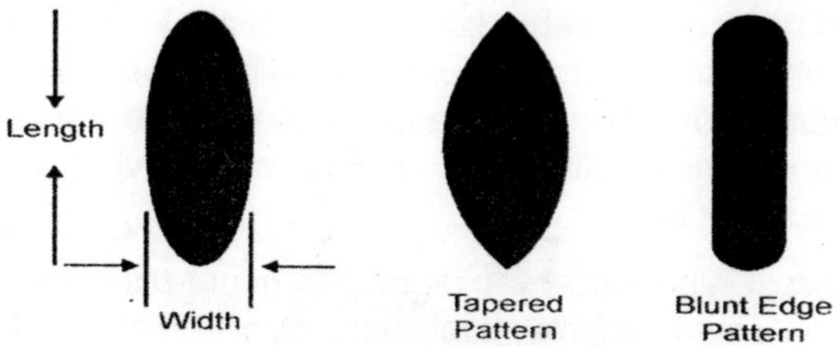

Figure 23.1 Spray pattern shapes and dimensions identification

apart when released through the orifice. Consequently, the paints and coatings used in airless have to be shearable. Most paints will atomize well with airless. Viscosity is a factor in sprayability to the extent that heavy paints or very viscous materials are difficult to atomize uniformly, whereas lower-viscosity paints break up very well. Examples of easy-toatomize formulations are alkyd flat and latex wall paints. Difficult-toatomize materials are adhesives, chlorinated rubber and similar cohesive types. Enamels and lacquers atomize and spray very well with the airless process.

Earlier, reference was made to the pattern of the atomized paint. The patterns formed by the air cap on a conventional gun and the spray cap on an airless gun are similar. Figure 23.1 shows typical patterns. The dimensions "length" and "width" are measured in inches. The size pattern produced by a cap is a matter of cap design. On a conventional cap, the jets of air from the horns define the pattern; on an airless cap, the angle machined at the orifice determines the pattern dimensions.

Since there are varied requirements to suit production needs, different caps are fitted on guns for wide or narrow patterns or for atomizing a high- or low-volume fluid flow. There is really no one universal cap. Consequently, the selection of the right cap for job conditions is important.

Hot Spray

This is the system of atomization of paint at elevated temperature. Note the use of the words "atomization of paint." The description is purposely made this way to clear up the common misconception that hot paint is applied onto a surface. The basis for hot spray is the result of paint being influenced by temperature changes and the way viscosity determines atomization. While paint is very receptive to temperature changes and readily accepts heat, it is not a good retainer of heat.

At the instant of atomization with a paint temperature of 1400 F, Figure how heat is lost as the pattern continues toward the surface with

Figure 23.2 Heat loss in spray pattern in hot spray process.

the paint arriving in a chilled-down condition. The primary reason for the heat dissipation is the refrigerating effect of solvent loss during atomization. This occurs because the paint within the heater is generally raised to a temperature beyond the boiling point of the fast-evaporating solvent. Immediately upon release, this hot solvent expands and vaporizes out of the pattern- this is a cooling action. The atomizing air also has a cooling effect.

Hot spray produces several very beneficial advantages, among which are viscosity control, lower spraying pressures and heavier film build when desired.

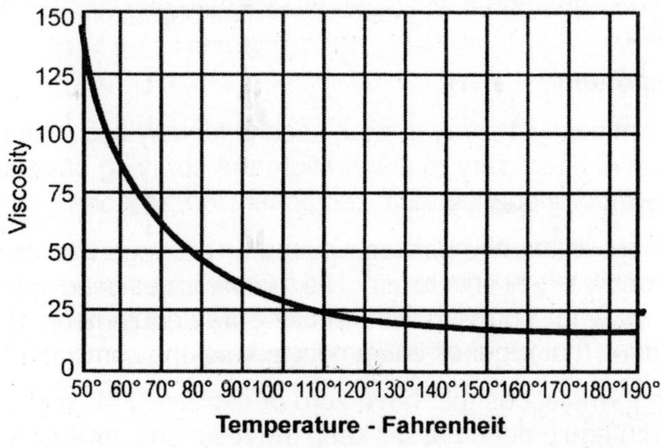

Fig. 23.3 Typical viscosity curve showing viscosity range when paint is heated.

Using heat for viscosity control eliminates the variables of viscosity due to spray area temperature changes and the possibility of incorrect viscosity due to human error in mixing.

There is naturally a limit to the mechanical capabilities of paint heaters, and their potential is approximately a 100° rise. This means if the temperature of the unheated paint is 50° F, the heater will raise it to 150° F.

It is not necessary to heat paint excessively to obtain viscosity benefits. Figure 23.3 illustrates the relationship between viscosity drop and heat applied. It is important to note that at about 130° F the lowest viscosity is attained and additional heat does not have any significant effect. In practice, most materials would be heated to a temperature range to overcome heat loss in the hose and to assure adequate temperature of paint at the gun.

Hot spray is an ideal system for lacquers, enamels, resins and solventtype paints, with a limitation to materials that are in the paint c'lassificac tion. Coatings of a mastic or similar extremely heavy viscosity are rarely hot sprayed.

Because atomizing air pressure in conventional spray and hydraulic pressure in airless spray are selected and adjusted to produce uniform atomization based on viscosity, it is evident that a lower-viscosity material can be atomized at lower pressures. Consequently, a heated and less viscous paint can be broken up at lower pressure. Lower pressures make for economy because a lower level of overspray is generated. Any reduction in overspray and bounce-off is advantageous because of less contamination to surroundings, better atmosphere for the operator, and fewer demands on the spray booth.

Dual Component

The term catalyst spray is often used to identify this system. However, a distinction is necessary to differentiate the spraying of catalyzed paints from true two-component or dual-component formulations.

There are many two-package paints or coatings that are mixed in a common container just prior to use. The mixture is designed with long enough pot life to allow for spraying with regular spray equipment. This is not the type of coating that requires equipment to keep the components separate.

Those formulations that have zero or extremely short pot life must be sprayed with equipment that will keep the resin and catalyst separate until the instant of application. This is dual-component equipment.

Both conventional and airless systems are available for spraying dual components. Since the heart of any system is the spray gun, this item is specially designed and manufactured with separate fluid passageways. Some models keep the components apart inside the gun so that mixing takes place in the atomized pattern outside the gun. In another type, the materials join in a mixing chamber in the gun and are emitted together from the gun. This type requires the attachment of a purge or cleaning line into the mixing chamber so that when spraying is stopped this gun area can immediately be flushed clean.

Use of dual-component spray equipment demands accurate controls, such as calibrated fluid ratios and more precise spraying techniques than used in ordinary spraying. Noncorrosive metals and durable plastics are used in the tanks, pumps, regulators, hoses and guns.

Electrostatic Spray

The most popular area for electrostatic spraying is in product finishing. While portable power sources and hand-operated guns are available, the electrostatic system is sometimes impractical for maintenance or refinish painting because, of surface, kind of paint or production speed.

The surface to be painted must be conductive. This means that if it is not conductive, it must be pretreated with a coating or solution that will attract the electrostatic charge. It is evident that many products from our factories lend themselves to electrostatic finishing because they are metal and conductive. In contrast, the various surfaces painted for maintenance or decorative reasons in too many cases are not conductive.

The types of paints used in product finishing are very economically and successfully applied by the electrostatic system.

Multiple gun setups are arranged on a production line to assure highspeed finishing. A single electrostatic spray gun is slow compared to a single conventional or airless setup; therefore, the latter systems are best for meeting the production speeds of maintenance painting.

Spraying Today's Paints

In today's technology, there are two major users of spray: product finishers and refinishers. This distinction is made for reasons of selling and distribution of the equipment itself and because of the types of paints and coatings applied.

These classifications influence the development, engineering and style of equipment. Product finishing spray equipment becomes part of a finishing department in a plant and is installed like other tools in a somewhat permanent location. Spray equipment for refinishing is more portable.

The spraying capacity of product finishing equipment is generally higher than refinishing setups because in factories the items to be sprayed are brought into the spray booth continuously at regular intervals either on powered conveyors or in batches. It is common on conveyorized spray lines to have a nozzle combination on a gun atomizing a quart of paint per minute distributed uniformly over a 14-inch-long pattern. Both manual and automatic guns are capable of sustained high production.

The product finishing paints used today on metal, plastic and wood surfaces are beautifully sprayed, meaning that the combination of paint chemistry and spray equipment style assures the user of preselected good results.

In the early days of spraying, different guns and nozzle combinations were needed to apply lacquer or enamel. Today because of similarity in viscosities in lacquer, enamel, epoxy and other product finishes in like

formulations, a standardized gun and nozzle combination will spray all of them.

In contrast, spraying of paints in the maintenance painting profession requires attention in a larger degree to selection of guns and nozzle com binations. This is necessary because of the wide range of viscosities of maintenance paints and coatings from lacquers to mastics. Too, while high production is important in maintenance painting, the fluid flow rate from a gun is adjusted to somewhere between 1 and 1 ~ pintsjmin for most jobs. Both conventional and airless systems are capable of spraying greater volumes than these, but the lower rates are mentioned in the interest of being practical.

Another division in the refinishing field is concerned with spraying automobiles, trucks, boats, business machines, canteen dispensers and similar renovated and repaired items. In this category are washing machines, dryers, freezers and separate electric and gas motors which are repainted after repair. These service operations represent a large share of the refinish market.

The spraying of automobiles and trucks is done by independent body shops and car dealers in standard design but specially engineered spray booths. The spraying of vehicle lacquers and enamels in these production shops is accomplished mostly with a suction feed gun. Pressure tank setups are used particularly in fleet repainting shops because all units in the fleet are painted the same color. Of course, this volume method of handling paint has advantages over the suction gun method which lends itself best to the rapid and frequent colour changes that are a necessary part of job shop spraying.

Figure 23.4 shows a typical auto refinishing spray booth with scientifically placed lights and an air replacement unit on the right at ceiling line and an exhaust outlet on the left. Clean, heat-tempered air in adequate volume is drawn across the car during the spraying operation.

Appliance refinishing is done in floor-type booths. The spraying is again suction feed for job work or pressure feed for volume repainting.

Automation and Spraying

The general subject of automation must be considered from the view point of product handling method, spray machines and spray equipment.

Automation starts with the handling method, and therefore, the selection of the spray machine is influenced by the plant's handling process.

The following is a list of types of handling methods and items to be sprayed:

Figure 23.4. Auto refinishing spray booth with air replacement unit on right and exhaust fan on left.

Chain-on-edge machines	Parts that can be sprayed as they remot but must be dried or baked on the machine can be handled on this type of deivce *Example :* Automobile weheels, electric motors, shells, and containers such as aerosol cans and 5-gallon pails.
Continous rolls	Coil steel, paper, fabric and other materials are sometimes coated as they are rewound. *Example :* Decorating fabric or paper, bonding foam to fabric.
Fabricating machine	Occasionally, it is desirable to spray on the part as it leaves the fabricating machine. *Example :* Coating or marking pipe, lubrication of abillet as it enters an extruding die, adding moisture to paper.
Lay down conveyor	Articles can be easily conveyed horizontly by laying them on a cross light, cable or pin type conveyor. *Example :* Coating plywood prcelain enameling stove parts, adhesive on panel and honeycomb for laminating
Overhead conveyor	This is the most popular because it makes vertical turns as well as horizontal end, therefore can be used to convey parts through many operations. The parts may be nonrotating, indexed or rotated. *Example :* Sheet metal parts such as washers, dryers, refrigerator, automobile fender and hoods are conveyed through the washers, metal preparations, paint application, bake (ovens can be overhead) and on through farbication.
Pallet type conveyor	Large and or heavy articles are often conveyed on platforms riding on chains or wheels. They can be at floor level or elevated. *Example :* Automobile bodies, furniture, case goods, caskets, heavy machinery.
Rotary table machines	Parts that must be rotating but can be removed

wet are sprayed on arotating table with workholder on spindles. The parts can be loaded and unloaded continuously for higher production.

Example : Decorating glassware, bonding cement on clutch disks.

The following is a listing of standard spray machines in relation to handling methods for various products and items :

Following mechanism	Following guns are sometimes used to coat small parts, to coat the interior of cavities not requiring on extension and to provide a longer spray duration. *Example* : Decorating glassware, coating inside of aerosol cans.
Rotary arm transverse	This devide is used to coat flatwork at the higher conveyor speeds up to approximately 450 ft/min. The coating is not as uniform as that obtained with the transeverse machine. *Example :* Plywood, leather, sheet steel.
Short stroke reciprocator	The device is used to provide a short reciprocating motion for electrostatic guns. *Example :* Any object on an overhead conveyor that can be sprayed electrostatically.
Stationary gun or guns	Ocasionally, a stationary gun or gang spray will apply a satisfactory coating to a product. It is the best expensive of the various machines. There is a minimum speed which will permit the required pattern length without flooding. However, there is no maximum speed since additional guns in series will provide adequate coverage. There is always the possibility of streaks whenever it is necessary to blend two or more patterns together to cover wide surfaces. Stationary guns are often used on rotating parts such as on the single spindle, rotary table and chain-on-edge machines. *Example :* Priming of lumber, coating pipe,

lubricating dies, spraying identification marks.

Transverse machines — The reciprocating guns of the horizontal and vertical transverse machines are used to produce a uniform coating on flatwork. However, a slight contour and some edges can be coated with the guns at compound angles. These machines will spary at the rate of about 120 sq. ft./ for a first class finish and about 240 sq. ft./ min for finishes such as ceiling tile and wallboard.

Example : Automobile sides and tops, stove parts, shingles (metal and wood), adhesive on metal, wood and fabric.

Vertical moving mechanism — This devise is used to move extensions and out of a part or a gun or guns over the outside of a part. it is necessary to use this is conjunction with the following devide or to have the part stationary at the time of spraying. It is generally used in the chain-on-edge machines. However, a slowly moving vertical transverse machine may be used for parts on an overhead conveyor.

Example : Shells, 5 gallon pails or other containers requiring extensions

The relationship of spray equipment to autonation is summed up as follows :

Airless — Although airless lacks the flexibility to easily accommodate the set conditions of an automatic process, it does have advantages, particularly where there ae limited exhauset facilities.

Conventional air spray — Convetional air spray is particularly well suited to automation because of its flexibility of adjustment and ability to handle nearly all materials. It can invariable be adjsuted to satisfy the conditons predetermined by an automatic process.

Additional film build, higher quality finishes and greater economy can be had by the addition of a paint heater.

Electrostatic — Electrostatic is ideally suited to automation since it recognizes the area rather than the particular shape of a part. Therefore, different parts with like areas can be intermixed on the line with the same equipment setting. It has the added advantages of being more economical than the other method.

The Professional Sprayman

The operation of spray equipment in many operations today requires trained personnel. Not only do the factors of economical use of paints and perfection of finishes dictate the need for know-how, but the high degree of mechanization of spray equipment itself demands technical aptitude.

24

Paints Formulae

PAINT BASES :

Dry Bases for Paints- The following colours and minerals mixed in the proportions given and then ground to find power, make excellent dry paints and may be thinned with terpentine oil, and a small percentage of cheap varnish to consistency required.

Buff.—

Yello Ocher	44	Pounds
Whiting	6	Pounds
Oxide zinc	5	Poinds
Plaster of Paris	½	Pounds

Brick Brown.—

Yellow ocher	26	pounds
Calcinedcoppears	4	pounds
Red hemitite	1¼	poiunds
Best silica	7	pounds
Whiting	18	pounds

Gray.—

Oxide zinc	30	pounds
White lead	6	pounds
Whitening	12	pounds
Bone black	¼	pound
Yellow ocher	2	pounds

Crimson.—

Indian red	25	pounds
Crocus martis	7	pounds
Oxide of zinc	6	pounds
Whiting	6	pounds

Vendyke Brown—

Yellow ocher	25	pounds
Whiting	18	pounds
Umber	4	pounds
Oxide of zinc	7	pounds
Purple oxide of iron	1	pounds

Blood red.—

Crocus martis	30	pounds
Whiting	20	pounds
Hemitit	3	pounds
Silica	6	pounds
Venetian red	2	pounds

Drab.—

Yellow ocher	40	pounds
Whiting	10	pounds
Oxide of zinc	8½	pounds
Sulphate of barytes	1	pounds

Paint of blackboard.—

Shellac	1	pound
Alcohol	1	gallon
Lampblack (fine quality)	4	ounces
Powdered emery	4	ounces
Ultramarine Blue	4	ounces

Dissolve the shellac in the alcohol. Place the lampblack, emery and ultramarine blue on a cheese-cloth stainer, pour on part of the shellac solution, pour on part of the shellac solution, stirring constantly and gradually adding the solution until all the powders have passed through the stainer.

Drak Green Paint for Blackboards- Mix 1 part Prussian blue and 1 part chrom green with equal part of gliders size and alcohol to a thin crean consistency. Apply with a large, stiff brush and after an hour a second coat is given. After 24 to 48 hours smooth the surface with a felt cloth. This renders it rich and velvety. The shade must be a deep black green and the quantities of the colours have to be modified accordingly if necessary. Old blackboards should be previously thoroughly cleaned with soda.

BRONZING SOLUTION FOR PAINTS.

I.– The so called "banana solution" (the name being derived from its odor) which is used in applying bronzes of various kinds, usually a mixture of equal parts of amyl acetate, acetone and benzine, with just enough pyroxiline dissolved therein to give it body. Powedered bronze is put into a bottle containing this mixture and the paint so formed applied with a brush. The thin covering of pyroxyline that is left after the evaporation of the liquid protects the bronze from the air and keeps it from being wiped off by the cleanly housemaid. Tarnished picture frames and tarnished chandeliers to which a gold bronze has been applied from such a solution will look fresh and new for a long time. Copper bronze as well as gold bronze and the various coloured bronze powders can be used in the "banana solution" for making very pretty advertising signs for use in the drug store. Lettering and bordering work upon the signs can be done with it. Several very small, stiff painters brushes are needed for such work and they must be either kept in the solution when not in use, or, better still, washed in benze or acetone immediately after use and put away for future service. As the "Banana solution" is volatile, it must be kept well corked.

II.– A good bronzing solution with paint tins, applied by dipping, is made by dissolving Syrian asphaltum is spirits of turpentine, etc., and thinning it down with these solvents to the proper bronze colour and consistency. A little good boned oil will increase the adherence.

Paint Brushes–To soften a hard paint brush, stand the brush overnight in a pot of soft soap and clean in warm water. Afterwards clean in benzen. If the brush is wrapped with a string do not let the string touch the soap.

Paint brushes which have dried up as hard as stone can be cleaned in the following manner: Dissolve 1 part soda in 3 parts water: pour the solution in a cylinder glass, and suspend in it the brushes to be cleaned, so that they are about 2 inches from the bottom of the vessel. Let it remain indisturbed at a temperature of 140° to 158° F. 12 to 24 hours, after which the most indurated brushes will have become soft so that they can be readily cleaned with soap. It is essential however to observe the temperature, as bristle brushes will be injured and spoiled if the heat is greater.

Black– A Permanent Black of rich Luster for Metal Boxes– Dissolve chlorate the potassium and blue vitriol, equal parts in 36 times as much water, and allow the solution to cool. The parts to be blacked may be either dipped in the solution, or the solution may be flowed on the allowed to remain until the metal becomes black, after which the fixtures should be rinsed in clean water and allowed to dry. those parts of the surface which show inperfections in the black should be recoated.

Dead White on Silver work etc– Bruise charcoal very finely and mix it with calcined borax in the proportion of 4 parts of charcoal to 1 of borzx. Of this make a past with water: apply this paste on the parts to be deadened; next expose the piece to the fire of well lit coal until it acquires a cherry red shade; allow to cool and then place it in water slightly acidulated with sulphuric acid. The bath must not be more than 5° Be Leave the piece in the bath about 2 hours then rince off several times.

White Coating for Signs etc.– A white cholor for signs and articles exposed to the air is prepared as follows for the last coat: Thin-so-called Dutch "stand" oil with oil of turpentine to working consistency, and grind in it equal parts of zinc white and white lead, not adding much siecative, as the white lead assists the drying considerably. If thepaint is smoothed well with a badger brush. A very durable white color of great gloss is obtained. Linseed oil or varnish which has thickened like "stand" oil by long open storing, Will answer euqally well.

To Prevent Crawling of Paints–Probably the best method to pursue will be to take an ordinary fannel rage and carefully rubt it over the work previous to varnishing, stripping or painting. This simple operation will obviate the possibility of crawling.

In some instance however, crawling may be traced to a defective varnish. The latter, after drying evenly on well prepared paint surface will at time crawl, leaving small pitmarks. For this, the simple remedy consists in purchasing varnish from a reputable manufacturers.

FIREPROOF PAINTS :

Fireproofing paints of effective quality are prepared in different ways. Naturally no oily or greasy substances enter into their composition, the blending agent being simply water.

I.– One of the standing paints consists of 40 pounds of powdered asbestoes, 10 pounds of lime, and 30 pounds of silicate of soda, with the addition of any non-rosinous colouring matter desired. The whole is thoroughly mixed with enough water to produce a perfect blend and render an easy application. Two or more coats of this is the rule in applying it to any wood surface, inside or outside of building.

II.- Another formula involves the use of 40 pounds of finely ground glass a like amount of ground porcelain, and similarly of China clay or the same quantity of powdered asbestos, and 20 pounds of quicklime. These materials are ground very fine and then mixed in 60 pounds of liquid silicate of soda with water, as in the preceding formula. Two or more coats, if necessary are given.

Each of these paints is applied with a brush in the oardinary way, the drying ebing accomplished in a few hours, and if colouring matter is desired, the above proportions are varied accordingly.

III.– A surface coated with 3 coats of water glass, these 3 coats being subsequently coated with water glass containing enough whiting or ground chalk to make it a trafile thicker than ordinary paint, is practically non-inflammable, only yielding to fierce consuming flames after a somewhat protected exposure.

IV.– Zine white, 70 pounds; airlaked lime, 30 pounds; white lead, 50 pounds; sulphate of zinc, 10 pounds; silicate of soda, 3 galions. The zinc white and lime are mixed together, then ground in elastic oil, after which the silicate of soda is added, this addition being followed by the white lead and sulphate of zinc. This white paint can be colored to meet any desired shade and itmay be classed as a good working paint and probably fireproof to the same extent that most of the pretentiously sounded pigments on the markets are.

Fireproof and Waterproof Paints.– The following recipes are claimed to resist both fire and water: A preparation for protecting wood against the action of fire and of moisture, and also for producing on the surface of wood and metal a coat, insulating with reference to electricity and preservative from corrosion, has been introduced in France by Louis Bethisyand Myrthil Rose. The bases of fundamental raw materials quite distinct from those hitherto employed for the same purpose are 100 parts, by weight of nitro-cellulose and 30 parts, by weight of chloride of lime, dissolved in 50 percent alcohol.

Preparation of the Bases–The cellulose (of wood, paper cotton, line, ramie, or hemp) is put in contact with two thirds part of sulphuric acid of 66° Be and one-third part of nitric acid of 42° Be. for some 20 or 30 minutes, washed with plenty of water, and kept for 24 hours in a tank of water supplied with an energetic current.

The nitro—cellulose thus obtained is bleached for this purpose, a double hypochlorite of aluminium and magnesium is employed. This is obtained by grinding together 100 parts of chloride of lime, 60 part of aluminium sulphate, 23 parts of magnesium sulphate, with 200 parts of water.

When the nitro–cellulose is bleached and rewashed, it is reduced to powder and dried as throughly as possible. It is then placed in a vat hermetically closed and put in contact with the indicated proportion of calcium chloride dissolved in alcohol. This solution of calcium chloride should be prepared at least 24 hours in advance and filtered.

Composition of the Coating– This has the following constituents; Bases (nitro cellulose and solution of calcium chloride), 1 part amyl actate (solvent of the bases), 5 parts, by weight; sulphuric ether of 65E, 1.650 parts by weight; alcohol 0.850 part by weight; one of these powders, alum, takc asbestos, or mica, 0.100 parts. Other solvents may be employed instead of amyl acetate; for example, acetone, acetic acetic acid, ether alcohol, or methlic alcohol. The ether alcohol furnishes a product drying very quickely. If a very pliant coating is desired, the amyl acetate is employed preferably, with addition of vaseline oil, 0.20 parts, and lavender oil, 0.010 parts.

Method of Operating – The sulphuric acid is mixed with the alcohol, and left for an hour in contact, shaking from time to time. Afterwards the amyl acetate is added, and left in contact for an other hour under similar agitation. In case of the employment of vaseline oil and lavender oil, these two are mingled in ether alcohol. The base is introduced and left in contact for 24 horus, with frequent agitation. The fluidity of the product is augemented by increasing the quantity of the solvent.

Properties– Wood covered with this coating is fireproof, non hygometric. and refractory to the electric current. It also resist the action of acids andalkalies. Metals covered with it are sheltered fromm oxidation, and effectually insulted on their surface from the electric current. The coating is liquid in form, the and applied like collodions, either by the brush or by immersion or other suitabnle method.

Paint Deadening– In order to obtain an even dullness of large walls, proceed as follows; After all the dirt has been carefully swept of, oil with 2 parts linseed oil and 1 part turpentine and rub down the smooth places in the wet part with pumice stone. When th eoil coating is dry, mix the ground paint consisting of whiting, 2 parts; and white lead, 1 part; both finely ground and diluted as above do not apply grounding too thin, because the chalk in itself possesses little covering power. It is not the mission of the chalk however, to adulterate the material, but to afford a hard, foundation for the subsequent coats. For the third coating take white lead, 1 part; and zinc white, 1 part; thin as above and blend with a soft hair pencil. For the final application use only zinc white, ground stiff in oil with any desired mixing colour and thinned with turpentine and rain water. Mix the water and the turpentine with the colour at the same time, and this coat may be dubbed instead of blended. By the addition of water the paint becomes dull more slowly and is a little more difficult to lay on; but it does nto show a trace of gloss after a few days and never turns yellow, even in places less exposed to the air, and besides excels by great permanency.

Another way is to add white wax instead of water to the last coating. This was paint also gives a handsome dillness but is more difficult of treatment. A nice matt coating is also obtained by addition of venetian soap, dissolved in water instead of the wax. This is very desirable for church decoration where exceptionally large surface are to be deadended

Paint Dryers

I.–	Ordinary barytes	25	pounds
	Whiting	4	pounds
	Litharge	2	pounds
	Sulphate of zinc	2	pounds
	Sugar of lead	2	pounds
	Boiled linseed oil	5	pounds
	Plastic of Paris	½	pounds
II.–	Whiting	16	pounds
	Barytes	16	pounds
	White lead	3	pounds
	Boiled linseed oil	3/4	gallon

PAINTS FOR GOLD AND GILDING :

Gold Paints – The formulas of the various gold paints on the market are carefully guarded trade secret. Essentially they consist of a bronze powder mixed with a varnish. The best bronze powder for the purpose is what is known in the trade as "French flake" a deep gold bronze. This bronze, as seen under the microscope, consists of tiny flakes or sspangles of the bronze metal. As each minute flake forms a facel for the reflection of colour, the paint made with it is much more brilliant than that prepared from finely powdered bronze.

For making gold paint this the socalled "washable gold enamel" that is gold by the manufacturers at the present time it is necessary to mix a celluloid varnish with the French flake bronze powder. This varnish is made by dissolving transparent celluloid in amyl acetate in the proportion of about 5 per cent of celluloid.

Transparent celluloid finely sharedded..... 1 ounce

Acetone sufficient, quantity.

Amyl acetate to make 20 ounces. Digest the celluloid in the acetone until dissolved and add the amyl acetate. From 1 to 4 ounces of flake bronze is to be mixed with this quantity of varnish. For silver paint or "aluminium enamel" flake aluminium bronze powder should be used in place of the gold. The celluloid varnish incloses the bronze particles in an imprevious coating, air tight and water-tight. As it contains nothing that will act upon the bronze, the latter retains its luster for a long period, until the varnished surface becomes owrn or abraded and the bronze thus exposed to atmospheric action.

All of the "gold" or more properly, gilt furniture that is sold so cheaply by the furniture and department stores is guided with a paint of this kind, and for that reason such furnitures can be offered at a modrate price. The finish is suprisingly durable and in colour and luster is a veryclose imitation of real gold leaf work. this paint is also used on picture frames of cheap and medium grades, taking the place of gold leaf or the lacquired silver leaf formerly used on articles o the better grades; it is also substituted for "Dutch metal." or imitation gold leaf on the cheapest class of work.

A cheaper gold paint is made by using an expensive varnish composed of gutta percha, gum dammer, or some other varnish gum, dissolved in benzole, or in mixture of benzole and benzene. The paint made with a celluloid amyl acetate varnish give off a strong banana like odor when applied, and may be readily recognized by this characteristics.

The impalpably powded bronzes are called "lining" bronzes. They are chiefly used for striping on lining by carriage painters; in bronzing gas fixtures and metal work; in fresco and other interior decoration, and in printing; the use of a very fine powder in inks or paints admits of the drawing and printing of very delicate lines.

Lincing bronze is also used in picutre frames or other plastic ornamental work. Mixed with a thin weak glud sizing it is applied over "burnishing clay" and when dry is polished with agate burnishers. The object thus treated, after receiving a finishing coat of a thin transparent varnish, imitates very closely in appearance a piece of finely cast antique bronze. To add still more to this effect the burnishing clay is colored the greenish black that is seen in the deep parts of real antique bronzes, and the bronze powder, mixed with sic. is applied only to the most prominent parts or "high lights" of the ornament.

Since the discovery of the celluloid amyl actate varnish or bronze liquid, and its preservative properties on bronze powders, manufacturers have discontinued the use of liquids containing oils, turpentine, or gums, since their constituents,or gums, since there dconstitutents corrode the bronze metal, causing the paint finally to turn black.

Grinding in Size– The old painters and gilders used to prepare the gold size themselves, but nowadays it is usually bought ready made, barring the white of egg additional. The best and most reliable, and especially suited for fine work, is undoubtedly the red French gold size. It is cleaned, as far as possible, of all impurities, and powdered. For 248 grains take 1 white of egg; put it into a glass, taking care of exclude the yolk entirely– otherwise the burnish will show black spots. Beat the white of egg to a forth with a long, well cleaned bristle bursh; add the froth to the size and grind finely together, which is soon done. When grinding, a little water and red size, if necessary, may be added (use only water for thinning). After being ground the size is forced through a very fine hari sieve into a perfectly clean vessel, and covered up well, for immediate or subesequent use.

The raw stuff of the red size is bolus, which is dug in France and Armenia in excellent quality. Besides the red size there are yellow, white (pipe clay), blue, and gray (alumina), which are used for certain purposes, to enumerte which here would lead too far.

For burnish gold, always take yellow size for ground work. Dip a finely ground bristle brush in the gold size prepared for use; fill a well-cleaned glass (holding 1 pint) half full of water, and add the size contained in the brush, also about 4 to 5 spoonfuls of pure alcohols. It is advisable not to take too much size; the liquid, when applied, must hardly have a yellow tint. When this is dry soon after, commence applying the size, for which a hari pencil is used. The essentials are to paint evenly and not too thickly, so that the tone remains uniform. Apply three coats of size.

When the size is laid on correctly and has become dry, brush the whole with a special brush, or rub with a flannel rage, so as to obtain the highest possible luster. The size must not stand too long; other wise no gloss can be developed. After brushing coat the work with weak glue water and wrap it up in tissue paper if the gilding is not to be done at once.

The strietest cleanliness is essential, as the red gold size is very sensitive. The parts where the size has been applied must not be touched with the hand, else grease spost will ensue, which will make a flawless gloss in gilding impossible. The least relaxation of the necessary attention may spot spoil the whole job, so that everything has to be ground off again.

The necessary tools for the application of gold leaf are; Hair pencils of various sizes, tip cusion, and gilding knife, as with oild-glding. Take pure alcohol or grain brandy, and dilute with two-thirds water. When ready to apply the gold leaf, dip a hair pencil of suitable size into the fluid, but do not have it full enough that the alcohol will run on the size ground. Moisten a portion of the ground surface as large as the gold leaf, which is laid on immediately after. Proceed in the same manner, first moistening, then applying the ready cut gold leaf. The latter must not be pressed on but marely laid down lightly, one leaf a little over the edge of the previous one, without using up too much gold. Technical practice in gold leaf gilding is presupposed; though this alone can any skill be acquired being of no avail.

The leaf of gold being applied, all dust must be swept off by means of a light fine hair pencil (but never against the overlapping edge), and the burnishing is commenced. For this purpose there are special agate tools of the shape of a wolf teeth are sometimes, but gradually more seldom, employed. Burnish till a full, fine luster appears; but very carefully avoid dents and lines, not to speak of scratches, which would be very hard to mend.

Gold Enamel Paints—

I.–	Pure turps...	6	pints
	Copal varnish...	1	pint
	Gold gold bronze	6½	pounds
	Calsis hydrate (dry slaked lime)...	½	ounce

Mix the varnish and turps at a gentle heat, then shake well with the lime, and settle for a few days, then pour off the clean portion and mix with the powder.

II.—	White hard varnish..	1	gallon
	Methylated spirit..	3/4	gallon
	Gold bronze...	12	pounds
	Finely powdered mica	3	ounces

Mix the varnish and spirit, reduce the mica to an impalapable powder, mix with the gold, then add to the liquid. Many bronze powders contain a goodly proportion of mica, as it imparts brilliancy. Powdered mother-of pearl is used also.

GRAINING WITH PAINT

Oak Graining— Prepare a paint of two-thirds of white lead and one-third of gold ocher with the requisite amount of boiled linseed oil and a little drier, and cover the floor twice with this mix ture, which possesses great covering power. When the last coating is dry, paint the floor with a thinly liquid paint consisting of varnish and sienna, applying the same in the longtitudinal direction of the boards. Treat a strip about 20 inches wide a time, and draw at once a broad paint brush or, in the absence of such, an ordinary brush or goose feather along theplanks through the wet paint, whereupon the floor will acquire a nicely grained appearance. The paint requires several days to dry. A subsequent coating of varnish will cause the graining to stand out still more prominently.

Birch— Imitations of birch are usefully employed for furniture. The ground should be a light, clean buff, made from white lead, stained with either yellow ocher or raw sienna inoil. In graining, brush over the surface with a thin wash of warm brown, making the panel of 2 or 3 broad colour shades. Then take a large mottler and mottle the darker parts into the light, working slantwise as for maple, but leaving a broad and stiff mark. While this is still wet soften the panel and then slightly mottle across the previous work of break it up. When thoroughly dry, carefully wet the work over with celan water and clean mottler, and put in darker overgrain with a thin oak overgrainer or overgrainer in tubes.

Maple— Sixty pounds white lead; 1 ounce deep vermilion; 1 ounce lemon chrome.

Ash.—Sixty pounds white lead; 1 ounce deep vermilion; 1 ounce lemon chrome.

Medium Oak.— Sixty pounds white lead; 2 pounds French ocher; 1 ounce burnt umber.

Light Oak.— Sixty pounds white lead; 1 ounce lemon chrome; ½ pound french ocher.

Dark Oak.— Sixty pounds white lead; 10 pounds burnt umber; 1¼ pounds medium Venetian red.

Satin Wood.— Sixty pounds white lead; 1 ounce deep vermilion; 1½ pounds lemon chrome.

Pollard Oak.— Seventy five pounds white lead; 20 pounds French ocher; 3 pounds burnt umber; 2½ pound medium Venetian red.

Pitch Pine.—Sixty pounds white lead; ¼ pound French Ocher; ¼ poundmedium Venetian Red.

Knotted Oak.— Sixty pounds white lead; 9 pounds French ocher; 3¼ pounds burnt umber.

Italina Walnut.—Sixty pounds white lead; 6 pound French ocher; 1¼ pound burnt umber; 1¼ pound smedium Venetian red.

Rosewood.— Nine and one half pound burnt umber; 40 pound medium Venetian red; 10 pound orange chrome.

Dark Mahogany— Nine and one half pounds burnt umber; 40 pounds medium Venetian red; 10 pounds orange chrome.

Light Mahogany— Sixty pounds white lead; 3 pounds burnt umber; 10 pounds medium Venetian red.

American Valnut— Thirty pounds white lead; 9 pounds French ocher; 4 pounds burnt umber; 1 pound medium Venetian red.

LUMINOUS PAINTS

The illuminating power of the phosphorescent masses obtained by heating strontium thiosulphate or barium thiosulphate is considerably increased by the addition, before heating, of small quantities of the nitrates of uranium, bismuth or thorium. Added to calcium thio sulphate, these nitrates do not heighten the luminosity or phosphorescence. The product from stronitum thiosulphate is more luminous than that of thebarium compound. Among the best luminous paints are the following :

I.— Lennord's– One hundred parts by weight of strontium carbonate; 100 parts, by weight of sulphur; 0.5 parts, by weight, of potassium chloride; 0.5 part, by weight, of sodium chloride; 0.4 parts, by weight of manganese chloride. The materials are heated for three quarters of an hour to one hour, to about 2.732° F. The product gives a violet light.

II.— Mourel's— One hundred parts, by weight of strontium carbonate; 30 parts, by weigh, of sulphur; 2 parts by weight, of sodium carbonate; 0.5 parts, by weight, of sodium chloride; 0.2 parts, by weight, of manganese sulphate. The method of treatment is the same as in the first, the phosphorescence deep yellow.

III.— Vanino's— Sixty parts, by weight of strontium thiosulphate; 12 parts, by weight, of a 0.5 per cent acidified alcoholic solution of bismuth nitrate; 6 parts, by weight of a 0.5 per cent alcoholic solution of uranium nitrate. The materials are mixed, dried, brought gradually to a temperature of 2.372° F., and heated for about an hour. The phosphorescence is emerald green.

IV.—Balmin's– Twenty parts, by weight, of calcium oxide (burnt lime), free from iron; 6 parts, by weight, of sulphur; 2 parts, by weight, of starch; 1 part, by weight of a0.5 per cent solution of bismuth nitrate; 0.15 parts, by weight, of potassium chloride; 0.15 parts by weight of sodium chloride. The materials are mxied, dried and heated to 1.300° C. (2.372°F.) The product gives a violet light.

To make these phosphorescent bustances effective, they are exposed for a time to direct sunlgith; or a mercury lamp may be used. Powerful incandescent gas light also does well, but requires more time.

PAINTS FOR METAL SURFACES :

Blackening Ornaments of Iron—

I.— To give iron ornaments a black brown to black colour, proceed in the following manner The articles are treated with corrosives, cleavned off all adherning grease, and placed in a 10 per cent solution of potassium bichromate, dried in the air and finally held over an open, wel glowing, non sooting fire for 2 minutes. The first coloring is usually black brown, but if this process is repeated several times, a pure black shade is obtained. Special attention has to be paid to removing all grease, otherwide the greasy, spots will not be touched by the liquid, and the coloring produced will become irregular. Benzine is employed for that purpose and the articles must not be touched with the fingers afterwards.

II.—This process protects the iron from rust for a long time. the treatments consists a coating the objects very uniformly with a thin layer of linseed oil varnish, and buring it off over a charcoal fire. During the deffagration the draught must be stopped. The varnish will first go up in smoke with a strong formation of soot, and finally burn up entirely. The process is repeated i.e. ater one coating is burned off a new one is applied, until theparts exhibit a uniformly handsome. deep black colour. Next wipe off the covering with a dry rag, and beat again, but only moderately. Finally, the articles are taken from the fire and rubbed with a rage well saturated with linseed-oil varnish. The black turns completely dull, and forms a red durable covering for the objects.

Black for Polished Iron Pieces.— Apply successive layers of a very concentrated solution of nitrate of maganese dissolved in alcohol over a gentle fire and the water bath. The surfaces to be blackened should be previously heated. By repeating the layers all the tints between brownish black and bluish black may be obtained.

Glossy Black for Bicycles, etc.—

Amber..	8	ounces
Linseed oil..................................	4	ounces
Asphaltum..................................	1½	ounces
Rosin..	1½	ounces
Oil turpentine.............................	8	ounces

Heat the linseed oil to boiling point, add the amber, asphaaltum and rosin and when all melted remove trom the fire and gradually add the turpentine.

Japan Black— The following is a good japan black for metal surfaces Take 12 ounces of amber and 2 ounces of asphaltum. Fuse by heat, and add ½ pint boiled oil and 2 ounces of rosin. When cooling add 16 ounces of oil of turpentine.

Brass and Bronze Protective Paint— As a protective covering especially for brass and bronze, objects a colorless celluloid solution is recommended, sch as is found in trade under the name of "Zapon" (q.v.)

Paint for Copper.—Dissolve 1 ounce of alum in 1 quart of warm soft water. When cold add flour to make it about the consistency of cream, then add ½ thimable of rosin and ½ ounce of sugar of lead.

Priming Iron.—The following oif carefully carried out, gives the best satisfaction; The first step consists in thoroughly cleaning the surface of the iron, removing all adhesions in theway of dirt, rust etc. before the question of priming is considered. As paint in this instance is applied more with a view of protecting the rion from atmospheric influences, rather than for a decorative effect, careful attention should be devoted for securing a base of surface which is calcuated to produce a thorough and permanent application. A great deal depends upon the nature of the metal to be painted. Common cast iron for instance, possessing a rough estensive with ordinary precautions can be more readily painted with the prospect of a permanent adhesion of the paint, than a planed steel or wrought iron surface. With the latter it has been demonstrated, that a hard and elastic paint is needed, while with regard to cast iron, other paints containing iron oxides ae more suitable. For good drying and covering properties, as well as elasticity, a good boiled oil to which has been added an adequate proportion of red lead will be found to form an excellent apint for smooth metal surfaces. The primary object is to protect the surface of the iron from moisture for the purpose of avoiding rust. The priming must therefore be carriied out so that it will stick, after which subsequent coats may be added if desired.

It is advisable that articles, made of iron should first be coated with linseed oil varnish. It dries slowly, hardens, and enables the operator afterwards to exercise an effect control over the condition of this metarial. Iron must be absolutely dry and free from rust when it is to be painted. It is best to apply next a coating of hot linseed oil; when dry this should be followed by a priming of pure red lead in good linseed oil; when dry this should be followed by a priming of pure red lead in good linseed oil, and the rion shoule then be painted a desired, using ground oil paints and leaving an interval ofa week between each coating. Cementing should be done after the red lead priming, but the last coat must not be given until the whole is thoroughly dry. Bright oil paints and an upper coating with plenty of oil resist the effect of heat better than thin coatings; moreover, rust can be detected in its early stages with the former. Coatings of tar and asphalt (asphalt dissolved in terpentine) are prectible for undergound pipes, exposed to the air, as they are quickly spoiled. Asphalt varnish, used for coating coatl secuttles fire screens, etc., consists of asphalt dissolved in linseed oil varnish. Iron stoves and stovepipes are best coated with graphites.

Galvanized Iron.—For galvanised iron there has been recommended a wash consisting simply of dilute hydrochloric acid, which produces chloride of zinc, that is combination with the oxygen of the air is said to produce a film upon which oil color takes as good a hold as it would upon ordinary sheet iron.

Another method which has been tested and found effective is to make a solution as follows : One ounces of chloride of copper; 1 ounce nitrate of copper; 1 ounce sal ammoniac, dissolved in 2 quarts of soft water, to which is added 1 ounce of crude or commercial hydrochloric acid. This solution should be made in an earthware dish or pot or in glass or stoneware, as tin will precipitate the copper salts and kae the solution imperfact. To large surfaces this solution is applied with a broad brush, when the surface assumes a deep black color, which in drying out in from 12 to 24 hours, becomes a gray white, upon which the properly prepared primer will take a permanent grip. On thefilm so produced a much thinner paint will cover very much better than a shouter paint would on the untrated galvanized or ordinary iron surface. A single trial will convince the craftsman that this treatment is a method that will give lasting results, provided he tries the same priming paint on the treated and untreated surface.

To paint wrought rion with Graphite— In order to make wrought iron look like new mix fine graphite with equal parts of varnish of turpentine oil, adding a little siccative. Paint the iron part with this twice, allowing to dry each time. Especially the second coating must be perfectly dry before further treatment. The latter consists in preparing graphite with spirit and applying it very thinly over the first coat. After the drying or evaporation of the spirit the graphite last applied is brushed vigorously whereby a handsome, durable gloss is produced.

Paint for iron bodies exposed to Heat— Dilute 1 part soda water glass with 2 parts water and mix intiamtely with the following pigments :

White. — White lead of sulphate of barium.
Yellow. — Chromate of barium, cocher, or uranium yellow.
Green. — Chromic oxide or ultramaine green.
Blue. — Ultramarine.
Brown. — Oxide of cadimum, oxide of maganese or terra di sienna.
Red. — English red or chrome red.

Bronze powder in a suitable quantity may be added to the mixture, but not more paint should be prepared than can be used up in a few hours. The bronze powder may also be strewn on the fresh paint, or applied with a dry brush to enhance the gloss. This paint is not affected by heat, and in inodorous.

Protective coating for bright Iron Articles.— Zinc white, 30 parts; lamp black. 2 parts; tallow, 7 parts; vaseline 1 part; olive oil 3 parts; varnish, 1 part Boil together ½ hour and add ½ part of benzine and ¼ part of turpentine; stirring the mass carefully and boiling for sometime. The finished paste-like substances can be readily removed with a rage with out the use of solvent.

Rust Paints.—

I.— A new rust paint is produced by the following process; Mix 100 parts dry iron sulphate and 87 parts sodium chlorate and heat to 1,500° to 1,800° F. The Chlorine set free seems to have a very favourable action on the colour of the simultaniously forming iron oxide. In order to avoid, however, too far reaching an effect of the chlorine gas, about 18 pounds of a substance which absorbs the same mechanically, such as kaoline, ground pumice stone,ocher, etc. are added to the mixture.

II.— A material known under the names of lardite, steatite, agalmatolite, pagolite, is excellently adapted a s substitute for the ordinary metallic protective agent of the pigemnts and has the property of protecting iron from rust in an effective manner. In China, lardite is used for protecting edifices of sandstone, which crumbles under the action of the atmosphere. Likewise a thin layer of a powdered steatite, applied in the form of paint has been found valuable there as a protector against the decay of obelinks, statues, etc. Lardite, besides possesses the quality of being exceedingly fine-grained which renders this material valuable for use in ship painting. Ground steatite is one fo the finest materials which can be produced, and no other so quickly and firmly adheres to the fibers of rion and steel, Furthermore, steatite is lighter than metallic covering agents, and covers, mixed in paint, a larger surface then zince white, red lead, or iron oxide. Steatite as it coccurs in Switzerland is used there and in the Tyrl for stoves, since it is fireproof.

Steel.— An excellent coating for steel, imitating the blue color of natural steel, is composed of white shellac, 5 parts; borax, 1 part; alcohol, 5 parts; water, 4 parts; and sufficient quantity of methylene blue. The borax is dissolved in water. The shellac in alcohol. The aqueous solution of the borax is heated to a boil and the alcoholi solution of the shellac is added with constant stirring. Next add the blue color, continuing to stir. Before this coating is applied to stir. Before this coating is applied to the steel, e.g., the spokes of a bycycle, the latter are first rubbed off with fine emery paper. The coat is put on with a soft rage. The quantity of pigment to be added is very small. By varying the quantity a paler or darker coloring of the steel can be produced.

Paints for roofs and roof paper :

Carbolineum.— This German preparation is made in three colors.

I.— **Pale.**— Melt together in an iron kettle, over a naked fire, 30 parts of American rosin F and 150 parts of pale paraffine oil and stir in 10 parts of single rectified rosin oil.

II.— **Dark.**—Melt 100 parts of anthracene oil and 20 parts of American rosin F on a slow fire. Next stir in 2 parts of Para rubber solution (or solution of caoutchoac waste) and keep on boiling until all is dissolved. When this is done thre should be still added 5 parts of crude concentrated carbolic caid and 5 parts of zinc chlorine lye. 50° Be stirring until cool. The last named admixture is not absolutely necessary but highly advisable owing to its extraordinary preservative and bactericidal properties.

III.— **Coloured.—** For, red melt 100 parts of coal tar oil, then stir in 50 parts of pale paraffin oil, and finally 75 parts of bole or iron minum, and pass through the paint mill. Although the addition of iron minium is very desirable, it is considerably more expensive. For gray, proceed as above, with the exception that metallic gray is used in place of the bole. For green, metallic green is employed. The colour are identical with those used in the manufacture of roof varnish To increase the antiseptic properties of the colored carbolineium, any desired addition of phenol or zinc chloride solutions may be made, but the chief requirement in the case of colored carbolineum is good covering power of the coating.

Paints for Roofs Covered with Tar Paper for Roofing Paper etc.—

I.—	Distilled coal tar....	70	parts
	Heavy mineral oil	10	parts
	(lubricating rosin)	20	parts
II.—	Distilled coal tar	52	parts
	Trinidad asphalt	15	parts
	Mineral oil, containing paraffin	10	parts
	Dry clay, finely ground	25	parts

Rubber base (Latex) Paints :

Withe the advent of synthetic rubber aquesous dispersions resulting from the emulsion polymerization of these synthetics become known as lates. This lates is now used to make waterproof, washable, and easy to apply paint, which is water thinned, reducing fire hazard. The good year Tire and Rubber Chemical Division has developed a base called Chemigum 101 (55 parts sytene to 45 parts budiene).

Latex Semi Gloss White.— To make a ten gallon batcn mix 22.58 lbs. of titanium oxide, 6.48 lbs. of lithopone, 3.23 lbs. of mica, 16 lb. of tetrasodium pyrophosphate, 6.08 lbs. of wetting agent, and 10.75 lbs of water. Then heat separately at 130-140°F., soybean protein (2.04 lbs.) Ammonia (0.2 lb), water (11.03 lbs.), and sodium pentrachlorophenate (0.34 lb.) The thickener is made with 0.2 lb. of ammonium alginate, 5.24 lbs. of water, and 0.03 lb. of sodium pentachlorophenate. After mixing the three separate preparation add 35.16 lbs. of Chemigum and 10.12 lbs. of water.

Yellow.— Chrome oxice, 49.7%; water, 49.7% wetting agent 0.35% tetrasodium pyrophosphate, 0.25%.

Blue.—Ultramarine blue, 49.7%; water, 49.7% wetting agent, 0.35%; and tetra sodium pyrophosphate, 0.25%

PAINTS, STAINS, ETC. FOR SHIPS :

Anti-Fouling composition— Make as agglutinant by by heating together.

	By weight	
White lead, ground in		
Oil	2	parts
Red lead dry	1	parts
Raw linseed oil	14	parts

While hot stir in yellow ocher, kaoline,baked clay in powder, or any inert body, such as silica, barytes, gypsum etc., ot form a stiff dough and without allowing this compound to become cold (the vessel should not be removed from the source of heat), dilute with more or less manganese linoleate to the required consistency.

Marine Paint to Resist sea Water.— First prepare the water resisting agglutinant by heating together

Dry white lead, crbonate only	1	part
Litharge	1	part
Linseed oil (fluid measure) ...	14	parts

Heat these and stir until of the consistancy of thick glud, and for every 36 parts, by weight of thsi compound add 3 parts, by weight of turpentine, and 1 part, by weight of mastic varnish (mastic rosin dissolved in turpentine); reheat the whole, and for every 32 parts, by weight, stir in and mix the following;

Black and powdered clay.....	4	parts
Portland cement	16	parts
Zinc White	1	parts
Red lead	1	part

After well mixing, dilute with more or less turpentine (not exceeding 25 per cent of the whole), or linoleate of manganese, the letter being preferable, as it has greater building powderpower. For colored paints use red oxide of iron or green oxide of chrome, but do not use chrome green or lead, as they will not stand the action of the sea water.

Composition of Ship's Bottoms.—

Green

Pale rosin	25	pounds
Prepared mineral green	8	pounds
D. L. Zinc	13	pounds
Boild oil	2	pounds
Mineral naphtha	1	gallon
Petoleum spirit	1½	gallons

Prepared Mineral Green.

Dry levigated mineral green	25	pounds
Turpentine	7	pounds
Turpentine varnish	7	pounds
Refined linseed oil	7	pounds

Copper Colour.

Pale rosin	25	pounds
Light italian ocher	15	pounds
D.L. Zinc	5	pounds
Turkey red paint	½	pound
Petoleum sourut	1½	pounds
Mineral naptha	1	pound

Pink

Pale rosin	25	pounds
D.L. Zinc	16	pounds
Deep vermilian	7	pounds
Mineral naphtha	1	gallon
Petrolium spirit	1½	gallon

PAINTS FOR WALLS OF CEMENT, PLASTER HARD FINISH ETC.

Coating for Bathrooms.— As a rule cement platering, as well as oil paint, suffices for the protection of walls and ceilings in bathrooms, but attention must be called to the desctructive action of medicinal admixtures. For such rooms as well as for laboratories, an application of sweedish wood dar, made into a flowing consistency with a little oil of turpentine and put on hot, has been found very excellent. It is of advantage previously to warm the wall slightly. To the second coat add some wax. A very durable coating is obtained, which looks so pleasing that it is only necessary to draw some strips with a darker paint so as to divide the surface into fields.

Cement, to Paint Over Fresh.— The wall should be washed with dilute, sulphuric acid several days before painting. This will charge the surplus caustic lime to sulphate for lime or gypsum. The acid should be about one-half chamber acid and one-half water. This should be repeated before painting, and a coat of raw linseed oil flwoed on freely should be given for the first coat. While this cannot be always guaranteed as effectual for making the paint hold, it is the best method our correspondent has heared of for the purpose, and is worth trying when it is absolutely necessary to paint over fresh cement.

Damp, Walls Coating for.— Thirsty parts of the tin are dissolved in 40 parts of hydrochloric acid, and 30 parts of alsammoniac are added. A powder composed of freestone, 50 parts, and calcined nagnesia, 5 parts is prepared and made into apaste with the liquid above mentioned. Coloring matter may be added. The composition may be used asa damp proof coating for walls, or for repairng stonework, or for molding statues or ornaments.

Facade Paint.— For this zinc oxide is especially adapted, prepared with size or casin. Any desired earth colors may also be added. The surfaces are coated 3 times with this mass. After the third application is dry, put on a single coating of zinc chloride solution of 30°C Be to which 3 per cent borax is added.

This coating is very solid, can be washed, and is not injured by hydrogen sulphide./

Hard-Finished Walls.— The treatment for hard-finished walls which are to be painted in flat colours is to prime with a thin coat of lead and oil well brushed into the wall. Next put on a thin coat of glue size; next a coat mixed with 1/3 oil and 2/3 turpentine; next a coat of flat paint mixed with turpentine. If you use any dry pigment mix it stiff in oil and thin with turps. If in either case the paint dries too fast, and is liable to show laps, put a little glycerine in, to retard the drying.

PAINTS, WATERPROOF AND WEATHERPROOF :

The following are claimed to be both waterproof and weatherproof :

I.— In 50 parts, by weight, of spirit of 86 per cent, dissolve 16 parts, by weight of shellac, orange, finely, powdered; 3 parts, by weight, of silver lake, finely powdered; and 0.6 parts, by weight of gamboge, finely powdered. This paint may be employed without admixture of any siccative, and is excellently adapted for painted objects which are exposed to the inclemencies of the weather, as it is perfectly weatherproof.

II.— Mix glue water with zinc oxide (zinc white) and paint the respective object with this mixture. When this is dry (after about 2 hours) it is followed up with a coating of glue water and zinc chloride in a highly diluted state. Zinc oxide enters into a chemical combination with zinc chloride, which acquires the hardness of glass and a mirror like bright surface. Any desired colors can be prepared with the glue water (size) and are practically imperishable. This zinc coating is very durable, dries quickly, and is 50 per cent cheaper than oil paint.

Water- and Acid Resisting Paint.— Caoutchouc is melted wth colophony at a low temperature, after the caoutcouc has been dried in a dryign closet (stove) at 158° to 176° F., until no more considerable increase in weight is preceptible, while the colophoney has caompletely lost its moisture by repeated melting. The raw products thus prepared will readily melt upon slight heating. To the melted colophony and caoutchouc add in ahot liquid state zinc white or any similar pigment. Thin with a varnish consisting of 50 parts of perfectly anhydrous colophony, 40 parts of absolute alcohol, and 40 parts of benzine. The whole syrupy mass is worked through in a paint mill to obtain a uniform product, at which operation more or less colophony varnish is added according to the desired consistency.

Water and Air Proof Paint.— An air proof and waterproof paint, the subject of a recent French patent, is a compound of 30 parts, by weight acetone; 100 parts acetic ether; 50 parts sulphuric ether; 100 parts camphor; 50 parts gum lac; 200 parts cotton; 100 parts paper dissolved in sulphuric acid); 100 parts mstic in drops. These proportions may fluctuate according to need. The paper is reduced well and dissolved in the acetone and the whole is mixed together with the other ingredients and stirred well. The application is performed as with any other varnish. The coating is said not to crack or shrink and to be particularly useful as a protection against moisture for all stuffs.

PAINT FOR WOOD :

Floor coating.— A new paint for floors. especially those of soft wood; Mix together 2.2 pounds joiners glue; a little over 1 ounce powdered bichromate of potash: 3½ ounces aniline brown; and 10½ quarts water in a tine vessel. After 6 hours have elapsed (when the glue is completely soaked), heat gradually the boiling point. The coating becomes perfectly water tight after 2 or 3 days; it is not opaque as the earthy body is lacking. The glue causes the wood fibers to be firmly united. It becomes insoluble by the addition of bichromate of potash, under the influence of light. Without this admixture a simple glue coat has formerly not been found satisfactory, as it dissolves if cleaned with water.

Durable House Paint.—

I.— New houseshould be primed ouce with pure linseed oil then painted with a thin paint from white lead and chalk, and thus gradually covered. The last coat is prepared of well-boiled varnish, while lead and chalk. The chalk has the mission to moderate the saponification of the linseed oil by the white lead. Mixing colours such as ocher and black, which take up plently of oil, materially assist in producing a durable covering.

II.— Prime with zinc white with let this be succedded by a coating with zinc chloride in glue water (size). The zinc oxide forms with the zinc chloride ian oxy-chloride of great hardness and glossy surface. The admixture of pigments any desired shade may be produced. The zinc coating is indestructible, dries quicly, does not peel, is free from the smell of fresh oil paint, and more than 5 per cent cheaper.

Ivory Coating for Smooth, Light Wood.— In order to cover the articles, which may be flat or round, with this coating, they must rist be polished quite smooth and clean; then they are coated with thin hot, white glue. When the coat is thoroughly dry, the glud is rubbed off again with fine glass paper. The mass is prepard a follows; Take 3 pounds (more or less, according to the number of articles) of the purest and best collotion; grind upon a clean grinding stone twice; the quantity that can be taken up with the point of knife of krems white, with enough good pale linseed oil as is necessary to grind the white smooth and fine. Take a clean bottle, into which one half of the collodian, is poured; to this adde the ground white, which can be removed clean from the stone by means of a good spatula and put in the bottle. Add about 100 drops of linseed oil, and stake the mass till it looks like milk.

Now painting with this milky substances may be commenced, using a fine hair pencil of excellent quality. The pencil is not dipped in the large bottle; but a glass is kept at hand with an opening of about 1 inch, so as to be able to immerse the pencil quickly. The substance is not flowering like the alcoholaquers, for which reason it may be pu on thick, for the ether, chiefly constituting the mass, evaporates at once and leaves but a very thin film which becomes noticeable only after about 10 such applications have been made. Shake the bottle well each time before filling the small glass, as the heavy Krems white is very apt to sink to the bottom of the bottle. It is observed that the substance becomes too thick, whch may be easily occur on account of the evaporation, a part of the remaining ether is added, to which in turn 30 to 40 drops of oil are added, shaking if will the oil a appears to be completely dissolved.

The operator must put on the mass in quick succession and rather thick; After about 10 coats have been applied the work is allowed to rest several hours; then 3 or 4 coats of pure collodion, to which likewise several drops of oil have been added, are given. Another pause of several hours having been allowed to intervene, application of the mass is once more begun.

When it is noticed that a lyaer of the thickness of paper has formed, the articles, after drying thoroughly, should be softly rubbed off with very fine glass paper, after which they require to be wiped off well with a clean linen rage, so that no dust remains. Then coating is continued till the work seems serviceable.

A few application of pure collodion should be made, and when this has become perfectly hard, after a few hours, it can be rubbed down with a rage, tripoli, and oil, and polished by hand, like horn or ivory. This work can be done only in a room which is entirely free from dust. The greatest cleanliness must be observed.

MISCELLANEOUS RECIPES, PAINTS ETC.

Bathtub Paint.— Take while keg lead, tint to any desired colour and then add say, ½ boiled oil (pure linseed) to 7/8 hard drying durable body varnish. Clean the surface of the tub thoroughly before applying the paing. Benzine or lime wash are good cleaning agents. Coat up auntil a satisfactorily strong, pure color is reached. This will give good gloss and will also wear durable.

Coating for Name Plates.— A durable coating for name plates in nurseries is produced as follows; Take a Woollen rage, saturate it with joiners's polish, lay it into a linen one, and rub the wooden surface with this for some time. Rub down with sandpaper and it can be written on almost like paper. When all is dry, coat with dammer lacquer for better protection. It the wood is to recive a color it is placed in the woolen rag before rubbing down, in this case chrome yellow.

To keep Flies from Fresh Paint.— For the purpose of keeping flies and other linsects away from freshly painted sufaces mix a little bay oil (laurel oil) with the oil paint, or place or receptacle containing same in the vicinity of the painted objects. The pungent odor keeps off the flies.

Heat Indicating Paint.— Heat indicating paint composed of a double iodide of coopper and mercury was first discovered years ago by a German physicist. At ordarny temperature the paint is red, but when heated to 206°F. it rurns black. Paper painted with this composition and warmed at a stove exhibits the charge in a few seconds. A yellow double iodine of silver and mercury is even more sensitive toheat, changing from yellow to dark red.

Silicone Paints.— The elements silicon and oxygen are found combined in nature in a substance called quarts, one of the most heat-resisting minerals. By treating quarts with organic compounds containing the methyl, ethyl or phenyl group, silicone resins are formed, which are incorporated in paints and varnishes to give them extraordinary heat and water resistant qualities as well as other remarkable properties.

These finishes can be applied by the conventional methods (brush, spray, dip, roller, or silk screen). The usual pigmets, such as ultramarine blue, titanium oxide, etc. can be used for coloring. they are used to colour incandescent, bulbs, and identity radio, tubs that attain temperatures too high for other resins. Silicone paints resisnt acids, oil corrosive agents, sunlight, bending etc.

Besides being so highly resistant to water, silicone compounds also repel other substances. When used as a glaze on bread pans in backeries, hundreds of "bakes" are possible without regreasing. Silicone paints are particularly suited to outdoor use, since they do not readily discolor nor chalk on exposure.

Peeling of Paints.— For the prevention of peeling of new coatings on old oil paintings or lakes, the latter should be rubbed with roughly ground pumice stone, wet by means of felt rages, and to the first now coat there should be added fine spirit in the proportion of aboud 1/10 of the thinning necessary for stirring (turpentine, oil, etc.) This paint dries well and has given good results, even in the most difficult cases. The subsequent coatings are put on with the customary paint. Fat oil glazes for graining are likewise mixed withspirit, whereby the cracking of the varnish coating is usually entirely obviated.

Polychroming of Figures.— This paint consists of white wax, 1 part, and powdered mastic, 1 part, melted together upon the water bath and mixed with rectified turpentine. The colors to be used are first ground stiffly in turpentine on the grinding slab, and worked into consisting with the above solution.

Priming Coat for Water Spots.—A good way to remove rain spots, or wuch caused by water soaking through ceilings, has been employed with good results. Take unslaked white lime, dilute with alcohol, and paint the spots with it. When the spots are dry— which ensues quickly, as the alcohol evaporates and the lime forms a sort of insulating layer— one can proceed painting with size color, and the spots will not show through again.

TIRE PRESERVING PAINT :

Mix thoroughly : 2 pounds Linseed Oil; 2 pounds Petroleium; 1 pound Cottonseed Oil.

Then to this mixture add just enough dry white lead to give it a colour simila to a new tire.

TACK RAG :

The surface of furniture or other wood work must be clean if enameling or vanishing is to be done succesfuuly. A "tack rag" can easily be made to do this. A lintless cloth, preferably with a hemmed edge (an old handkerchief is excellent), is dipped in water, wrung out, and then sprinkled with varnish. The tack rag should be used on the woodwork or furniture just before the application of the finish.

25

Paint, Varnish and Enamel Removers

To remove Old oil, Paint or Varnish Coats.—

I.— Apply a mixture of 1 part 2 per cent ammonia water, 36 parts sand, 3 parts of 40 per cent soda lye. The composition dissolves the old varnish coat, as well as the paint, down to the bottom. The varnish coatings which are to be removed may be brushed off or let for days in a hardened state. Upon being throughly moistened with water the old varnish may be readily washed off, the lacquer as well as the oil paint coming off completely. The ammonia otherwise employed dissolves the varnish, but not the paint.

II.— Apply a mixture of 1 part oil of turpentine and 2 parts of ammonia. This is effective, even if the coatings withstand the strongest lye. The two liquids are shaken in a bottle until they mix like milk. The mixture is applied to the coating with a little oakum; after a few minutes the old paint can be wiped off.

To clean Brush and Vessels of Dry Paint.—The cleaning of the brushes and vessles in which the varnish or oil paint had dried is usually done by boiling with soda solution. This frequently spoils the brushes or craks the vessles if of glass; besides, the process is rather slow and dirty. A much more suitable remedy is amyl acetate, which is a liquid with a pleasant odor of fruit drops, used mainly for dissolving odor of fruit drops, used mainly for dissolving and cementing celluloid. If amyl acetate is poured over a paint brush the varnish or hardened paint dissolves almost immediately and the brush is again rendered serviceable at once. If necessary, the process is repeated. For cleaning vessles shake the liquid about in them, which softens the paint so that it can be readily removed with paper. In this manner much labour can be saved. The amyl acetate can be easily removed from the brushes etc., by alcohol or oil of turpentine.

Varnish and Paint Remover.—Dissolve 20 parts of caustic soda (9 per cent) in 100 parts of water, mix the solution with 20 parts of mineral oil and stir in a kettle provided with a mechanical stirrer, until the emulsion in complete. Now add with stirring, 20 parts of sawdust and pass the whole through a paint mill to obtain a uniform intermixture. Apply the past moist.

To remove Varnish from Metal.— To remove old varnish from metals, it suffices to dip the articles in equal parts of ammonia and alcohol (95 per cent).

To remove Water Stains from Varnished Furniture.— Pour olive oil into a dish and scrape a little white wax into it. This mixture should be heated until the wax metals and rubbed sparingly on the stains. Finally, rub the surface with a linen rag until it is restored to brilliancy.

To Remove Paint, Varnish, etc., from Wood.— Varnish, paint etc. no matter how old and hard may be softened in a few minutes so that they can be easily scraped off, by applying the following mixture :

Water Glass..........	5	part
Soda lye. 40°B. (27 percent)............	1	Part
Ammonia water..............	1	parts Mix.

Removing Varnish etc.— A patent has heen taken out in England for a liquid for removing varnish, lacuer, tar, and paint. The composition is made by mixing 4 ounces of benzol, 3 ounces of fusel oil, and 1 ounce of alcohol. It is stated by the inventor that this mixture, if applied to a painted or varnished surface, will make the surface quite clean in less than 10 minutes, and that a paint soaked brush : as hard as iron" can be made as soft and pliable as new by simply soaked for an hour or so in he mixutre.

To Remove Enamel and Tin Solder.— Pour enough of oil and vitriol (concentrated sulphuric acid) over powdered fluorspar in an earthen or lead vessel, so as just to cover the parts whereby hydrofluoric acid is generated. For use, dip the article suspended on a wire into the liquid until the enamel or the tin is eaten away or dissolved, which does not injure the articles in any way. If heated, the liquid acts more rapidly. The work should always be conducted in the open air, and care should be taken not to in hale and fumes, which are highly injurious to the health, and not to get any liquid on the skin, as hydrofluroric acid is one of the most dangerous poisons. Hydrofluoric acid must be kept in earthen or leaden vessles, as it destroys glass.

Removing Paint and Varnish from Wood.— The following compound is given as one which will clean paint or varnish from wood or stone without injuriing the material :

Benzol	50	parts
Paraffin	3	parts
Denatured alcohol	25	parts
Acetone	25	parts

This mixture is applied to the surface and left on for some time. It is then brushed off, and brings the paint away with it. Benzine or alcohol rubbed on with a rag will remove the wax.

Paste for Removing Old Paint or Varnish Coats.—

I.—	Sodium hydrate	5	parts
	Soluble soda glass	3	parts
	Flour paste	6	parts
	Water	4	parts
II.—	Soap	10	parts
	Potassium hydrate	7	parts
	Potassium silicate	2	parts

To Remove Old Enamel.—Lay the articles horizontally in a vessel, containing a concentrated solution of alum and boil them. The solution should be just sufficient to cover the pieces. In 20 or 25 minutes the old enamel will fall into dust, and the article can be polished with emery. If narrow and deep vessels are used the operation will require more time.

26

Paint Mixing and Grinding

PAINT MIXING AND GRINDING

As a general rule the ingredients of the paint to be made which consist of the various colours or pigments are mixed together with the linseed oil in a paste blade mixer which is elevated six or seven feet above the floor level and fastened securely on a stron platform. Steps lead up to this platform and the workman can get to the mixer at any time he chooses. The heavy cans or pails or tanks of raw materials are hoisted up to the mixer by the use of a pully arrangment. They are dumped in and thoroughly mixed.

Then the mixture is ready for grinding and the grinding mill is located on a floor just below the mixer so that the thick paste can be run through a funnel right into the mill below and be ground. Various kinds of mills are used by different manufacturers. There are the toils for paste grinding and those for liquid grinding, the latter being used for thinner materials. Two types of mills are commonly used today, the Stone or sometimes called Burr Mill and the Pebbie or Ball Mill.

The paint, whichever type of mill it is to be ground in must be very finely ground and samples can be taken from the mill from time to time to determine the smoothless. Using the pallette or a knife one can spread a little on a clean piece of glass and allow it to dry and by feeling of it and looking at it can one readily determine how smooth the particles have been ground. It is important that the pigment be very smooth although for some cheap paints manufacturers are not nearly as particular as for good paints. Especially is this true when grinding a barn paint as compared with architectural enamel. The enamel must be ground finer than even any ordinary paint or the oil or varnish will not cover over the small unground particles.

There is still another type of mill to he mentioned and that is the Roller Mill. This mill is used for grinding exceedingly heavy pastes such as pigment pastes, putties, etc., although regular commercial putty is usally ground in what we call a putty chaser which really is not a grinding machine. Very thick pastes can be ground up in a Roller mill.

Different pigment require different lengths of time in which to be ground for some are harder to crush than others. Experimentation by the mixer will soon teach him this. One pigment will require more oil to make up a paste than others. Different pigments have different oil absoprtion, consequently you might mix the same amount of oil with the last amount of both Zinc Oxide and Lithophone but you would find that you would have a nice smooth workable mass with the Zinc Oxide but with the Lithophone you have such a stiff paste that you could not work it at all. Because Lithophone absorbs more oil than Zinc Oxide.

HOUSE PAINTS

House Paints should consist of the best materials that can be found but it is regrettable that the marked is loaded with cheap, poor covering paints that will not give satisfaction. Since there is a demand for a cheap house paint we will give herewith a formula for one but always recommened the use of the high grade material. there is little doubt but that the old lead and oil combination is better than the factory prepared cheap paints but the guaranteed high grade machine grond and mixed house paint is better than the hand mixed lead and oil. It is impossible for one to throughtly mix lead and oil by hand and do it as satisfactorily as it can be done in the mixing machine.

Highest Grade White Outside Paint—

White Lead (Carbonate)	33	pounds
White lead (Sulphate)	7	pounds
Zinc Oxide	26	pounds
Pure Linseed oil	30	pounds
Turpentine	3	pounds
Drier	1	pound

Cheap Grade Outside White.—

White lead (Carbonate)	25	pounds
Zinc oxide	20	pounds
Calcium Carbonate	20	pounds
Blown Linseed Oil	25	pounds
V.M.P. Naptha	10	pounds
Drier	3/4	pounds

Inside White Gloss Paint.—

White lead (ground in linseed oil) ...	10	pounds
Zinc Oxide (ground in linseed oil) ..	10	pounds
Pure linseed oil	1½	gals.
Turpentine	1½	gals.
Liquid Paint Drier	½	pint.

Preparation of Mixed Paints.— The usual custom in factory practice in to mix the pigments with the oil and grind same in a roller mill until the desired smoothness is obtained. A regular heavy duty mixer is employed after which the paste is run into the roller mill. Where the paint is thinner and not so thick, a stone or burr mill is quicker and more satisfactory as a paste paint often times requires more than one grinding ina roller mill. After it is ground it may be reduced although in a thick paste paint all of the ingredients can be mixed together in the first place.

Coloured Outside and Inside Paints.—(Tints) Simply grind the various pigment colors in linseed oil to obtain the so-called colours in oil. Then add the amount of colour s in oil. Then add the amount of colour to the white that is necessary to produce the shade or tint required.

RED BARN PAINTS.

No. 1

Spanish Red Oxide	85	pounds
Magnesia Silicate	150	pounds
Linseed Oil	15	gallons

Mix the above ingredients together and then grind for as long a time until paint is smooth. This mixture may be too thick for satisfactory grinding and in such a case add a little V.M.P. Naptha until mixture is thin enough to grind. After it is finely ground add the following :

Improved Boiled Linseed

Oil	4	gallons
Water Solution	4	gallons
Sipes Japan Oil	15	gallons
Camphor or Mineral Spirits	5	gallons

No. 2

Spanish Red Oxide	100	pounds
Calcium Carbonate	80	pounds

Magnesia Silicate	60	Pounds
Linseed Oil	13	gallons

Thin the linseed oil down to Naptha, Varnolene or turpentine and then mix the above ingredients and grind in the paint mill. After they are ground add the following ingredients :

Improved Linseed Oil	24	gallons
Sipes Japan Oil	5	gallons
Naptha, V.M.P.	2½	gallons
Wate Solution (free alkali)	5	gallons

1 to 2% Caustic in the water is plenty strong enough. Add the water Solution after the 24 gallons of linseed oil has been added and not before.

RUST AND WEATHER PROOF PAINTS.

Many experiments have been made, trying to find a combination of materials that would produce a paint which would to a great degree withstand the salt air, a product that could be used on smoke stacks on the waterfrongs, etc. Up to the rpesent time the best known formulas for a paint to give the desired results and stand the exposure are as follows :

Black Paint

Asbestine	20	pounds
Red Lead	25	pounds
Black Lead	10	pounds
Blown Fish Oil	40	gallons
V.M. & P. Naptha	20	gallons
Liquid Cobalt Drier	½	galloon
(more or less as required)		

Dark Gray Paint

Asbestine	75	pounds
White Lead	90	pounds
Blue Lead	80	pounds
Zinc Oxide	10	pounds
Blown Fish Oil	150	gallons
Naptha or Mineral Spirits as desired	90	gallons
Liquid Cobalt Drier	1½	gallons
(more or less as required)		

The pigments are mixed together and ground in a roller or stone mill until the necessary smoothness is obtained. As a rule the same smoothness is not required as in an house paint since this calss of paint is used on outside, rough work. It is understood that the pigments are ground in the fish oil. More or less fish oil can be added or deducted as desired. Likewise with the thinner and drier. The formula is simply suggestive and since there is very wide range fo requirements for paints of this type we merely give a tentative formula for same.

Varnish and Oil Enamels and Undercoats

Light Amberol F-7	23	pounds
Extra Light Amberol BSI	26	pounds
China Wood Oil	18	gallons
Bodied Linseed Oil	6	gallons
Sugar of Lead	1 3/4	pounds
Liquid Cobalt Drier	1	quart
V.M.P. Naptha or Mineral Thinners	50	gallons

Into a gallon of this grind approximately 7 pounds of White Pigment consisting of 3 pounds highest grade Zinc Oxide and 4 pounds Titanox. Amounts can be varied according to density and covering capacity of enamel desired. For undercoats increase the amount of pigment to 10 pounds consisting of the following, 2 pounds Calcium Cabronate, 8 pounds Lithophone. All products must be bleached with Blue Pigment, By tinting.

Some slower drying, easier flowering architectural enamels are made simply by grinding.

ROOFING PAINTS.

Red Liquid Asbestos Coating.—

Pitch	50	pounds
Naptha (49 degree)	24	gallons
Aluminium Steareate	2	pounds
Bright Red Oxide (Yellow tone)	100	pounds
Fibrous Asbestos	25	pounds
Blown Linseed Oil	8	gallons
Kerosene	4	gallons
V.M. & P. Naptha or Gasoline	10	gallons

This makes a batch of 52 gallons, Melt pitch in iron varnish pot until it is fluid. Remove from the fire and stir in one ingredient at a time in the order given in formula, very slowly.

Black Liquid Asbestos Coating.—

Liquid Coal Tar	50	gallons
Fibrous Asbestos	40	pounds
Solvent Naptha (Straw Color)	5	gallons
Blown Linseed Oil	2	gallons

This makes a batch amounting to 53 gallons. Liquid coal tar should be free from ammonia and water. If not put to in pot and slowly raise temperature to 250°F. and hold there until fumes are gone. Mix in the asbestos. Caution. Take away from the fire when mixing or adding Naptha or Gasoline.

Dust Colour Paint for Floors etc.

5	gallons	Boiled Linseed Oil
10	gallons	Natural Gum Varnish
5	gallons	Japan Dryer
5	gallons	Turpentine
3	gallons	V.M. & P. Naptha
100	pounds	Zinc White in Oil
100	pounds	White Lead in Oil
3	pounds	Black Color No. 1
6	pounds	Red Color No.1
20	pounds	Ochre Color No. 1
10	Pounds	Green Color No. 1

Formula for Colours.—

Black Colour No. 1 :

25 gallons Lamp Black in Oil
2½ gallons Linseed Oil
½ gallon V.M. P. Naptha
1 pint Liquid Paint Drier

Red Colour No. 1 :

25 pounds Red Oxide in Oil (light)
3 gallons Linseed Oil
¼ gallon V.M. & P. Naptha
1 Pint Liquid Drier

Ochre Colour No. 1 :

25 pounds Ochre in Oil (French)
4 gallons Linseed Oil

¼ gallon V.M.&P. Naptha
1 pint Liquid Drier

Green Colour No. 1 :

25 pounds Medium Chrome Green in Oil
5 gallons raw Linseed Oil
¼ gallon V.M. & P. Naptha
1 pint liquid Drier

You can take a mixture of White lead or Zinc as a base and by intermixing these various colours can get a paint with any desired shade.

To Get More Gloss and Body in Paints.—

By passing air through linseed and other oils what is known as Blown Oil is obtained. It appears to have more body but in reality this is false for it does not have. It does produce a paint with more gloss and one which will dry more rapidly and is being used very extensively today by leading paint manufacturers.

TOUCH UP BLACK.

The simplest way to make up a touch up Black is to purchase a high grade quality of tear outside coach varnish, one that will stand the weather fairly well. There are any number of varnish makers who will sell you very reasonabley what you need.

If you get it in five gallons cans you can get a real good FOUR HOUR Varnish (driers in four hours) for around $1.25 a gallon. To this you simply add from five to eight ounces or Carbon Black ground fine in Japan and stir it up and this will give you a touch up Black. This will dry quicker than four hours because the pigment causes the film to dry faster. it actually sets up in an hour so that in that amount of time will be practically dust free. (We mean to add from five to eight ounces on the Black to each gallon of varnish).

TOP DRESSINGS.

There are two kinds particularly of dressings. Lacquers Type and Varnish Type. From these types hundreds of formulas originate, some good and some poor.

VARNISH TYPE DRESSING.

To a gallon of LONG OIL OUTSIDE SPAR Varnish add 6 ounces of Carbon Black, ground in Japan. Some finishers add a ½ pint of linseed oil of this but if your varnish is long in oii enough you need not do this. The linseed or china wood oil gives the film more flexibility as does Castor Oil. Soya Bean and Fish Oil are also good especially the later but it smells too much. The higher the gloss you want the less black you add.

LACQUER TYPE DRESSING.•

It's cheaper to buy a ready made Lacquer Solution than to make it yourself if you just are goint to make up some top dressing. Get the following formulas : 10 ounces Coton, 8 Ounces Easter Gum in a gallon of 25% Butyl Acetate, 35% Butyl Alcohol, 40% Toluol. To this add 3 or 3¼ ounces finely ground Carbon Black. Then after you have added the Black and stirred it in with a gallon of Clear Lacquer, you add ¼ pint linseed or china wood oil to give the film flexibility. Castor Oil is sometimes used but is not so good for out door exposure.

COMMERCIAL PUTTY.

350	pounds Putty Whiting
450	pounds Marble Dust
12½	gallons Putty Oil

Mix thoroughly in a putty chaser for large quantities. Putty oil, consists of 6 gallons Raw Linseed oil, 11 gallons Paraffine Oil, ½ galloon Japan Oil. This is similar to all well known cheap putties put out by large paint manufacturers.

OIL STAINS :

Early English Oil Stain.—

Oil Black	10	ounces
Oil Brown	¼	ounces
Oil Yellow	1	ounce

Linseed Oil

(Pure)	16	ounces (Liquid)
Turpentine	10	ounces
Naptha	½	gallon

The turpentine is heated, preferably on a water bath, and the colours are dissolved, Then add the linseed oil and when it is cooled off the naptha is added. Be very careful to avoid a fire when heating the turpentine.

Antwerp Oil Stain.—

Oil Black	2	ounces
Oil Yellow	2	drams

Oil Red	37	grains
Linseed Oil	17	Liquid ounces
Turpentine	17	liquid ounces
Naptha	½	gallons

Prepare in the same manner as directions give more.

Fumed Oak Oil Stain.—

Oil Brown	15	ounces
Oil Black	½	ounce
Oil Mahogany	1/8	ounce
Benzol	½	pint
Acetone	¼	ounce

WATER STAINS.

There are three classes of stains most commonly used, Oil, Water and Spirit. While Oil Stains are used greatly by the painters and decorators, Water Stains are used almost entirely by furniture and other manufacturers of products requiring stains. It will not be outy of place to list a few Water Stains. Water soluble colors ae of course used in Water Stains.

Mahogany Stain Water.—

Brown Mahogany	7	ounces
Red Mahogany	4	ounces
Water	1¼	gallons

Adam Brown Mahogany.—

Brown Mahogany	1	ounces
Jet Black Nigrosine	¼	ounce
Bichromate of Potash	1/8	ounce

Antique Mahogany.—

Mahogany Brown	1	ounce
Mahogany Red	½	ounce
Potassium Bichromate	¼	ounce
Water	2	quarts

There are numerous antique mahoganies. The wood in this case is usually filled with a very dark paste filler and two coats of the stain are applied in the regular manner.

Mahogany Water Stain for Birch.—

Brown Mahogany	2	ounces
Red Mahogany	3	ounces
Water	3	quarts

Usually the wood is first sponged with a weak lye solution, sanded, stained shellaced and varnished.

27

Pigments Formulae

Natural Source, and Manufacture of Pigments.— A pigment is a dry earthy by clayey substance that, when mixed with oil, water, etec. forms a paint. Most pigments are of mineral origin, but there are vegetable pigments as longwood, and animal pigments as cohineal. In modern practice the colours are produced mainly by dyeing certain clays, which excel in a large percentage of silicic acid, with aniline dyestuffs. The coloring matters best adapted for thsi purpose are those a basic character. The colors obtaine in this manner excel in a vivid hue, and fastness to light and water.

Following is a general outline of their manufacture: one hundred parts, by weight, of washed clay in paste from are finely suspended in 6 to 8 times the volume of water and acidulated with about 1½ parts, by volume, of 5 per cent hydrochloric or acetic acid, and heated by means of steam almost to the boiling temperature. There is next introduced, according to the shade desired, 1 to 2 parts, by weight, of the dyestuff, such as auramin, diamond greens, Victoria blue, etc., with simultaneous stirring and heating for 1 to 2 hours, or until a sample filtered off from the liquor shows no dyestuff. Next the clay dyed in this manner is isolated by filtration and washed with hot water and dried. The colors thus obtained may be used as substitues for mineral colours of all discription.

The method of manufacture varies greatly. According to the Bennet and Mastin English patent the procedure is as follows : Grind together to a paste in water, substances of a clavey, stony, earthy, or vitreous nature and certain metallic oxides, or "prepared oxides", such as are commonly used in the pottery trades; dry and powder the paste, and subject the powder to the heat of a furnace, of such a temperature that the requisite colour is obtained, and for such length the whole substance. For example, 8 parts of black oxide of cobalt, 12 parts of oxide of zinc, and 26 parts of alumina, when incorporated, with 20 times their combined bulk of clay and treated as described, yield a rich blue pigment in the case of a white clay, and a rich green in the case of a yellow clay. Long continued firing in this case improves tne colour.

Many minerals included in formulas for pigments have little or no colouring power in themselves; nevertheless they are required in producing the most beautiful shades of colour when blended one with another, the colour being brought out by calcination.

Mixing Oil Colours and Tints.—It must not be expected that the formulas given will produce the exact effect desired, because the strength of the various brands of colours vary to a great extent, and therefore the painter must exercise his own judgement. The table simply gives an idea of what can be produced by following the formulas given, when chemically pure material is employed in the mixing. It is also recommended that the parts mentioned be weighed out in paste form, and the white or black and each colour, separately thinned and strained before mixing them together, because the arriving at the proper hue of colour or depth and tone of tint will be simplified by using that precautions. By thinning is not meant that they should be quite ready for application, but of such consistency that they will pass an ordinary stainer with the aid of a brush.

Unless otherwise indicated, the materials are understood to be ground fine in paste form.

Note.— The majority of the following are by Joseph Griggs, in the *Painters*

:

GROUNDS FOR GRAINING COLOURS :

Ash Ground.— Four hundred parts white lead; 4 parts French ocher; 1 part raw Turkey umber.

Ash.— Raw umber; raw sienna; and a little black or vandyke brown.

Hungarian Ash.— Raw Sienna and raw and burnt umber.

Bun Ash.— Raw sienna; burnt umber; and Vandyke brown.

Cherry Ground.— One hundred parts white lead; 5 parts burnt sienna; 1 part raw sienna.

Natural Cherry.— Raw and burnt sienna and raw umber.

Stained Cherry.— Burnt sienna; burnt umber; and Vandyke brown.

Chestnut.— Raw sienna; burnt umber; Vandyke bronw; and a little burnt sienna.

Maple.— Raw sienna and raw umber.

Silver Maple.— Ivory black over a nearly white ground.

Light Maple Ground.— One hundred parts white lead; 1 part French ocher.

Dark Maple Groun.— One hundred parts which lead; 1 part dark golden ocher.

Oak.— Raw Sienna; Burnt Umber, a little black.

Pollard Oak.—Raw and burnt sienna, or burnt umber and Vandyke brown.

Light Oak Ground.— Buty partw white lead; 1 part French ocher.

Dark Oak Ground.— Fifty parts while lead; 1 part dark golden ocher.

Satinwood.— Add a little ivory black to maple colour.

Mahogany.—Burnt sienna; bunt umber; and Vandyke brown.

Mahogany Ground.— Tea parts white lead; parts orange chrome and 1 part bunt sienna.

Rosewood.—Vandyke brown and a little ivory black.

Rosewood Ground.—Drop Black.

Walnut Ground.—Fifty parts white lead; parts dark golden ocher; 1 part dark Venetian red; and 1 part drop black.

Black Walnut.— Burnt umber with a little Vandyke brown for dark parts.

French Burl Walnut.— Sam as black walnut.

Hard Pine.— Raw and burnt sienna; add a little burnt umber.

Cyprens.— Raw and burnt sienna and burnt umber.

Whitewood.—Ground same as for light ash; graining color, yellow ocher, adding raw umber and black for dark streaks.

POSITIVE COLOURS :

Blue.—Twelve parts borate of lime; 6 parts oxide of zinc; 10 parts litharge; 9 parts feldspar; 4 parts oxide of cobalt.

Blue Black A.— Nine parts lamp black; 1 parts Chinese or Prussian blue.

Blue Black B.— Nineteen parts drop black; 1 part Prussian Blue.

Bright Mineral.— Nine parts light venetian red, 1 part red lead.

Brilliant Green.— Nine parts Paris green; 1 part C.C. chrome green, light

Bronze Green Light.— Three parts raw Turkey umber; 1 part medium chrome yellows.

Bronze Green, Medium.— Five parts medium chrome yellow; 3 parts burnt Turkey umber; 1 part lampblack.

Bronze Green, Dark.— Twenty parts drop black; 2 parts medium chrome yellow; and 1 part dark orange chrome.

Bottle Green.— Five Parts commercial chrome green, medium and 1 part drop black.

Brown.— Ten parts crude antimony; 12 parts litharge; 2 parts manganese; 1 part oxide of iron.

Brown stone.— Eighteen parts burnt umber; 2 part dark golder ocher; and 1 part bunt sienna.

Cherry Red.— Equal parts of best imitation vermilion and No. 40 carmine.

Citron A.—Three parts medium chrome yellow and 2 parts raw umber.

Citron B.— Six parts commercial chrome green, light and 1 part medium chrome yellows.

Coffee Brown.— Six parts burnt Turkey umber; 2 parts french ocher; and 1 part burnt sienna.

Emerald Green.— Use Paris Green

Green.— Twenty parts litharge, 12 parts flint; 2 parts oxide of copper; 2½ parts ground glass; 2½ parts whitingl; 1½ parts oxide of chrome.

Flesh Colour.— Ninteen parts French ocher; 1 parts deep English Vermilion.

Fern Green.— Five parts lemon chrome yellow and 1 part each of light chrome green and drop black.

Foliage Green.— Three parts medium chrome yellow and 1 part of ivory of drop black.

Foliage Brown.— Equal parts of vandyke brown and orange chrome yellows.

Golden Ocher.— Fourteen parts french yellow ocher and 1 part medium chrome yellow for the light shade, and 9 parts Oxford ocher and 1 part orange chrome yellow for the dark shade.

Gold Russet.— Five parts lemon chrome yellow and 1 part slight Venetian Red.

Gold Orange.— Equal parts of dry orange mineral and light golden ocher in oil.

Indian Brown.— Equal parts of light Indian red, French Ocher, and lamp black.

Mahogany, Cheap.— Three parts dark golden ocher and 1 part of dark Venetian red.

Maroon, Light.— Five parts dark Venetian Red; 1 part drop black.

Maroon, Dark.— Nine parts dark Indian Red; 1 part lampblack.

Olive Green.— Seven parts light golden ocher; 1 part lampblack.

Ochrous Olive.— Nine parts French cher; 1 part raw umber.

Orange Brown.—Equal parts burnt sienna and orange chrome yellow.

Oriental Red.— Two parts Indian Red, light, in oil; 1 part dry red lead.

Purple A.—Eight parts crocus martis; 2 parts red hematite; 1 part oxide of iron.

Purple B.— Two parts rose pink; 1 part ultramarine blue.

Purple Black.— Three parts lampblack and 1 part rose pink, or 9 parts drop black and 1 part rose pink.

Purple Brown.— Five parts Indian Red, Dark and 1 Part each of ultramarine blue and lampblack.

Roman Ocher.—Twenty three parts French ocher and 1 part each burnt sienna and burnt umber.

Royal Blue, Dark.— Eighteen parts ultramarine blue and 2 parts Prussian blue. To lighten use as much white lead or zinc white as is required.

Royal Purple.— Two parts ultramareine blue; 1 part No. 40 carmine or carmine lake.

Russet.— Fourteen parts orange chrome yellow and 1 part C.P. chrome green, medium.

Seal Brown.— Ten parts burnt umber; 2 parts golden ocher, light; 1 part burnt sienna.

Snuff Brown.— Equal part burnt umber and golder ocher, light.

Terra Cotta.—Two parts white lead; 1 part burnt sienna, also 2 parts French ocher to 1 part Venetian red.

Turkey Red.— Strong Venetian red or red oxide.

Tuscan Red. Ordinary.— Nine Parts Indian red to 1 part rose pink.

Brilliant.— Four parts Indian red to 1 part red madder lake.

Violet.— Three parts ultramareine blue; 2 parts rose lake; 1 part best ivory black.

Yellow.— Four and one half parts tine ashes; 1 part crude antimony; 12 part litharge, and 1 part red ocher.

Yellow, Amber.— Ten parts medium chrome yellow; 7 parts burnt umber; 3 parts burnt sienna.

Yellow, Canary.— Five parts white lead; 2 parts permanent yellow; 1 part lemon chrome yellow.

Yellow, Golffin.— Ten parts lemon chrome yellow, 3 parts orange chrome, dark; 5 parts white lead.

Yellows, Brimstone.— Three parts white lead; 1 part lemon chrome yellow; 1 part permanent yellows.

Azure Blue.— Fifty parts white lead; 1 part ultramarine blue.

Blue Gray.— One hundred parts while lead; 3 parts Prussian blue; 1 part lamp black.

Bright Blue.— Twenty parts zinc white; 1 part imitation cobalt blue.

Blue Grass.—Seven parts white lead; 2 parts Paris green; 1 part Prussian Blue.

Deep Blue.—Fifteen parts white lead; 1 part Prussian blue or Antwerp blue.

French Blue.— Five parts imitation cobalt blue; 2 part French zinc white.

Green Blue.— One hundred parts white lead; 5 parts lemon chrome yellow; 3 parts ultramarine blue.

Hazy Blue.— Sixty parts white lead; 16 parts ultramarine blue; 1 part burnt sienna.

Mineral Blue.— Five parts white lead; 4 part imitation cobalt blue; 2 parts red madder lake; 1 part best ivory or drop black.

Orient Blue.— Twenty five parts white lead; 2 parts Prussian Blue; 1 part lemon chrome yellows.

Royal Blue.— Thirty four parts white lead; 19 parts ultramarine blue; 2 parts Prussian blue; 1 part rose madder or rose lake.

Sapphire Blue.— Two parts French zinc white and 1 part best Chinese blue.

Turquoise Blue.— Twenty parts white lead; 3 parts ultramarine blue; 1 part lemon chrome yellow.

RED TINTS :

Cardinal Red.— Equal parts of white lead and scarlet lake.

Carnation Red.— Fifteen parts white lead; 1 part scarlet lake.

Claret.— Twenty one parts oxide of zinc; 4 parts crocus martis; 4 parts oxide of chrome; 3 parts red lead; 3 parts borric acid.

Coral Pink.— Fifteen parts white lead; 2 parts bright vermilion; 1 part deep orange chrome.

Deep Rose.— Ten parts white lead; 1 part red lake.

Deep Purple.— Five parts white lead; 1 part ultramine blue ; 1 part rose pink.

Deep Scarlet.— Fifteen parts bright vermilion; 2 parts red lake; 8 parts white lead.

Flesh Pink.—One hundred parts white lead; 1 part orange chrome yellow; 1 part red lake.

Indian Pink.— One hundred parts white lead; 1 part light Indian red.

Lavender.— Fifteen parts white lead; 2 parts ultramarine blue; 1 part red lake.

Light Pink.— Fifty parts white lead; 1 part bright vermilion.

Lilac.— Fifty parts white lead; 1 part best rose pink.

Mauve.— Fifteen parts white lead; 2 parts ultramarine blue; 1 part caramine lake or red lake.

Orange Pink.— Two parts white lead; 1 part dark orange chrome or American vermilion.

Purple.—Five parts white lead; 2 parts ultramarine blue; 1 part red madder lake.

Royal Pink.—Five parts white lead, 1 part caramine lake or red madder lake.

Royal Rose.—Twenty parts white lead; 1 part rich rose lake.

Red Brick.—Ten parts white lead; 3 parts light Venetian red; 1 part yellow ocher.

Reddish Terra Cotta.— Two parts white lead; 1 part rich burnt sienna.

Salmon.—Fifty partw white lead; 5 parts deep orange chrome.

Shell Pink.— Fifty parts white lead; 2 parts bright vermilion; 1 part orange chrome; 1 part burnt sienna.

Violet.— Fifteen parts white lead; 4 parts ultramarine blue; 3 parts rose lake; 1 part drop black.

GREEN TINTS :

Apple Green.— Fifty parts white lead; 1 part chrome green, light or medium shade.

Citrine Green.— One hundred parts, white lead; 2 parts medium chrome yellow; 1 part drop black.

Citron Green.— One hundred parts white lead; 3 parts medium chrome yellow; 1 part lampblack.

Emerald Green.— Ten parts white lead; 1 part Paris (emerald) green.

Grass Green A.—Ten parts white lead; 7 parts Paris Green.

Grass Green B.— Ten parts oxide of chrome; 2 parts tin ashes; 8 parts whiteing; 1 part crocus martis; 1 part bichromate potash.

Gray Green.— Five parts white lead; 1 part verona green.

Marine Green.— Ten parts white lead; 1 part ultramarine green.

Nile Green.— Fifty parts white lead; 6 parts medium chrome green; 1 part Prussian blue.

Olive Green.—Fifty parts white lead, 2 parts medium chrome yellow; 3 parts raw umber; 1 part drop black.

Olive Drab.— Fifty parts white lead; 8 parts raw umber; 5 parts medium chrome green; 1 part drop black.

Pea Green.— Fifty parts white lead; 1 part ligtt chrome green.

Satin Green.— One hundred white lead; 1 part Milori green.

Sage green.— One hundred parts white lead; 3 parts medium chrome green; 1 part raw umber.

Sea Green.—Fifty parts white lead; 1 part dark chrome green.

Stone Green.— Twenty five parts white lead; 2 parts dark chrome green; 3 parts raw umber.

Velvet Green.— Twety parts white lead; 7 parts medium chrome green; 2 parts burnt sienna.

Water Green.— Fifteen parts white lead; 10 parts French ocher; 1 part dark chrome green.

BROWN TINTS :

Chocolate.— Twenty five parts white lead; 3 parts burnt umber.

Cocoanut.— Equal parts white lead and burnt umber.

Cinnamon.— Ten parts white lead; 2 parts burnt sienna; 1 part French ocher.

Dark Drab.—Forty parts white lead; 1 part burnt umber.

Dark Stone.—Twenty parts white lead; 1 part raw umber.

Fawn.—Fifty parts white lead; 3 parts burnt umber 2 parts French ocher.

Golden Brown.— Twenty five parts white lead; 4 parts French ocher; 1 part burnt sienna.

Hazel Nut Brown.— Twenty parts whtie lead; 5 parts burnt unber; 1 part medium chrome yellow.

Mulberry.—Ten parts manganese; 2 parts cobalt blue; 2 parts saltpeter.

Purple Brown.— Fifty parts white lead; 6 parts Indian red; 2 parts ultramarine blue; 1 part lampblack.

Red Brown.— Twelve parts hematite ore; 3 parts manganese; 7 parts litharge; 2 parts yellow ocher.

Seal Brown.— Thrity parts white lead; 5 parts burnt umber; 1 part medium chrome yellows.

Snuff Brown.— Twenty five parts white lead; 1 part burnt umber; 1 part Oxford ocher.

GRAY TINTS :

Ash Gray.— Thirty partw white lead; 2 parts ultramarine blue; 1 part burnt sienna.

Cold Gray.— Five hundred parts white lead; 6 parts lampblack; 1 part Antwerp blue.

Dove Color.— Twelve parts manganese; 5 parts steel fillingsl 3 parts wihting; 1 part oxide of cobalt.

Dove Gray.— Two hundred parts white lead; 5 parts ultramarine blue; 2 parts drop black.

French Gray.— One hundred and fifty parts white lead; 2 parts lampblack; 1 part orange chrome yellow; 1 part chrome red (American vermilion).

Lead Color.— Fifty parts white lead; 1 part lampblack (increase proportion of white lead for light tings).

Lustrous Gray.— Ten parts white lead; 1 part graphite (plumbago).

Olive Gray.— Two hundred parts white lead; 2 part lampblack; 1 part medium chrome yellow.

Pure Gray.— Pure hundred parts white laed; 1 part drop black.

Pearl Gray.— One hundred parts white lead; 1 part ultramarine blue; 1 part drop black.

Silver Gray.— One hundred and fifty leads; 2 parts lampblack; 3 parts Oxford ocher.

Warm Gray.— One hundred parts whit elead; 3 parts drop black; 2 parts French ocher; 1 part light Venetian red.

Note.— For inside work and whenever desirable, the white lead may be replaced by zinc white or a mixture of the two white pigments may be used. Be it also remembered that pure colours, as a rule will produce the cleanest tints and that fineness of grinding is an important factor. It will not be amiss to call attention to the fact that the excessive use of driers, especially of dark japans or liquid driers, with delicate tints is bad practice, and liable to ruin otherwise good effects in tints or delicate solid colors.

COLOUR TESTING.

Expense and trouble deter many a painter from having a colour examined

Although such as exámination is often very necessary. For the practical man it is less important to know that percentage of foreign matter a paint contains, but whether substances are contained therein, 'which may act injuriously in some way or other.

If a pigment is to be tested for arsenic, pour purified hydrochloric acid into a test tube or a U-shaped glass vessel which withstands heat, add a little of the pigment or the coloured fabric, wall paper, etc. (of pigment take only enough to stongly colour the hydrochloric acid simply in the first moment), and finally a small quantity of stannous chloride. Now heat the test tube with its contents moderately over a common spirit lamp. If the liquid or mass has assumed a brown or brownish colour after being heated, arsenic is present in the pigment or fabric etc.

An effective but simply test for the durability of a colour is to paint strips of thick paper and nail them on the wall in the strongest light possible. A strip of paper should then be nailed over one half of the samples of colour so as to protect them from the light. On remcving this the difference is shade between the exposed and unexposed portions will be very apparent. Some colours, such as the vermilionettes, will show a marked difference after even a few weeks.

Testing Body colours for Gritty admixtures.— The fineness of the powdered pigment is not a guaranteed of the absence of gritty admixtures. The lattr differ from the pigment proper in their specific gravity. If consisting of metallic oxides or metallic sulphides the sandy admixtures are lighter than the pigments and rise to the surface upon a systematic shaking of the sample. In the case of other pigments e.g., aluminas and iron varnish colours, they collect at the bottom. For carrying out the test, a smoothly bored metallic tube about ½ to 3/4 inch in diameter and 6 to 7 inches long is used. Both ends are closed with screw caps and at one side of the tube some holes about 1/6 of an inch in diameter are bored, closed by pieces of a rubber hose pushed on. The tube is filled with the pigment powder, screwed up and feebly shaken for some time in a vertical position (the length of time verying according to the fineness of the powder). Samples may now be taken from all parts of the tube. Perhaps glass tubes would be preferable, but lateral apartures cannot be so readily made. After necessary samples have been collected in this manner, they must be prepared with a standard sample, which is a accomplished either by feeling the powder between the fingers or by inspecting it under a microscope, or else by means of the scratching test, which last named is the usual way. The requisites for these scratch tests consists of two soft, well polished glass plates (2½ X 2¼ inches) which are fixed by means of cement in two stronger plates of hard wood suitably hollowed out. The surface of the glass must project about ½ inch over the wooden frame If a sample of the pigment powder is placed on such a glass plate, another plate is laid on top and both are rubbed slowly together; this motion will retain a soft, velvety character in case of pigment is free from gritty admixtures; if otherwise the glass is injured and a corresponding sound becomes audible. Next the powder is removed from the plate, rubbing the latter with a soft rage, and examining the surface with a microscope. From the nature of scratches on the plate the kind of gritty ingredients on the plate the kind of gritty ingredients can be readily determined. The human finger is sufficiently sensitive to detect the presence of gritty sensitive to detect the presence of gritty substances, yet it is not capable of gritty substances, yet it is not capable of distinguishing whether they consist of imperfectly reduced or badly sifted grains of pigment or real gritty admixtures.

To Determine the Covering Power of Pigments.— To determine the covering power of whitelead, or way other pigment, take equal quantities of several varieties of white lead and mix them with a darker pigment, black, blue etc. the latter also in equal proportions. The white lead which retains the highest colour is naturally the most opaque. In a similar manner, or the other hand, the mixing power of the dark pigments can be ascertained. If experimments are made with a variety of white lead or zinc white, by the admixture of dark pigments, the color which tints the white lead or zinc white most, also the possesses the greatest covering or mixing power..

To detect the Presence of Aniline in a Pigment.— Lay a little of the colour upon letter paper and pour a drop of spirit on it. If it is mixed, with aniline the paper is coloured right through thereby, white a pure pigment does not alter the shade of the paper and will never penetrate it.

Vehicle for Oil Colours.— Petroleum 20 to 30 pounds; tallow, 3 to 5 pounds; cotton seed oil, 5 to 7 pounds; colophony, 5 to 7 pounds. The pigment having been grounded up with the mixture, the mixed paint can be made still better by adding to it about a sixth of its weight of the following mixture; Vegetable oil, 8 to 20 pounds, saponified rosin, 6 to 16 pounds; turpentine, 4 to 30 ounces.

Frankfort Black.— Frankfort black, also known as German black, is a name applied to a superior grade of lampblack. In some districts of Germany it is said to be made by calcining wine lees and tartar. The material is heated in large cylindrical vessels having a vent in the cover for the escape of smoke and vapors that the evolved during the process. When no more smoke is observed, the operation is finished. The residium in the vessels is then washed several times in boiling water to extract the salt contained therin and finally is reduced to the proper degree of fineness by grinding on a porphyry.

Paris Green.— Emerald or Paris green is rather permanent to light, but must not be mixed with pigments containing sulphur, because of the tendency the blacken when so mixed. It will not resist acids, ammonia, and caustic.

PILE OINTMENTS.

I.—	"Extract" witch hazel...........	2	fluidounces
	Lanum	2	ounces
	Petrolatum	6	ounces
	Glycerine	4	fludounces
	Tannic acid	1	dracm
	Powdered opium	1	drachm
II.—	Tannic acid	20	grains
	Bismuth subnitrate	1	drachm
	Powdered opium	10	gains
	Lanum	3	drachms
	Petrolatum	5	drachms

PLANT PARASITES :

A spray which will destroy most plant parasites can be made as follows : dissolved 5 rounds of copper sulphate, 5 pounds quicktime in 50 gallons of water.

You can use this spray on pear, apple and cherry tree with good results.

PLANTS :

Temperature of Water for Watering Plants.—

Experiments were made several years ago at the Visconsin Agricultrual Experiment Station to determine whether cold water wad detrimental to palnts. Plants were grown under glass and in the open field, and in all cases the results were similar. Thus cleus planted in lots of equal size and vigor were watered with water at 35°, 50°, 65° and 86°F. At the end of 60 days it was impossible to not any difference, and when the experiment was repeated with water at 32°, 40°, 70° and 100°F the reusult was the same Bans worked with water at 32º, 40°, 70° and 100°F were equally vigorous; in fact, water at 32° and 40° F. gave the best results. Lettuce watered with water at 32°F yielded slightly more than the other lots. From those experiments it was concluded that for vegetable and flowering plants commonly grown under glass, ordinary well or spring water may be used freely at any time of the year without warming.

28

Paint Making Machinery Suppliers

Deepak Engineers
Shop No. 6-2-111/ B/2,
Road No. 6, Shobana Colony,
Balanagar,
Hyderabad - 500042,
Telangana, India
Mobile: +(91)-9849075217
Phone: +(91)-(40)-23772705

Chem Maco
408, Jessore Road, Bus Stop,
Barat Colony
Kolkata - 700055,
West Bengal, India
Mobile: +(91)-9830052076
Phone: +(91)-(33)-25221544
Fax: +(91)-(33)-25222153
Email: chemmaco@yahoo.com
chemmaco@gmail.com

Surya Engineering Co.
2, Dr. R. N. Tagore Road,
Dunlop & Dakhineshwar
Kolkata - 700076,
West Bengal, India
Mobile: +(91)-9830217654
+(91)-9830091468
Phone: +(91)-(33)-25632032
+(91)-(33)-25443898
Fax: +(91)-(33)-28430370

Biomate India
436,Shahabad Daulatpur
New Delhi - 110042, India
Mobile: +(91)-9910896223
+(91)-9818648066
+(91)-9312130119
Phone: +(91)-(11)-27298066
Email: salesbiomate@gmail.com

Sivaram Industries
Mobile: +91-7299946605
No. 3/643, Parivakkam Road,
Vettalaithottam, Seneerkuppam,
Nearby Bisleri Water Company
Chennai, Tamil Nadu, India

MAC-Tools
Phone: +91-22-22662312
+91-22-40787878
Office No. 33, 2nd Floor,
Dossa House, No. 5,
Gunbow Street, Fort
Mumbai - 400001 (MS), India

SBS Group
Phone: +91-8407977718
+91-832-2330282
Plot No. 121,
Bethora Industrial Estate
Ponda - 403409, Goa, India

Wel Fab & Engineers
Mobile: +91-9825025496
Plot No. 1009, Phase-IV,
Near Royal Electricals,
G. I. D. C
Vitthal Udyognagar - 388 121
Gujarat, India

29

Paint Mixer Suppliers

Blastech
No. 102, Dattar Mansion,
Shivaji Nagar Road,
Vakola Bridge,
Santacruz East,
Mumbai - 400055,
Maharashtra, India
Mobile: +(91)-9920280939
+(91)-9920591113
+(91)-9773597578
Phone: +(91)-(22)-26684375
Fax: +(91)-(22)-26684376
Email: blastechindia@vsnl.net
info@blastech.in

Modern Engineering Co.
Plot No. I - 33 Phase - IV,
G. I. D. C. Estate, Vitthal,
Udyognagar
Anand - 388121, Gujarat, India
Mobile: +(91)-9227135851
Phone: +(91)-(2692)-229542
+(91)-(2692)-229543
Fax: +(91)-(2692)-235812

Mohindra Engineering Co.
RZ- 73, Nursing Garden,
Near Khyala Village
New Delhi - 110018, India
Mobile: +(91)-9999778804
+(91)-9312944733

Alpha Marketing, New Delhi
C- 199, Nariana Industrial Area,
Phase No. 1,
New Delhi - 110028,
Delhi, India
Mobile: +(91)-9810146910
+(91)-9811307703
Phone: +(91)-(11)-45578023
+(91)-(11)-41412023
+(91)-(11)-25794116
Fax: +(91)-(11)-45578023

R. K. Industries, Sameypur
Radha-Krishan Mandir Road
Gali No. 10, Near K. K. India,
Sameypur, Delhi - 110042, India
Mobile: +(91)-9212140991,
+(91)-9212140992
+(91)-9212140717

Kapal Enterprises
Mr. Navjot Singh Kapoor
Plot No. 38/2/9, Site-4,
Sahibabad Industrial Area
Ghaziabad - 201010,

Uttar Pradesh, India
Mobile: +(91)-9899732009
+(91)-7042395777
Phone: +(91)-(120)-4233061

Beetax
Kala Sangha Road,
Basti Sheikh
Jalandhar - 144002,
Punjab, India
Mobile: +(91)-9815928288
Phone: +(91)-(181)-2252429
+(91)-(181)-5092410
Fax: +(91)-(181)-2483024
+(91)-(181)-2431365
Email: beetax@jla.vsnl.net.in
beetaxenterprises@gmail.com

T. R. Sharma Engineering Works
A-156, Hari Nagar, Clock Tower
New Delhi - 110064.
Delhi, India
Mobile: +(91)-9810137555
+(91)-9818125123

Rama & Company
Harish Dhawan
Call Us: 08049443808
Kala Singha Road,
Village Kot Sadiq,
P.O Basti Guzan,
Jalandhar - 144002
Punjab, India

Forgings & Chemicals Indstries
Niru Kumari
Call Us: 08045137572
G.T. Road, Bye-Pass
Jalandhar - 144004
Punjab, India

Jagdambay Forgings
Phone: +91-181-2203425
+91-181-5052625
+91-181-3254615
120, Feet Road,
Babu Jagjivan Ram Chowk,
Basti Guzan,
Jalandhar - 144002
Punjab, India

M. S. Babbar & Company
Mobile: +91-9872140653
+91-181-5007080
Phone: +91-181-5007081
M- 9/10, Industrial Area
Backside Telephone Exchange
Jalandhar - 144004
Punjab, India

Bellota Hand Tools
Ram Babu Prasad
Mobile: +91-9811854346
C14/17, Shiv Shakti Apartment,
Janta Flat, Noida - 422112
Uttar Pradesh, India

30

Chemical Storage Tank Suppliers

Deft Engineering
D- 2/12, Ganga Triveni Apartment,
Sector- 9, Rohini,
New Delhi - 110085,
Delhi, India
Mobile: +(91)-9811527432
+(91)-9555164400

Ashoo Model Arts
Krishna Kuteer, 21/13,
East Punjabi Bagh
New Delhi - 110026,
Delhi, India
Mobile: +(91)-9891444846
Phone: +(91)-(11)-28312984
Fax: +(91)-(11)-28312984

Sangam Plastic Industries Pvt. Ltd
No. 110, Satya Bhawan, 36,
Community Center,
Wazirpur Industrial Area
Delhi - 110052, India
Mobile: +(91)-9810026034
+(91)-9810057441
+(91)-9871747570
+(91)-9818138481
Phone: +(91)-(11)-27372565
+(91)-(11)-27372566
Fax: +(91)-(11)-27372565

Uma Shankar Engineer
K-55B, LGF, Kalkaji
New Delhi -110 019, India
Phone: +(91)-(11)-41613675
41058584
Mobile: +(91)-9810088622
9871188622

Super Chemfab Engineers & Consultants
J - 7/59A, Rajouri Garden
New Delhi - 110027,
Delhi, India
Mobile: +(91)-9868226398
+(91)-9899126926
Phone: +(91)-(11)-25104759
+(91)-(11)-25435035
Fax: +(91)-(11)-25435035
+(91)-(11)-25104759

Apex Thermotech Technologies Private Limited
No. 101, Surya Niketan
New Delhi - 110092,
Delhi, India
Mobile: +(91)-9810214195
+(91)-9313478350

Phone: +(91)-(11)-22377889
Fax: +(91)-(120)-2701583
Email:
info@apexthermotech.com
sales@apexthermotech.com
apexthermotech@hotmail.com

Exch Therm Engineering Co.
C-10 Ashoka Tower, C - Block
Community Center, Janakpuri
New Delhi - 110058,
Delhi, India
Mobile: +(91)-9810057612
Phone: +(91)-(11)-25506190
+(91)-(11)-25573756
Email: exch.therm@gmail.com

Shiv Shakti Road Equipments Pvt. Ltd.
52/12, Swarn Park,
Udyog Nagar,
Mundika,
New Delhi - 110041,
India
E-mail: shivshakti@ssrepl.com
Phone: +(91)-(11)-65454808
28343198
Fax: +(91)-(11)-28341702
Mobile: +(91)-9810113481

31

Ball Mill Suppliers

Stockdale Process Engineers
Plot No. 105, Phase 2,
Badli Industrial Area, Samaypur,
Badli, Delhi - 110042, India
Mobile: +(91)-9899880911
+(91)-9868017877
Phone: +(91)-(11)-27297522
+(91)-(11)-27854414
Email:
stockdales105@yahoo.co.in,
sales@stockdale.in

SGM Lab Solutions
BA-15, Mangolpuri Industrial Area,
Phase- 2, New Delhi - 110034,
India
Mobile: +(91)-8130897474
9811565000
8130897434
Phone: +(91)-(11)-48481414
48481415
48481411
Fax: +(91)-(11)-43852040
E-mail: sales@lab360.co.in,
info@lab360.co.in

M. S. & Company
Plot No. 94, Pocket - B,
Sector - 3,
DSIDC Industrial Area, Bawana
New Delhi - 110039, Delhi, India
Mobile: +(91)-9810772313
+(91)-9886742555
+(91)-8375932007

Macro Scientific Works Pvt. Ltd.
B- 35/3, G. T Karnal Road,
Industrial Area,
Near Gola Banquet Hall,
Delhi - 110033, India
Mobile: +(91)-9810110476
+(91)-9910660476
+(91)-9650000476
Phone: +(91)-(11)-48494849
Fax: +(91)-(11)-42385201

M.H. Spice And Food Machinery
B- 485, Street No. 6,
Nehru Vihar,
Dayalpur, Delhi - 110094, India
Mobile: +(91)-9811933786
+(91)-9899624046
+(91)-9555212120
+(91)-8860692658

GRR Steel Fabs
Plot No. 14, Lane No. 7,
Anand Parbat Industrial Estate,
New Rohtak Road
New Delhi - 110005,
Delhi, India
Mobile: +(91)-9873463966
+(91)-9811151890
Phone: +(91)-(11)-43073778
+(91)-(11)-45536233

Harrisons Pharma Machinery Private Limited
No. 4675/21, Ground Floor,
Ganpati Bhawan, Darya Ganj
Delhi - 110002, India
Mobile: +(91)-9811053588
+(91)-9311053588
+(91)-9311053533
Phone: +(91)-(11)-23278924
+(91)-(11)-41564433
Email: sales.harrisons@gmail.com
harrisons@vsnl.com

Scientific & Technological Equipment Corporation
M11, Street No. 10,
Anand Parbat Industrial Area,
New Rohtak Road
New Delhi - 110005,
Delhi, India
Mobile: +(91)-9868275312
+(91)-9212189333
+(91)-9868275310
Phone: +(91)-(11)-28762949

T. R. Sharma Engineering Works
A-156, Hari Nagar, Clock Tower
New Delhi - 110064,
Delhi, India
Mobile: +(91)-9810137555
+(91)-9818125123

R. K. Industries, Sameypur
Radha- Krishan Mandir Road,
Gali No. 10, Near K. K. India,
Sameypur, Delhi - 110042, India
Mobile: +(91)-9212140991
+(91)-9212140992
+(91)-9212140717

Bandi Technology
Block- A/419, Minto Road,
Daryaganj, Central Delhi
Delhi - 110002, India
Mobile: +(91)-9891673394
+(91)-9716963092
+(91)-9643975180

32

Triple Roll Suppliers

Danyal Engineering Company
No. 3022, Nal Bandan Street,
Chowk Shahganj, Ajmeri Gate
Delhi - 110006, India
Mobile: +(91)-9811174981
+(91)-9899861156
+(91)-9899913201
Ohone: +(91)-(11)-23212102
+(91)-(11)-23217244

Golden Heavy Engineering Co.
Village Majri Kishne Wali,
Khanna Road,
Amloh, Khanna - 141402,
Punjab, India
Mobile: +(91)-8872166000
+(91)-9876063162
Phone: +(91)-(1765)-232789

Advanced Technocracy Inc.
ATICO House, 5309,
Grain Market,
Nr. B. D. Senior Secondary School
Ambala - 133001,
Haryana, India
Mobile: +(91)-9996186555
+(91)-9896793832
+(91)-9034949132
Email: aticoexport@gmail.com
aticoindia@gmail.com

Khusboo Engineering Works
Gala No. 3, Plot No. 318/ 6,
40 Shed Area,
Near Vijay Transport
Vapi - 396195, Gujarat, India
Mobile: +(91)-9825532678
+(91)-8401618040

Fluid Tech Engineers India Private Limited.
No. 113/2, Vandalur
Kelambakkam Road,
Rathinamangalam, Beside
Tagore Engineering College
Chennai - 600048,
Tamil Nadu, India
Mobile: +(91)-9444046437
+(91)-9444046447
+(91)-7299922107
Phone: +(91)-(44)-27498088
Fax: +(91)-(44)-27498088

Promas Engineers Pvt. Ltd.
R - 877, T. T. C.,
M. I. D. C. Industrial Area,
Thane Belapur Road, Rabale
Mumbai - 400701,
Maharashtra, India
Mobile: +(91)-9819991078
+(91)-9820529488
Phone: +(91)-(22)-27694287
+(91)-(22)-27694285
+(91)-(22)-27694275
+(91)-(22)-27694276

Manu Enterprises, Chennai
No. 11, Reddy Street,
Madurametttupalayam,
Puzhal, Chennai - 600066,
Tamil Nadu, India
Mobile: +(91)-9840295194
Phone: +(91)-(44)-26591397
Fax: +(91)-(44)-26591397

EIRI PROCESS TECHNOLOGY BOOKS

CHEMICAL/ DYES/ PETROCHEMICALS/ LUBRICANT/ ELECTROPLATING

01 Small Medium & Large Chemical Industries
02 Industrial Chemicals Technology Hand Book
03 Modern Technology of Organic & Inorganic Chemicals
04 Hand Book of Electroplating Anodizing & Surface Finishing Technology
05 Hand Book of Agro Chemical Industries (Insecticides & Pesticides)
06 Technology of Synthetic Dyes, Pigments Intermediates
07 Petrochemicals, Lubricants, Greases & Petroleum Refining
08 Hand Book of Lubricants, Greases & Petrochemicals Technology

GUMS, ADHESIVES AND SEALANTS

01 Technology Of Gums, Adhesives & Sealants With Formulations
02 Hand Book Of Adhesives With Their Formulaes
03 Adhesives Technology & Formulations Hand Book (Hand Book of Adhesives)
04 Technology of Glue and Adhesives with Adhesives Bonding and Formulations

SMALL SCALE INDUSTRIES/ STATIONERY/PAPER/ INKS/ CANDLES & EXPORT BUSINESS

01 Start Your Own Export Business (How To Export)
02 Start Your Own Small Business And Industry
03 Candle Making Processes & Formulations Hand Book
04 Stationery, Paper Converting & Packaging Industries
05 Modern Inks Formulations & Manufacturing Industries
06 Profitable Businesses To Start For Entrepreneurs
07 Modern Small & Cottage Scale Industries
08 Profitable Small Cottage Tiny & Home Industries

BIO FUEL & BIOPROCESSING

01 Technology Of Bio-Fules (Ethanol & Biodiesel)
02 Modern Technology Of Bioprocessing

PRINTING, SCREEN PRINTING & PACKAGING

01 Hand Book of Printing Processes Technologies & Industries
02 Hand Book Of Printing Technology (Offset, Screen, Flexo, Gravure, Inkjet & Digital)
03 Hand Book Of Offset Printing Technology
04 Screen Printing With Processes & Tech.
05 Hand Book Of Prepress
06 Hand Book Of Packaging Technology
07 Modern Packaging Technology for Processed Food, Bakery, Snack Foods, Spices and Allied Food Products
08 Hand Book Of Food Packaging Technology
09 Modern Technology of Printing Inks

PAINT, VARNISH, SOLVENTS, COATING & LACQUERS, POWDER COATING

01 Paint Pigment Varnish & Lacquer Manufacturing
02 Paint Varnish Solvents & Coating Technology

EIRI PROCESS TECHNOLOGY BOOKS

03 Paint, Pigment, Solvent, Coating Emulsion, Paint Additives & Formulations
04 Technology Of Coating, Resins, Pigments & Inks Industries
05 Manufacturing Technology & Formulations Hand Book On Thinners, Putty, Wall & Industrial Finishes And Synthetic Resins
06 Technology of Synthetic Resins and Emulsion Polymers
07 Technology of Paints and Coatings with Formulations
08 Powder Coating Technology Hand Book

PLASTIC/POLYMER PROCESS, COMPOUNDING, INJECTION MOULDING, ROTATIONAL MOULDING, PLASTIC FILM, FIBRE GLASS, PLASTIC WASTE RECYCLING, MOULDS, PET & RESINS INDUSTRIES

01 Moulds Design & Processing Hand Book
02 Hand Book Of Plastic Materials & Processing Technology
03 Injection Moulding Of Plastics
04 Plastic Processing and Packaging Industries
05 Plastic Waste Recycling Technology
06 Technology Of Plastic Films
07 Rotational Moulding Technology Hand Book
08 Plastic Compounding, Master Batches, Pet & Other Plastics
09 Synthetic Resins Technology With Formulations
10 Technology Of PVC Compounding And Its Applications
11 Hand Book of Polymer And Plastic Technology
12 Hand Book of Fibre Glass Moulding
13 Technology of Reinforced Plastics
14 Plastic Additives Technology Hand Book
15 Technology of Pet Bottles, Preform and Pet Recycling
16 Modern Technology of Extrusion & Extruded Products
17 Technology of Synthetic Resins & Emulsion Polymers
18 Technology of Plastic Additives with Processes and Packaging
19 Technology of Disposable Medical Products

BAKERY, CONFECTIONERY & BREAKFAST, PASTA & CEREALS

01 Hand Book Of Bakery Industries
02 Hand Book Of Confectionery With Formulations
03 Breakfast, Dietary Food, Pasta & Cereal Products Technology
04 Hand Book Of Modern Bakery Products
05 Modern Bakery Technology & Fermented Cereal Products With Formulae
06 Technology of Confectionery, Chocolates, Toffee, Candy, Chewing & Bubble Gums, Lollipop and Jelly Products with Formulations

AGRO CULTIVATION, ANIMAL FARMING, AGRO PLANTATION & AGRO CHEMICAL/ PESTICIDES/ FLORICULTURE & BEE KEEPING

01 Poultry Farming & Feed Formulations
02 Hand Book of Pig Farming
03 Agro Based Hand Book of Plantation, Cultivation & Farming
04 Agro Based Plantation Cultivation & Farming
05 Agro Chemical Industries (Insecticide & Pesticides)
06 Modern Bee Keeping & Honey Processing

EIRI PROCESS TECHNOLOGY BOOKS

07 Technology Of Modern Rice Milling And Basmati Rice
08 Hand Book Of Goat Farming
09 Floriculture Hand Book (Flowers Growing Technology)
10 Aloe Vera Cultivation, Processings, Formulations And Manufacturing Technology
11 Poultry Farming, Hatchery and Broiler Production

DAIRY FARM, MILK PROCESSING AND ICE CREAM

01 Hand Book of Dairy Formulations, Processes & Milk Processing Industries
02 Milk Processing And Dairy Products Industries
03 Hand Book Of Dairy Farming to Produce Milk with Packaging
04 Hand Book Of Ice Cream Technology And Formulae
05 Hand Book Of Milk Processing Dairy Products And Packaging Technology
06 Dairy Farming for Milk Production Technology
07 Commercial Dairy Farming with Project Profiles

HERBS & MEDICINAL CULTIVATION

01 Herbs, Medicinal & Aromatic Plants Cultivation
02 Aushidhi And Sungndhit Paudho Ka Vaysayik (Hindi)
03 Hand Book Of Aromatic & Medicinal Plants And Biodiesel (Jatropha)
04 Hand Book Of Medicinal & Aromatic Plants (Cultivation, Utilisation & Extraction Processed)

FOOD & AGRO PROCESSING, PRESERVATION, SNACK FOOD, DEHYDRATION, FRUIT BEVERAGE, POTATO, MAIZE, MEAT PROCESS

01 Fruits & Vegetables Processing Hand Book
02 Fruit Beverage & Processing With Mango
03 Food Processing & Agro Based Industries
04 Manufacturing Technology of Snacks Food, Namkeen, Pappad & Potato Products
05 Preservation & Canning Of Fruits and Vegetables
06 Hand Book of Food Dehydration & Drying
07 Meat Processing & Meat Products Hand Book
08 Technology of Food Preservation & Processing
09 Hand Book of Food Packaging Technology
10 Agro Based & Processed Food Products
11 Potato & Potato Processing Technology
12 Technology of Maize & Allied Com. Products
13 Technology of Food Processing Industries
14 Technology of Sweets (Mithai) with Formulae
15 Modern Technology of Frozen Food Products
16 Technology of Water and Packaged Drinking water
17 Complete Hand Book on Frozen Food Processing and Freeze Drying Technology
18 Technology of Sweets (Mithai), Namkeen and Snacks food with Formulae
19 Complete Book on Banana Cultivation, Dehydration, Ripening, Processing, Products and Packaging Technology

EIRI PROCESS TECHNOLOGY BOOKS

20 Technology of Chicken Meat and Poultry Products
21 Agro Food Processing and Packaging Technology
22 Modern Technology of Tomato Processing and Dehydration (Ketchup, Juice, Paste, Puree, Soup and Drying)
23 Modern Technology of Agro Processing and Food Packaging Products with Project Profiles
24 Start Your Own Coffee and Coffee Processing

SOAPS & DETERGENTS

01 Household Soap. Toilet Soap & Other Soap
02 Profitable Small Scale Manufacture Of Soaps & Detergents
03 Synthetic Detergents With Formulations
04 Modern Technology of Acid Slurry, Surfactants, Soap and Detergents with Formulae

ORGANIC FARMING AND FOOD

01 Hand Book Of Organic Farming And Organic Foods With Vermi-Composting And Neem Products

FISH FARMING & FISHERY PRODUCTS

01 Hand Book Of Fish Farming And Fishery Products

COSMETIC (SYNTHETIC & HERBAL)

01 Cosmetics Processes & Formulations
02 Herbal Cosmetics & Beauty Products With Formulations
03 Profitable Small Scale Manufacture Of Cosmetics (Synthetic & Herbal)
04 Hand Book Of Synthetic & Herbal Cosmetics (How to Make Beauty Products)
05 Technology Of Herbal Cosmetics & Toiletries Products With Formulae

OIL AND FATS

01 Hand Book of Oils, Fats And Derivatives With Refining & Packaging Technology
02 Technology of Oilseeds Processing, Oils & Fats and Refining

ESSENTIAL OILS & AROMATIC

01 Essential Oils Manufacturing & Aromatic Plants
02 Modern Technology Of Essential Oils
03 Technology Of Perfumes, Flavours & Essential Oils
04 Essential Oils Processes & Formulations

PERFUMES AND FLAVOURS

01 Hand Book Of Flavours & Food Colourants Technology
02 Hand Book Of Perfumes & Flavours
03 Hand Book of Perfumes With Formulations
04 Technology Of Perfumes, Flavours & Essential Oils
05 Hand Book Of Flavours Technology

BUILDING MATERIALS & CHEMICALS

01 Technology Of Building Materials & Chemicals With Processes

EIRI PROCESS TECHNOLOGY BOOKS

TEXTILE, GARMENTS, DYEING

01 Modern Technology Of Bleaching, Dyeing, Printing & Finishing Of Textiles
02 Technology Of Textiles (Spinning & Weaving, Dyeing, Scouring, Drying, Printing And Bleaching)
03 Garments Manufacturing Technology

SPICES & COLD STORAGE

01 Spices & Packaging With Formulaes
02 Start Your Own Cold Storage Unit

PULP & PAPER TECHNOLOGY

01 Hand Book Of Pulp & Paper, Paper Board & Paper Based Technology

NON WOVEN TECHNOLOGY

01 Complete Technology of Nonwovens Fabrics, Carry Bags, Composite, Geotextiles, Medical Textiles, Fibres, Felts, Apparels, Spunlace and Absorbent Nonwoven

TEXTILE AUXILIARIES & CHEMICALS

01 Textile Auxiliaries And Chemicals With Processes And Formulations

PHARMACEUTICALS & DRUGS

01 Pharmaceuticals And Drugs Technology With Formulations

LEATHER & LEATHER PRODUCTS

01 Hand Book Of Leather & Leather Products Technology

BIOTECHNOLOGY

01 Hand Book Of Biotechnology

CERAMICS

01 Hand Book of Ceramics and Ceramics Processing Technology

TREE FARMING

01 Hand Book Of Tree Farming

MUSHROOM CULTIVATION/ PROCESS

01 Hand Book Of Mushroom Cultivation, Processing and Packaging

BIOFERTILIZERS & VERMICULTURE

01 Hand Book Of Biofertilizers & Vermiculture

MINERAL AND MINERALS

01 Hand Book Of Minerals And Minerals Based Industries

RUBBER CHEMICALS, COMPOUND & RUBBER INDUSTRIES

01 Rubber Chemicals & Processing Industries
02 Modern Rubber Chemicals, Compounds & Rubber Goods Technology
03 Technology Of Rubber & Rubber Goods Industries

AYURVEDIC MEDICINES

01 Ayurvedic & Herbal Medicines With Formulaes
02 Hand Book Of Ayurvedic Medicines With Formulations (A

EIRI PROCESS TECHNOLOGY BOOKS

Complete Hand Book Of Ayurvedic & Herbal Medicines)

STEEL, S.S., NON FERROUS METALS, ROLLING MILL

01 Modern Technology of Non Ferrous Metals and Metal Extraction

02 Processing Technology of Steels and Stainless Steels

03 Modern Technology of Rolling Mill, Billets, Steel Wire, Galvanized Sheet, Forging & Castings

04 Manufacturing Technology of Non-Ferrous Metal Products

WOOD, VENEER, PLYWOOD, PARTICLE, BOARD, FIBREBOARD, BAMBOO & FOREST PRODUCTS

01 Modern Technology Of Wood, Veneer, Plywood, Particle Board, Fibreboard, Bamboo & Forest Products

BIO GAS PRODUCTION

01 Modern Technology of BIOGAS Production

WASTE BASED PRODUCTS INCLUDING INDUSTRIAL, AGRICULTURE, MEDICAL, MUNICIPALITY, ORGANIC & BIOLOGICAL

01 Technology Of Products From Wastes Industrial, Agriculture, Medical, Municipality, Organic & Biological

02 Products from Waste Technology Handbook

FOOD CHEMICALS, FOOD ADDITIVES, PIGMENTS, AROMA, SWEETENERS AND FOOD EMULSIFIERS

01 Technology of Food Chemicals, Pigments and Food Aroma Compounds

02 Modern Technology of Food Additives, Sweeteners and Food Emulsifiers

SOYBEAN

01 Technology of SOYBEAN Products with Formulae

02 Technology of Soya Milk, Tofu, Hydrlyzate and allied Soyabean Products with Project Profiles

EIRI Multiple Project Reports in CD ROM

01 92 New Lucrative Project Reports In Cd

02. 45 Infotech/It, Hospitality, Hospital, College, School & Club

03. 23 Profitable Construction Projects

04. 56 Agro Based & Food Processing Projects

05. 52 Food, Dairy, Bakery, Confectionery & Snacks Foods

06. 45 New Chemicals & Allied Project Reports

07. 100 Profitable Plastic, Polymers & Allied Projects

08. 44 Textile, Garments, Hosiery & Allied Products In Cd

09. 23 Dairy Farming (Buffalo & Jersey Cow, Dairy Products & Other Milk Processing Ind.

10. 42 Paper, Pulp & Paper Converting Products Reports